Rand McNally

ATLAS OF WORLD HISTORY

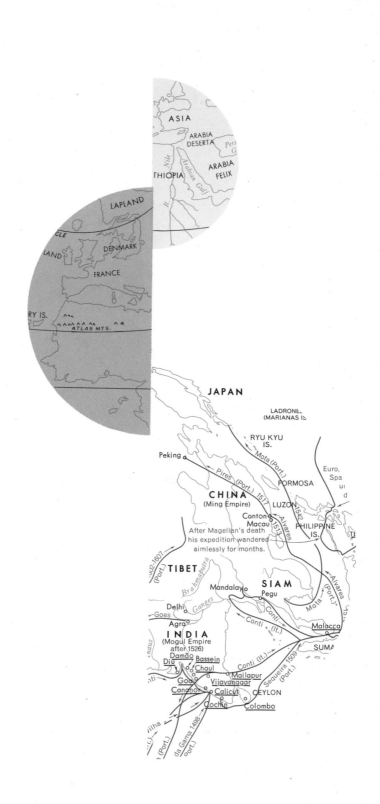

RAND McNALLY

Atlas
of
World
History

EDITED BY **R. R. PALMER**, PRINCETON UNIVERSITY

Contributing Editors

Knight Biggerstaff, CORNELL UNIVERSITY

John W. Caughey, UNIVERSITY OF CALIFORNIA AT LOS ANGELES

Charles Jelavich, UNIVERSITY OF CALIFORNIA AT BERKELEY

Tom B. Jones, UNIVERSITY OF MINNESOTA

Charles E. Nowell, UNIVERSITY OF ILLINOIS

Sidney Painter, THE JOHNS HOPKINS UNIVERSITY

RAND McNALLY & COMPANY

NEW YORK   •   CHICAGO   •   SAN FRANCISCO

RAND MᶜNALLY HISTORY SERIES

Fred Harvey Harrington   CONSULTING EDITOR

PREFACE

IN THIS BOOK we have tried to produce an atlas illustrating the history of all parts of the world since ancient times, within limits of size and cost that may make it available and convenient to a large number of readers. There are about 120 maps, large and small, including the insets. Asia is represented at successive periods of its history, and we have given attention to Africa and Latin America, but since the book is designed primarily for use in the United States the treatment of North American and European history is admittedly more detailed. All maps have been newly conceived and produced for this volume, though like all makers of atlases we are heavily dependent on our predecessors.

We have aimed less at novelty than at usefulness, and have sought to give both fulness of information and attractiveness of design. There has long been a trend in map-making to reduction of detail and boldness of general impact. With due regard for this trend, by which very striking maps can be produced, we have held to the view that an atlas, to have lasting value, should after all be more a reference book than a picture book. The most widely used of all maps today are probably road maps; the mass of their minutiae suggests that readers have no objection to details in which they are interested. The present maps are meant both to illustrate general ideas and to supply particular information.

Interest in history today ranges well beyond political history, though political facts, such as the size of states, the location of boundaries, and the territorial changes brought about by wars and treaties, are the most susceptible of all historical facts to representation by mapping. Many of our maps are primarily political. Others have an economic, social, or religious content. We have also devised a series of maps illustrating the civilization of Europe and the United States at significant periods, since readers of history today are often interested in whole civilizations, including movements of ideas and of literature and the arts. Thus, for example, there are maps of the Renaissance and of the Enlightenment.

Obviously, much of the intellectual or creative activity that goes under the name of civilization does not especially lend itself to cartographic treatment. Maps, like other media of expression, have their own advantages and limitations; they show location or distribution in space. The civilization maps in this book show, for various periods, the concentration of civilization in certain places, or its distribution, or the movement of its center of gravity from time to time. The map of the Enlightenment, for example, shows a clustering in England and France, and indeed in London and Paris, while the map of nineteenth-century civilization shows a greater dispersion in central, eastern, and northern Europe. Civilization, in each case, is represented by concrete data of a kind that may be plotted, such as the location of buildings, institutions, and collective enterprises, and the birthplaces of writers, artists, and thinkers whose very names evoke the civilization of their day. Thus Renaissance civilization is signified by the Sistine Chapel, the Collège de France, and the birthplaces of Michelangelo and many others. It is true that place of birth in individual cases may have little significance, since a man's productive work may have been done elsewhere. It is nevertheless the birthplace that is plotted on each of these civilization maps, except for earlier periods where birthplace is sometimes unknown. It must be remembered that birthplace is usually also the place of upbringing, training, or education. If a great many persons whose achievements make up the culture of a period are born in one locality, and few or none in another, then we have an indication—barring such statistical oddities as the birth of El Greco in Crete—that some localities were at some periods nurseries of "civilization," and others not.

Pages of explanatory text interleaved with the maps are another feature of the atlas. While it is hoped that these text pages will make interesting connected reading and convey important general ideas, they are also frankly intended as condensed factual statements to elucidate the maps themselves. The statistical appendix may also be of use; here the data for population, emigration, the size of cities, etc., are projected in historical time, so far as known.

Division of labor among the coeditors has been as follows: for ancient history (except India and East Asia), Mr. Jones; medieval European history and the Renaissance, Mr. Painter; Asian history, Mr. Biggerstaff; United States history, Mr. Caughey; European expansion, Latin America, Canada, and Africa, Mr. Nowell; Russia, Eastern Europe, the Ottoman Empire, and the world map on pages 190-91, Mr. Jelavich; modern European history, myself, except that the maps on pages 175–79 and 186 originated with Mr. Jelavich. Mr. Carl H. Mapes, chief map editor of Rand McNally & Company, has played a creative and important role from the beginning, as has Mr. F. E. Peacock. It has been my privilege to act as co-ordinator and spokesman, in a sense, for colleagues in six other universities and for all those at Rand McNally & Company, with their diverse skills and functions, by whose combined efforts this *Atlas of World History* has come into being.

Princeton, New Jersey   R. R. PALMER

CONTENTS

OLD MAPS

▶ MAPS ON PAGES 10, 11, AND 12

A HISTORICAL ATLAS is a collection of modern maps illustrating past periods of time, not a collection of old maps made in times past. On the following pages a few old maps are nevertheless reproduced. They reveal an important chapter in the history of thought, for they show how men at different times have conceived the world in which they lived. The oldest known map (not reproduced here) is a clay tablet made in Babylonia about 2300 B.C. Cartographic knowledge has had an uneven and often interrupted progress ever since.

Ptolemy's Map

▶ MAP ON PAGE 10

Centuries of Greek and Near Eastern thought are summarized in the map made by Ptolemy at Alexandria about 150 A.D. It is a truly scientific effort. Ptolemy knew that the earth is a sphere, but he believed that only about a third of the northern hemisphere was habitable. His map represents this habitable portion of the globe. He understood the principles of projection, that is of representing a curved surface on a flat page, and he located places according to longitude and latitude, defining longitude by distance east from the Fortunate Islands (the Canaries), and latitude by the length of the longest day in the year. His map is defective not in conception but simply in information. People, of course, lived in most of the places shown on Ptolemy's map, but few of them, even Greeks, had any contact with scientific circles. Hence, although latitude could be determined, there were only a few places from which reports of latitude were available. Longitude, or east-west distance, could not be measured with exactness until the invention of the chronometer about 1740 A.D.

Medieval Maps

▶ MAPS ON PAGES 10 AND 12

After the decline of Greco-Roman civilization Ptolemy's geographical work was unknown in Europe until about 1400. Meanwhile, during the Middle Ages, men of learning were preoccupied with abstract or spiritual questions, in which so mundane a matter as mapping the physical details of the earth seemed unimportant. A common form of map—a diagram rather than a true map—is the one shown from the twelfth century. The outer circle represents the Ocean. The vertical radius containing fourteen oblong islands is the Mediterranean Sea. East is at top. The Holy Land is in the center. The medieval person using this map could get a rough sense of direction: facing east from a point in the Mediterranean, he knew that Europe was on his left, Africa on his right, and Asia ahead, with the Garden of Eden presumably in the extreme east. But he would have no idea of distance, size, shape, or proportion for any part of the world.

At the other extreme, sea captains of the western Mediterranean in the Middle Ages, without contact with science or learning, but simply by solving their own practical problems, developed an amazingly exact knowledge of the Mediterranean and Black Sea coasts. This appears in a series of "portolans" or navigator's manuals which began before the year 1300. The upper map on page 12 is from a portolan prepared by Dulcert about 1339. It will be seen that Dulcert's knowledge of the coasts was more accurate than that of two geographers, one Christian and one Moslem, whose work appeared much later.

Behaim's Globe

▶ MAP ON PAGE 11

Martin Behaim of Nuremberg, in 1492, constructed the earliest surviving globe. It is represented on page 11 in two hemispheres on a much reduced scale. Behaim had learned more of Asia than Ptolemy knew, thanks to such travels as those of Marco Polo; and he may have been associated with the explorations sponsored in his own time by Portugal. His globe shows the state of geographical knowledge generally available on the eve of Columbus' first voyage.

Behaim's conception of the Mediterranean and European coasts, except in the north, shows no real improvement on Ptolemy, though allowance must be made for the small scale of these regions on a globe. Like Ptolemy, Behaim has Italy running mainly east and west; his British Isles and Black Sea seem less accurate than Ptolemy's. For the interior of Africa he seems unaware of recent Italian discoveries (see pages 62–63), but reproduces the Mountains of the Moon from ancient sources. He had more knowledge than Ptolemy of the East Asian islands, which in fact bulked very large in his imagination. He even put a pepper forest in "Java Major," which no known European had ever seen. Like Ptolemy, Behaim had no sense of India as a peninsula, and believed in a huge island of Taprobane, or Ceylon.

Bartholomew Diaz in 1488 had reached the tip of Africa, which Behaim already knew as the Cape of Good Hope. Da Gama had not yet completed the voyage to India, to which Behaim hopefully indicated the way by an imaginary passage into the Indian Ocean, where the islands of Madagascar and Zanzibar loomed equally large. On the whole, however, because of the fifteenth-century Portuguese explorations, Behaim's Africa was surprisingly accurate in shape and size.

In the Atlantic Behaim placed the Canary Islands, the old Fortunate Islands of the ancients, rediscovered by Europeans in the Middle Ages; and the Azores and Cape Verde islands, which ancient geographers had never known, but which fourteenth-century navigators had made known to Europe. He included also the mythical island of Antilia, whose name was soon to be transferred to the Antilles discovered by Columbus. Behaim, it is to be noted, greatly underestimated the distance from Europe westward to Asia. In this he only perpetuated a misconception which Ptolemy and the geographers of Behaim's day shared; Eratosthenes of Alexandria, in the third century B.C., had made a more exact estimate of the earth's true circumference. From the Azores to Japan, on Behaim's globe, was no farther than the length of the Mediterranean. Such supposed knowledge gave confidence to Columbus when he set out to probe the Ocean Sea.

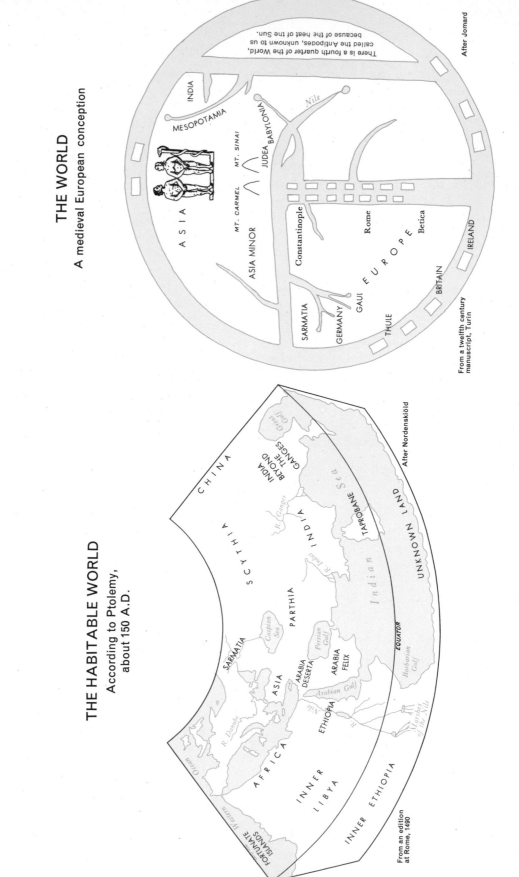

THE WORLD
A medieval European conception

ASIA

INDIA

MESOPOTAMIA

MT. CARMEL   MT. SINAI

JUDEA

BABYLONIA

Nile

ASIA MINOR

Constantinople

Rome

Betica

EUROPE

SARMATIA

GERMANY

GAUL

THULE

BRITAIN

IRELAND

There is a fourth quarter of the World,
called the Antipodes, unknown to us
because of the heat of the Sun.

After Jomard

From a twelfth century
manuscript, Turin

Copyright by Rand McNally & Company. Made in U.S.A.

THE HABITABLE WORLD
According to Ptolemy,
about 150 A.D.

CHINA

INDIA
BEYOND
THE
GANGES

Great Gulf

SCYTHIA

R. Ganges

INDIA

Indian Sea

TAPROBANE

PARTHIA

R. Indus

UNKNOWN LAND

After Nordenskiöld

SARMATIA

Caspian Sea

ASIA

ARABIA
DESERTA

Persian Gulf

ARABIA
FELIX

EQUATOR

Barbarian Gulf

Arabian Gulf

R. Danube

ETHIOPIA

Nile

R. Marshes of the Nile

AFRICA

Western Ocean

INNER
LIBYA

INNER ETHIOPIA

FORTUNATE ISLANDS

From an edition
at Rome, 1490

10

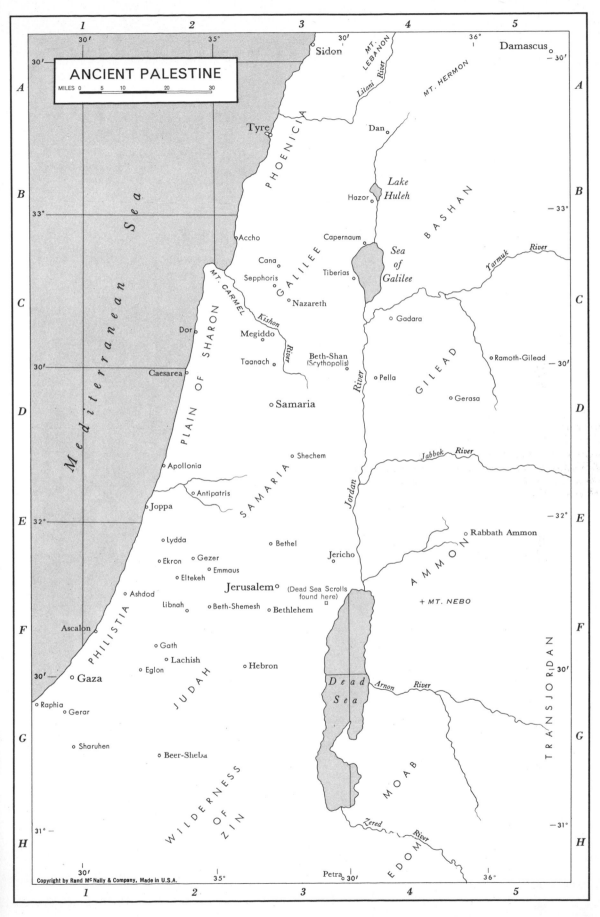

ANCIENT PALESTINE

MILES 0 5 10 20 30

Damascus

Sidon

MT. LEBANON

Litani River

MT. HERMON

Tyre

PHOENICIA

Dan

Lake Huleh

MT. HERMON

BASHAN

Hazor

Accho

Capernaum

Sea of Galilee

Cana

Sepphoris

GALILEE

Tiberias

Nazareth

Gadara

Dor

MT. CARMEL

Kishon River

Megiddo

Taanach

Beth-Shan (Scythopolis)

Caesarea

PLAIN OF SHARON

Pella

GILEAD

Ramoth-Gilead

Gerasa

Samaria

Mediterranean Sea

Shechem

Jabbok River

Apollonia

Antipatris

SAMARIA

Jordan River

Joppa

Lydda

Bethel

Jericho

Rabbath Ammon

Ekron

Gezer

Emmaus

AMMON

Eltekeh

Jerusalem

(Dead Sea Scrolls found here)

+ MT. NEBO

Ashdod

Libnah

Beth-Shemesh

Bethlehem

Ascalon

PHILISTIA

Gath

Lachish

Hebron

Eglon

JUDAH

Gaza

Dead Sea

Arnon River

TRANSJORDAN

Raphia

Gerar

Sharuhen

Beer-Sheba

WILDERNESS OF ZIN

MOAB

Zered River

Petra

EDOM

Copyright by Rand McNally & Company, Made in U.S.A.

25

MODERN MAPS:
PROJECTION AND SCALE

▶ MAPS ON PAGES 14–15, 18–19, 62–63, AND 190–91

MODERN MAPS DIFFER from old maps in being more exact in projection and in scale. To convert the curvature of the earth to the flat surface of a printed page is somewhat like squaring the circle; it cannot really be done, and whatever method is used presents disadvantages. A good map should give a clear idea of true *direction* and *distance*, and of the *area* and *shape* of land and water masses. At least one of these four qualities must be sacrificed on any flat map of a region large enough to have perceptible curvature on the globe—for example, a large country, a continent, or the earth as a whole.

Projection

The method by which points on the curved surface of the earth are plotted on the flat surface of a page is called the projection. With different projections, the four basic desirable qualities are realized or sacrificed in different ways. The world map on pages 190–91 (a modified Mercator projection) is excellent for direction, all north-south meridians being vertical and all east-west parallels being horizontal; but it greatly exaggerates distances and areas in proportion as one departs from the equator, and it cannot represent the shapes of the two polar regions at all. The map on pages 62–63 gives a better idea of the shape of north Atlantic, north polar, and adjoining regions, and is fairly accurate for areas; but shapes are distorted away from the center, direction must be read with reference to the North Pole, and the identity of the Pacific Ocean is lost. This map is not really more distorted than the more familiar one on pages 190–91; indeed, it suggests the true rotundity of the earth more effectively. It is necessary in reading any map of a large area to make a mental correction for the projection.

In a well-planned atlas, projections are carefully chosen with a view to the purpose of each map. For example, on the map of Eurasia on pages 18–19 Europe seems larger with respect to Asia than it really is, and northeast Asia is greatly compressed and distorted; but this projection has the great advantage—for the purpose of this map—of keeping the lines of latitude horizontal, and of avoiding distortion of shape in areas where the data are to be plotted. For the *Age of Discovery*, pages 62–63, the projection has been selected to show how the discoveries radiated from the north Atlantic area as from a center, and because distortion of the Pacific Ocean is not for this particular purpose any great disadvantage.

Scale

Scale is simply the ratio between distance on the map and the real distance which is represented. Thus an inch on paper may represent a mile or a thousand miles on the surface of the earth. Since a mile is 63,360 inches, a scale of an inch to a mile may also be indicated as about 1:63,000. A scale of 1:630,000 would signify an inch to ten miles. This way of indicating scale is most useful in countries using the metric system, in which 1:100,000 simply means that a centimeter on the map represents a kilometer on the earth's surface. Geographers often prefer this system, which has the advantage of making it easier to compare maps of diverse origins. In this book, however, except on the two following pages, scale is indicated by the familiar device of a bar marked off in miles.

A scale is "large" if the space on the page is large in proportion to the real space represented. Thus a scale of one inch to a mile is much larger than a scale of one inch to a thousand miles. In general, the larger the scale the better, and small scales are often merely unavoidable necessities. Within the limits of a portable book, areas of continental size can only be portrayed on a very small scale. But both large and small scales have their advantages. Where large scale allows the presentation of more detail, small scale allows one to see the relationships between big geographical regions in one convenient sweep of the eye.

London and England on Four Scales

▶ MAPS ON PAGES 14–15

The following pages show the effects obtained by the use of different scales. By using a very large scale, it is possible to show streets and buildings in eighteenth-century London within a panel of five and one-half by four inches. One may see, for example, that from Grub Street, the haunt of small literary men, it was only a moment's walk to "Bedlam," the famous asylum for the insane. With a somewhat smaller scale the whole of London, except the East End, comes into view in a panel of the same size. The West End, with its fashionable squares, is now seen in relation to the business center, the old "city" proper. The Drury Lane theater district and the government and ecclesiastical centers also appear. Reducing the scale a hundred times, we are able to get south England and the Midlands into the panel. We now see London in its true position in the southeastern part of the country, at that point on the Thames where seagoing vessels could come up the river and where land traffic could yet easily cross it. On this scale the new manufacturing towns and the new canal system, characteristic of the beginning of the Industrial Revolution, can also be shown, as can the fashionable centers of Bath or Tunbridge Wells, so often mentioned in the literature of the period. Let us again reduce the scale. We are beginning to have projection trouble, for on this scale, to avoid distortion of areas, we must make the north-south meridians (except the one in the middle) slant a little. But we can see London in its relation to the Continent and to the ocean. It is clear that London faced the European Continent across the "Narrow Seas"; that it had easy access to the ocean if these Narrow Seas were not controlled by a hostile power; and that it was closer to Paris than to Scotland. If these facts seem obvious, it is only because we have learned from maps since childhood. They would not be obvious to the author of the twelfth-century map shown on page 10, nor in any society that was not map minded.

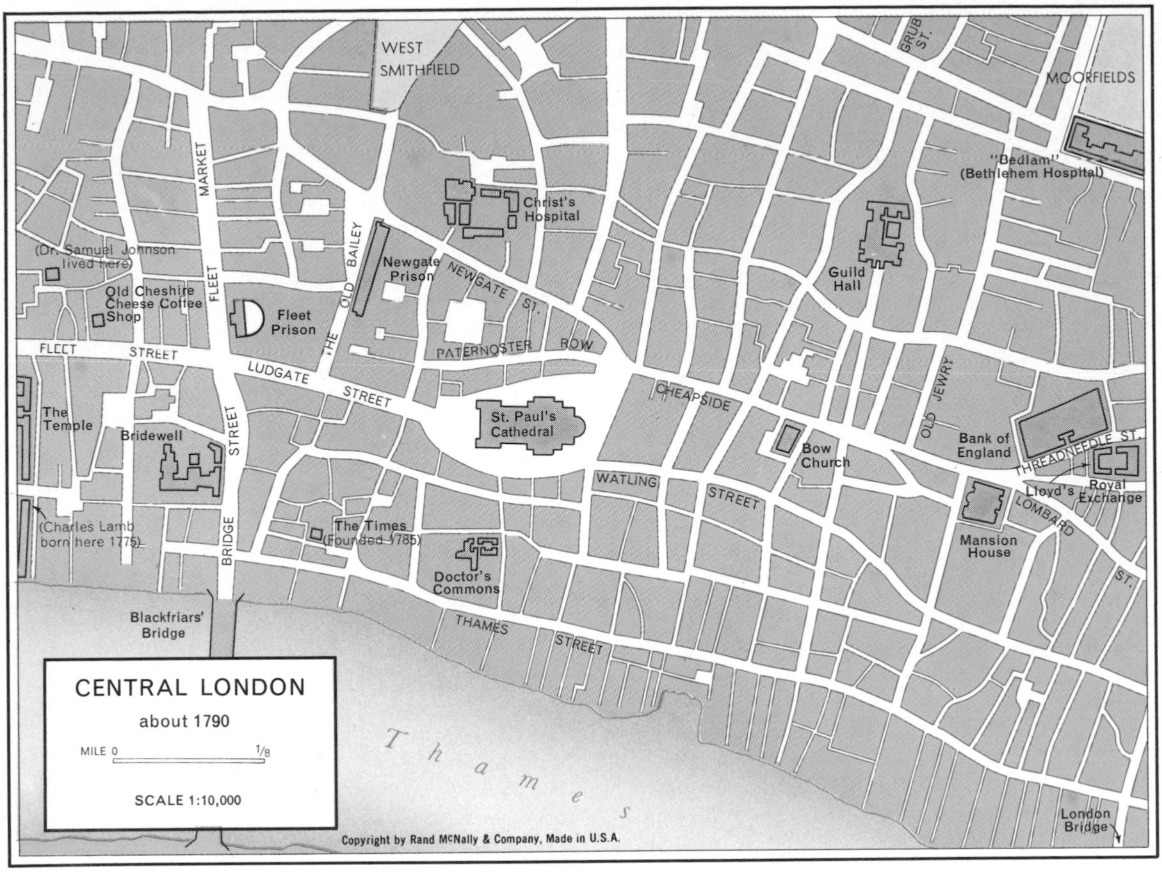

CENTRAL LONDON

WEST SMITHFIELD

MOORFIELDS

GRUB ST.

"Bedlam" (Bethlehem Hospital)

Christ's Hospital

Guild Hall

MARKET

FLEET

Newgate Prison

THE OLD BAILEY

NEWGATE ST.

(Dr. Samuel Johnson lived here)

Old Cheshire Cheese Coffee Shop

Fleet Prison

PATERNOSTER ROW

CHEAPSIDE

OLD JEWRY

FLEET STREET

LUDGATE STREET

St. Paul's Cathedral

Bow Church

Bank of England

THREADNEEDLE ST.

Royal Exchange

The Temple

Bridewell

WATLING STREET

LOMBARD

Lloyd's

BRIDGE STREET

(Charles Lamb born here 1775)

The Times (Founded 1785)

Mansion House

ST.

Doctor's Commons

Blackfriars' Bridge

THAMES STREET

London Bridge

CENTRAL LONDON

about 1790

MILE 0   1/8

SCALE 1:10,000

Copyright by Rand McNally & Company, Made in U.S.A.

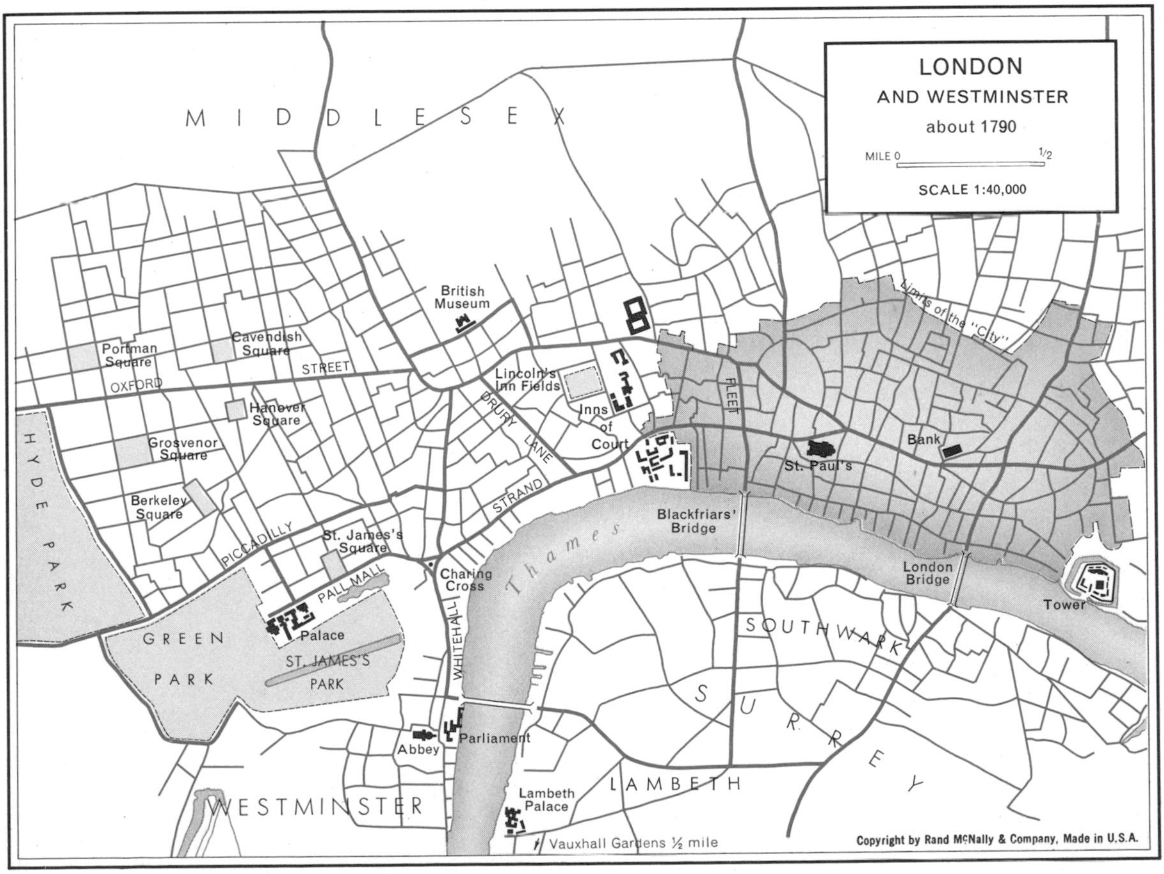

T h a m e s

LONDON AND WESTMINSTER

M I D D L E S E X

LONDON
AND WESTMINSTER
about 1790

MILE 0   1/2

SCALE 1:40,000

British Museum

Limits of the "City"

Portman Square

Cavendish Square

OXFORD STREET

Lincoln's Inn Fields

FLEET

HYDE PARK

Hanover Square

DRURY LANE

Inns of Court

St. Paul's

Bank

Grosvenor Square

Berkeley Square

STRAND

Blackfriars' Bridge

London Bridge

PICCADILLY

St. James's Square

Charing Cross

Thames

Tower

PALL MALL

WHITEHALL

SOUTHWARK

GREEN PARK

Palace

S U R R E Y

ST. JAMES'S PARK

Abbey

Parliament

L A M B E T H

WESTMINSTER

Lambeth Palace

Vauxhall Gardens 1/2 mile

Copyright by Rand McNally & Company, Made in U.S.A.

14

IN SCALE

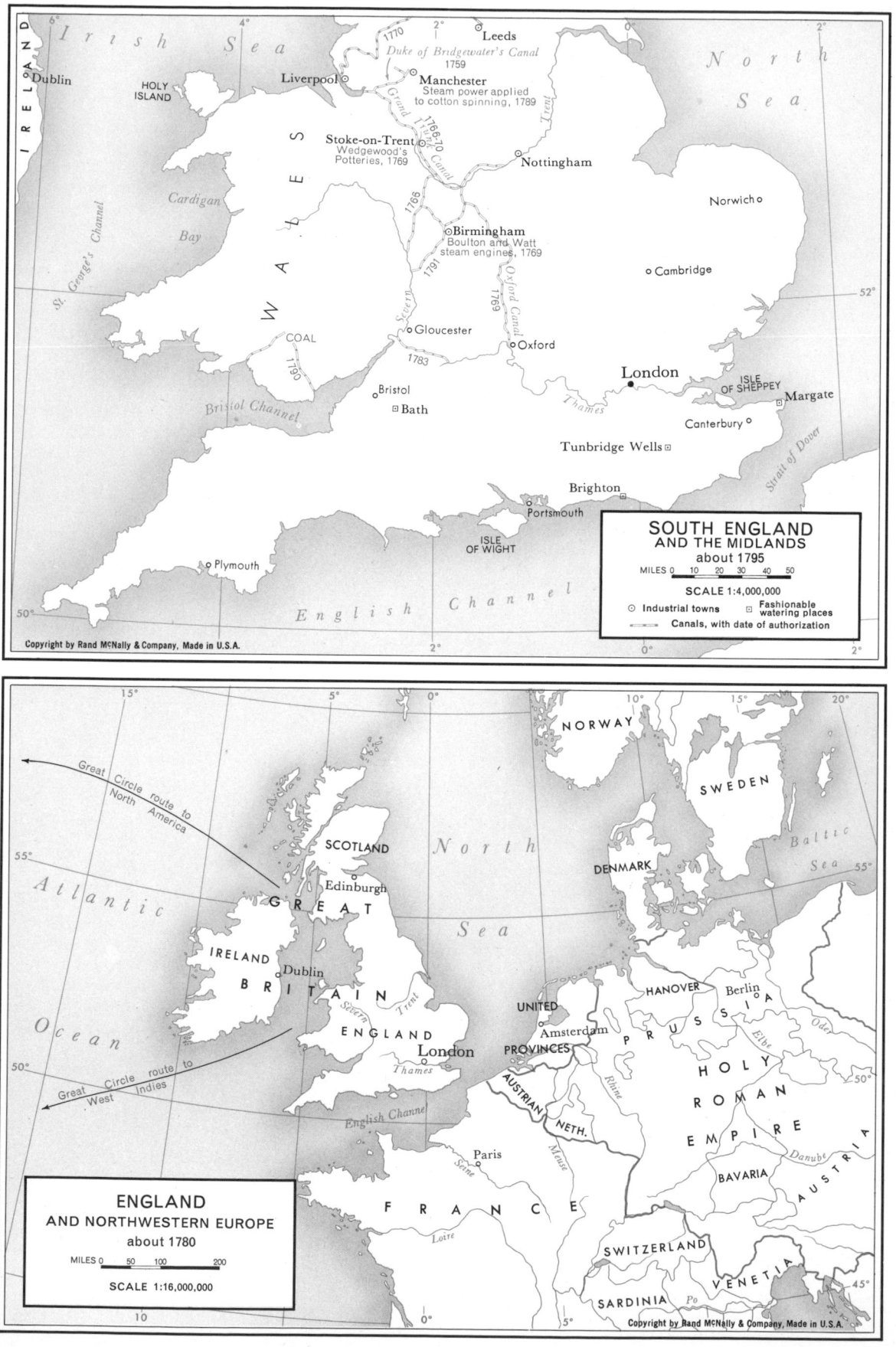

Dublin

Irish Sea

HOLY ISLAND

Leeds

1770 *Duke of Bridgewater's Canal* 1759

Liverpool

Manchester
Steam power applied
to cotton spinning, 1789

1766-70

Grand Trunk Canal

Stoke-on-Trent
Wedgewood's
Potteries, 1769

Nottingham

1766

W A L E S

Cardigan Bay

St. George's Channel

Norwich

Birmingham
Boulton and Watt
steam engines, 1769

1791

Cambridge

1769

Severn

Oxford Canal

Gloucester

1783

Oxford

London

COAL
1790

Bristol

Bath

Thames

ISLE
OF SHEPPEY

Margate

Canterbury

Tunbridge Wells

Bristol Channel

Brighton

Portsmouth

ISLE
OF WIGHT

*North
Sea*

Strait of Dover

52°

Plymouth

E n g l i s h   C h a n n e l

50°

Copyright by Rand McNally & Company, Made in U.S.A.

SOUTH ENGLAND
AND THE MIDLANDS
about 1795

MILES 0 10 20 30 40 50

SCALE 1:4,000,000

⊙ Industrial towns   ⊡ Fashionable
                           watering places

━ Canals, with date of authorization

NORWAY

Atlantic

Great Circle route to
North America

SWEDEN

*Baltic
Sea*

55°

SCOTLAND

North

Edinburgh

DENMARK

Sea

GREAT

HANOVER

Berlin

Ocean

IRELAND

BRITAIN

Dublin

UNITED

Amsterdam

PROVINCES

PRUSSIA

Oder

Severn

Trent

HOLY

Elbe

ENGLAND

London

50°

Thames

AUSTRIAN

ROMAN

Great Circle route to
West Indies

NETH.

Rhine

EMPIRE

Danube

English Channel

Meuse

AUSTRIA

Paris

BAVARIA

Seine

ENGLAND
AND NORTHWESTERN EUROPE
about 1780

MILES 0 50 100 200

SCALE 1:16,000,000

F R A N C E

SWITZERLAND

Loire

VENETIA

45°

SARDINIA

Po

Copyright by Rand McNally & Company, Made in U.S.A.

THE FIRST CIVILIZATIONS

▶ MAPS ON PAGES 18–19, 20, 21, 22, AND 25

A HUNDRED THOUSAND YEARS of human history (though such estimates of time are very uncertain) are summarized by the map on pages 18–19, which shows the growth of culture from the Old Stone Age through the expansion of the ancient civilizations. Fossil human remains of much older date have been found all over the Old World, as at Heidelberg and Peking and in Rhodesia; but these human creatures, presumably anterior to *homo sapiens*, had no culture, and were distinguished from other animals only by their physical form.

It is by the possession and transmission of a culture that man differs from other animals, and the first culture began with the habitual use of tools and of articulate speech. In the Old Stone Age, or Paleolithic era, man lived a precarious existence by the hunting of animals and gathering of vegetable food. The map shows important Old Stone Age sites: Altamira in Spain, where the first cave paintings were found in 1879; Chelles, St-Acheul, Le Moustier, Aurignac, and Solutré in France, where Stone Age cultures were classified, named, and put into a chronological sequence; Mt. Carmel in Palestine, where there is especially good evidence of long continued occupation; and Gafsa in North Africa, the type site for microflints of the Capsian or late Paleolithic period. Paleolithic sites from other widely separated places in Eurasia-Africa are also indicated. Old Stone Age man in fact spread to all parts of the world. The known sites of his remains depend more on where modern men have looked for him than on his actual distribution.

About 6000–5000 B.C., in some places, the Paleolithic culture was transformed into the Neolithic. Instead of hunting and gathering, men began to produce their own food. The transition can be seen at Mt. Carmel, where the last people to inhabit the caves were "incipient farmers" (about 6000 B.C.) who kept young wild animals in pens and cut wild grasses with sickles. It is not known where the sowing and domestication of plants—that is agriculture—began. It may have been at Jarmo, in the grassy foothills of eastern Iraq. In any event, shortly before 4000 B.C. settled peasant villages existed all over the Near East—at Merimde, Badari, and Naqada in Egypt, at Jericho in Palestine, at Judeidah in Syria, Tell Halaf in upper Mesopotamia, and Quetta and other places farther east. It is significant that Neolithic sites, unlike Paleolithic, are concentrated geographically. They occur in places where civilization began soon thereafter. This is a measure of the great economic revolution brought in by the invention of agriculture, with its consequences of settled village life.

About the fourth millennium B.C. agriculturists moved into the river valleys of the Nile, the Tigris-Euphrates, and the Indus. Here the climate was arid, but the soil was fantastically rich if only water could be brought to it. It could therefore support a denser population than human beings had heretofore known. The remains at Eridu in Mesopotamia show a sequence from peasant villages just after 4000 B.C. to civilization just before 3000.

Civilization began, then, shortly before 3000 B.C. in the Nile and Tigris-Euphrates valleys, and perhaps not until about 2500 B.C. along the Indus. These third-millennium civilizations are shown in green on the map. They were characterized by city life, writing, and trade, by which culture was diffused to surrounding areas. Metallurgy also began. Bronze appears with civilization in Mesopotamia, spread to Greece before 2000 B.C., and to Italy soon after. The use of iron seems to have originated in Asia Minor shortly after 1500 B.C. Before 1000 it was diffused to Europe, where the type sites of the Iron Age are Hallstadt, La Tène, and Villanova.

The extent of civilization in the second millennium B.C. is shown on the map in purple. At Troy and Cnossus, in this area, we may see the remains of peasant villages of the fourth and third millenniums which became civilized towns in the second. In China the peasant villages began to produce what we know as Chinese civilization about 1500 B.C.

The period from 1000 B.C. to 200 A.D. saw a further expansion of the area of civilization, which now reached in an almost continuous belt across the Old World continent. The silk routes connected China with India and with central Asia and the West. Sea routes connected the civilizations of the Indian subcontinent with those of the Near East and the Mediterranean.

The ancient civilizations of the Near East and Europe are shown in the following pages, those of India and China on pages 118–19. The American Indian civilizations, less advanced and of later date than 200 A.D., appear on page 140.

Egypt

▶ MAP ON PAGE 20

It is important to remember that Egypt, often represented as a large area of 400,000 square miles, really consists of the cultivated land of the delta and valley of the Nile to the First Cataract, an area probably not exceeding 10,000 square miles in ancient times—not very much larger than Massachusetts. Away from the river all was, and still is, desert.

In the predynastic period (before 3100 B.C.) there were many small independent communities, eventually brought together into the two kingdoms of Upper Egypt, in the valley, and Lower Egypt, in the delta. With the union of these two kingdoms under Menes began the First Dynasty and the history of Egypt as such. The following periods may be distinguished:

Old Kingdom (Dynasties III–VI), 2700–2200 B.C.
Middle Kingdom (Dynasty XII), 2000–1800 B.C.
New Kingdom (Dynasties XVIII–XX), 1570–1100 B.C.
Saite Period (Dynasty XXVI), 663–525 B.C.
Persian Period, 525–332 B.C.
Ptolemaic Period, 323–30 B.C.
Roman and Byzantine Period 30 B.C.–639 A.D.

The Old Kingdom had its capital at Memphis. This was the Pyramid Age, most of these structures being located at Gizeh, Sakkara, Meidum, and Dahshur. Thebes was the capital of the Middle Kingdom, during which trade and political contacts with the outside world increased. Cedar was brought

from Lebanon, copper from Sinai, and trade reached to Crete and southward above the First Cataract. In the New Kingdom the Egyptians acquired an empire along the eastern Mediterranean (see page 22). The famous Ikhnaton, often called the first monotheist, had his capital at Akhetaton.

Greco-Roman influence began as early as the seventh century with the founding of Naucratis by Greek traders. Alexandria, founded by Alexander the Great in 331 B.C., became the capital of Ptolemaic and Roman Egypt. Thousands of Greek papyri have been discovered at Oxyrhynchus.

Mesopotamia and the Indus
▶ MAP ON PAGE 21

Little is known of Mesopotamia before 2500 B.C., though its civilization is at least as old as that of Egypt, the earliest examples of writing, from Jemdet Nasr, being dated shortly after 3500 B.C. During the fourth millennium Sumerians from the northeast settled at the head of the Persian Gulf, while Semites from Arabia settled near Babylon.

During the third millennium the south was called Sumer, the north Akkad. There was an Early Dynastic period from about 3100 to 2350 B.C., dominated by the Sumerians, whose chief city states were Eridu and Ur, at that time on the seacoast, and Lagash, Erech, and Umma. From 2350 to 2200 Sumer and Akkad were united by Sargon and the Akkadian Semites in an empire of Akkad. This was followed by a Sumerian empire, called the Third Dynasty of Ur (2125–2025 B.C.), which made its power felt as far north as Assyria. This empire in turn dissolved before new invaders, but the plain was again united in the Amorite or Old Babylonian Kingdom (1890–1595 B.C.), chiefly by the famous Hammurabi, who reigned at the end of the eighteenth century B.C. From 1595 to about 1200 B.C. Babylonia was ruled by the Kassites (see page 22). Archeological sites in Mesopotamia are too numerous to mention, but of especial interest are Shuruppak, home of the Sumerian Noah, and Bisitun, where a famous trilingual inscription gave a clue to the decipherment of cuneiform writing. It should be added that some experts prefer a "short chronology" for Mesopotamia, in which all dates prior to Hammurabi are reduced one or two hundred years.

In the third millennium the only other center of civilization, besides Egypt and Mesopotamia, was the slightly less ancient and today less known civilization of the Indus valley in India. It probably developed from indigenous villages with some influence from Sumer. Its chief cities were Harappa and Mohenjo-daro.

The Near East and Greece about 1400 B.C.
▶ MAP ON PAGE 22

About 1400 B.C. the then civilized world reached an apex of peace and prosperity. The Egyptian empire under Amenhotep III was the greatest power, extending through Palestine and Syria to the upper Euphrates. The Kassite kings in Babylonia, having vanquished the descendants of Hammurabi, courted the friendship of Egypt and offered their daughters to the Pharaoh. Above Babylonia lay the mysterious kingdom of Mitanni, where Indo-Aryan rulers held sway over a mixed Semite and Hurrian population. The Mitannians too sought alliance with Egypt. In Crete and the Aegean, where a brilliant civilization had risen during the second millennium, the Mycenaeans had overcome the previously dominant Minoans of Crete. These Mycenaeans lived mainly on the Greek mainland, where kings and princes of Homeric type dwelt in handsome palaces on fortified hilltops at Mycenae, Tiryns, Pylos, and the Acropolis of Athens. Mycenaeans were also in Miletus, Rhodes, Cyprus, and the Palace of Minos in Crete, and traded with merchants of Egypt, Ugarit, and the Phoenician towns on the east coast of the Mediterranean.

After 1400 B.C. came the deluge. The Hittites, who had lurked north of the Taurus in Asia Minor in a great feudal empire with its capital at Hattusas, had long plotted with Syrian princes against Egypt. They now burst into Syria. The monotheist Ikhnaton, mainly interested in religion, was unable to maintain the power of Egypt, whose boundaries were pushed back to Palestine. The Assyrians revolted against Mitanni, which disappeared. Many raiders struck at Egypt, including the Philistines, who occupied the east Mediterranean coast (see page 23), and from whose name the word "Palestine" is derived. The Hittite empire itself vanished, as did the Kassite. Troy fell. Barbaric Dorian Greeks overran Greece; other Indo-European tribes invaded Asia Minor. Greece entered a Dark Age, and the whole Near East was ravaged by plague, earthquake, invasion, and the burning of cities.

By 1200 B.C. a whole era of civilization had come to an end.

Palestine
▶ MAP ON PAGE 25

This is a reference map of Palestine for all periods of the Old and New Testaments. A small country, only fifty miles from Dan to Beer-Sheba, it has three main regions: a coastal plain, a hill country where elevations rise to over 3,000 feet, and the Jordan valley, where Jericho is 700 feet and the Dead Sea 1,286 feet below sea level.

Palestine was occupied in the Old Stone Age. About 2000 B.C. the Canaanites, a Semitic group, came in from the Arabian Desert. It was from them that the Hebrews conquered the Promised Land between 1300 and 1200, during the great overturn of civilization described above. Politically the great period of the Hebrews was under David (c. 1000 B.C.) and Solomon (c. 950 B.C.), after whose death the kingdom was divided into two—Judah and Israel. Israel, with its capital at Samaria, fell to the Assyrians in 721, while Judah, whose capital was Jerusalem, fell to Nebuchadnezzar of Persia in 597. Palestine later belonged to the Persian Empire (530–332 B.C.); Alexander's Empire (332–323 B.C.); Ptolemaic Egypt (323–198 B.C.); the Seleucids of Syria (198–63 B.C.); the Roman Empire after 63 B.C., though at times governed by its own dependent kings; and to the Byzantine, Arab, and Ottoman states in medieval and modern times.

For the New Testament period see also page 40.

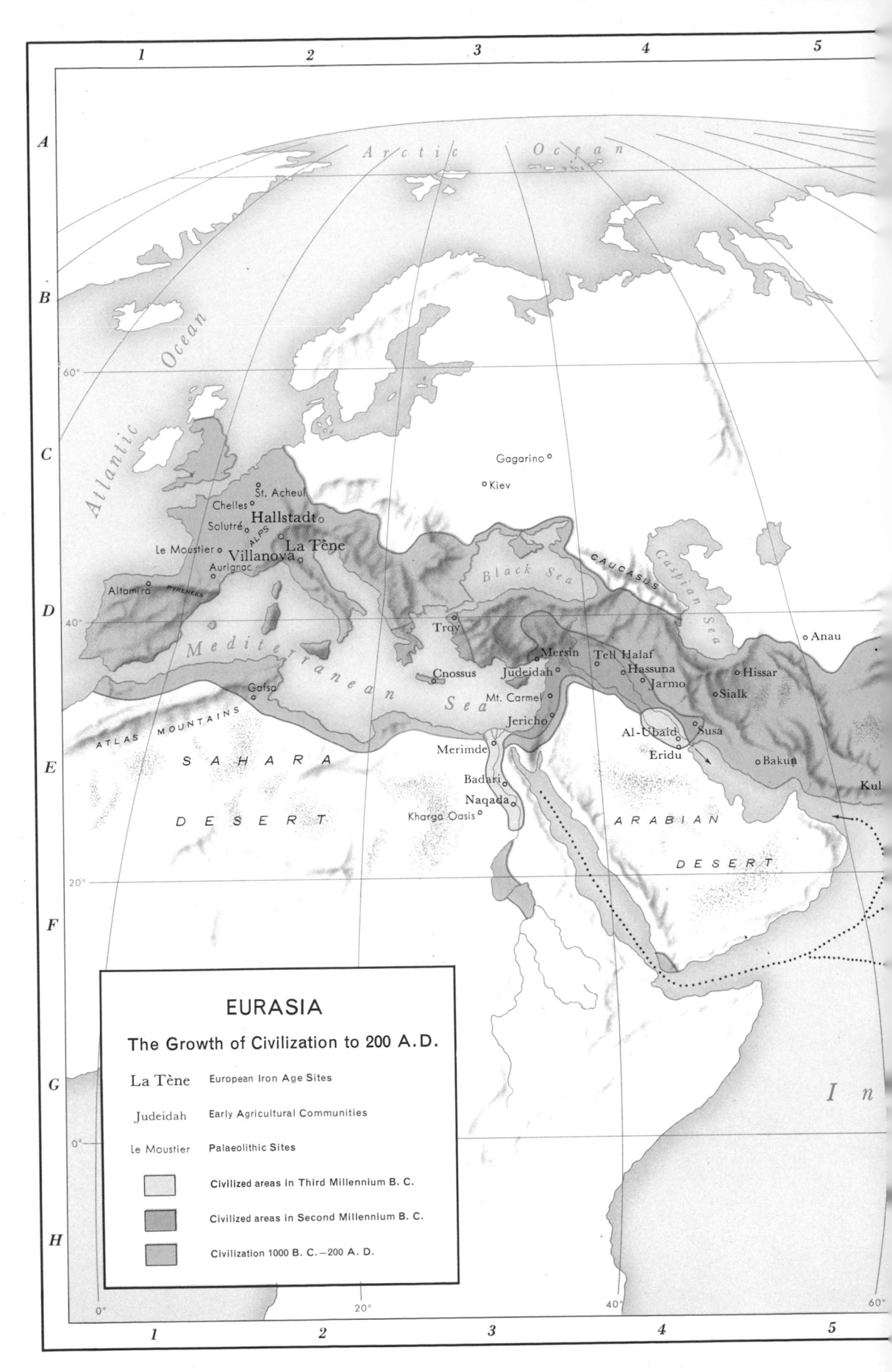

EURASIA

The Growth of Civilization to 200 A.D.

La Tène   European Iron Age Sites

Judeidah   Early Agricultural Communities

Le Moustier   Palaeolithic Sites

Civilized areas in Third Millennium B. C.

Civilized areas in Second Millennium B. C.

Civilization 1000 B. C.—200 A. D.

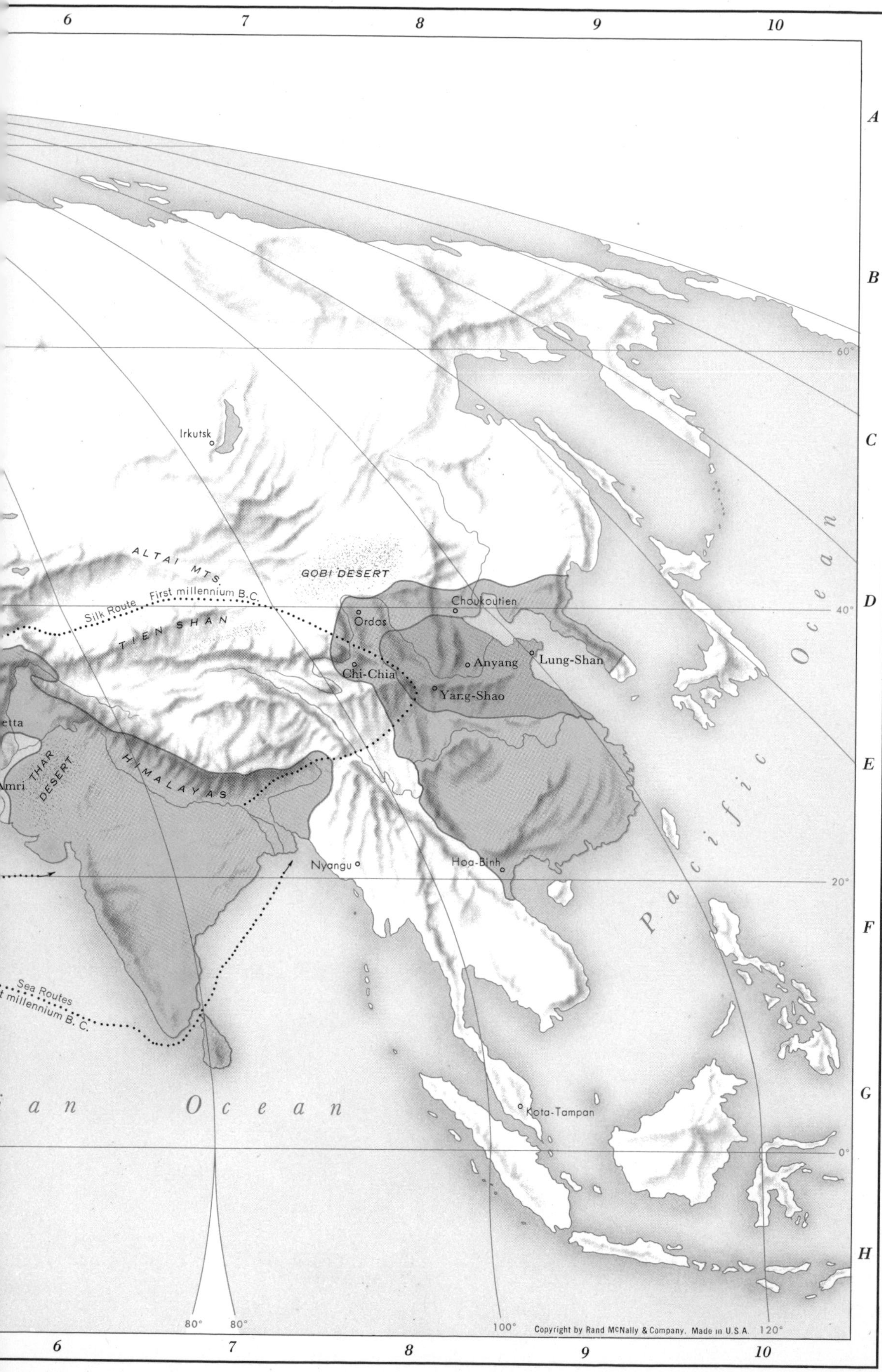

A

B

60°

C

Irkutsk

ALTAI MTS.

GOBI DESERT

D

40°

Silk Route   First millennium B.C.

TIEN SHAN

Choukoutien

Ordos

Anyang   Lung-Shan

Chi-Chia

Yang-Shao

etta

THAR DESERT

HIMALAYAS

E

Amri

Nyangu   Hoa-Binh

20°

F

Sea Routes
t millennium B.C.

an   Ocean

Pacific Ocean

G

Kota-Tampan

0°

H

80°   80°

100°   Copyright by Rand McNally & Company. Made in U.S.A.   120°

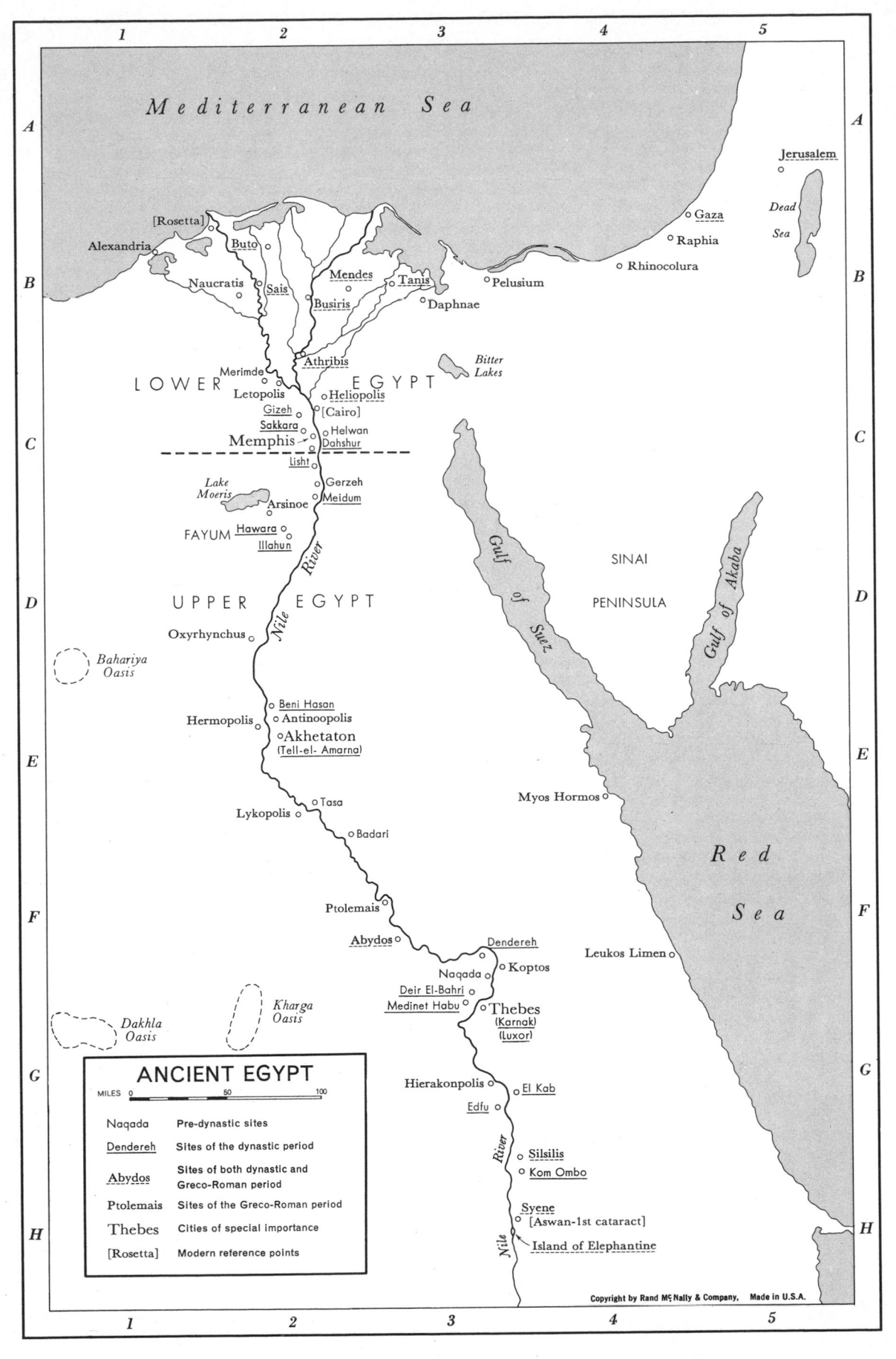

ANCIENT EGYPT

Naqada	Pre-dynastic sites
<u>Dendereh</u>	Sites of the dynastic period
<u>Abydos</u>	Sites of both dynastic and Greco-Roman period
Ptolemais	Sites of the Greco-Roman period
Thebes	Cities of special importance
[Rosetta]	Modern reference points

MILES 0   50   100

Copyright by Rand McNally & Company,   Made in U.S.A.

Mediterranean Sea

Jerusalem

Dead Sea

Gaza
Raphia
Rhinocolura

[Rosetta]
Alexandria
Buto
Naucratis
Sais
Mendes
Tanis
Busiris
Pelusium
Daphnae

LOWER EGYPT
Merimde
Athribis
Letopolis
Heliopolis
Gizeh
[Cairo]
Sakkara
Helwan
Memphis
Dahshur
Lisht
Gerzeh
Lake Moeris
Meidum
Arsinoe
FAYUM
Hawara
Illahun

Bitter Lakes

SINAI PENINSULA

Gulf of Suez

Gulf of Akaba

UPPER EGYPT
Oxyrhynchus

Bahariya Oasis

Hermopolis
Beni Hasan
Antinoopolis
Akhetaton
(Tell-el- Amarna)

Tasa
Lykopolis
Badari

Myos Hormos

Red Sea

Ptolemais
Abydos
Dendereh
Koptos
Naqada
Deir El-Bahri
Medinet Habu
Thebes
(Karnak)
(Luxor)

Leukos Limen

Dakhla Oasis
Kharga Oasis

Hierakonpolis
El Kab
Edfu

Nile River

Silsilis
Kom Ombo

Syene
[Aswan-1st cataract]
Island of Elephantine

Nile River

20

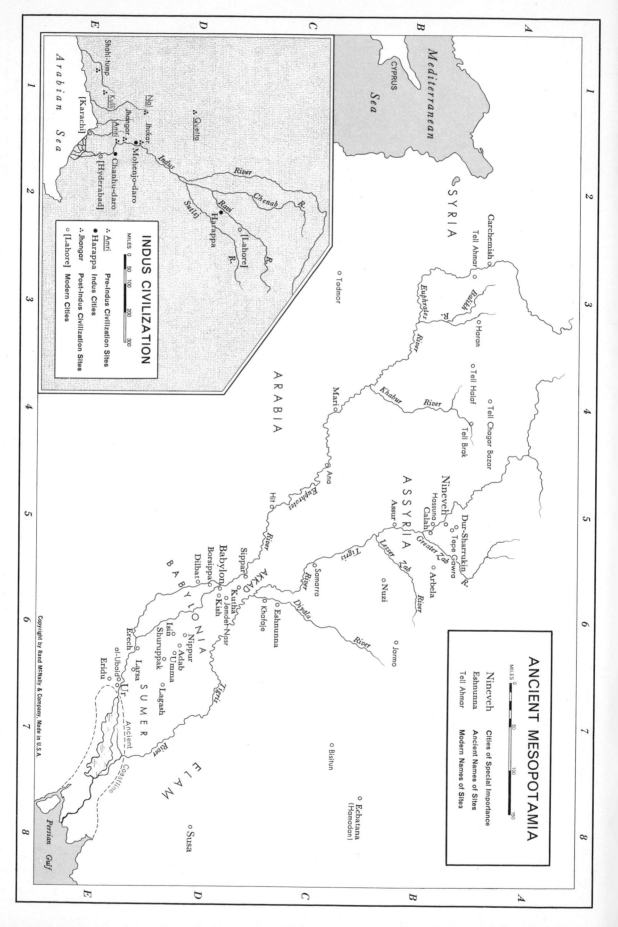

ANCIENT MESOPOTAMIA

	Cities of Special Importance
Nineveh	Ancient Names of Sites
Eshnunna	Modern Names of Sites
Tell Ahmar	

MILES 0   50   100   150

INDUS CIVILIZATION

MILES 0   50   100   200   300

Amri	Pre-Indus Civilization Sites
Harappa	Indus Cities
Jhangar	Post-Indus Civilization Sites
[Lahore]	Modern Cities

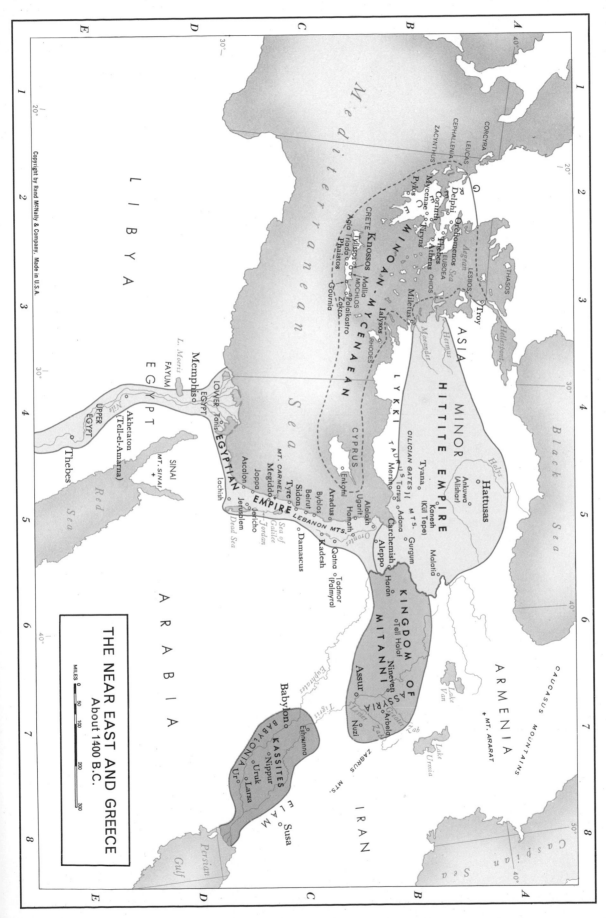

THE NEAR EAST AND GREECE
About 1400 B.C.

MILES
0 50 100 200 300

LIBYA

EGYPT

L. Moeris
FAYUM
Memphis
LOWER EGYPT
Tanis

UPPER EGYPT

Akhetaton (Tell-el-Amarna)

Thebes

SINAI
MT. SINAI

Red Sea

ARABIA

EGYPTIAN EMPIRE

Lachish
Ascalon
Joppa
Jerusalem
Jericho
Jordan
Sea of Galilee
Megiddo
MT. CARMEL
Tyre
Sidon
Beirut
Byblos
Aradus
Damascus
Kadesh
Qatna
Tadmor (Palmyra)

Dead Sea
LEBANON MTS.

Mediterranean Sea

CRETE
Knossos
Tylissos
Agia Triada
Phaistos
Gournia
Mallia
MOCHLOS
Palaikastro
Zakro

MINOAN - MYCENAEAN

Ialysos
RHODES

CYPRUS
Enkomi

CORCYRA
LEUCAS
CEPHALLENIA
ZACYNTHUS
Delphi
Orchomenos
Corinth
Mycenae
Tiryns
EUBOEA
Thebes
Athens
Pylos

Aegean Sea

LESBOS
CHIOS

THASOS

Troy

Hellespont

ASIA MINOR

Maeander
Hermus
Habs

Miletus
LYKII

HITTITE EMPIRE
Hattusas
Ankuwa (Alishar)
Kanesh (Kül Tepe)
Tyana
CILICIAN GATES
TAURUS MTS.
Tarsus
Adana
Mersin
Gurgum
Malatia
Carchemish
Aleppo
Haran

Ugarit
Alalakh
Hamath
Orontes

Black Sea

ARMENIA
+ MT. ARARAT

Lake Van
Lake Urmia

CAUCASUS MOUNTAINS

Caspian Sea

KINGDOM OF MITANNI
Tell Halaf
Nineveh
ASSYRIA
Arbela
Assur
Nuzi
Upper Zab
Lower Zab

ZAGROS MTS.

IRAN

Euphrates
Tigris

Babylon
BABYLONIA
KASSITES
Eshnunna
Nippur
Uruk
Ur
Larsa
ELAM
Susa

Persian Gulf

23

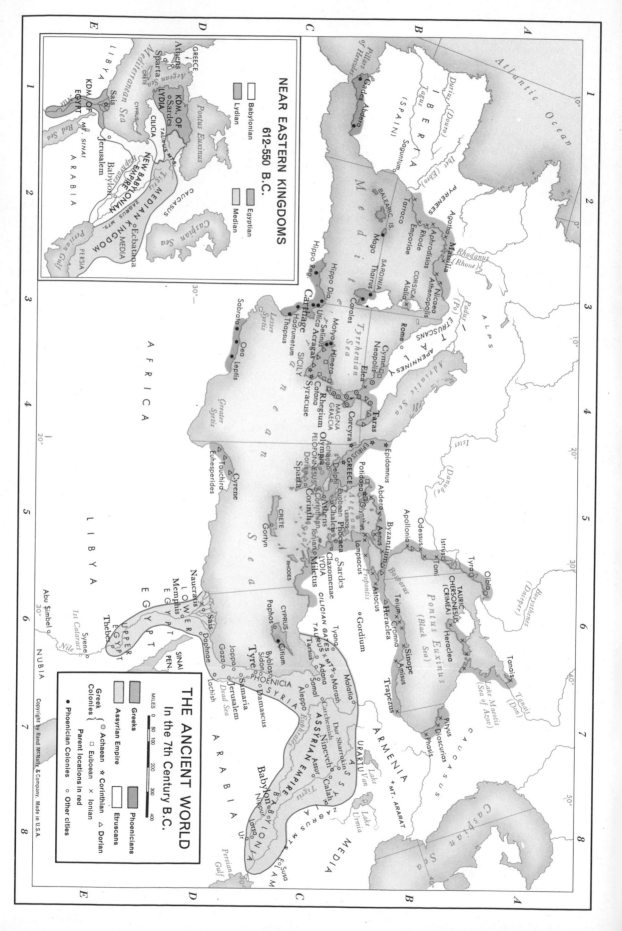

NEAR EASTERN KINGDOMS
612-550 B.C.

Babylonian

Lydian

Egyptian

Median

THE ANCIENT WORLD
In the 7th Century B.C.

MILES 0 50 100 200 300 400

Greeks

Assyrian Empire

Phoenicians

Etruscans

Greek Colonies:
○ Achaean
☆ Corinthian
□ Euboean
× Ionian
△ Dorian

Parent locations in red

● Phoenician Colonies
○ Other cities

Copyright by Rand McNally & Company, Made in U.S.A.

CLASSICAL ANTIQUITY:
THE GREEKS AND THE PERSIANS

▶ MAPS ON PAGES 23, 26, AND 27

THE COMMERCIAL AND CULTURAL contacts of the civilized world were broken up for several centuries from 1200 to 750 B.C. Greece was plunged into semibarbarism by the Dorian invasion, and in the Near East there were many small separate kingdoms, like that of the Hebrews.

The Ancient World in the Seventh Century B.C.
▶ MAP ON PAGE 23

Economic recovery set in as the Phoenicians by sea, and the Aramaeans by land, contributed to the revival of long-distance trading. The Phoenicians established colonies at widely scattered points as far west as Spain. The most famous of these was Carthage, founded about 800 B.C. Meanwhile, the Assyrians grew in strength, and established an empire about 750 B.C. under Tiglath Pileser III (the Pul of the Old Testament), who was followed by the more famous Sennacherib and Ashurbanipal. The map shows the Assyrian empire at its height under Ashurbanipal. With his death, in 626, the empire began to disintegrate. In 612 Nineveh fell to the Babylonians and Medes. For a time there were four more or less equal kingdoms in the Near East: the Saite Dynasty in Egypt; the Medes ruling Iran and part of Asia Minor; the Lydian kingdom in Asia Minor; and the neo-Babylonian kingdom, comprising Babylonia, Assyria, Syria, and Palestine. In the next century, the sixth, these came under the Persians (see page 27).

The Greeks
▶ MAP ON PAGE 26

The revival of trade, and the political unity imposed by Assyria, brought the Aegean area back into contact with the Near East—a contact interrupted since Mycenaean times—and stimulated the cultural development of the half-barbarian Greeks. The Greek Dark Age, lifting about 750 B.C., was succeeded by the Archaic Period of the Greeks as we know them in literature and history. The first stirrings among the Greeks of western Asia Minor and the islands soon spread to the Greek mainland. Voyages to the Black Sea and the western Mediterranean, undertaken for trade or to discover new copper, iron, and silver deposits, led to the founding of trading posts, which became permanent colonies.

Colonization is the key to this early phase of Greek history. The colonies of Miletus and other Ionian towns were mainly commercial foundations, though after the Persian advance many Greek refugees went to them. The colonies of Euboea and the mainland states, though originally inspired by trade, became a means of relieving overpopulation. Corinth and Megara led the Greek world in the number of their colonies, and hence became great centers of industry and trade. The accumulation of capital in the home cities, made possible by trade and colonization, laid a foundation for the culture of the Archaic Period.

The west was for the first time brought within the sphere of civilization by Phoenician and Greek expansion. Greek cities were established in Sicily, south Italy, and on the modern Spanish and French coasts, where Massilia, the modern Marseille, was founded about 600 B.C. Greek and Phoenician (later Carthaginian) colonists struggled in the western Mediterranean. The latter kept the Greeks from settling in southern Spain and in Corsica. In Italy the Etruscans, becoming hostile, confined the Greeks to the southern part of the peninsula.

The age of colonization in Greece was followed by a period dominated by relations with Persia. The Persian kings Darius and Xerxes attacked in turn. Xerxes invaded with a huge army and fleet, broke through the pass of Thermopylae, and pressed into Attica, only to be defeated by the Greek naval victory at Salamis (480 B.C.) and land victories at Plataea and at Mycale in Asia Minor (479 B.C.).

The period of the Persian Wars, in which Greeks had combined against an outside danger, was followed by a century and a half in which Greek fought Greek. After the Persian defeat Athens took the lead in forming an alliance to liberate the islands. When the other members sought to withdraw Athens prevented them, turning the alliance into an Athenian empire, at its height under Pericles about 456 B.C. Athenian culture reached its zenith in this and the following generations (a map of the city appears on page 29). Athenian ascendancy provoked the opposition of Sparta and Corinth, which led to the Peloponnesian War (431–404 B.C.) and the end of the Athenian empire. Vain attempts by Sparta and Thebes to dominate Greece were followed by the success of Macedon, whose king, Philip, taking advantage of Greek disunity, crushed all resistance in the battle of Chaeronea (338 B.C.), and so opened the way for his spectacular son, Alexander the Great (see pages 30–31).

The Persian Empire
▶ MAP ON PAGE 27

The Persians were one of the many Indo-European-speaking tribes whose movements disturbed the world at the close of the second millennium. Others were the Dorians who invaded Greece, the rulers of Mitanni, and the Indo-Aryans who invaded India at about this time (see page 118; for the Indo-European languages of modern Europe see pages 94–95).

Cyrus the Great conquered Media, Lydia, and Babylonia about 550 B.C.; Cambyses added Egypt in 525; Darius extended his power to the Indus valley and to European Thrace; Xerxes invaded Greece in 480. The Persian Empire, giving for the first time a political unity to the whole area from the Indus to the Aegean, had a magnificent capital at Persepolis, and was administered through about thirty great satrapies. A Persian minority ruled over a conglomerate population and so issued bilingual and even trilingual documents, one of which was the Bisitun inscription, mentioned above.

The Persian Empire weakened after Xerxes. The fact that a famous expedition of 10,000 Greeks, in 401 B.C., could safely march through its sprawling domains was an intimation of the subsequent conquest by Alexander.

MEDITERRANEAN AND OTHER COASTS

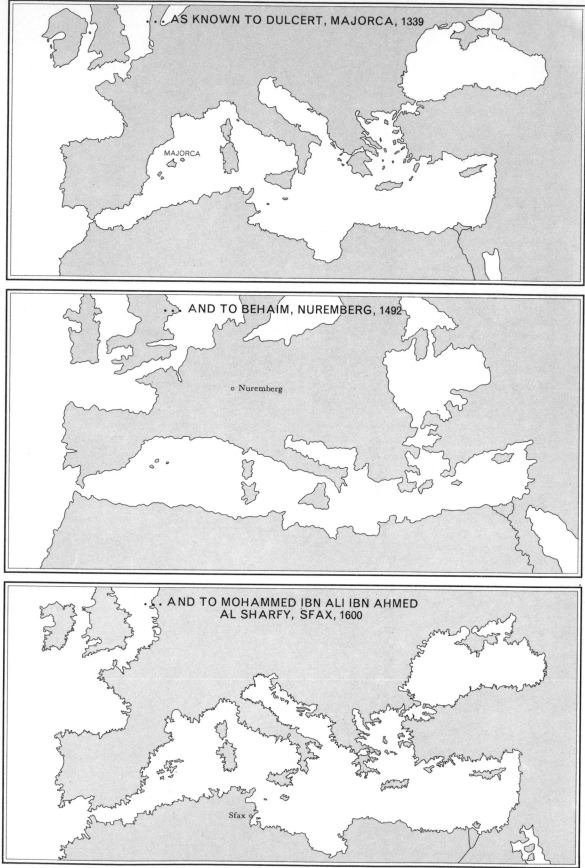

... AS KNOWN TO DULCERT, MAJORCA, 1339

MAJORCA

... AND TO BEHAIM, NUREMBERG, 1492

o Nuremberg

... AND TO MOHAMMED IBN ALI IBN AHMED
AL SHARFY, SFAX, 1600

Sfax o

THE WORLD
According to Behaim, 1492

The original globe is
twenty inches in diameter

After Jomard

Copyright by Rand McNally & Company, Made in U.S.A.

11

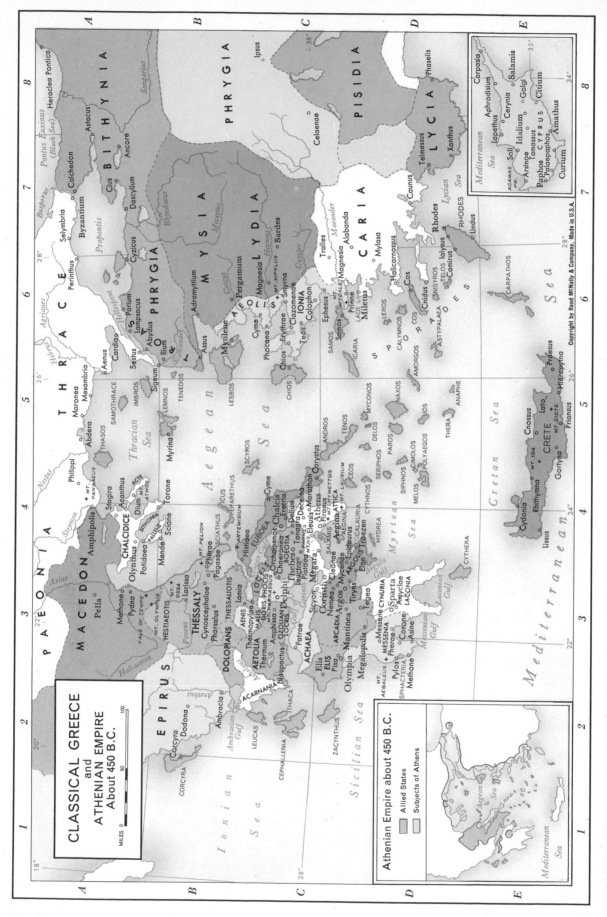

CLASSICAL GREECE and ATHENIAN EMPIRE About 450 B.C.

MILES
0   50   100

Copyright by Rand McNally & Company, Made in U.S.A.

Athenian Empire about 450 B.C.

Allied States
Subjects of Athens

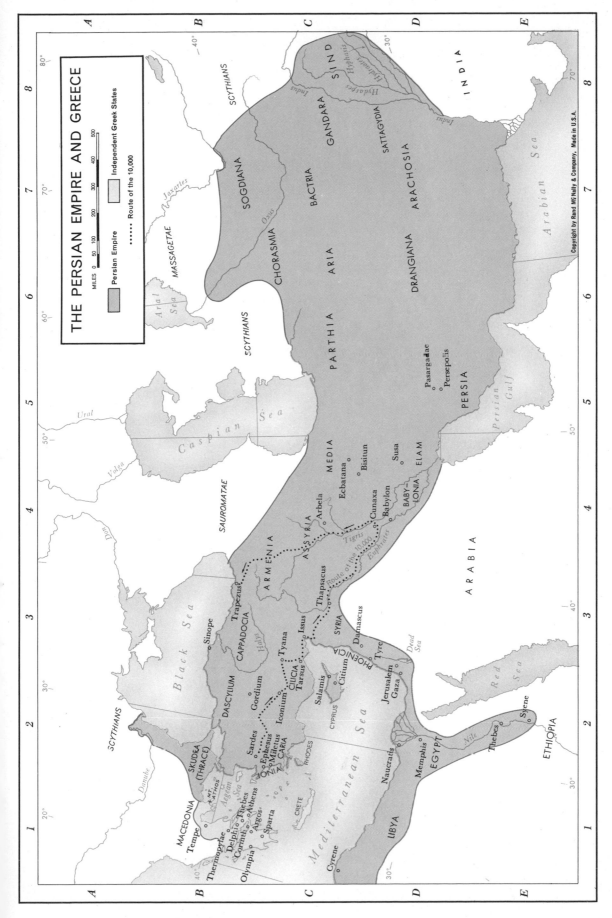

THE PERSIAN EMPIRE AND GREECE

MILES 0 50 100 200 300 400 500

Persian Empire

Independent Greek States

..... Route of the 10,000

Copyright by Rand McNally & Company, Made in U.S.A.

SCYTHIANS

MASSAGETAE

SOGDIANA

S I N D

GANDARA

BACTRIA

SATTAGYDIA

ARACHOSIA

I N D I A

Indus

Hyphasis

Hydaspes

Indus

Jaxartes

Aral Sea

Ozus

CHORASMIA

ARIA

DRANGIANA

Arabian Sea

SCYTHIANS

Ural

Volga

Caspian Sea

SAUROMATAE

Don

PARTHIA

PERSIA

Pasargadae

Persepolis

Persian Gulf

MEDIA

Ecbatana

Bisitun

Susa

ELAM

BABY-LONIA

Babylon

Cunaxa

Arbela

ASSYRIA

ARMENIA

Route of the 10,000

Tigris

Euphrates

ARABIA

Black Sea

Sinope

Trapezus

CAPPADOCIA

Halys

Gordium

Thapsacus

SYRIA

Damascus

Tyana

Iconium

CILICIA

Tarsus

Issus

PHOENICIA

Tyre

Dead Sea

Red Sea

DASCYLIUM

Sardes

Ephesus

Miletus

IONIA

CARIA

RHODES

Salamis

Citium

CYPRUS

Jerusalem

Gaza

Naucratis

Memphis

EGYPT

Nile

Thebes

Syene

ETHIOPIA

SCYTHIANS

SKUDEA (THRACE)

MACEDONIA

Tempe

MT. ATHOS

Thermopylae

Delphi

Corinth

Olympia

Thebes

Athens

Argos

Sparta

Aegean Sea

CRETE

Mediterranean Sea

LIBYA

Cyrene

40°

30°

70°

80°

60°

50°

40°

30°

20°

70°

50°

40°

30°

ALEXANDER'S EMPIRE
AND THE HELLENISTIC KINGDOMS

▶ MAPS ON PAGES 29, 30–31, AND 32

PHILIP OF MACEDON, after conquering Greece, formed additional plans to invade Asia with the combined manpower and resources of the Greek states; but he was assassinated in 336 B.C., so that the execution of his plans fell to his son, Alexander.

In 334 Alexander crossed into Asia Minor. As resistance collapsed before him, he passed on through the Cilician Gates in the Taurus Mountains to Tarsus, near which he met and defeated the Persian king, Darius III, at Issus in 333. Alexander then proceeded down the coast, taking Tyre and Gaza in 332, and spent about a year in Egypt, where he made a famous trip across the desert to consult the priests at the Oasis of Siwah. The year 331 found him in Assyria, where he again defeated Darius at Gaugamela. He occupied Babylonia and wintered at Persepolis. Darius fled toward Bactria, but was murdered by his own people somewhere south of the Caspian Sea. Alexander pushed on ever eastward, crossed the Hindu Kush into Bactria and Sogdiana in 329, recrossed it and reached the upper Indus in 327, descended the river, and returned to Babylon in 325, where he died two years later, at the age of thirty-three.

The brevity of Alexander's meteoric career left him no time to organize his conquests. A compromise regency under his son and half brother was followed by a struggle between Alexander's generals, of whom Ptolemy, Seleucus, and Antigonos were ultimately the most successful. Ptolemy, sent to Egypt as Alexander's viceroy in 323, made himself king in 306 and established a dynasty which lasted until the death of Cleopatra in 30 B.C. Seleucus founded a dynasty which lasted until 63 B.C. Originally the Seleucids controlled most of the former Persian Empire, but in the third century local revolts led to the independence of Pergamum (250 B.C.), Parthia (250), and consequently of the more remote Bactria (225). In Macedonia itself Antigonos Gonatas, son of Alexander's general of similar name, established an Antigonid kingdom in 277. The third century was the great age of the Hellenistic states, the most important being the Ptolemaic, Seleucid, and Antigonid kingdoms, the lesser ones Bithynia, Pontus, Pergamum, Epirus, and the Aetolian and Achaean leagues in the old Greece.

Alexander's amazing conquests did not, in fact, carry him beyond the limits already reached by the Persian Empire. The Persians had already provided a certain unity and intercommunication for most of the ancient world of the Near East. Alexander's conquests brought all this into relation with Greece. Greeks settled in the Near East, and the Greek language became an international medium. The resulting mixture of Greek and "Oriental" culture (that is, the culture of the ancient Near East) resulted in an amalgam called Hellenistic. Alexander himself founded many cities, such as Alexandria in Egypt. Others founded by or named after him included an Alexandria on the Indus, whence cultural influences were diffused further east to the Ganges, and an Alexandria on the Jaxartes, the jumping-off place for the silk route to China, two thousand miles away (see pages 118–119).

Greek Civilization
▶ MAPS ON PAGES 29 AND 32

The map on page 32 suggests the geographical distribution of Greek civilization in the classical and Hellenistic ages. The Greek spirit first showed itself in poetry and philosophical speculation, and first of all, from the eighth to the sixth centuries, in Ionia on the Asia Minor coast, and in the islands. Here the poems of Homer originated, and "burning Sappho" loved and sung; here, too, with men like Thales and Heraclitus in the sixth century, Greek science as we know it first appeared. In the fifth and fourth centuries Athens assumed its extraordinary lead, particularly in philosophy, dramatic poetry, sculpture, oratory, and history. Aristotle, called the "Stagirite" from his birthplace in Macedonia, actually lived and worked at Athens, as did Socrates and Plato. Athens declined in creative powers as suddenly as it had risen; no one is shown on the map for Athens after the fourth century B.C. The Greek colonies began to contribute to Greek civilization as early as the fifth century, especially in philosophy and science. In the third century Archimedes lived in Syracuse, and the geometer Euclid at Alexandria; it was also at Alexandria that Eratosthenes, born in Cyrene, calculated the size of the earth with more accuracy than his successor Ptolemy four centuries later.

Athens
▶ MAP ON PAGE 29

Buildings and monuments of Athens from the sixth century B.C. to the second century A.D. are shown on the facing page. The two most prominent natural features were the Areopagus and the Acropolis. The hill called Areopagus was the meeting place of the council of the same name. The steep rock of the Acropolis was in the classical period the religious center of the city. Here the Erechtheum and the Parthenon (Temple of Athena) were planned by Pericles in the fifth century. The fifth-century approach to the Acropolis, leading to the Propylaea (Gates), is shown by dotted lines; the Beule Gate belongs to the Roman period.

The center of everyday life was the market place or Agora. The famous Long Walls, built after the Persian Wars, formed a corridor down to the Peiraeus (Piraeus), the seaport of Athens. Long after the ebbing of its creative vitality the city continued to grow in size. The Hellenistic period saw the addition of the Middle Stoa, the Stoa of Attalus, and the Odeum. In the Roman period the Agora expanded eastward. The Roman market was built in the first century A.D., the Library of Pantainos about 100 A.D., the Library of Hadrian in the following century. At this time, at the height of the Roman Empire, Athens was an active center of learning, famous mostly, however, for a past already ancient. For Greek culture of the Roman period see page 37.

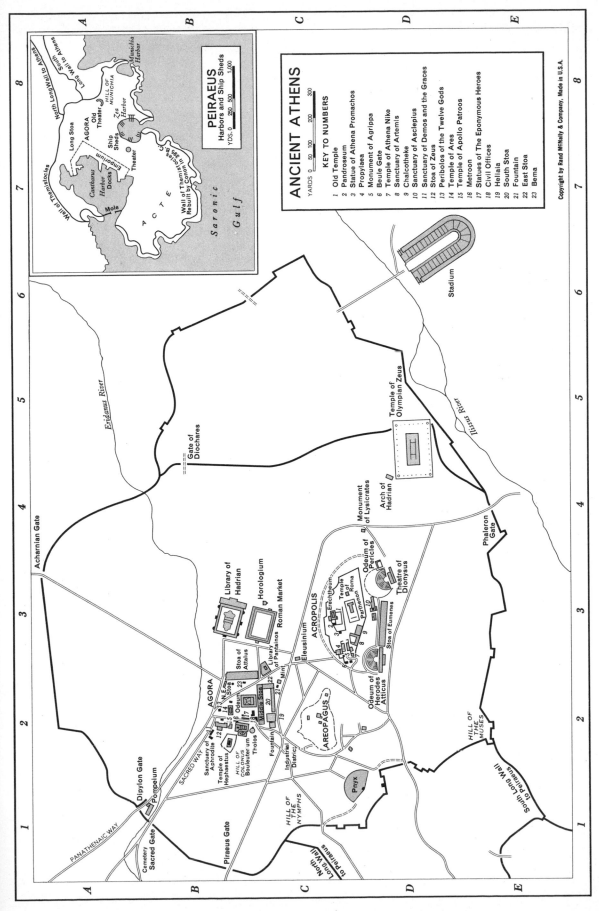

ANCIENT ATHENS

YARDS 0 50 100 200 300

KEY TO NUMBERS

1 Old Temple
2 Pandroseum
3 Statue of Athena Promachos
4 Propylaea
5 Monument of Agrippa
6 Beule Gate
7 Temple of Athena Nike
8 Sanctuary of Artemis
9 Chalcotheke
10 Sanctuary of Ascleplus
11 Sanctuary of Demos and the Graces
12 Stoa of Zeus
13 Peribolos of the Twelve Gods
14 Temple of Ares
15 Temple of Apollo Patroos
16 Metroon
17 Statues of The Eponymous Heroes
18 Civil Offices
19 Heliaia
20 South Stoa
21 Fountain
22 East Stoa
23 Bema

Copyright by Rand McNally & Company, Made in U.S.A.

PEIRAEUS
Harbors and Ship Sheds

YDS. 0 250 500 1,000

29

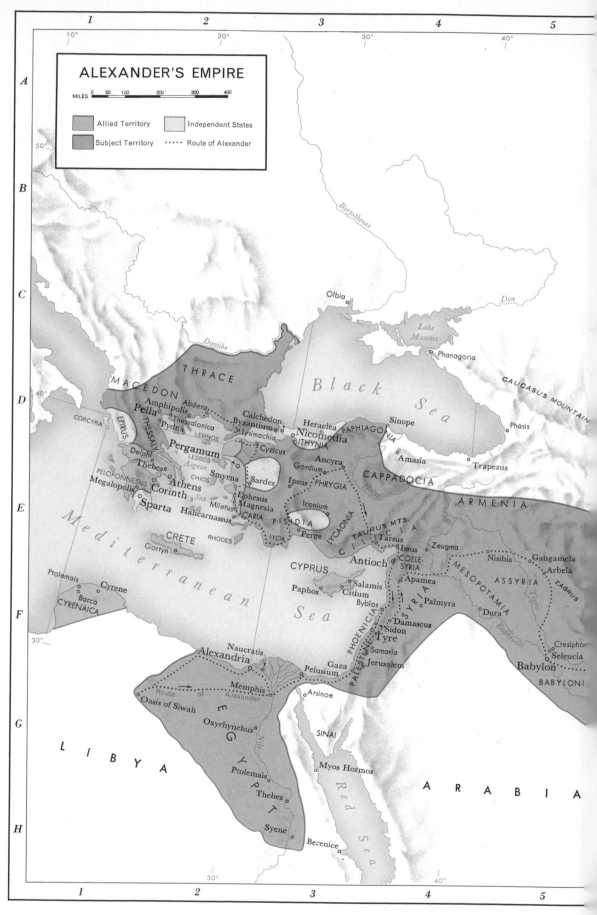

ALEXANDER'S EMPIRE

MILES 0 50 100 200 300 400

Allied Territory   Independent States
Subject Territory   ····· Route of Alexander

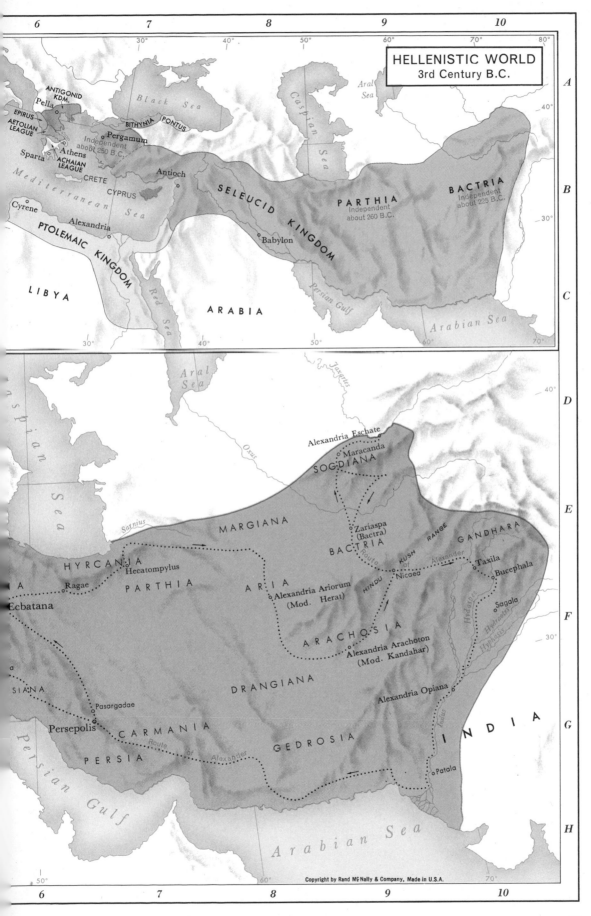

HELLENISTIC WORLD
3rd Century B.C.

Aral Sea

Black Sea

Caspian Sea

ANTIGONID KDM.
Pella
EPIRUS
AETOLIAN LEAGUE
Sparta
Athens
ACHAIAN LEAGUE
CRETE

BITHYNIA
PONTUS
Pergamum
Independent about 250 B.C.

Antioch
CYPRUS

Mediterranean Sea

Cyrene
Alexandria
Babylon

SELEUCID KINGDOM

PARTHIA
Independent about 260 B.C.

BACTRIA
Independent about 225 B.C.

PTOLEMAIC KINGDOM

LIBYA

ARABIA

Persian Gulf

Arabian Sea

Aral Sea

Jaxartes

Oxus

Caspian Sea

Alexandria Eschate
Maracanda
SOGDIANA

MARGIANA

Zariaspa (Bactra)
BACTRIA

HINDU KUSH RANGE

GANDHARA

Sorníus

HYRCANIA
Hecatompylus
Ragae
PARTHIA

ARIA

Alexandria Ariorum
(Mod. Herat)

Route

Nicaea
Alexander
Taxila
Bucephala

Ecbatana

Sagala

ARACHOSIA

Alexandria Arachoton
(Mod. Kandahar)

Hydaspes
Hydraotes
Hyphasis

a

SIANA

DRANGIANA

Alexandria Opiana

Pasargadae
Persepolis
CARMANIA

PERSIA

Route of Alexander

GEDROSIA

Indus

INDIA

Persian Gulf

Patala

Arabian Sea

Copyright by Rand McNally & Company, Made in U.S.A.

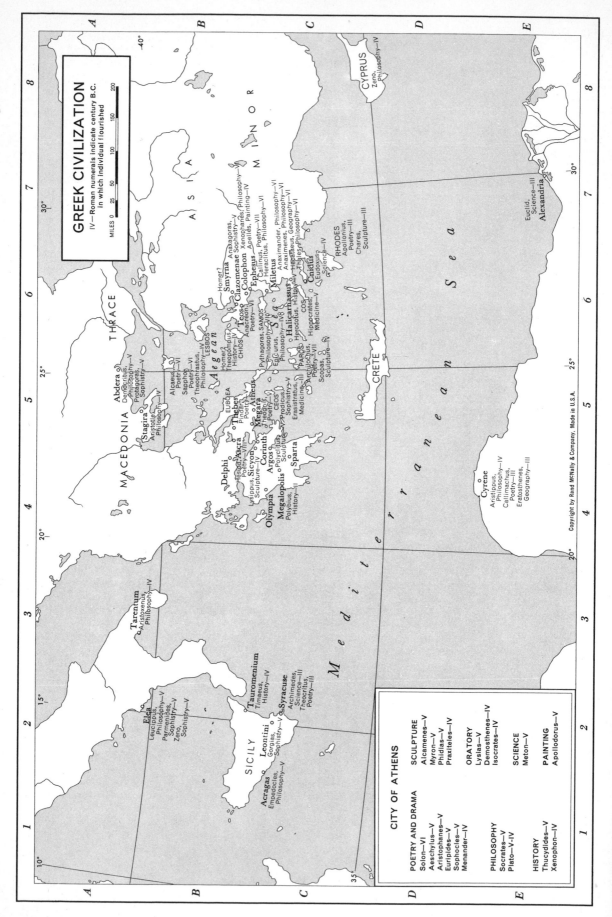

GREEK CIVILIZATION

IV—Roman numerals indicate century B.C.
in which individual flourished

MILES 0 25 50 100 150 200

CYPRUS
Zeno, Philosophy—IV

ASIA MINOR

Homer?
Smyrna Anaxagoras,—V
Clazomenae Sophistry—V
Teos **Colophon** Xenophanes, Philosophy—
Anacreon **Ephesus** Apelles, Painting—IV
Poetry—V Callinus, Poetry—VII
CHIOS Heraclitus, Philosophy—VI
Pythagoras, SAMOS **Miletus** Anaximander, Philosophy—VI
Philosophy—VI Anaximenes, Philosophy—VI
Epicurus, IV O Thales, Philosophy—VI
Philosophy—IV **Halicarnassus** Herodotus, History—V
PAROS **Cnidus** Hippocrates,
Scopas, Medicine—V
Sculpture—IV Eudoxus?
Poetry—VII Science—IV

RHODES
Apollonius,
Poetry—III
Chares,
Sculpture—III

Alexandria
Euclid,
Science—III

THRACE

MACEDONIA

Abdera o Democritus,
Philosophy—V
Protagoras,
Sophistry—IV

Stagira o
Aristotle,
Philosophy—IV

Alcaeus,
Poetry—VI
Sappho,
Poetry—VI
Theophrastus,
Philosophy—IV
LESBOS

EUBOEA
Thebes
Pindar,
Hesiod Ascra Poetry—V
o Poetry—VII
Lysippus, Sicyon
Sculpture—IV
Delphi **Corinth**
Polyclitus,
Argos Sculpture—V
Sparta

Olympia
Megalopolis o
Polybius,
History—II

Megara
Poetry
Prodicus,
Sophistry—V
Erasistratus,
Medicine—

Aegean Sea

CRETE

Cyrene
Aristippus,
Philosophy—IV
Callimachus,
Poetry—III
Eratosthenes,
Geography—III

Tarentum o
Aristoxenus,
Philosophy—IV

Elea
Leucippus,
Philosophy—
Parmenides,—V
Zeno,
Sophistry—V

SICILY

Acragas o
Empedocles,
Philosophy—V

Leontini
Gorgias,
Sophistry—V

Tauromenium
Timaeus,
History—IV

o **Syracuse**
Archimedes,
Science—III
Theocritus,
Poetry—III

Mediterranean Sea

Copyright by Rand McNally & Company, Made in U.S.A.

CITY OF ATHENS

POETRY AND DRAMA
Solon—VI
Aeschylus—V
Aristophanes—V
Euripides—V
Sophocles—V
Menander—IV

PHILOSOPHY
Socrates—V
Plato—V-IV

HISTORY
Thucydides—V
Xenophon—IV

SCULPTURE
Alcamenes—V
Myron—V
Phidias—V
Praxiteles—IV

ORATORY
Lysias—V
Demosthenes—IV
Isocrates—IV

SCIENCE
Meton—V

PAINTING
Apollodorus—V

THE ROMAN REPUBLIC

▶ MAP ON PAGES 34–35

THE FOLLOWING MAP SHOWS the extent of Roman territory at the close of the republic in the first century B.C.

According to its own traditions Rome was founded in 753 B.C. Actually little is known of it before the year 400. Archeology confirms that the site of Rome was occupied in the tenth century B.C., and that in the seventh century it was an Etruscan stronghold, ruled by kings. So much is in accord with tradition. Sometime after 500 (the traditional date is 509) the kings were replaced by a republic. For two centuries the city, with its allies of the Latin League, maintained its independence and slowly extended its influence in central Italy, until, soon after 300, the Romans conflicted with the powerful Greek city-state of Tarentum. Against the Romans the Tarentines enlisted the famous general, Pyrrhus, king of Epirus, who defeated them at Heraclea in 280. But the Romans overcame Pyrrhus at Beneventum (275) and subdued the Tarentines.

The Punic Wars

Thus involved with the Greeks of south Italy, the Romans came into increasing contact with the Greeks of Sicily, who looked to them for protection against Carthage, archenemy to Sicilian and all western Greeks. The First Punic War between Rome and Carthage thus began at Messana in 264. Building a fleet, the Romans won the naval battle of Mylae with the aid of a novel boarding bridge. When the war ended in 241, the Romans had acquired their first province outside Italy, namely Sicily, and with civil disturbance weakening Carthage they seized Sardinia and Corsica as well.

Expanding northward, the Romans about 220 B.C. conquered the Po valley, known as Cisalpine Gaul. At the same time the Carthaginians were expanding northward along the coast of Spain. The Greek colonies of that area were alarmed; again it seemed to be the fate of Rome to identify itself with Greek civilization against a Carthaginian threat. Rome declared war when the Carthaginian Hannibal attacked Saguntum. The Second Punic War ensued, fought in Spain, Italy, Sicily, and Africa. Hannibal crossed the Alps in 218 (the famous elephants that he took on this expedition suggesting the far-flung connections of Phoenician Carthage), descended into the Po valley, and beat the Romans at Trebia, Lake Trasimene, and Cannae (217–216). Only Hannibal's distance from home, and Roman superiority in manpower and sea power, turned the tide. The brilliant young Scipio, after victories in Spain, was able to invade Africa and at last to defeat Hannibal and end the war at Zama in 202.

In Greece itself the Romans were now able to offer themselves as protectors. They defeated a Macedonian king at Cynocephalae in 197, and in 192 repelled an invasion of Greece by the Seleucid Antiochus III, whom they pursued into Asia Minor and overwhelmed at Magnesia in 190. In 149–146 revolts flared up, and were suppressed, in Macedonia, Greece, and Carthage. Corinth and Carthage were destroyed and abandoned, though later rebuilt. Macedonia was reorganized as a Roman province, and the territory around Carthage became the Roman province of Africa. Soon thereafter the king of Pergamum, Attalus I, bequeathed his kingdom to the Romans, who in 129 B.C. converted it into the province of Asia.

From Republic to Empire

This century of rapid expansion, by introducing the Romans to Greek civilization, produced a Roman or Latin culture closely related to the Greek, and also, by creating new sources of wealth and power, led to political and social strife at Rome itself. An invasion of Italy by the Cimbri and Teutones was stopped in southern Gaul at Aquae Sextiae (102 B.C.) and Vercellae (101 B.C.) by the Roman general Marius, who had also distinguished himself in the Jugurthine war in Numidia. Marius and his rival Sulla both served in the Social War (90–88 B.C.), in which the Italian allies (*socii*) of Rome attempted to revolt and set up a capital at Corfinium. Marius and Sulla then became opponents in the conflict between the senatorial and popular factions at Rome. Marius and the popular party seized the government while Sulla campaigned in Asia, but when Sulla returned in 83 B.C. he triumphed over Marius and held a dictatorship until his retirement in 79 B.C.

The king of Bithynia willed his kingdom to Rome in 75 B.C., but the Romans, to obtain the bequest, had to fight a new war with the king of Pontus, Mithradates, against whom Sulla had campaigned, and who now claimed Bithynia as his own. The new war with Mithradates was terminated in 66 by Pompey. Bithynia became a Roman province, other states of Asia Minor became vassals, and the dwindling Seleucid kingdom was annexed as the province of Syria.

Pompey, Crassus, and Julius Caesar formed a First Triumvirate in 60 B.C. to govern Rome. Caesar, made proconsul or governor of Cisalpine and Transalpine Gaul, used this position to conquer Gaul as a whole (58–51 B.C.). Crassus meanwhile was killed at Carrhae (53 B.C.) in a campaign against the Parthians. Caesar and Pompey drifted apart, Caesar becoming the popular leader, while Pompey allied with the senatorial party. In 49 B.C. Caesar crossed the Rubicon, the boundary of Cisalpine Gaul, south of which he had no lawful authority. Thus precipitating civil war, he defeated Pompey at Pharsalus and Pompeian forces at Thapsus (46 B.C.) and Munda (45 B.C.). Caesar was assassinated in 44 B.C. A Second Triumvirate (Antony, Lepidus, Octavian) defeated the assassins of Caesar at Philippi in 42 B.C. A struggle then developed between Octavian and Antony, the latter allied with the Ptolemaic Queen of Egypt, Cleopatra. Octavian crushed the forces of Antony and Cleopatra in the naval battle of Actium in 31 B.C. Antony and Cleopatra fled to Egypt and committed suicide. Egypt became a Roman province. Octavian emerged as the first Roman emperor, Augustus Caesar.

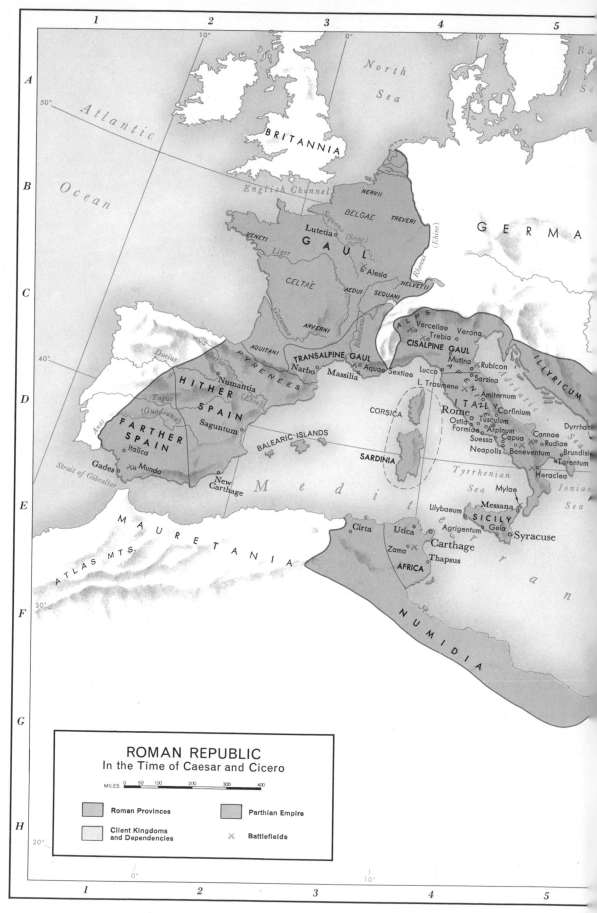

ROMAN REPUBLIC
In the Time of Caesar and Cicero

MILES 0 50 100   200   300   400

Roman Provinces

Client Kingdoms
and Dependencies

Parthian Empire

✕ Battlefields

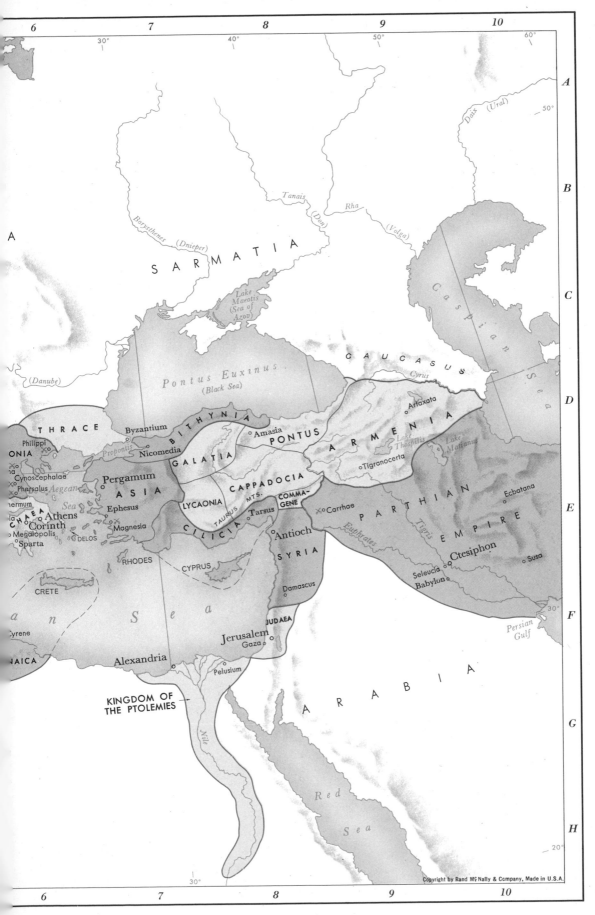

	6	7	8	9	10	
	30°	40°	50°	60°		A

A

S A R M A T I A

Borysthenes (Dnieper)

Tanais (Don)

Rha (Volga)

Daix (Ural)

Lake Maeotis (Sea of Azov)

C A U C A S U S

Cyrus

Caspian Sea

B

(Danube)

Pontus Euxinus (Black Sea)

C

THRACE

Byzantium

BITHYNIA

Amasia

PONTUS

A R M E N I A

Artaxata

Lake Thospitis

Lake Mattanus

Philippi

ONIA

Nicomedia

GALATIA

Tigranocerta

D

Cynoscephalae

Propontis

Aegean

Pergamum

CAPPADOCIA

Pharsalus

ASIA

LYCAONIA

COMMA-GENE

PARTHIAN

Carrhae

Ecbatana

Sea

Ephesus

TAURUS MTS.

Tarsus

EMPIRE

E

CHAEA

Athens

Corinth

Magnesia

CILICIA

Antioch

Tigris

Euphrates

Ctesiphon

Susa

Megalopolis

DELOS

SYRIA

Seleucia

Sparta

RHODES

CYPRUS

Damascus

Babylon

F

CRETE

Persian Gulf

a   n   S   e   a

JUDAEA

Cyrene

Jerusalem

NAICA

Gaza

Alexandria

ARABIA

Pelusium

KINGDOM OF THE PTOLEMIES

G

Nile

Red

Sea

H

Copyright by Rand McNally & Company, Made in U.S.A.

	6	7	8	9	10

THE ROMAN EMPIRE

▶ MAPS ON PAGES 37, 38–39, AND 40

THE EMPIRE AS FOUNDED by Augustus for a long time preserved many republican forms, which were gradually discarded until, after the turmoil of the third century A.D., the government became an autocracy under Diocletian (285–305). The map on pages 38–39 shows the Empire with its provinces and chief cities from Augustus to Diocletian. At this time the civilized world of western Eurasia, except for those territories now under the Parthians (or Persians after 225), was united under a single administration and enjoyed a high level of material activity and cultural exchange. The whole Mediterranean was alive with shipping, and roads ran uninterruptedly from the Euphrates to the English Channel.

Augustus had annexed Egypt even before he became *princeps* or "first citizen" in 27 B.C. Between that date and his death in 14 A.D. he completed the occupation of Spain, closed the gap between Italy and Gaul by forming the Alpine provinces, effected the conquest of Raetia, Noricum, Pannonia, Illyricum, and Moesia, and in Asia Minor took over Galatia, Lycaonia, and Pisidia.

The main strategic problem of the Empire was to find defensible frontiers to the north and east. The Rhine and Danube formed obvious boundaries, but to gain a shorter line Augustus attempted between 9 B.C. and 9 A.D. to reach the Elbe. A revolt in Illyria and a disastrous defeat of Varus in Germany persuaded him to withdraw to the Rhine-Danube and to forego plans for the conquest of Britain, which Julius Caesar had briefly visited in 55 B.C. In the east the great problem was the rising power of the Parthians. Augustus was content to hold the upper Euphrates and the edges of the Arabian Desert as natural frontiers.

His immediate successors adhered to these policies, except for the annexation of Cappadocia by Tiberius and of Mauretania by Caligula. Claudius (41–54 A.D.) adopted a more vigorous course; he annexed Thrace and Lycia, and, more important, Britain. The Flavian emperors (69–96 A.D.) incorporated Lesser Armenia, extended the Syrian frontier, and took the very important step of occupying the Agri Decumates, by which the Rhine-Danube line was shortened and Roman civilization introduced into south Germany.

The Empire reached its maximum extent under Trajan, 98–117 A.D. Trajan annexed Dacia, thus pushing north of the lower Danube; and, after conquering Arabia Petraea, moved on eastward against the Parthians, temporarily occupying Armenia and Mesopotamia. A Jewish revolt and Trajan's death forced the surrender of these provinces. It was not until the reign of Septimius Severus (193–211 A.D.) that the Romans organized a province in upper Mesopotamia. Meanwhile, at the other end of the Empire in northern Britain, the frontier was short enough to be protected by a wall, first by the wall of Hadrian (117–138 A.D.) and then by the wall of Antoninus Pius (138–161 A.D.), which ran from the Firth of Forth to the mouth of the Clyde.

In the second century A.D., the Age of the Good Emperors, the Roman power was at its height. In the next century there was a turbulent fifty-year period, 235–285 A.D., during which the Empire came near to disintegration. For a time, in fact, Gaul and Britain constituted a separate realm, and Egypt and Syria were governed from Palmyra. Unity was restored by Aurelian (270–75 A.D.) and his successors. With the reorganization accomplished by Diocletian and his successor Constantine, under whom the ruling authority became officially Christian, the Empire took on enough new life to last another century and a half in the west, and another millennium in the east.

Roman Civilization
▶ MAP ON PAGE 37

The map on page 37 exhibits something of the state of civilization under the Romans. Though Rome remained the capital and drew much cultural activity to itself, it is significant that from early times many creative writers and thinkers were born and brought up in distant places. Thus, in the republican era, Plautus came from Sarsina, and Terence as a slave from Carthage. Of the great lights of the Ciceronian era, the poet Catullus was born at Verona, the historian Sallust at Amiternum, and Cicero himself at Arpinum, though he never willingly left Rome in later years.

A common culture was widely diffused under the Empire. Greece itself fell into an intellectual poverty, but the Hellenized Near East remained much alive, with vigorous centers of learning at Alexandria, Antioch, and Pergamum. A Strabo could come from Amasia, the former capital of barbaric Pontus. The penetration of Roman civilization into the west is shown by the contributions to Latin literature of recently barbaric regions, notably Spain in the first century A.D., followed by Africa and Gaul. It was in what was then called Cisalpine Gaul that both Virgil and Livy were born. Literature in the imperial period was essentially bilingual, most educated people in all parts of the Empire knowing both Latin and Greek, so that a clear dividing line would give a false emphasis. Though Greek writers were concentrated in the east and Latin in the west, Marcus Aurelius wrote his *Meditations* in Greek, and Ammianus Marcellinus composed his history in Latin. Literacy was remarkably widespread; in the second century there were public schools supported by the state and by private philanthropy. For this large reading public a huge literature was produced, much of it trivial. What we have today of this Greek and Latin writing is a mere fragment of what once existed.

Travels of Paul
▶ MAP ON PAGE 40

Civilized communications aided the spread of Christianity and other religions. The map on page 40 shows the cities in which Christian communities are known to have existed as early as the lifetime of St. Paul. Probably there were Christians also in Galatia, Cappadocia, Bithynia, Pontus, Crete, and Cyrenaica. The four journeys of Paul, as shown here, took place respectively about 45, 55, 60, and 65 A.D.

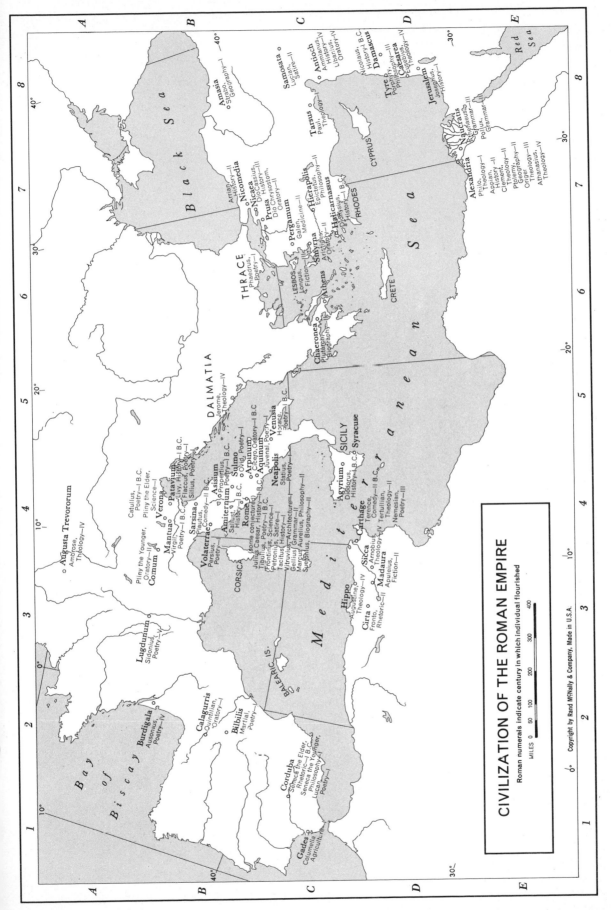

CIVILIZATION OF THE ROMAN EMPIRE

Roman numerals indicate century in which individual flourished

MILES 0 50 100   200   300   400

Copyright by Rand McNally & Company, Made in U.S.A.

Roman City Names and Modern Equivalents

ROMAN NAME	MODERN NAME	ROMAN NAME	MODERN NAME
Ancyra	Ankara	Londinium	London
Aquincum	Budapest	Lugdunum	Lyon
Arelate	Arles	Lugdunum Batavorum	Leiden
Augusta Treverorum	Trier, Treves	Lutetia	Paris
Augusta Vindelicorum	Augsburg	Malaca	Malaga
Augustodunum	Autun	Massilia	Marseille
Bononia	Bologna	Mazaca Caesarea	Kayseri
Burdigala	Bordeaux	Mediolanum	Milan
Caesar Augusta	Saragossa	Moguntiacum	Mainz
Camulodunum	Colchester	Nemausus	Nimes
Carales	Cagliari	Olisipo	Lisbon
Colonia Agrippina	Cologne	Patavium	Padua
Deva	Chester	Salmantica	Salamanca
Eburacum	York	Thessalonica	Salonika
Emerita Augusta	Merida	Toletum	Toledo
Gades	Cadiz	Tolosa	Toulouse
Hispalis	Seville	Valentia	Valencia
Lindum	Lincoln	Vindobona	Vienna

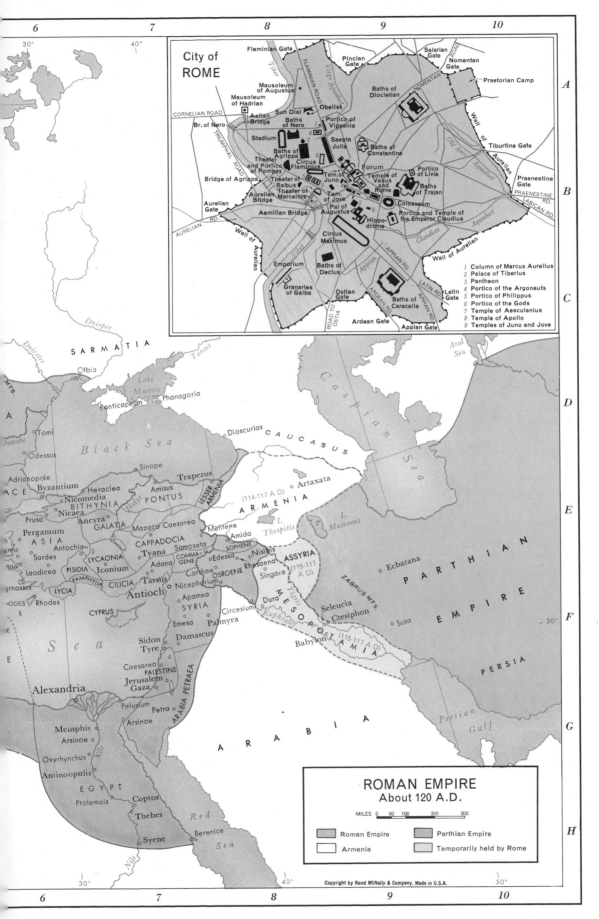

City of ROME

Flaminian Gate
Pincian Gate
Salarian Gate
Nomentan Gate
Praetorian Camp
Mausoleum of Augustus
Mausoleum of Hadrian
Sun Dial
Obelisk
Baths of Diocletian
Aelian Bridge
Br. of Nero
Baths of Nero
Portico of Vipsania
Stadium
Saepta Julia
Baths of Constantine
Baths of Agrippa
Theater and Portico of Pompey
Circus Flaminius
Forum
Temple of Venus and Rome
Portico of Livia
Baths of Trajan
Bridge of Agrippa
Theater of Balbus
Tem. of Juno
Tem. of Jove
Theater of Marcellus
Colosseum
Aurelian Gate
Aurelian Bridge
Pal of Augustus
Portico and Temple of the Emperor Claudius
Aemilian Bridge
Hippodrome
Circus Maximus
Emporium
Baths of Declus
Granaries of Galba
Ostian Gate
Baths of Caracalla
Ardean Gate
Applan Gate

CORNELIAN ROAD
TRIUMPHAL ROAD
AURELIAN RD.
Wall of Aurelian
ROAD TO OSTIA
Tiber
FLAMINIAN ROAD
Virgo Aqueduct
NOMENTAN ROAD
Old Anio Aqueduct
Wall of Aurelian
Tiburtine Gate
Aurelian
Praenestine Gate
PRAENESTINE
LABICAN RD.
Claudian Aqueduct
Wall of Aurelian
Appian
APPIAN RD.
LATIN RD.
Latin Gate
Ardean RD.

1 Column of Marcus Aurelius
2 Palace of Tiberius
3 Pantheon
4 Portico of the Argonauts
5 Portico of Philippus
6 Portico of the Gods
7 Temple of Aesculanius
8 Temple of Apollo
9 Temples of Juno and Jove

ROMAN EMPIRE
About 120 A.D.

MILES 0 50 100 200 300

Roman Empire	Parthian Empire
Armenia	Temporarily held by Rome

Copyright by Rand McNally & Company, Made in U.S.A.

SARMATIA
Dnieper
Dniester
Tanais
Lake Maeotis
Olbia
Panticapeum
Phanagoria
Aral Sea
Dioscurias
CAUCASUS
Caspian Sea
Tomi
Danube
Odessus
Black Sea
Adrianople
Byzantium
Sinope
Trapezus
Artaxata
(114-117 A D)
Heraclea
Amisus
LESSER ARMENIA
ARMENIA
Nicomedia
BITHYNIA
PONTUS
Prusa
Nicaea
Ancyra
GALATIA
Melitene
L. Thospitis
L. Matianus
Ecbatana
PARTHIAN
Pergamum
ASIA
Mazaca Caesarea
CAPPADOCIA
Amida
Antiochia
Tyana
SOPHENE
Sardes
LYCAONIA
COMMA-GENE
Samosata
Nisibis
ASSYRIA
EMPIRE
Laodicea
PISIDIA
Iconium
Carrhae
Edessa
Rhesaena
(115-117 A D)
RHODES
Rhodes
PAMPHYLIA
CILICIA
Adana
OSROENE
Singara
ZAGRUS MTS.
Susa
LYCIA
Tarsus
Nicepherium
Dura
Seleucia
Ctesiphon
Antioch
Apamea
SYRIA
Circesium
MESOPOTAMIA
Babylon
(115-117 A D)
PERSIA
Sea
Emesa
Palmyra
Euphrates
Tigris
Sidon
Damascus
Tyre
30°
Caesarea
PALESTINE
Jerusalem
ARABIA PETRAEA
Persian Gulf
Gaza
Alexandria
Pelusium
Petra
ARABIA
Memphis
Arsinoe
Arsinoe
Oxyrhynchus
Antinoopolis
EGYPT
Ptolemais
Coptos
Red
Thebes
Syene
Berenice
Nile
Sea

39

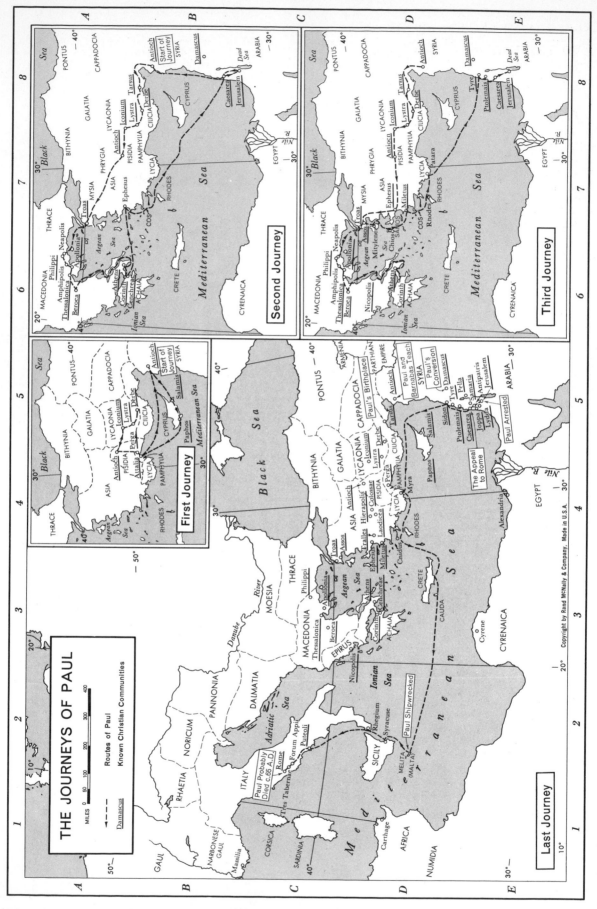

THE JOURNEYS OF PAUL

MILES
0   50 100   200   300   400

- - - Routes of Paul
Damascus   Known Christian Communities

Copyright by Rand McNally & Company, Made in U.S.A.

First Journey

Start of Journey
Antioch
Salamis
Paphos
Perga
Attalia
Antioch PISIDIA
Iconium
Lystra
Derbe

Second Journey

Start of Journey
Antioch
Tarsus
Iconium
Lystra
Derbe
Antioch
Ephesus
Troas
Neapolis
Philippi
Amphipolis
Thessalonica
Apollonia
Beroea
Athens
Corinth
Cenchreae
Caesarea
Jerusalem

Third Journey

Antioch
Tarsus
Iconium
Lystra
Derbe
Antioch
Ephesus
Miletus
Troas
Assos
Mitylene
Chios
Samos
Cos
Rhodes
Patara
Tyre
Ptolemais
Caesarea
Jerusalem
Neapolis
Philippi
Amphipolis
Thessalonica
Apollonia
Beroea
Nicopolis
Athens
Corinth

Last Journey

Paul's Birthplace
Paul and Barnabas Teach
Paul's Conversion
Damascus
Sidon
Tyre
Ptolemais
Pella
Samaria
Antipatris
Jerusalem
Joppa
Lydda
Caesarea
Paul Arrested
The Appeal to Rome
Paphos
Myra
Cnidus
Paul Shipwrecked
MELITA (MALTA)
Syracuse
Rhegium
Puteoli
Forum Appii
Tres Tabernae
Rome
Paul Probably Died c.65 A.D.

40

THE ROMAN EMPIRE ABOUT 400 A.D.
AND THE BARBARIAN INVASIONS

▶ MAP ON PAGES 42–43

DIOCLETIAN AND HIS SUCCESSORS in the fourth century subjected the Roman Empire to such a thorough reorganization that by 400 A.D. it was very different from what it had been two centuries before. The provinces were smaller and more numerous. There were now over a hundred of them, too many to show on this map. The Mediterranean coast of Gaul, for example, was divided between First Narbonnensis, west of the Rhone River, and Second Narbonnensis, east of it. Above the provinces were "dioceses"—whose names are given on the map— and the dioceses were organized into larger units called "prefectures." The four prefectures of Gaul, Italy, Illyricum, and the East are shown in color. Each province was ruled by a governor, each diocese by a vicar, and each prefecture by a praetorian prefect.

At the top of this structure, as envisaged by Diocletian, were to be two senior emperors called Augusti, and two junior emperors called Caesars, who were to succeed the Augusti. There would thus be a senior emperor to watch each of the main frontiers—against the Germans and the Persians—and a junior emperor for less exposed posts. Although this plan was not strictly followed after Diocletian, there was usually more than one emperor. Whenever there were two Augusti, one ruled in the eastern and the other in the western part of the Empire. In 400 there were two Augusti, Honorius in the west and Arcadius in the east, the sons of Theodosius I, the Great. Officially, there were two capitals, Rome and Constantinople, but Rome was so far from the German frontier that the emperor ruling in the west often maintained his capital elsewhere, as Theodosius did at Milan and Honorius at Ravenna. Though one often finds references to an Eastern and a Western Roman Empire, these terms are technically incorrect; for although there might be two emperors and two capitals there was considered to be only one single empire, and when one Augustus died the other in principle became ruler of the whole.

The Barbarians

The Romans used the word "barbarians" to describe peoples who lived outside the pale of the Empire. These outside peoples included the Sassanids, successors to the Parthians and older Persians; the primitive Picts and Scots of the extreme northwest; and many Germanic groups, tribal and agricultural, extending from what is now Denmark, along the Rhine and Danube, to the north coast of the Black Sea. Anglo-Saxons, Franks, Alamanni, Burgundians, Lombards, and Goths were all Germans.

In the fourth century these peoples exerted a steady pressure on the Empire. The Sassanids held Mesopotamia and Armenia. Britain was assailed by Scots from Ireland, Picts from Scotland, and the Germanic Anglo-Saxons from across the North Sea. The Franks lived along the lower Rhine, some within the Empire on the left bank, hired by the Romans to hold at bay other Franks living east of the river. The Germanic assaults long remained no more than raids, easily repulsed by frontier troops. The state of relative equilibrium was broken about 375 A.D., and was followed by about two centuries of "barbarian invasions," shown on the map, in which Germanic bands wandered over the territory of the Empire, devastated, settled down, and in some cases, by the sixth century, established somewhat indeterminate kingdoms.

What broke the equilibrium was the appearance of the Huns, a fierce Asiatic people who had originated on the frontiers of China. About 375 A.D., having swept through the grasslands north of the Caspian, the Huns fell upon the easternmost Germans, the Ostrogoths (or East Goths), who were living peacefully north of the Black Sea. The Ostrogoths recoiled on the Visigoths (or West Goths), who in terror of the Huns sought refuge within the Empire. The Huns, moving west, threw the other Germanic peoples into confusion, and started them on a great wave of migrations.

The map shows the routes of the Huns and the chief Germanic peoples. Here and there a date indicates when a people reached a certain point. Two dates show a pause in migration. An underlined date shows when a people permanently settled down. Thus the Visigoths crossed the Danube in 375; remained in Macedonia and Thrace until 395; moved on through Greece and into Italy, where they plundered Rome in 410; sojourned in southern Gaul from 412 to 507; and settled in Spain about 415. Other important Germanic peoples are traced in the same way, except for the Alamanni and Suevi. The Alamanni simply crossed the upper Rhine. Half the Suevi went with the Vandals to Spain, settled in the mountainous north, and held their own against the Visigoths and later against the Moslems.

The chief Germanic kingdoms founded within the territory of the Empire were as follows:

Visigoths—Southern Gaul, 412–507;
         Spain, 415–711.
Ostrogoths—Italy, 489–554.
Vandals—Spain, 400–424; Africa, 429–548.
Franks—Northern Gaul, 486;
         Southern Gaul, 507.
Lombards—Italy, 568.

Small Anglo-Saxon kingdoms were formed in Britain in the sixth century. It is possible that when the Roman legions left Britain shortly after 400 Scots from Ireland overran parts of the country before the Anglo-Saxon conquest, but this is by no means certain. Indeed our knowledge of all these barbarian invasions is limited.

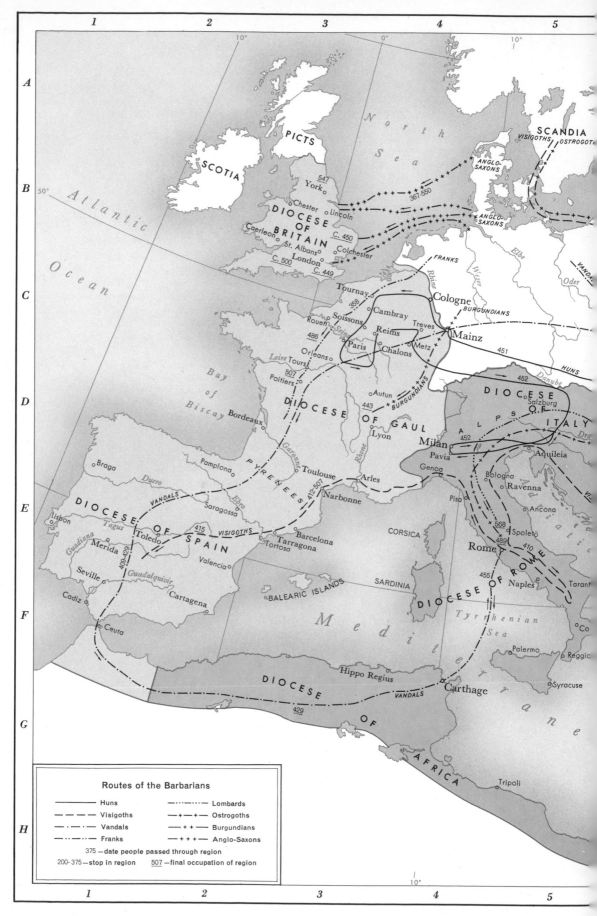

Routes of the Barbarians

—————— Huns	—·—··—··— Lombards	
— — — — Visigoths	—+—+—+ Ostrogoths	
—·—·—·— Vandals	+ + + Burgundians	
—··—··—·· Franks	+++++ Anglo-Saxons	

375 —date people passed through region

200-375 —stop in region   <u>507</u> —final occupation of region

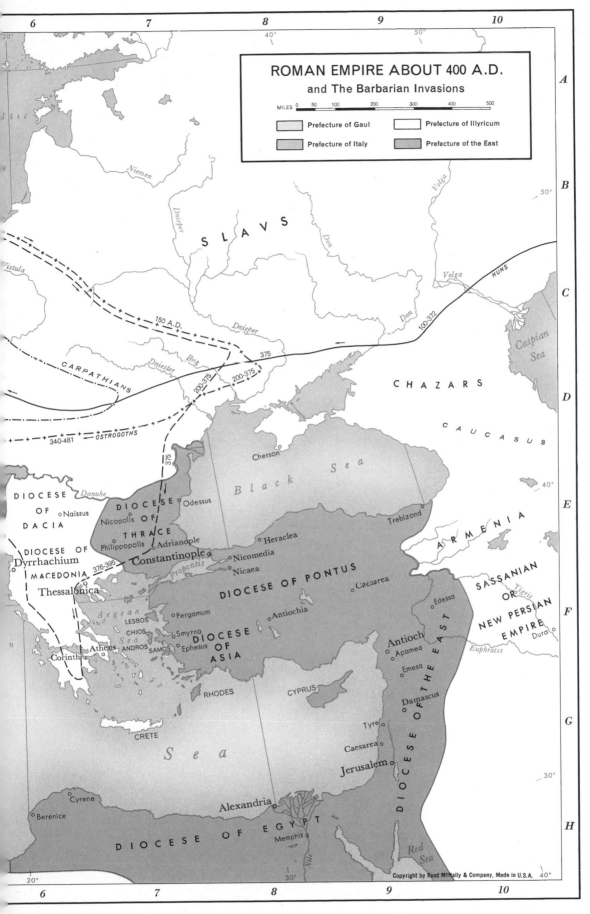

ROMAN EMPIRE ABOUT 400 A.D.
and The Barbarian Invasions

MILES 0 50 100 200 300 400 500

Prefecture of Gaul

Prefecture of Italy

Prefecture of Illyricum

Prefecture of the East

SLAVS

Niemen

Dnieper

Volga

Don

Volga

HUNS

50°

Caspian Sea

150 A.D.

Dnieper

375

100-372

CHAZARS

CARPATHIANS

Dniester

Bug

200-375

200-375

CAUCASUS

Cherson

Black Sea

40°

340-481 OSTROGOTHS

375

DIOCESE OF DACIA

Danube

Naissus

Odessus

Trebizond

ARMENIA

DIOCESE OF THRACE

Nicopolis

Adrianople

Heraclea

SASSANIAN OR NEW PERSIAN EMPIRE

Philippopolis

DIOCESE OF DYRRHACHIUM

Dyrrhachium

MACEDONIA

376-396

Constantinople

Nicomedia

Nicaea

Propontis

DIOCESE OF PONTUS

Caesarea

Edessa

Dura

Thessalonica

Aegean

LESBOS

Pergamum

Antiochia

Tigris

CHIOS

Smyrna

DIOCESE OF ASIA

Antioch

Euphrates

Athens ANDROS SAMOS

Ephesus

Apamea

Corinth

Sea

RHODES

CYPRUS

Emesa

DIOCESE OF THE EAST

CRETE

Damascus

Sea

Tyre

30°

Caesarea

Jerusalem

Cyrene

Alexandria

Berenice

DIOCESE OF EGYPT

Memphis

Nile

Red Sea

40°

Copyright by Rand McNally & Company, Made in U.S.A.

43

MEDIEVAL EUROPE TO 1200

▶ MAPS ON PAGES 44, 45, 46–47, AND 49

B Y 800 A.D. the Germanic Anglo-Saxons had occupied the shaded area in the map below. They had established a number of kingdoms, with boundaries too vague and fluctuating to be indicated. Bernicia and Deira were sometimes separate, sometimes joined into Northumbria. Kent was often divided among brothers. Occasionally one king would defeat the others and be called "bretwalda" or chief of the Anglo-Saxon kings, but without forming a unified Anglo-Saxon kingdom. The unshaded portion of the map was occupied by the older pre-Anglo-Saxon peoples, the Picts in the north, whose origin is unknown, and the Celts of western Britain and of Ireland. King Offa of Anglo-Saxon Mercia (757–96) built a "dyke" or ditch to mark off his kingdom from the tribesmen of Wales. West Wales, the modern Cornwall, had in 800 been recently conquered by Wessex. "Scots" from Ireland had conquered from the Picts the region called Dalriada, the ancestor of the Scottish state which emerged in the ninth century. Ireland was a land of tribal chiefs; it had been Christianized in late Roman times, and had sent out missionaries to convert the Picts and the Anglo-Saxons. The island of Iona contained a famous monastery, founded in the sixth century by the Irish monk St. Columba. A synod at Whitby in 664, decided that England should follow Roman rather than Celtic Christianity. England thus came into closer relationship with the Continent.

Charlemagne's Empire

▶ MAP ON PAGES 46–47

The most immediately successful of the Germanic invaders of the Roman Empire were not the Anglo-Saxons but the Franks, who by 814 A.D., at the death of Charlemagne, had assembled the empire shown in the inset on page 47. Its heartland was Austrasia, the ancient Frankish homeland astride the lower Rhine. Neustria, Aquitaine, Alamannia, and Burgundy were added by Clovis and his successors to form the Merovingian state. The Carolingians greatly enlarged it, beginning with Charles Martel, Charlemagne's grandfather, who began the conquest of Saxony and Thuringia, and Pepin, who subdued Bavaria. Charlemagne (742–814) completed the conquest of Saxony, Thuringia, and Frisia, incorporated Bavaria, and added the adjoining Nordgau. He made war against the Moslems, whose expansion in the seventh century had brought them into Spain (711 A.D.), and gained back for the Christian world the region called the Spanish March, later known as the March of Barcelona. He also conquered the Lombard kingdom, while his sons, with his Lombard cavalry, took Carinthia and Carniola from the Avars. Pepin had created the States of the Church, which Charlemagne enlarged and confirmed to the pope.

Charlemagne began his reign as king of the Franks. When he overthrew the Lombard state, he took the additional title King of the Lombards. In 800 he assumed the title of Roman Emperor and was crowned by the pope. He remained, however,

(Continued on page 48)

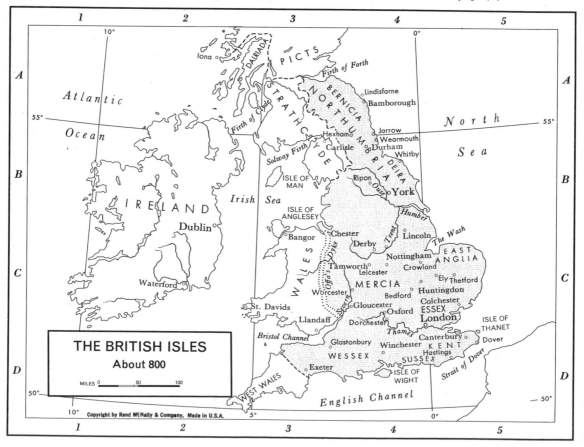

THE BRITISH ISLES
About 800

MILES 0   50   100

Copyright by Rand McNally & Company, Made in U.S.A.

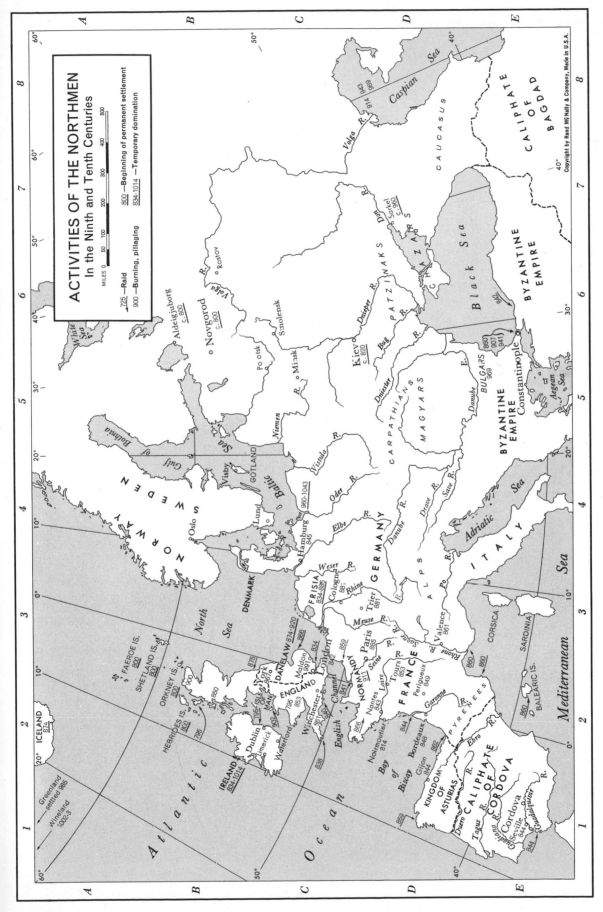

ACTIVITIES OF THE NORTHMEN
In the Ninth and Tenth Centuries

MILES 0 50 100 200 300 400 500

725 —Raid
900 —Burning, pillaging
800 —Beginning of permanent settlement
834-1014 —Temporary domination

Copyright by Rand McNally & Company, Made in U.S.A.

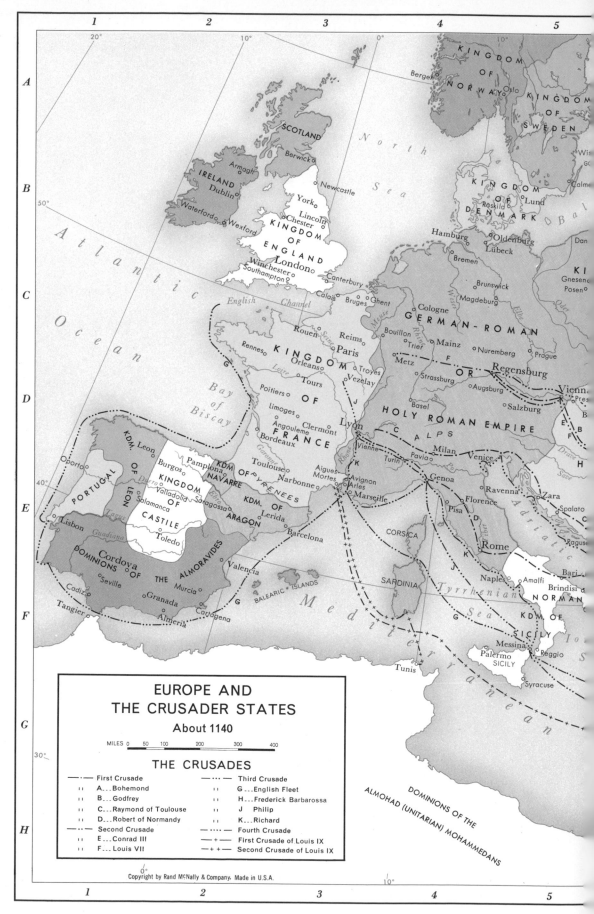

EUROPE AND
THE CRUSADER STATES

About 1140

MILES 0 50 100   200   300   400

THE CRUSADES

—·—·— First Crusade	——·—— Third Crusade
ıı A...Bohemond	ıı G...English Fleet
ıı B...Godfrey	ıı H...Frederick Barbarossa
ıı C...Raymond of Toulouse	ıı J Philip
ıı D...Robert of Normandy	ıı K...Richard
———— Second Crusade	········ Fourth Crusade
ıı E...Conrad III	—+—+— First Crusade of Louis IX
ıı F...Louis VII	—++— Second Crusade of Louis IX

CHARLEMAGNE'S EMPIRE 814
Showing Division by Treaty of Verdun 843

West Frankish
Kingdom of
Charles the Bald

East Frankish
Kingdom of
Louis the German

Central Kingdom
of Lothaire

States of
the Church

North Sea

WILTZI

ENGLAND
WALES
London
Winchester
Canterbury
Crediton
Chester
Thetford
Dublin

FRISIA
Bremen
Verden
Utrecht
SAXONY
Detmold
Corvey
Paderborn
THURINGIA
Cologne
Heristal
Aachen
Triero
Mainz
Ingleheim
Fulda
NORDGAU
Worms
ALAMANNIA
Ratisbon
Strassburg
Augsburg
Passau
Salzburg
BAVARIA
St. Gall
CARINTHIA

WENDS

AVARS

SERBS

MARCH OF NEUSTRIA
BRITTANY
Rennes
Nantes
Tours
Orleans
Paris
St. Denis
Soissons
Rouen
Reims
Verdun
Metz
Thion-ville
Langres
Auxerre
Luxeuil
Basel
Geneva

St. Riquier
Quierzy
AUSTRASIA

ALPS
LOMBARDY
Milan
Pavia
Venice
MARCH OF FRIUL
Aquileia

CARNIOLA

Atlantic
Ocean

AQUITAINE
Limoges
Clermont
Perigueux
Bordeaux
Chasseneuil
Poitiers
Bourges
Autun
BURGUNDY
Lyon
Vienne
Genoa
Bologna
Florence
Pisa
Ravenna
Spoleto
DUCHY OF
SPOLETO

Adriatic Sea

PYRENEES
Pamplona
Roncesvalles
Toulouse
SPANISH MARCH
CALIPHATE
Saragossa
OF CORDOVA
Barcelona
Nimes
Arles
Marseille
Narbonne

Mediterranean Sea
CORSICA
STATES OF THE CHURCH
Rome
DUCHY OF
BENEVENTO

LITHUANIA

RUSSIA

CUMANS OR POLOVZIANS

CHAZARS

Caspian Sea

CAUCASUS

KDM. OF BULGARIA
Danube
Varna
Cherson
Black Sea
Trebizond

SERBIA
Belgrade

Arezzo
Thessalonica
Adrianople
Constantinople
Nicomedia
Nicaea
Dorylaeum
Angora
SELJUK KINGDOM
OF
ICONIUM

Mosul

BYZANTINE
EMPIRE
Aegean Sea
Thebes
Athens
Smyrna
Iconium
Heraclea
ARMENIA
EDESSA
COUNTY
OF EDESSA
Aleppo
Antioch
PRIN.
OF
ANTIOCH
Euphrates
Tigris
CALIPHATE
OF
BAGDAD
Bagdad

RHODES
Candia
CRETE
Nicosia
CYPRUS
Limasol
Famagosta
CO. OF
TRIPOLI
Tripoli
Hamah
Homs
Beirut
Tyre
Acre
Tiberias
Jaffa
Ascalon
Jerusalem
Kerak
KINGDOM
OF
JERUSALEM
SULTANATE
OF
DAMASCUS
Damascus

Damietta
Mansurah
Alexandria
Cairo
CALIPHATE
OF
CAIRO

Nile
Red Sea

47

essentially a Germanic monarch, with his capital at Aachen; and his own royal estates, on which his power rested, were mostly in Austrasia and Neustria, though he had an important one in Aquitaine also.

After the death of Charlemagne's son, Louis the Pious (814–40), Louis' three sons divided the empire by the Treaty of Verdun in 843, as shown in color on the inset map. In 870 the central portion, called Lotharingia or Lorraine, was again divided, the eastern portion going to Louis the German, the western to Charles the Bald, and Italy remaining outside their dominions.

The Northmen
▶ MAP ON PAGE 45

From the eighth to the tenth centuries Europe was disturbed by another general movement of pagan barbarians, the Northmen or Vikings. All places on the map on page 45 were either attacked, plundered, or settled by Northmen. There were many others, now unknown. It will be seen that these expeditions, originating in southern Scandinavia, reached as far as Iceland, Seville, Kiev, and Constantinople. Northmen settled even in Greenland, and they sighted America about the year 1000. The grant of Normandy to Rollo in 911 practically ended the attacks on northern France, but Aquitaine suffered a severe raid as late as the early eleventh century. Ireland was dominated by Danes until 1014, and England was ruled by kings of Denmark from 1013 to 1042. The principalities founded by the Swedes in Russia were the beginnings of the later Russian state (see page 109).

Twelfth-Century Europe
▶ MAP ON PAGES 46–47

By the twelfth century, as shown on pages 46–47, some of the principal states of Europe, as we have since known it, had come into being. Within the area of Latin Christianity there were kingdoms of England, Scotland, France, Denmark, Poland, Hungary, and Sicily, several Spanish kingdoms, and the Holy Roman or German-Roman Empire. Many towns had arisen, either reviving after a long period of decay in the lands of the former Roman Empire, or built for the first time in the central and eastern European regions that had lain outside ancient civilization. In the east still subsisted the Byzantine Empire, the surviving eastern portion of the old Roman Empire; the kingdom of Bulgaria was much more recent. The Near East, North Africa, and southern Spain were Moslem.

The Crusades
▶ MAP ON PAGES 46–47

The map shows the Christian counterattack against Islam. After the death of Mohammed in 632 Islam had spread very rapidly. Moslems in the eighth century conquered all Spain except a northern fringe and poured across the Pyrenees into France. Pepin, king of the Franks, had driven them back into Spain, and Charlemagne had conquered the Spanish March. In the following century, the ninth, the Moslems had occupied the Balearic Islands, Corsica, Sardinia, and Sicily, and had invaded southern Italy many times. They repeatedly plundered Rome and besieged the pope in his own fortress.

By the eleventh century the Christians were strong enough to begin a counteroffensive. The kings of Leon, Castile, Aragon, and Navarre, with the aid of knights from France, conquered about half of Moslem Spain. French knights under a Burgundian leader founded the kingdom of Portugal. Seamen from Genoa and Pisa captured Corsica and even attacked Tunis. A Norman adventurer, Roger de Hauteville, settled in Italy and conquered Sicily between 1061 and 1091—it was at this same time that another Norman, William, conquered England. Roger's son, Roger II, founded the Norman kingdom of Sicily.

The First Crusade to recover the Holy Land began in 1096. The map shows the routes, some overland, some by sea, of the chief crusades. The First Crusade, 1096–99, won back western Asia Minor for the Byzantine Empire, and established the Latin crusader states of Jerusalem, Tripoli, Antioch, and Edessa in the Syria-Palestine region. These outposts of the Latin West were at their height in 1140; they were lost in the following century. Islam was divided at this time. In the west two reforming sects essentially Berber in composition were dominant, the Almoravides in Spain and the Almohades in North Africa. Egypt was ruled by the Fatimite caliph of Cairo. The rest of western Islam was in theory under the Abbasid caliph of Bagdad, but the Turkish sultans who were his subordinates were actually independent rulers and the caliph a figurehead.

Feudal Europe
▶ MAP ON PAGE 49

On the facing page the feudal monarchies of France and Germany about the year 1200 are shown in some detail. To give linear boundaries for feudal states may be more misleading than helpful; the solid boundary for France simply represents the area within which homage was done to the French king, and for the subordinate lordships no bounds are indicated at all. The towns in the larger type sizes were mostly the capitals of named fiefs or places from which lesser lords took their titles. Thus Bordeaux was the seat of the duke of Gascony. There were twelve "peers of France"—six secular lords, the dukes of Normandy, Aquitaine, and Burgundy, and the counts of Flanders, Champagne, and Toulouse; and six ecclesiastical lords, the archbishop of Reims, and the bishops of Beauvais, Noyon, Laon, Chalons, and Langres. In Germany the chief lordships were the great duchies, Saxony, Lorraine, Franconia, Swabia, and Bavaria, but bishops were also important feudal figures, and the king of Bohemia was a vassal to the emperor.

There were no national political entities. In 1200 the duke of Normandy, Aquitaine, and Gascony and count of Maine and Anjou was none other than King John of England, who was also overlord to the duke of Brittany. The king of France had no real authority in these territories. The Holy Roman Empire, founded in the tenth century, included not only Germany but Bohemia and certain Italian regions as shown. The same lord might hold lands in both France and the Empire: the count of Toulouse held the marquisate of Provence, and the count of Flanders was also count of Hainaut.

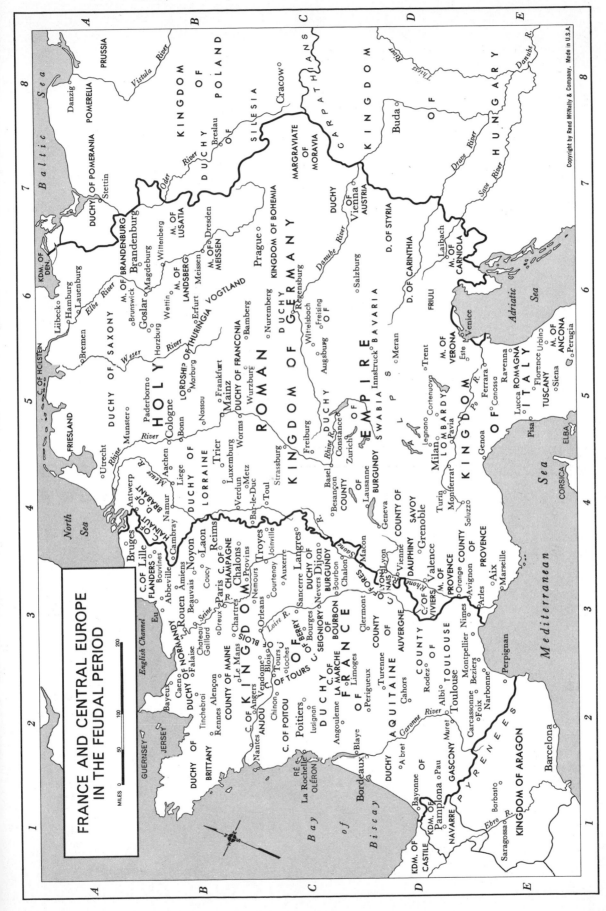

FRANCE AND CENTRAL EUROPE
IN THE FEUDAL PERIOD

MILES 0   50   100   200

Copyright by Rand McNally & Company. Made in U.S.A.

49

EUROPE
About 1360

MILES 0   50   100   200   300

—— Boundary of Holy Roman Empire
- - - Boundary of France

FAEROES

N O R W A Y

S

Bergen

Oslo

Upsal

ORKNEY
ISLANDS

SHETLAND
ISLANDS

HEBRIDES

Colmar

DENMARK

Copenhagen

SCOTLAND   Aberdeen

Bannockburn
Falkirk   Edinburgh
Berwick

Armagh

Lubeck
Stralsund
POMERANIA

Hamburg

IRELAND   Carlisle

Dublin

York
Lincoln
Chester

Bremen

Magdeburg   BRANDENBURG

Gne

Po

Wexford

WALES
ENGLAND

Cork

Norwich

North

Sea

HOLLAND

H O L Y

SILESI

Prague

Atlantic

London

Bruges

Calais
BRABANT
Ghent
Cologne

Rhine

Agincourt
Harfleur   Crecy   HAINAUT
Rouen
Caen   Reims
Bretigny   Compiegne
Paris   Vaucouleurs
Orleans   Troyes
Chinon   Dijon
Poitiers

Trier   Frankfurt
Mainz

R O M A N

BOHEMIA

Regensburg   MORAVI

English Channel

BRITTANY
Rennes

Thames

Elbe

LUXEMBURG

PALATINATE

FRANCE

Domremy
Strassburg
Basel

BAVARIA   Munich

Vienna

Salzburg

Nantes

Loire

Seine

LORRAINE

Ocean

*Bay of
Biscay*

Limoges

Bordeaux   AQUITAINE

BURGUNDY

Lyon

Besancon
SWISS
CONFED
Constance

E M P I R E

AUSTRIA

B

Danube

Bayonne
Toulouse
Pau

Garonne

Avignon

Rhône

SAVOY
DAUPHINY

LANDS
OF THE
Turin   Milan
Ferrara   Trieste
VISCONTI
Genoa   Venice
Bologna   REPUBLIC

BOS

PORTUGAL

Santiago

Leon

Salamanca

Ebro

NAVARRE

Duero

Toledo

CASTILE

Saragossa

ARAGON

Narbonne
PROVENCE
Marseille

Florence

OF

VENICE

Adriatic

Ro

Lisbon

Tagus

Guadiana

Seville

Cordova

Guadalquivir

Cadiz

Gibraltar

Valencia

Barcelona

BALEARIC ISLANDS

(To Aragon)

Granada

GRANADA

M A R I N D S

CORSICA
(To Genoa)

Rome

PAPAL STATES

Naples

KINGDOM   OF

NAPLES   To

SARDINIA
(To Aragon)

Mediter

Algiers

M O S L E M   S T A T E S

Z I A N I D S

Tunis

H A F S I D S

Palermo   Messina
KINGDOM
OF
SICILY   Reggio

ranean

MALTA

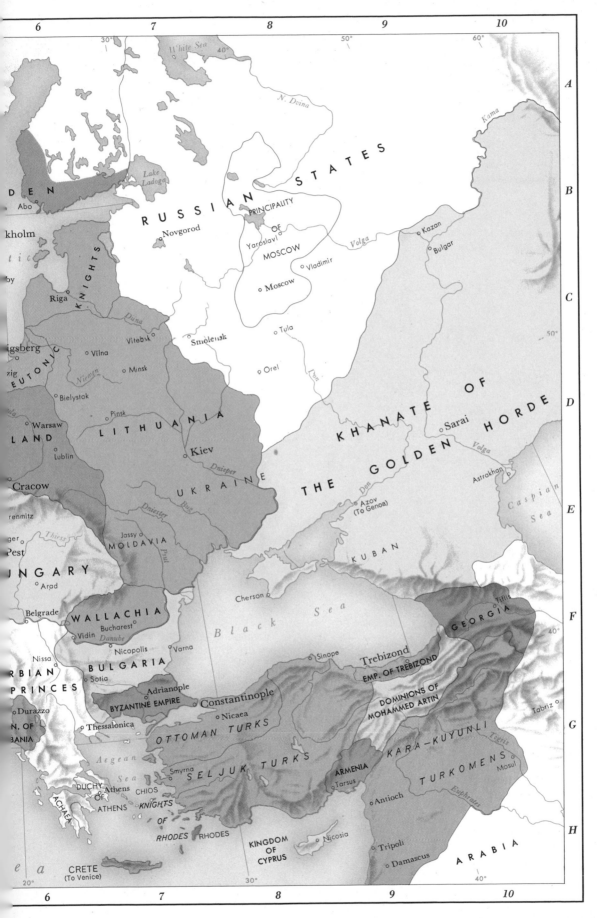

6 **7** **8** **9** **10**

A

White Sea

N. Dvina

Kama

R U S S I A N   S T A T E S

B

DEN

Abo

kholm

by

ic

PRINCIPALITY

Novgorod

OF

Yaroslavl

MOSCOW

Volga

Kazan

Bulgar

C

KNIGHTS

Riga

Vitebsk

Dvina

Smolensk

Vladimir

Moscow

Tula

Orel

Don

igsberg

zig

EUTONIC

Vilna

Minsk

LITHUANIA

Bielystok

Pinsk

Niemen

D

K H A N A T E   O F

Sarai

LAND

Warsaw

Lublin

Kiev

Dnieper

T H E   G O L D E N   H O R D E

Volga

Cracow

UKRAINE

Bug

Astrakhan

renmitz

Thiess

Dniester

Jassy

MOLDAVIA

Pruth

Azov
(To Genoa)

Don

E

Caspian Sea

ger

Pest

JNGARY

Arad

KUBAN

Cherson

Black   Sea

F

Belgrade

WALLACHIA

Bucharest

Vidin

Danube

Nicopolis

Varna

GEORGIA

Tiflis

Nissa

RBIAN

PRINCES

BULGARIA

Sofia

Adrianople

Sinope

Trebizond

EMP. OF TREBIZOND

Tabriz

Durazzo

BYZANTINE EMPIRE

Constantinople

DOMINIONS OF
MOHAMMED ARTIN

N. OF

BANIA

Thessalonica

Nicaea

G

Aegean

O T T O M A N   T U R K S

KARA–KUYUNLI

DUCHY

OF

ATHENS

Athens

Smyrna

Sea

S E L J U K   T U R K S

ARMENIA

Tarsus

T U R K O M E N S

Mosul

Euphrates

Tigris

ACHAEA

CHIOS

KNIGHTS

OF

RHODES   RHODES

Antioch

H

e a

CRETE
(To Venice)

KINGDOM
OF
CYPRUS

Nicosia

Tripoli

Damascus

A R A B I A

6 **7** **8** **9** **10**

EUROPE ABOUT 1360

▶ MAPS ON PAGES 50–51, 53, AND 60

BY THE THIRTEENTH and fourteenth centuries medieval Europe was fully formed. The process of its Christianization was now virtually complete. As long ago as the fourth century the lands within the Roman Empire had been officially Christian, but most of the barbarian invaders had been pagans when they burst into the Empire, and Spain and the Mediterranean islands had fallen under the Moslems.

The Christianizing of Europe
▶ MAP ON PAGE 53

It was the work of the Middle Ages, over almost a thousand years, to convert the invading barbarians, to repel the Moslems, and to extend Christianity to the north and east far beyond the limits of the old Roman Empire and the ancient church. In general, the Franks were converted in the sixth century, the Angles and Saxons in the seventh, the Germans between the Rhine and Elbe in the eighth and ninth, the Scandinavians, Czechs, Poles, and Magyars in the tenth and eleventh. The trans-Elbian and east Baltic region was the last part of Europe to become Christian; here the German order of Teutonic Knights conquered and converted the non-German tribes variously called Pomeranian, Prussian, and Lithuanian. Ireland, meanwhile, had been Christian since late Roman times; almost all of Spain and the Mediterranean islands were won back for Christendom by 1250. All these regions looked to Rome. Meanwhile, from Constantinople, the Greek church had also carried on a great mission of conversion, Christianizing the Bulgarian and Serb invaders of the Eastern Empire in the ninth and tenth centuries, and then, about the year 1000, reaching to the Russian and other peoples north of the Black Sea. Beginning about 1050, the Greek Orthodox and Roman Catholic churches drifted apart.

Medieval Trade Routes
▶ MAP ON PAGE 53

By 1360 a complex network of trade had also arisen. The lower map on page 53 shows the more important trade routes, products, and commercial towns. In general, development over the medieval period was somewhat as follows: In the early Middle Ages, before the eleventh century, western Europe had no direct contact with the Near Eastern markets for spices, sugar, silks, and the like. Such goods were brought first to Constantinople, then shipped from Constantinople either to Venice or to Kiev. Venice in the early Middle Ages was subject to the Byzantine Empire, Kiev culturally dependent on it. From Venice the Eastern goods went on to southwestern Europe. Northwestern Europe was supplied from Kiev. Every spring the Vikings of Kiev loaded boats with forest products, went down the Dnieper and across the Black Sea to Constantinople (or to Trebizond), where they collected the wares of the East. Bringing these back to Kiev, they passed them on by way of Novgorod and Wisby to northern Europe.

In the eleventh century Venice, Genoa, and Pisa began to trade directly with Syria and Egypt. Eastern goods began to find their way from Italy to the north through the Rhone valley into France. Hence grew up in the twelfth and thirteenth centuries the famous fairs of Champagne, of which that at Troyes was the most important. At these fairs Italian and northern merchants would meet to do business. New routes to the north were developed in the fourteenth century: merchandise was increasingly carried overland through towns like Augsburg to such places as Hamburg and Lübeck; and the Venetians and Genoese began also to send galley fleets by way of the Atlantic to Southampton and Bruges. Bruges became the greatest commercial center of the north, with most of the great Italian mercantile houses maintaining offices there. The British Isles at this time were mainly exporters of raw materials, especially wool, while the textile centers, working up English wool, were in Flanders and Italy. Hence, the route from Bruges to London was of great importance. North European commerce in the late Middle Ages was largely controlled by the Hanse, a league principally of German towns, which had its agents and affiliates in England, at Bruges, and throughout the Baltic as far east as Novgorod (see page 60).

Political Boundaries About 1360
▶ MAP ON PAGES 50–51

A political map of Europe about 1360 appears on the preceding pages. Boundaries indicate independent states, except that in France and Germany the important semi-independent feudal principalities are shown. The king of England had lost his other domains in France, but still held Aquitaine as a vassal of the French king. Dauphiny was theoretically part of the Holy Roman Empire, but was actually the personal province of the heir to the French throne, and is therefore shown as part of France. The popes at this time resided at, and ruled over, Avignon. The Holy Roman Emperor was now largely a figurehead, enjoying power only in his own hereditary lands. The chief princely states of the Empire are shown. Seven great lords, by the Golden Bull of 1356, had the right to elect the Emperor—the king of Bohemia, the duke of Saxony, the margrave of Brandenburg, the count palatine of the Rhine, and the archbishops of Cologne, Mainz, and Trier. The Christian kingdoms in the Iberian peninsula had expanded southward, driving the Moslems back into Granada. Christendom in the east, however, was yielding before the Mongols and the Turks. The Golden Horde had reduced the Russian princes to tribute-paying vassals. (For the Mongol empire as a whole see pages 126–27.) The Byzantine Empire, still an important nucleus of civilization, had been driven out of Asia Minor by the Ottoman Turks. The simultaneous growth of the Christian Slavic kingdoms, on the European side, had squeezed the Byzantine power into a small region immediately adjacent to Constantinople.

Place names associated with the Hundred Years' War and with Joan of Arc are shown in France.

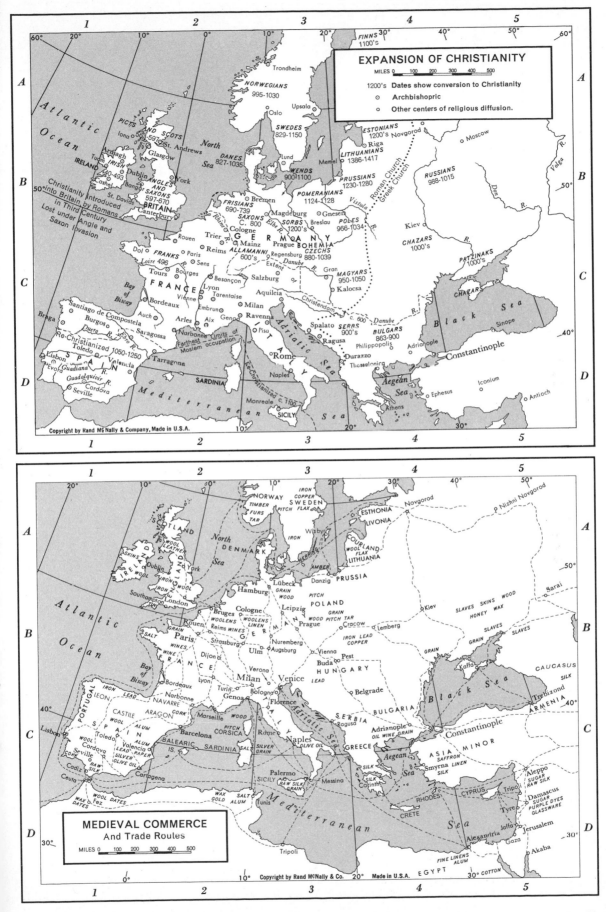

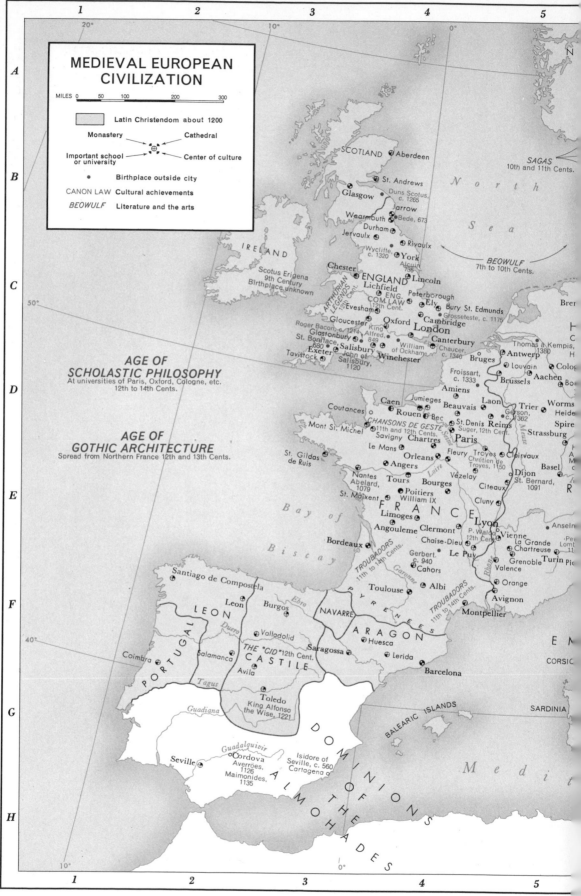

MEDIEVAL EUROPEAN CIVILIZATION

MILES 0 50 100   200   300

Latin Christendom about 1200

Monastery ——————→ ⊕ ←—————— Cathedral

Important school
or university ——→ ⊕ ←—— Center of culture

• Birthplace outside city

CANON LAW Cultural achievements

BEOWULF Literature and the arts

SCOTLAND • Aberdeen

SAGAS
10th and 11th Cents.

• St. Andrews
Duns Scotus,
c. 1265
Glasgow Jarrow
Wearmouth • Bede, 673
Durham
Jervaulx • Rivaulx

North

Sea

Wycliffe, York
c. 1320 Alcuin
735

BEOWULF
7th to 10th Cents.

IRELAND

Chester ENGLAND • Lincoln
Scotus Erigena Lichfield
9th Century • ENG. Peterborough
Birthplace unknown COM. LAW • Ely Bury St. Edmunds
12th Cent. Grosseteste, c. 1175
Evesham Bren
Roger Bacon, Gloucester King Oxford Cambridge
c. 1214, Alfred, London
St. Boniface, Glastonbury 849 Thomas à Kempis,
680 Salisbury Canterbury c. 1380
Exeter William Chaucer, Antwerp
Tavistock John of of Ockham c. 1340 Bruges Colog
Salisbury, Winchester Louvain
1120 Froissart, Brussels Aachen
c. 1333 Bo

AGE OF
SCHOLASTIC PHILOSOPHY
At universities of Paris, Oxford, Cologne, etc.
12th to 14th Cents.

Amiens Trier Worms
Caen Jumieges Beauvais Laon Gerson, Heide
Coutances Rouen Bec c. 1362
CHANSONS DE GESTE St. Denis Reims Spire
Mont St. Michel 11th and 12th Cents. Suger, 12th Cent. Strassburg
Savigny Chartres Paris
Le Mans Troyes Clairvaux Basel

AGE OF
GOTHIC ARCHITECTURE
Spread from Northern France 12th and 13th Cents.

St. Gildas Fleury Chrétien de Dijon R
de Ruis Orleans Troyes, 1150 A
Nantes Angers Vézelay St. Bernard,
Abelard, Tours Bourges Citeaux 1091
1079 Poitiers Cluny
St. Maixent William IX

Bay of Limoges FRANCE Lyon Anselm
Angouleme Clermont P. Wald Vienne
TROUBADORS Chaise-Dieu 12th Cen La Grande Lomb
11th to 14th Cents. Bordeaux Gerbert, Le Puy Chartreuse 11
c. 940 Valence Grenoble Turin Pic
Cahors Orange

Biscay Toulouse • Albi *TROUBADORS* Avignon
11th to 14th Cents.
Montpellier

Santiago de Compostela E
CORSIC
Leon Burgos NAVARRE
PORTUGAL LEON ARAGON • Huesca
Valladolid Saragossa
THE "CID" 12th Cent. Lerida
Coimbra Salamanca CASTILE
Avila Barcelona
Tagus Toledo SARDINIA
King Alfonso BALEARIC ISLANDS
Guadiana the Wise, 1221

DOMINIONS

Guadalquivir Isidore of
Seville Cordova Seville, c. 560
Averroes, Cartagena a
1126 *Medit*
Maimonides, *OF THE ALMOHADES*
1135

Upsala

SWEDEN

20°

30°

Novgorod

A

GOTLAND

ESTHONIA

LIVONIA

REPUBLIC
OF
PSKOV

Volga

MARK

Copenhagen

Baltic Sea

LITHUANIA

Dvina

PRINCIPALITY
OF
SMOLENSK

B

Rostock

Lübeck

Elbe

PRUSSIA

Nieman

R U S S I A

PRINCIPALITY OF
NOVGOROD-SYEVERSKI

C

Y

Magdeburg

Oder

Vistula

P O L A N D

50°

Leipsic

Meister Eckhart, c. 1260

Erfurt

NELUNGENLIED
n to 12th Cents.

Bamberg

Prague

Cracow

PRINCIPALITY
OF
KIEV

Kiev

Dnieper

D

Wurzburg

Huss,
c. 1369

Regensburg

Danube

Vienna

Pressburg

Dniester

C A R P A T H I A N S

C U M A N S

Tegernsee

Buda

H U N G A R Y

Treviso

Aquileia

Padua

Marsiglio,
1270 Po

Venice

Marco Polo
c. 1254

Black
Sea

E

Ferrara

ogna

Ravenna

Peter Damian,
1007

Florence

Dante, 1265

Arezzo

Emperor Frederick II,1194

Petrarch,1303

Danube

B U L G A R I A

mbrosa

Siena

Gratian,
12th-
Cent.

Assisi

St. Francis,
1182

Perugia

St. Benedict, 480

Farfa

S E R B I A

B Y Z A N T I N E

Constantinople

Nicaea

40°

Rome

Boethius, c. 480

Adriatic Sea

Thessalonica

Mt. Athos

Roccasecca
Thomas Aquinas,
1227

Monte Cassino

Naples

Salerno
MEDICAL SCHOOL
12th Cent.

E M P I R E

CORPUS JURIS CIVILIS
(Justinian's codification of Roman Law)
528-565 A.D.
Fully known in the West at Bologna,
12th Cent.

G

Tyrrhenian

SICILY

Aegean
Sea

Sea

Joachim of Flora
c. 1145

Cassiodorus, c. 468

Athens

Palermo

Messina

Monreale

Ionian

SICILY

Catania

Sea

RHODES

H

anean

Sea

CRETE

30°

20°

Copyright by Rand McNally & Company, Made in U.S.A.

55

MEDIEVAL EUROPEAN CIVILIZATION

▶ MAP ON PAGES 54–55

THE FIRST STRICTLY EUROPEAN civilization was that of Latin Christendom in the Middle Ages. Under the Roman Empire the north and south shores of the Mediterranean had been culturally alike, and the ancient world had always retained a strong orientation toward the Hellenized Near East. Medieval civilization had its center of gravity farther north. It was confined to Europe, but at the same time, by spreading over Germany, Hungary, Poland, and Scandinavia, it incorporated more of Europe than ancient civilization had ever directly touched. Its area was the region within which Christians used the Latin language and recognized the bishop of Rome as their head.

The preceding map is the first of a series of five, in which European civilization is shown at five periods from the Middle Ages to the nineteenth century. Each map sets forth cultural features of its time, and the names and birthplaces of persons who illustrate this culture. Place of birth is of course in some cases irrelevant to a man's later career, but since birthplace is most frequently the place of upbringing, and hence of the environment and opportunities of one's youth, a region with a high concentration of such birthplaces or of other cultural features may be regarded as a center of civilized activity, and regions with few such birthplaces or other features may be thought of as provincial or outlying. The preceding map thus suggests that medieval civilization lay along an axis from the British Isles to south Italy, with extensions in the middle into Germany and Spain.

Some of the persons shown on the map for the fifth and sixth centuries, like Isidore of Seville or St. Benedict and Cassiodorus in Italy, really reflect the expiring civilization of the ancient world. A few, like Alcuin of York, flourished in the half-millennium commonly called the Dark Ages that followed the dissolution of the Roman Empire. Most of what is on the map refers to the period from about 1050 to 1400, the great period of medieval civilization properly speaking.

European Beginnings

The earliest literary works in the modern European languages appeared at this time, mostly heroic poems of unknown authorship, and at first transmitted by word of mouth, like the epics of Homer. English has the oldest traditions of all the European languages, the Old English Beowulf having begun to take form as early as the seventh century among bards in both England and Denmark. The Scandinavian sagas, the German Nibelungenlied, the French chansons de geste, the Spanish Cid, and the Arthurian legends of Celtic Wales developed from the tenth to the twelfth centuries, though they generally referred to a more distant past, Carolingian or even pre-Christian, which survived in folk memories or popular stories. A little later came the troubadours in southern France, and then, after 1300, the works of Dante in Italy and Chaucer in England.

While the various European national cultures thus began, the higher culture was more truly international, or nonnational, than at any time since. Latin was everywhere the language of learning and even of practical administration; scholars and churchmen moved from one country to another with great ease. Two archbishops of Canterbury, Anselm and Lanfranc, were Italians. The theologians Albertus Magnus, Thomas Aquinas, and Duns Scotus, who came respectively from Germany, Italy, and Scotland, all taught at the universities of both Paris and Cologne.

The universities were among the most typical creations of the Middle Ages. All those founded in the thirteenth and fourteenth centuries are shown on the map. The oldest were those of Paris, Bologna, and Oxford, which date from before 1200. Paris became the great center for theology and scholastic philosophy; Bologna for Roman law and the closely related canon law; Salerno for medical studies. Many of these had begun as cathedral schools or abbey schools before incorporation as universities; a few such schools which never became universities, as at Chartres, Laon, and Bec, are also shown.

Gothic architecture, today the chief remaining visible symbol of medieval civilization, originated in the twelfth century in northern France, whence it spread, with effects diminishing with distance, to all parts of the Latin world. Notable abbeys and cathedrals are indicated. Abbeys are chosen for their importance at the time, whether standing today or not. Nothing remains today of Cluny, the mother house of a great monastic order. St-Denis was the royal abbey of France, the favorite church of the French kings. Abelard was for a time abbot of St-Gildas-de-Ruis in Brittany, and St. Bernard was abbot of Clairvaux in eastern France. The cathedrals chosen for inclusion on the map all survive as important examples of medieval architecture. Anyone planning a tour had best consult a guidebook, but the map may suggest which regions will prove architecturally most rewarding.

Europe in the Middle Ages was strongly influenced by both Islam and the Byzantine Empire, both of which long enjoyed a more developed culture than Europe. The Arab philosopher Averröes and the Jewish philosopher Maimonides flourished in Moslem Spain in the twelfth century. It was from the Arabs, through contacts in Spain and Sicily, that medieval Europeans drew much of their knowledge of Aristotle and the ancient Greeks. Some of the works of Aristotle and of Arabic writers were known in the first European universities. Byzantine culture was highly concentrated at Constantinople, Thessalonica, and Mt. Athos, the last a great mass of monastic establishments, many of which still survive. Mongol and Turkish invasions disrupted the Arab and Byzantine worlds, so that by the end of the Middle Ages Latin Christians possessed, in many ways, the most vigorous civilization of western Eurasia.

THE RENAISSANCE

▶ MAPS ON PAGES 58–59 AND 60

THE NEXT MAP ILLUSTRATES the civilization of Europe from 1400 to 1550, a transitional period between medieval and modern, characterized by the Renaissance, the beginnings of the Reformation, and the great geographical discoveries. As an artistic movement the Renaissance had two main centers, Italy and the Low Countries, from which it spread northward and southward to France and south Germany. The inset reveals the extraordinary predominance of Italy and especially of Florence and its surrounding country. The Sistine Chapel in Rome may be taken to signify the artistic splendors which no map can show, and the cluster of luminaries of the first magnitude—Donatello, Botticelli, Leonardo, Michelangelo, Raphael, Titian—must serve as a pale representation of the galaxy of genius that made the Quattrocento. In the north the chief painters before 1550 were the Van Eycks in the Netherlands, and in Germany Albrecht Dürer of Nuremberg and Hans Holbein of Augsburg. France also had its art centers, but most painters of the Fontainebleau school are not known by name, and those of the Dijon school were not native to France.

Humanism

In literature and in learned studies the work of the Renaissance is known as humanism, which began in Italy, where it produced men like Alberti and Lorenzo Valla, and then spread to other countries. The most notable of all humanist writers was Erasmus of Rotterdam. While the humanists were interested mainly in the classical works of Greece and Rome, the new attention to ancient texts contributed also to intensive Biblical studies. Erasmus translated the Greek New Testament into Latin, Ximenes sponsored Biblical studies in Spain, Tyndale and Coverdale translated the Bible into English, Luther into German, others less known into other languages. Biblical study merged into the religious movement of the Protestant Reformation, as suggested by the names of Luther, Zwingli, Calvin, and Knox on the map (see also page 68). The Catholic Reform was furthered by Ignatius Loyola, born in Spain, who obtained papal recognition of his newly founded Society of Jesus in 1540.

The printing of books by movable type was introduced into Europe about the middle of the fifteenth century. The first such printer was probably Gutenberg of Mainz; other early printers were Caxton in England and Aldus Manutius who founded the Aldine Press at Venice. The printing of books, and even more, at first, the eager search of the humanists for old manuscripts, led to the formation of libraries on a scale unknown in the Middle Ages. The most famous libraries founded at this time are the Vatican Library and the French National Library or Bibliothèque Nationale, which began as the Royal Library about 1480.

The Renaissance States

The Renaissance was a period of state building, and the map shows political boundaries as of about the year 1477. In that year Charles the Bold, duke of Burgundy, was killed in battle. For a time it had seemed that the miscellaneous Burgundian domains might become a lasting state, but with Charles' death they ceased to have independent existence, and most of them soon passed into the inheritance of the House of Hapsburg (see page 64). In 1477, however, the Hapsburgs stood only at the threshold of their greatness, possessing no territories outside their ancestral duchy of Austria; the long line of Hapsburg Holy Roman Emperors (1440–1806) had begun with Frederick III, but the Holy Roman Empire had little unity or effectiveness. John II ruled as king of Aragon and Sicily, but his heir Ferdinand was married to Isabella, queen of Castile, so that the union of the Spanish crowns was soon to be accomplished. In England the internal struggles of the Wars of the Roses were at their height, to be terminated about 1485. In France Louis XI mended the damage left by the Hundred Years' War, and carried on the long rivalry of the French kings with the dukes of Burgundy. In 1477 the "duchy" of Burgundy, the region around Dijon, was annexed to France; the "free county" of Burgundy, or Franche Comté, east of the duchy, did not become French for another two hundred years. Italy is shown in the inset with boundaries as of the Peace of Lodi, 1454. Here a half-dozen states of nearly equal importance engaged in a balance-of-power politics which was later to become typical of Europe as a whole. In this Italian political atmosphere, where states rose and fell by a combination of luck and cold calculation, Machiavelli wrote his famous handbook of statecraft, *The Prince*.

Eastern Europe was dominated by Casimir IV, king of Poland and grand duke of Lithuania, whose son, Vladislav, was king of Bohemia. Prussia, the domain of the Teutonic Knights, had been reduced both in size and in power, becoming vassal to Poland. Constantinople had fallen in 1453 to the Ottoman Turks, who by 1477 overran all Greece, Serbia, and Wallachia. The only remaining Christian outposts in the eastern Mediterranean were now Rhodes, Cyprus, and Crete.

The Medici and the Fuggers

▶ MAP ON PAGE 60

The Renaissance was also a classic age of merchant princes, notably the Fuggers in Germany and the Medici in Italy. Both families made their fortune first in textiles, then turned to banking, the Fuggers at Augsburg, the Medici at Florence. The Medici always considered trade more important than banking; they reached their height in the fifteenth century, but disappeared as a business firm about 1500, after which they figured as a political family of European importance. The Fuggers began their rise in 1473, a century after the Medici; they made many loans, especially to kings and princes, in return for which they got control of a good many enterprises. Among these were their mines in Hungary, Germany, and southern Spain. After Augsburg, their headquarters, Antwerp was their principal base; but there were large Fugger establishments at Nuremberg and Venice also. The Fuggers were ruined by 1600, mainly through the defaulting of princes who owed them money.

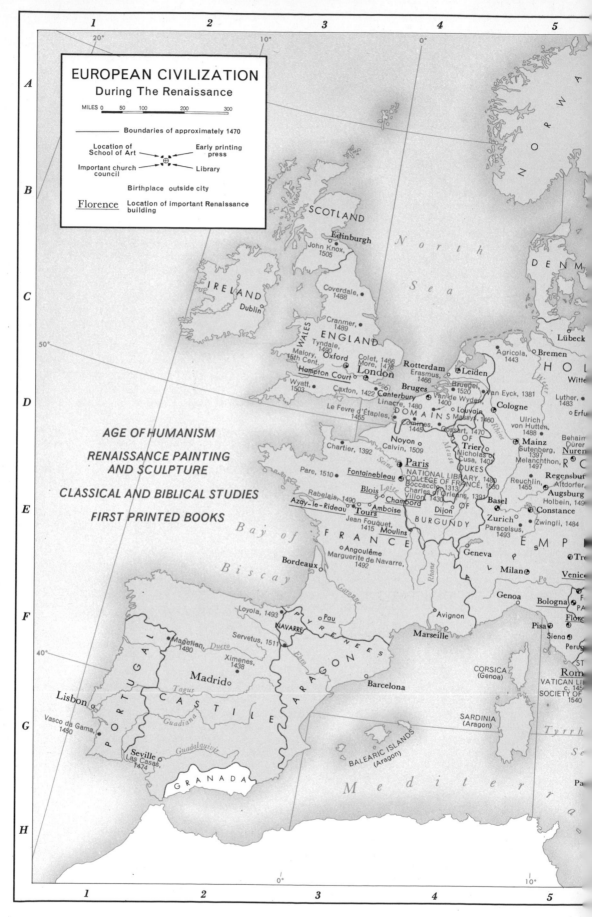

EUROPEAN CIVILIZATION
During The Renaissance

MILES 0 50 100   200   300

───── Boundaries of approximately 1470

Location of School of Art   Early printing press

Important church council   Library

Birthplace outside city

Florence Location of important Renaissance building

SCOTLAND

Edinburgh

John Knox, 1505

North Sea

NORWAY

DENM

Coverdale, 1488

Lübeck

IRELAND

Dublin

Cranmer, 1489

WALES ENGLAND

Tyndale, 1490

Malory, 15th Cent. Oxford

Hampton Court

Wyatt, 1503

Caxton, 1422

Canterbury

Colet, 1466

More, 1478

London

Le Fevre d'Étaples, 1455

Rotterdam

Erasmus, 1466

Bruges

Linacre, 1480

Comines, 1445

Leiden

Agricola, 1443

Bremen

HOL

Witte

Bruegel, 1520

Van Eyck, 1381

Van de Wyden, 1400

DOMAINS

Massys, 1460

Gossart, 1470

Cologne

Luther, 1483

Erfu

AGE OF HUMANISM

RENAISSANCE PAINTING AND SCULPTURE

CLASSICAL AND BIBLICAL STUDIES

FIRST PRINTED BOOKS

Chartier, 1392

Noyon

Calvin, 1509

OF

Trier

Nicholas of Cusa, 1401

Mainz

Gutenberg, 1397

Melanchthon, 1497

Ulrich von Hutten, 1488

Behaim

Dürer

Nuren

R C

Pare, 1510

Fontainebleau

Paris

NATIONAL LIBRARY, 1480

COLLEGE OF FRANCE, 1530

Boccaccio, 1313

Charles d'Orleans, 1391

Reuchlin, 1455

Regensbur

Altdorfer

Bay of

Biscay

Rabelais, 1490

Azay-le-Rideau

Blois

Chambord

Villon, 1430

Tours

Amboise

Jean Fouquet, 1415

Moulins

Dijon

BURGUNDY

Augsburg

Holbein, 149

Basel

Zurich

Constance

Paracelsus, 1493

Zwingli, 1484

Angoulême

Marguerite de Navarre, 1492

Geneva

E S M P

Tre

Bordeaux

Milan

Genoa

Venice

F

PA

Flore

PORTUGAL

Loyola, 1493

Pau

NAVARRE

PYRENEES

Avignon

Marseille

Pisa

Siena

Perus

ST

Magellan, 1480

Servetus, 1511

Ximenes, 1438

ARAGON

CORSICA (Genoa)

Rom

VATICAN LI

c. 145

SOCIETY OF

1540

Madrid

CASTILE

Barcelona

Lisbon

Tagus

Guadiana

SARDINIA (Aragon)

Tyrrh

Se

Vasco da Gama, 1450

Seville

Las Casas, 1474

Guadalquivir

BALEARIC ISLANDS (Aragon)

GRANADA

Mediterra

Pa

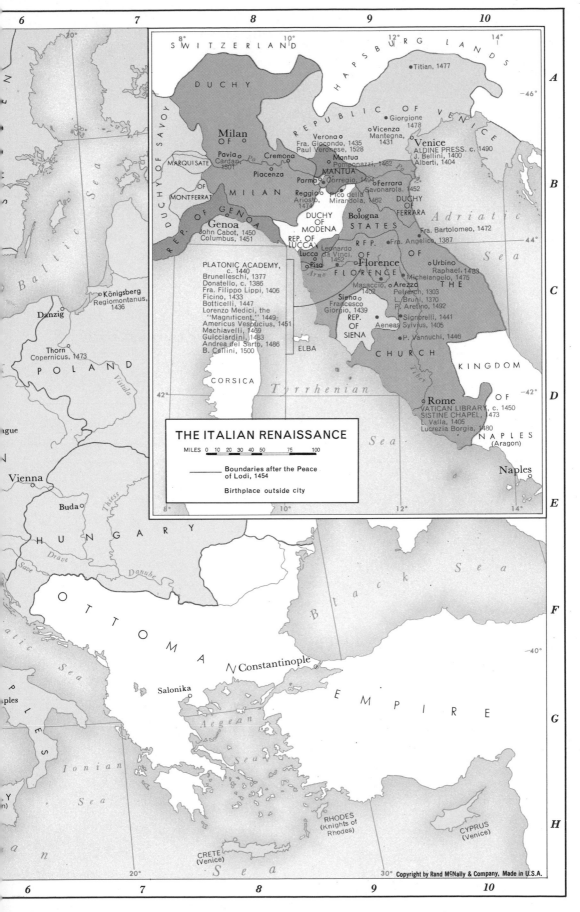

THE ITALIAN RENAISSANCE

MILES 0 10 20 30 40 50   75   100

——————— Boundaries after the Peace
of Lodi, 1454

Birthplace outside city

PLATONIC ACADEMY,
c. 1440
Brunelleschi, 1377
Donatello, c. 1386
Fra. Filippo Lippi, 1406
Ficino, 1433
Botticelli, 1447
Lorenzo Medici, the
"Magnificent," 1449
Americus Vespucius, 1451
Machiavelli, 1469
Guicciardini, 1483
Andrea del Sarto, 1486
B. Cellini, 1500

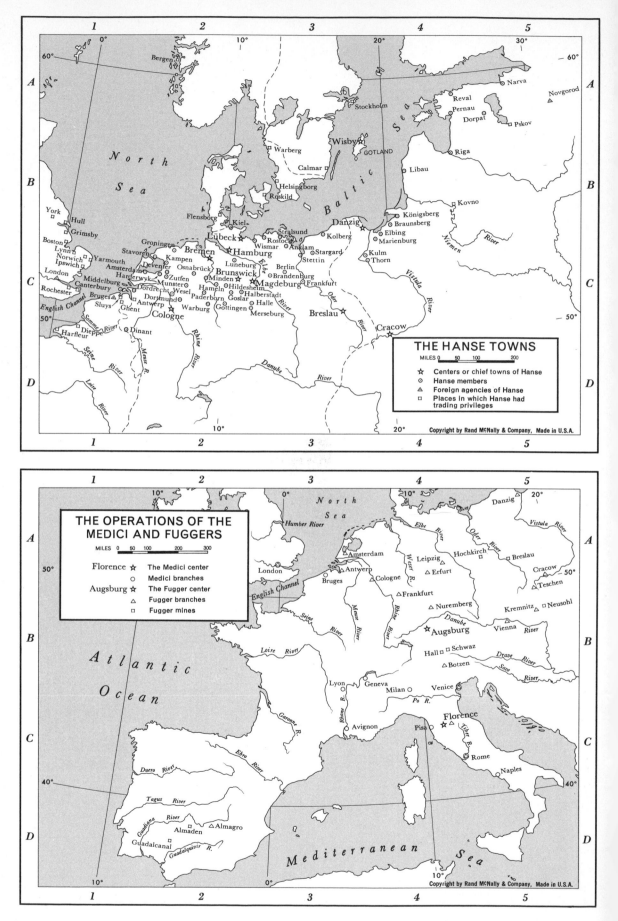

THE HANSE TOWNS

MILES 0   50   100   200

☆ Centers or chief towns of Hanse
⊙ Hanse members
△ Foreign agencies of Hanse
▫ Places in which Hanse had trading privileges

Copyright by Rand McNally & Company, Made in U.S.A.

North Sea

Baltic Sea

GOTLAND

Bergen
Narva
Novgorod
Stockholm
Reval
Pernau
Dorpat
Pskov
Warberg
Wisby
Riga
Calmar
Libau
Helsingborg
Roskild
Kovno
York
Hull
Flensborg
Königsberg
Braunsberg
Grimsby
Kiel
Danzig
Elbing
Marienburg
Boston
Lübeck
Stralsund
Rostock
Kolberg
Kulm
Lynn
Groningen
Bremen
Wismar
Anklam
Stargard
Thorn
Norwich
Stavoren
Hamburg
Stettin
Ipswich
Kampen
Luneburg
Berlin
London
Deventer
Osnabrück
Brandenburg
Rochester
Amsterdam
Munster
Minden
Magdeburg
Frankfurt
Middelburg
Harderwyk
Zutfen
Hildesheim
Canterbury
Dordrecht
Wesel
Goslar
Bruges
Dortmund
Paderborn
Halberstadt
Breslau
Sluys
Ghent
Antwerp
Hameln
Halle
Warburg
Göttingen
Merseburg
Cracow
Cologne
Brunswick
Dieppe
Dinant
Harfleur
Brandenburg

Niemen River
Vistula River
Oder River
Elbe
Rhine River
Meuse R.
Somme River
Seine River
Loire River
Danube River

English Channel

THE OPERATIONS OF THE MEDICI AND FUGGERS

MILES 0   50   100   200   300

Florence ☆   The Medici center
        ⊙   Medici branches
Augsburg ☆   The Fugger center
        △   Fugger branches
        ▫   Fugger mines

Copyright by Rand McNally & Company, Made in U.S.A.

North Sea

Atlantic Ocean

Mediterranean Sea

Danzig
Amsterdam
Antwerp
Leipzig
Hochkirch
Breslau
London
Bruges
Cologne
Erfurt
Cracow
Frankfurt
Teschen
Nuremberg
Kremnitz
Neusohl
Augsburg
Vienna
Hall
Schwaz
Botzen
Lyon
Geneva
Milan
Venice
Avignon
Pisa
Florence
Rome
Naples
Almagro
Almaden
Guadalcanal

Humber River
Elbe River
Oder River
Vistula River
Weser R.
Rhine River
Meuse River
Seine River
Loire River
Danube River
Drave River
Save River
Rhone R.
Po R.
Tiber R.
Garonne R.
Ebro River
Duero River
Tagus River
Guadiana River
Guadalquivir R.

English Channel

THE AGE OF DISCOVERY

▶ MAP ON PAGES 62–63

WITH THE GREAT Age of Discovery a knowledge of the earth as a whole for the first time became possible. The first men to have this knowledge were the Europeans of the fifteenth and sixteenth centuries, who, in their attempts to reach Asia by sea, felt out the shapes and sizes of the continents and oceans. The northeastern Atlantic became a center from which voyages went out in all directions.

In the later Middle Ages European knowledge of east Asia had actually declined, while knowledge of Africa had grown. The breakup of the Mongol empire (see pages 126–27) made European travel to the Far East no longer feasible. There was less contact with the Near East after the failure of the Crusades. The attention of Europeans turned west and south. As early as 1291 the Vivaldi of Genoa passed through the Strait of Gibraltar to seek "the Indies"; they never returned. Others, probably Italian, rediscovered the Canaries, known to the ancients, and discovered the Madeiras and Azores in the fourteenth century. Italians also penetrated the Sahara, reached Tombouctu, and even visited Abyssinia, which they now identified as the Christian kingdom of the legendary Prester John.

The Portuguese

Prince Henry of Portugal (the "Navigator") began to sponsor a series of expeditions early in the fifteenth century. His men colonized the Madeiras and Azores, discovered the Cape Verde Islands, and charted the African coast to Sierra Leone by the time of his death in 1460. King John II resumed the work in 1481. His captains, Cão and Dias, discovered the Zaire (Congo) river and the Cape of Good Hope respectively in 1482 and 1488. Meanwhile, another of the king's agents, Covilhã, traveling via the Red Sea, reconnoitered the east African and Indian coasts. The way was thus prepared for Vasco da Gama, who in 1498 reached India by sailing around the Cape of Good Hope. Very rapidly, within twenty years, the Portuguese explored and partly conquered as far east as Malacca, and established contact with the East Indies, Siam, and China. They first visited Japan in 1542.

In 1492, before the Portuguese expeditions had reached their objective with da Gama, the Spanish had laid a claim to certain West Indian islands by backing the Genoese Christopher Columbus. Portugal and Spain, by the treaty of Tordesillas of 1494, agreed to a demarcation line in the Atlantic, Spain to have sole rights to non-Christian countries west of this line, Portugal to the east. The Portuguese Cabral, touching Brazil in 1500, claimed it for Portugal.

America: The Search for Passages

Columbus, seeking Japan and China in the west, died in 1506, after four voyages, in the belief that he had reached Asia. Actually, he had discovered the principal West Indian islands, Venezuela, and Central America. Others suspected the truth before his death, notably the Florentine Amerigo Vespucci, who first called South America the *Mundus Novus*, or New World. An Alsatian geographer, Martin Waldseemüller, in 1507 proposed to call this new world "America" after Amerigo Vespucci, who used the Latinized name Americus Vespucius.

Since the *Mundus Novus* was regarded as an annoying obstruction in the way of the real Asia, which was by now monopolized by the Portuguese, the problem for all other nationalities was to circumvent it. Spain employed the Portuguese Magellan, who believed that the extreme of east Asia, the Spice Islands, might legitimately lie within the Spanish zone as established at Tordesillas. Magellan discovered the straits of his name, crossed the Pacific, and died in the Philippines, which in fact proved to lie on the Spanish side of the demarcation line. His subordinate, El Cano, completed the first circumnavigation of the globe, although this had not been the original purpose of the expedition.

Other Spaniards meanwhile tried to make what they could of America. Cortés conquered the Aztecs; Pizarro the Incas; Ulloa and Gamboa ranged along the Pacific coast; Orellana descended the Amazon as early as 1541. An expedition from Mexico assured Spanish rule over the Philippine natives in 1565.

John Cabot, born in Genoa a year before Columbus, reached North America for the English in 1497. His son Sebastian probably entered Hudson's Bay in 1508. English enterprise began in earnest a half-century later. Willoughby and Chancellor, seeking a Northeast Passage to east Asia, discovered the White Sea for western Europeans and opened contact with Russia. In the following years Anthony Jenkinson passed over the same route through Russia, across the Caspian, to Bokhara. A series of English voyages to find a Northwest Passage to Asia—led by Frobisher, Davis, Baffin, and Hudson—found no such passage but established the main outlines of the North American continent in this area.

French merchants sent out the Florentine Verrazano to find a strait through North America. After his failure, in 1524, Jacques Cartier shifted the search to the north, where he discovered the St. Lawrence River.

The Dutch, like the English, attempted to find a Northeast Passage; their navigator, Barents, discovered Spitzbergen and explored the Barents Sea. The English Henry Hudson, while in Dutch service, sailed up the Hudson River in 1609. After 1580 Portugal and its empire belonged to the crown of Spain, against which the Dutch were in rebellion; they used the opportunity to penetrate directly into the Portuguese colonial area, and so acquired Java and the lucrative East Indian islands. The Dutch government created an East India company, to which it gave a trading monopoly via both the Cape of Good Hope and the Straits of Magellan. Other Dutchmen, to evade the monopoly, thereupon sailed around Cape Horn in 1616, and named it after the small Dutch town of Hoorn where the enterprise had been planned.

Voyages of discovery in this period, by the nationality of sponsors, tended in general to determine the location of the Spanish, Portuguese, English, French, and Dutch colonial empires for three hundred years. For colonial enterprise and further exploration after 1600 see pages 144 and 149. For exploration of the Pacific Ocean see page 132.

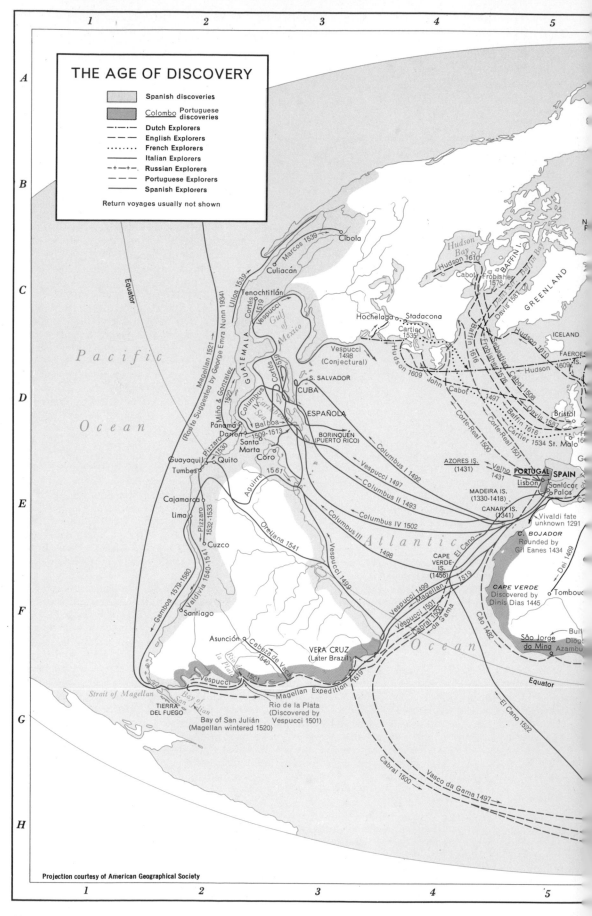

THE AGE OF DISCOVERY

Spanish discoveries
Colombo Portuguese discoveries
—·—·— Dutch Explorers
— — — English Explorers
·········· French Explorers
———— Italian Explorers
—+—+— Russian Explorers
— — — Portuguese Explorers
———— Spanish Explorers

Return voyages usually not shown

Pacific

Ocean

Equator

Cibola
Marcos 1539
Culiacán
Ulloa 1539
Tenochtitlán
Cortés 1519
Vespucci 1519

Hudson Bay
Hudson 1610
BAFFIN I.
Cabot Frobisher 1576
GREENLAND
Davis 1587
Baffin 1616
Hudson 1610
ICELAND
Sebastian Cabot 1508
FAEROES
Hudson 1609

Gulf of Mexico

Hochelaga Stadacona
Cartier 1535
Hudson 1609 John Cabot
1497
Davis 1585
Corte-Real 1500
Corte-Real 1501
Cartier 1534 St. Malo
Baffin 1616
Bristol

GUATEMALA
Cortés
Columbus
IV
Caribbean Sea
Vespucci 1498 (Conjectural)
S. SALVADOR
CUBA
ESPAÑOLA
BORINQUÉN (PUERTO RICO)
Columbus I 1492
Columbus 1497
Vespucci 1497
Columbus II 1493
Columbus IV 1502
Columbus III 1498

AZORES IS. (1431)
Velho 1431
PORTUGAL SPAIN
Lisbon
Santander
MADEIRA IS. (1330-1418)
CANARY IS. (1341)
Vivaldi fate unknown 1291

(Route Suggested by George Emra Nunn 1934)
Magellan 1521

Panamá
Niño & Gonzalez 1522
Darien
Pizarro 1509-1513
Balboa
Santa Marta
Coro
Guayaquil
Quito
Tumbes
Aguirre 1561

Cajamarca
Lima
Pizarro 1532-1533
Cuzco
Orellana 1541
Vespucci 1499

Atlantic
El Cano

CAPE VERDE IS. (1456)
El Cano 1519
Magellan 1519

C. BOJADOR
Rounded by Gil Eanes 1434
Del 1469
CAPE VERDE
Discovered by Dinis Dias 1445
Tombouc

Gamboa 1579-1580
Valdivia 1540-1541
Santiago

Asunción
Cabeza de Vaca 1540
Rio de la Plata
VERA CRUZ (Later Brazil)
Vespucci 1501
Magellan 1519

Vespucci 1499
Vespucci 1501
Cabral 1500
da Gama
Cão 1482

São Jorge da Mina
Bull Diogo Azambu

Ocean
Equator

Strait of Magellan
Bay of San Julián
TIERRA DEL FUEGO
Vespucci
Bay of San Julián (Magellan wintered 1520)
Magellan Expedition
Rio de la Plata (Discovered by Vespucci 1501)

El Cano 1522
Cabral 1500
Vasco da Gama 1497

Projection courtesy of American Geographical Society

62

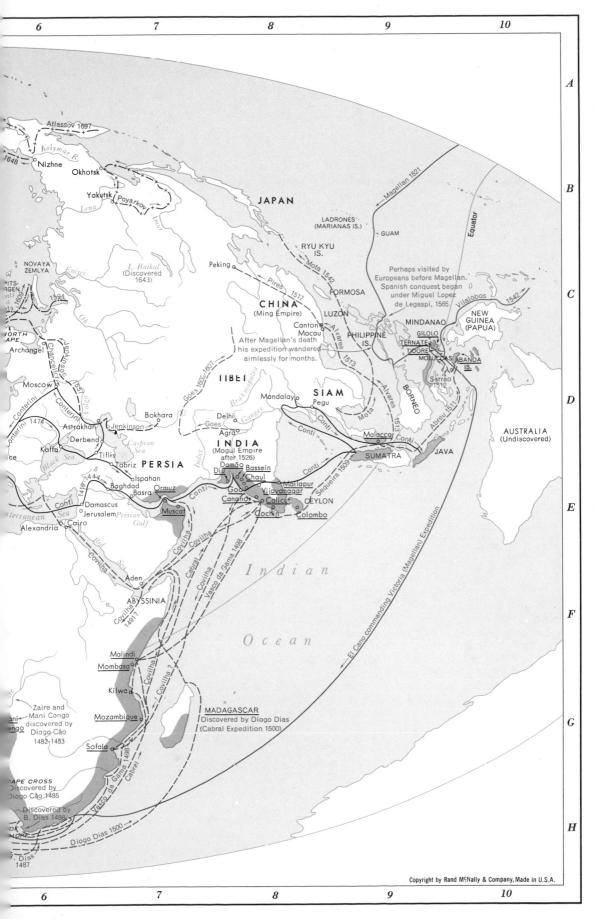

A

6 **7** **8** **9** **10**

Atlassov 1697
1648
Nizhne
Kolyma R.
Okhotsk
Yakutsk · Poyarkov
Lena
Amur

JAPAN

LADRONES
(MARIANAS IS.)
GUAM

Magellan 1521

Equator

B

NOVAYA
ZEMLYA
L. Baikal
(Discovered
1643)

Enisei
Ob

1594

RYU KYU
IS.

Mota 1542

Peking
Pires 1517

FORMOSA

CHINA
(Ming Empire)

Canton
Macau

After Magellan's death
his expedition wandered
aimlessly for months.

LUZON

Alvares

Perhaps visited by
Europeans before Magellan.
Spanish conquest began
under Miguel Lopez
de Legaspi, 1565.

Vilalobos
1542

MINDANAO
GILOLO
TERNATE
TIDORE
MOLUCCAS
Serrao
1512

**NEW
GUINEA
(PAPUA)**

C

NORTH
APE
Archangel

SPITS-
RGEN
IS

Chancellor

Yermak

Moscow
1557

Contarini
Contarini
Contarini 1474

Astrakhan
Jenkinson
Derbend

Goes 1602-1607

TIBET

Brahmaputra

Delhi
Goes
Agra

Mandalay
Ganges

SIAM
Pegu

Conti
Conti
Conti

Mota

Alvares 1513

Abreu 1511

BORNEO

PHILIPPINE
IS.

BANDA
IS.

D

Kaffa
Black Sea
ice

Tiflis
Tabriz

PERSIA

Caspian
Sea

Bokhara

INDIA
(Mogul Empire
after 1526)

Indus

Damão
Diu
Bassein
Chaul

Malacca

Conti

SUMATRA

Conti

Sequeira 1509

JAVA

Conti

AUSTRALIA
(Undiscovered)

E

Ispahan
1444
1419
Baghdad
Basra
Ormuz
Conti

Damascus
Jerusalem
Cairo
Alexandria

Mediterranean Sea
Conti

Muscat
Persian Gulf
Red Sea

Goa
Cananor
Cochin

Marlapur
Vijayanagar
Calicut

CEYLON

Colombo

Covilha
Cabral
Covilha
Vasco da Gama 1498

Covilha

Indian

F

Aden

ABYSSINIA
Covilha
1491?

El Cano commanding Victoria (Magellan) Expedition

Ocean

Malindi
Mombasa
Kilwa

Covilha
Covilha

G

Zaire and
Mani Congo
discovered by
Diogo Cão
1482-1483

Mozambique

MADAGASCAR
Discovered by Diogo Dias
(Cabral Expedition 1500)

Sofala
Vasco da Gama 1498
Cabral

APE CROSS
Discovered by
Diogo Cão 1485

Discovered by
B. Dias 1486

H

Diogo Dias 1500

. Dias
1487

6 **7** **8** **9** **10**

EUROPE IN THE SIXTEENTH CENTURY: POLITICAL AND RELIGIOUS

▶ MAPS ON PAGES 66 AND 68

THE MAP OF EUROPE about 1560 shows the Turkish penetration almost to Vienna. Note, too, the extent of Poland, which by union with Lithuania in 1569 became the largest state in Europe; the miscellaneous holdings of the king of Denmark; and the chain of Venetian islands reaching east to Cyprus. It may be recalled that the action in *Othello* has to do with the Venetian defense of Cyprus against the Turks.

The Hapsburgs
▶ MAP ON PAGE 66

For central and western Europe the main political fact in 1560 was the extent of the Hapsburg power. The Hapsburg family had ruled the small archduchy of Austria since 1276. Its rise to predominance after 1500, through a series of marriages and inheritances, illustrated the "dynasticism" which characterized European politics from this time until the French Revolution. In the person of the emperor Charles V four inheritances came together. From his paternal grandfather he received Austria, and from his paternal grandmother the "Burgundian inheritance," comprising Franche Comté and the Netherlands. His maternal grandparents were Ferdinand and Isabella of Spain. From the former he received Aragon and its Mediterranean dependencies, from the latter Castile and its new American empire. In addition, in 1519, Charles was elected Holy Roman Emperor; and in 1526 both Bohemia and Hungary, hoping for help against the Turks, elected Charles' brother Ferdinand as their king. Charles abdicated in 1556, leaving some of his possessions to his son Philip II of Spain, and some to his brother Ferdinand. Thus arose the Spanish and Austrian branches of the Hapsburg house. France, to oppose their joint predominance, extended the principle of the balance of power over Europe, seeking allies against the Hapsburgs in Turkey, Poland, Sweden, and the member states of the Holy Roman Empire. A first round in this encounter between France and the Hapsburgs (which went on for two centuries) was ended by the Treaty of Cateau Cambrésis in 1559. France by this treaty occupied the three bishoprics of Metz, Toul, and Verdun, thus beginning to eat away the western border of the Empire.

The Protestant Reformation
▶ MAP ON PAGE 68

The age of Charles V was also the period of the Protestant Reformation. In fact, Charles' most serious problem—except possibly for the Turkish advance—was this great revolution in the world of medieval Latin Christendom. At the Peace of Augsburg, in 1555, Charles was obliged to let each member state of the Holy Roman Empire be either Catholic or Lutheran as it locally chose. The map on page 68 shows the religious situation about 1600.

At this time the Catholic Church had already won back some German territories which had been Protestant a generation before. The Hapsburg ambition to re-Catholicize England had failed with the loss of the Spanish Armada (1588); but the situation was still fluid. In general, there were four types of territorial or established churches, supported by governments, but in all countries north of the Alps and Pyrenees there were significant numbers of people who did not accept this officially preferred religion.

Lutheran and Anglican churches originated in the action of governments, with varying degrees of consent or pressure from their peoples. Many states of the Holy Roman Empire, the two Scandinavian monarchies, and the German duchies of Prussia and Courland set up Lutheran churches. In England, under Henry VIII, Parliament passed an Act of Supremacy in 1534, and a similar act for Ireland in 1541, repudiating the authority of the pope. Lutheranism did not permanently spread beyond the German and Scandinavian orbit, nor Anglicanism beyond the range of English influence, in both cases including America in later times.

Calvinism often arose as part of a rebellion against governments, though where they obtained power, as in Scotland, the Dutch provinces, some of the Swiss city states, and Puritan Massachusetts, the Calvinists set up territorial churches. Calvinism was the great international form of Protestantism. In 1600 there were strong Calvinist or Puritan influences in England. In France, mostly in the south, 142 towns had been designated as Protestant by the Edict of Nantes. A few German rulers had turned Calvinist. In Hungary, Transylvania, and Poland many of the landed nobility were Calvinist; there were over a thousand Protestant churches and two thousand noble Protestant families in Poland-Lithuania alone. Lutheranism in eastern Europe spread mostly among German-speaking townsmen settled in the eastern Baltic, Poland, and Transylvania.

The radicals of the religious revolution were the Anabaptists. They demanded individual religious freedom, and denied the need for any territorial church. They were found in many countries, and included the "Pilgrims" who reached Plymouth in 1620. Socinians, who denied the Trinity, were not numerous except in Poland. Indeed Poland, largely because of weak government and the mixed ethnic character of the population, both of which promoted toleration, was the most heterogeneous part of Europe in religion. Many Jews fled or emigrated to Poland, which became the main center of European Jewry at this time. In western Europe the largest Jewish communities were at Amsterdam, Frankfurt, and Venice.

The Catholic or Counter Reformation went on for about a century after 1600. The Hapsburg dynasty re-Catholicized Bohemia, the French monarchy repealed the Edict of Nantes, and Jesuit and other missionaries restored Catholicism in Poland. At this time, also, many Greek Orthodox Christians in southern Poland, while retaining their own religious practices, consented to accept the authority of the pope. They were called Uniates, and have continued into our own time.

THE OTTOMAN EMPIRE

▶ MAP ON PAGE 67

THE HIGH POINT of the Ottoman Empire, so far at least as western Europeans were concerned, came in 1529, when the Turks, having crushed the Hungarians, laid siege to Vienna, the capital of the Holy Roman Empire and the bastion of central Europe. They abandoned the siege after a few weeks. But they long remained powerful, and were again to besiege Vienna in 1683. Their empire at its farthest extent, shown by the heavy red line on the map, reached from Hungary and the Ukraine to Egypt and Persia, and in east-west direction almost from Gibraltar to the Caspian Sea. The weakening of control over so large a territory, in later centuries, raised a long series of international crises until the expiration of the empire in 1923.

The Rise of the Ottoman Empire

The Ottoman branch of the Turkish peoples had first become organized as a military-religious unit in northwestern Anatolia about 1290. With the enfeeblement of the Byzantines, the Ottoman Turks secured their first foothold on the European continent in 1354 at Gallipoli. They were able to make Adrianople their capital in 1366, and in 1389 they defeated their first serious European opponent, the medieval Serbian empire, at the battle of Kosovo, by which Serbian independence was lost for almost five hundred years. Christians under Hungarian leadership organized a crusade against these militant Moslems, but were unsuccessful, so that Bulgaria and the mainland of Greece, by 1400, followed Serbia into a long dependency on Turkish rule. A second attempt by the Hungarians to lead a crusade was defeated at Varna in 1444. Thereafter, except for mountainous Montenegro and parts of Dalmatia held by Venice, the whole Balkan peninsula south of the Danube was held by the Turks. In 1453 they took Constantinople itself. The thousand-year history of the Byzantine or East Roman Empire thus came to an end in this greatest of all Moslem victories over the Christian world. Constantinople has remained Turkish ever since.

In the first decades after 1500 the Turks turned their efforts not to Europe but to the East. Here they had been defeated by Tamerlane at Angora in 1402, but they now proceeded to a succession of triumphs, as Selim I defeated the Persians (1514) and conquered Armenia and Kurdistan (1515), Syria (1516), Egypt (1517), far-off Algeria (1519), and the holy places of Mecca itself (1517). The western part of the Moslem world, with its great historical and religous centers, thus passed under Ottoman rule.

Suleiman the Magnificent, greatest of the sultans, began his reign in 1520. The Turks again turned to Europe. In 1521 they captured the fortress of Belgrade, in 1522 the island of Rhodes. In 1526 they brought the Hungarians to final defeat at the battle of Mohacs, from which they pressed on to the siege of Vienna. They soon became (and long remained) a factor in the European balance of power, as the French king Francis I, putting politics before religion, joined with the Turks against their common enemy, Charles V.

Vicissitudes of the Ottoman Empire

The Ottoman system required a succession of strong leaders in its sultans, which it seldom had after Suleiman's death in 1566. It nevertheless remained powerful for a century or more. The Christians won the naval battle of Lepanto in 1571, but failed to exploit their victory. The Turks strengthened their hold on Hungary, penetrated Poland, subdued the north coast of the Black Sea, and took Cyprus in 1573 and Crete in 1669.

It was in fact the Persians who first turned the Turkish tide, by annexing Armenia and Georgia in 1618. The failure of the Turks to capture Vienna in 1683 left them on the defensive in Europe. Austrians, Poles, Venetians, and Russians were now better able to work together than in the past, and the Ottoman army and administration suffered from increasing degeneracy and corruption. The old crusade against Islam was now taken up by Austria, which in 1699 forced the Turks to sign the treaty of Karlowitz (Karlovac). The Austrian Hapsburgs received Hungary (except for the Banat), where along the southern border they set up the special zone called the Military Frontiers. Transylvania, Croatia, and Slavonia also went to the Austrians in 1699, the region around Bar to Poland, the Morea to Venice. Nineteen years later, by the Peace of Passarowitz in 1718, Austria was able to take the Banat and much of Serbia south of the Danube, but the reviving Turks, in 1739, reoccupied Serbia and restored the Danube frontier, which lasted until the next century (see pages 78–79 and 174).

Gradually Russia replaced Austria as the chief enemy of the Turks. Peter the Great had taken Azov in 1702, but soon had to relinquish it. A long series of Russo-Turkish wars was really launched by Catherine the Great, who in 1768 sent her armies into Moldavia and Wallachia, and in 1770 defeated the Turkish fleet at Chesme in the Aegean. The Ottoman Empire was obliged to sign the epochal treaty of Kuchuk-Kainardji, by which Moldavia and Wallachia were returned to Turkey, but under a vague Russian protectorship, the Crimea was to be considered "independent," and Russia acquired the territory between the Bug and Dnieper rivers, gained the right to sail in Ottoman waters, including the straits that led to Constantinople itself, and obtained the privilege also, at least by one interpretation, of speaking for all the diverse and numerous Orthodox Christians throughout the Ottoman Empire. Russia annexed the Crimea in 1783, and by another war pushed its boundaries to the Dniester in 1792. By the time of the French Revolution it was clear that the Ottoman Empire, though still enormous, could with difficulty defend its possessions. Bonaparte's expedition to Egypt, the Serb revolt, and the loss of Bessarabia to Russia led to a period of dissolution punctuated by attempts at reform. (See pages 86–87, 91, 174.)

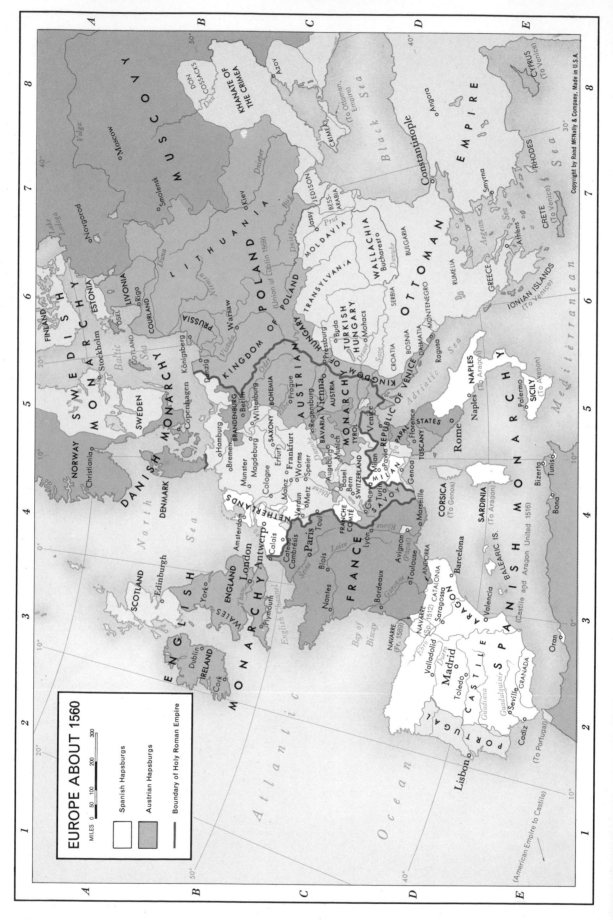

EUROPE ABOUT 1560

MILES 0 50 100   200   300

Spanish Hapsburgs
Austrian Hapsburgs
Boundary of Holy Roman Empire

Copyright by Rand McNally & Company, Made in U.S.A.

MUSCOVY

SWEDISH MONARCHY

NORWAY

SWEDEN

FINLAND

ESTONIA

LIVONIA

COURLAND

OSEL

GOTLAND

Riga

Stockholm

Christiania

DANISH MONARCHY

DENMARK

Copenhagen

Hamburg

Bremen

BRANDENBURG

Berlin

Münster

Magdeburg

Wittenburg

SAXONY

BOHEMIA

Prague

Cologne

Erfurt

Frankfurt

Mainz

Worms

Speier

Verdun

Metz

Toul

NETHERLANDS

Amsterdam

Antwerp

London

ENGLAND

ENGLISH MONARCHY

Plymouth

York

Dublin

IRELAND

Cork

SCOTLAND

Edinburgh

WALES

Calais

Cateau Cambrésis

Paris

Blois

Nantes

FRANCE

Bordeaux

Toulouse

Lyon

FRANCHE COMTÉ

SWITZERLAND

Basel

Bern

Geneva

Turin

SAVOY

MILAN

Genoa

Marseille

Avignon (Papal)

NAVARRE (Fr. 1589)

ANDORRA

Barcelona

CATALONIA

ARAGON

Saragossa

Valencia

NAVARRE (Sp. 1512)

Valladolid

Madrid

Toledo

CASTILE

Seville

Cadiz

GRANADA

Oran

PORTUGAL

Lisbon

(To Portugal)

SPANISH MONARCHY

(Castile and Aragon United (1516))

(American Empire to Castile)

BALEARIC IS. (To Aragon)

SARDINIA (To Aragon)

CORSICA (To Genoa)

Bizerta

Tunis

Bona

SICILY (To Aragon)

Palermo

NAPLES

Naples NAPLES (To Aragon)

PAPAL STATES

Rome

TUSCANY

Florence

Venice

REPUBLIC OF VENICE

Milan

Regensburg

Munich

BAVARIA

Augsburg

TYROL

AUSTRIA

Vienna

AUSTRIAN MONARCHY

KINGDOM OF HUNGARY

Pressburg

Buda

Mohacs

Drave

TURKISH HUNGARY

TRANSYLVANIA

Sava

CROATIA

BOSNIA

DALMATIA

Ragusa

MONTENEGRO

SERBIA

RUMELIA

BULGARIA

WALLACHIA

Bucharest

MOLDAVIA

Jassy

BESS-ARABIA

JEDISON

Danube

KINGDOM OF POLAND

POLAND

Warsaw

PRUSSIA

Königsberg

Danzig

Union of Dublin 1569

LITHUANIA

Kiev

Smolensk

Novgorod

Moscow

Lake Ladoga

Volga

Don

DON COSSACKS

KHANATE OF THE CRIMEA

CRIMEA

(To Ottoman Empire)

Azov

OTTOMAN EMPIRE

Constantinople

Angora

Smyrna

GREECE

Athens

CRETE (To Venice)

RHODES (To Venice)

CYPRUS (To Venice)

IONIAN ISLANDS (To Venice)

Black Sea

Aegean Sea

Mediterranean Sea

Adriatic Sea

Baltic Sea

North Sea

English Channel

Bay of Biscay

Atlantic Ocean

Ebro

Duero

Guadiana

Guadalquivir

Rhine

Rhône

Loire

Seine

Garonne

Elbe

Oder

Vistula

Niemen

Düna

Dnieper

Bug

Dniester

Prut

Save

Danube

Don

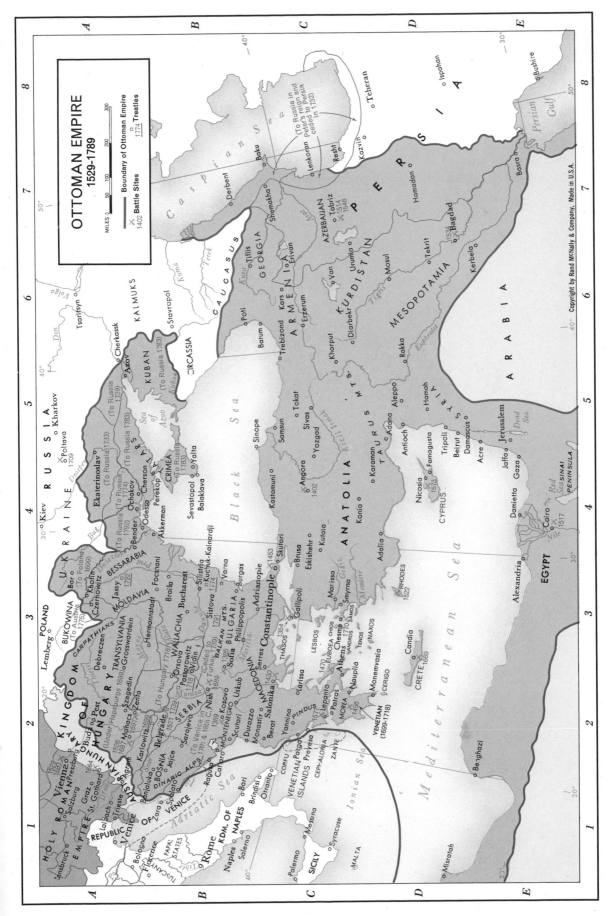

OTTOMAN EMPIRE
1529-1789

MILES 0   50   100   200   300

—— Boundary of Ottoman Empire
✗ Battle Sites
1402
□ 1774 Treaties

Copyright by Rand McNally & Company, Made in U.S.A.

A   B   C   D   E

P E R S I A

Ispahan
Bushire
Persian Gulf

(To Russia in Peter's reign and ceded in 1732)

Baku
Lenkoran
Resht
Kazvin
Basra
Bagdad
Tekrit
Kerbela
Mosul
Hamadan

Teheran

C a s p i a n S e a

Shemakha
Derbent
Tabriz ✗1514 1548
AZERBAIJAN
Erivan
Tiflis
Kars
Erzerum
Van
Urumia ✗ KURDISTAN
Diarbekr ✗1534
GEORGIA
ARMENIA
Poti
Batum
Trebizond
Kharput
Rakka

Euphrates

M E S O P O T A M I A

A R A B I A

S Y R I A

Aleppo
Hamah
Damascus
Beirut
Tripoli
Acre
Jaffo
Jerusalem
Gaza
Dead Sea

Antioch
Adana
Karaman
Famagusta
Nicosia ✗1573
CYPRUS

Stavropol
Cherkassk
KALMUKS
KUBAN
(To Russia 1783)
Azov (To Russia 1739)
CIRCASSIA
CAUCASUS
T A U R U S MTS.

Tsaritsyn
Volga
Don
Kuma
Terek

Kharkov
Poltava ✗1709
Kiev
R U S S I A
U K R A I N E
Dnieper
Bug

Ekaterinoslav
(To Russia 1733)
Kherson (To Russia 1774)
Ochakov (To Russia 1792)
Odessa
Perekop (To Russia 1783)
Yalta
CRIMEA
Sevastopol
Balaklava
Akkerman

S e a o f A z o v

B l a c k S e a

Sinope
Samsun
Kostamuni
Tokat
Sivas
Yozgad
Angora ✗1402
Kizil Irmak

A N A T O L I A

Konia
Adalia
Kutaia
Eskishehr
Brusa

Smyrna ✗1770
Morissa
Sardes
Mendere
SAMOS
ANDROS
TENOS
NAXOS
Candia
CRETE ✗1669
RHODES ✗1522

Adrianople
Gallipoli
Constantinople ✗1453
Skutari
Silistria
Varna
Burgas
B U L G A R I A
Philippopolis
Sofia
Serres
Saloniki
MACEDONIA
Uskub
Monastir
Berat
PINDUS
Larissa
Yanina
Arta
Lepanto ✗1571
Patras
MOREA
Nauplia ✗1456
Monemvasia
CERIGO
Athens ✗1770
EUBOEA
CHIOS
LESBOS
THASOS ✗1354

VENETIAN (1699-1718)

Prevesa ✗1538
CORFU
VENETIAN ISLANDS
CEPHALONIA
ZANTE
PAXO

I o n i a n S e a

Benghazi
Misratah
Alexandria
Damietta
Cairo ✗1517
Nile
Red Sea
SINAI PENINSULA

E G Y P T

M e d i t e r r a n e a n S e a

Benghazi

POLAND
Lemberg
BUKOWINA (To Austria 1775)
CARPATHIANS
Debreczen
Grosswardein
TRANSYLVANIA
Hermannstadt
Czernowitz
Kholm
Jassy □1792
MOLDAVIA
Focshani
Braila
BESSARABIA
Bender
WALLACHIA
Bucharest
Sistova □1791
Giurgevo
Orsova
Viddin
BALKAN MTS.
Nish
Kosovo ✗1389
SERVIA
Semendria
Belgrade
Passarowitz □1718
Karlowitz □1699
(To Venice in 17th & 18th C.)
Vidin
Morava
Maritsa

H U N G A R Y
KINGDOM OF
(Under Habsburgs 1699)
Pest
Buda ✗1686
OBuda
Mohacs ✗1526 1687
Szegedin
Zenta ✗1697
Grosswardein
Debreczen
Temesvar (Ceded to Hungary 1718)
Tisza
Theiss

Vienna ✗1529 1683
A U S T R I A
Pressburg
Graz
Salzburg
St. Gothard ✗1664
Innsbruck
H O L Y R O M A N E M P I R E
Laibach
Trieste
Bologna
Florence
TUSCANY

BOSNIA
Banialuka
Jaice
Serajevo
DINARIC ALPS
MONTENEGRO
Scutari
Durazzo
Cattaro
Ragusa
A d r i a t i c S e a

Zara
VENICE
REPUBLIC OF
Venice
PAPAL STATES
Rome
Tiber
KDM. OF NAPLES
Naples
Salerno
Bari
Brindisi
Otranto
Messina
Palermo
Syracuse
SICILY
MALTA

1   2   3   4   5   6   7   8

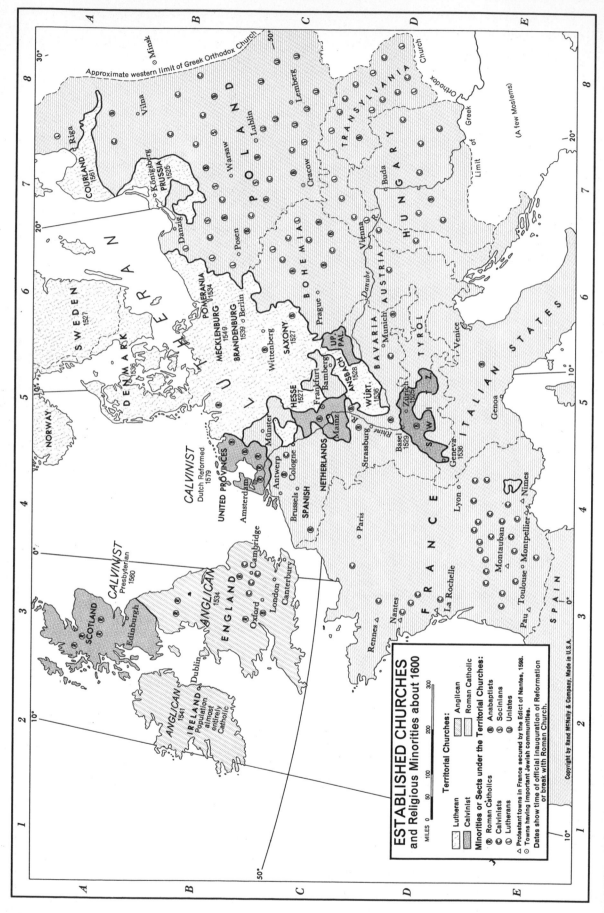

ESTABLISHED CHURCHES
and Religious Minorities about 1600

MILES 0 50 100 200 300

Territorial Churches:

Lutheran
Calvinist
Anglican
Roman Catholic

Minorities or Sects under the Territorial Churches:

Ⓡ Roman Catholics   Ⓐ Anabaptists
Ⓒ Calvinists   Ⓢ Socinians
Ⓛ Lutherans   Ⓤ Uniates

△ Protestant towns in France secured by the Edict of Nantes, 1598.
○ Towns having important Jewish communities.

Dates show time of official inauguration of Reformation or break with Roman Church.

Copyright by Rand McNally & Company. Made in U.S.A.

EUROPEAN CIVILIZATION, 1550–1700

▶ MAP ON PAGES 70–71

THE FOLLOWING MAP suggests the main developments in European civilization from 1550 to 1700. It may be compared with the maps for the preceding period of the Renaissance (pages 58–59) and the following period of the Enlightenment (pages 82–83). This intermediate age enjoys no such distinctive name as the other two, but it was, if anything, the most fundamentally creative of the three. Its art is called "baroque," which has come to signify a certain grandness of style, as in the paintings of Rubens or in the opera which arose at this time, or especially in a monumental architecture which made use of outdoor spaces as a setting for great buildings. It was a formal age, with a taste for arches and colonnades adapted from ancient models, majestic sweeping staircases both indoors and out, sculptured facades and detached statuary, ornamental gardens, fountains, and open city squares. St. Peter's church in Rome, though begun earlier, was mainly constructed at this time, as was St. Paul's in London. Other buildings testified to the growing institutions of monarchy. The Escorial in Spain, though hardly baroque, illustrated the greatness of the Spanish crown; and a century later the chateau and gardens of Versailles, in their combination of architecture, sculpture, painting, woodworking, and landscape design, gave expression to the French monarchy at its height.

Coming after the troubles of the Reformation, the period was also a great age of religion, both Protestant and Catholic. Its church architecture was second only to the Gothic. Religion inspired the paintings of Rembrandt and El Greco, the *Acta Sanctorum* or saints' lives written by the Bollandist fathers in Belgium (who are still at work), and the writings of Pascal in France, of the Spanish theologian Suarez, and of the English Puritan and poet John Milton.

The "Classical" Modern Literatures

In countries along the Atlantic seaboard of Europe, the modern languages were perfected to convey exact thought and finer shades of feeling, and standard forms of the languages effectively replaced dialectical variations. This process had occurred earlier in Italy, where the literary tradition went back to Dante and Petrarch. It was to come later in Germany, where politico-religious dissension and the Thirty Years' War had a retarding effect. In England, Holland, France, Portugal, and Spain the years from 1550 to 1700 were the literary golden age. England saw its great sequence of writers from the Elizabethans to Dryden; France produced Molière and Racine; Spain, Cervantes and Calderon. The greatest of Dutch poets, Vondel, was born near Cologne of Dutch parents; and Camoëns composed the national epic of Portugal, inspired by the recent discoveries and conquests, and in fact written at Macao on the coast of China.

Academies were founded to promote literature and to improve language itself. The first literary academies were in Italy, but the most famous was the French Academy, established in 1635 with government support. Often the same academy concerned itself with all the arts. In France, separate academies were set up for painting and sculpture, music, architecture, and the dance. The founding of the French Academy at Rome, in 1666, shows how even France in the *grand siecle* still looked to Italy for inspiration.

Modern Science

From the point of view of world history the greatest achievement of this period was the development of modern science. The scientific revolution of the seventeenth century replaced old concepts, derived from the Greeks, with new concepts of matter and its properties, new applications of mathematics to physics, and new methods of experimentation. By 1700 a new world view had taken form.

The map suggests the international scope of scientific thought and discovery. The Polish Copernicus appears on the map of the Renaissance, but the present one shows the Scandinavian Tycho Brahe, the German Kepler, the Anglo-Irish Robert Boyle, and the Scottish Napier, the inventor of logarithms. Mainly, science at this time was developed by the Italians, French, Netherlanders, and English. Galileo and Newton were the most famous of physicists; Descartes, Pascal, Fermat, and Newton were great mathematicians; Malpighi and Leeuwenhoek, using the newly invented microscope, laid foundations for biology.

Modern science rested on the interchange and mutual verification of scientific ideas and information by inquirers in many countries, and these needs were met by the scientific societies and publications which now appeared. Scientific academies are shown on the map. Some academies combined scientific and literary interests; some were predominantly scientific, like the sharp-eyed "lynxes" organized at Rome in 1603; others were exclusively scientific, like the English Royal Society and French Academy of Sciences, founded in the 1660's. Scientific publications included the *Acta Eruditorum*, which lasted for a century; and the *Philosophical Transactions* of the Royal Society, the *Memoirs* of the French Academy of Sciences, and the *Journal des Savants*, all three of which have gone on into our own time.

As for the geographical distribution of men and activities contributing to European civilization, the map shows, if compared with that for the Renaissance, that Italy no longer enjoyed its extraordinary primacy of the preceding era. The center of gravity now lay in northern France, southern England, and Holland. London and Paris emerged as intellectual and cultural capitals for all Europe. The bareness of the present map in eastern and northern Europe, and even in northern England, Scotland, and Ireland, gives a fair enough representation of the cultural provincialism of these regions in the seventeenth century. The maps on pages 82–83 and 106–7 show how these areas increasingly contributed, in the following centuries, to the main stream of civilization in Europe.

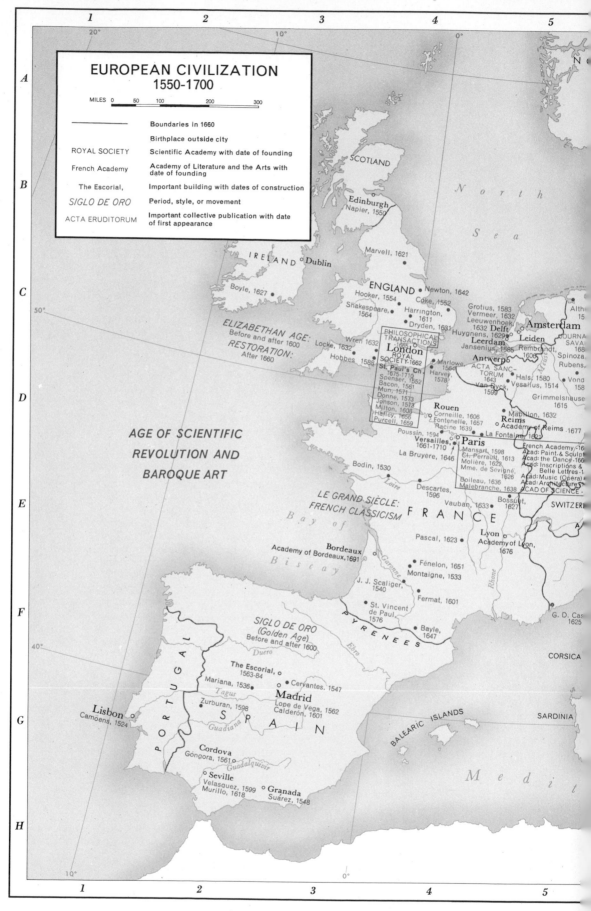

EUROPEAN CIVILIZATION
1550-1700

MILES 0   50   100   200   300

Boundaries in 1660

Birthplace outside city

ROYAL SOCIETY — Scientific Academy with date of founding

French Academy — Academy of Literature and the Arts with date of founding

The Escorial, — Important building with dates of construction

SIGLO DE ORO — Period, style, or movement

ACTA ERUDITORUM — Important collective publication with date of first appearance

SCOTLAND

North

Sea

IRELAND   o Dublin

Edinburgh
Napier, 1550

Marvell, 1621

ENGLAND   • Newton, 1642

Hooker, 1554   • Coke, 1552
Boyle, 1627 •   Grotius, 1583
Shakespeare,   • Harrington,   Vermeer, 1632
1564   1611   Leeuwenhoek,   Alth
                                           1632 Delft   o Amsterdam   15
ELIZABETHAN AGE: • Dryden, 1631   Huygnens, 1629 o   JOURNA
Before and after 1600   Wren 1632   PHILOSOPHICAL   Leerdam   o Leiden   SAVA
RESTORATION: Locke, 1632   TRANSACTIONS   Jansenius, 1585   Rembrandt,   168
After 1660   1665   o   1606   Spinoza,
                 Hobbes, 1588   London   • Marlowe,   Antwerp   Rubens,
                              ROYAL   1564   o   ACTA SANC-
                        St. Paul's Ch.   SOCIETY-1662   Harvey,   TORUM   Hals, 1580   Vond
                        1675-1710   Spenser, 1552   1578   1643   Vesalius, 1514   158
                        Bacon, 1561   Van Dyck,   1599
                        Mun, 1571   Grimmelshause
                        Donne, 1573   1615
                        Jonson, 1573   Rouen   Mabillon, 1632
                        Milton, 1608   • Corneille, 1606
                        Halley, 1656   • Fontenelle, 1657   Reims
                        Purcell, 1659   Racine 1639   Academy of Reims 1677
                                   Poussin, 1594 •   • La Fontaine, 162
                                   Versailles,   French Academy -16
AGE OF SCIENTIFIC   1661-1710   • Paris   Acad. Paint.& Sculpt
                        Mansart, 1598   Acad: the Dance-166
REVOLUTION AND   La Bruyère, 1646   Cl. Perrault, 1613   Acad: Inscriptions &
                        Molière, 1622   Belle Lettres -1
BAROQUE ART   Bodin, 1530 •   Mme. de Sévigné,   Acad: Music (Opera)
                                   1626   Acad: Architecture
                                   Boileau, 1636   ACAD OF SCIENCE -
                                   Descartes,   Malebranche, 1638
                                   1596   SWITZER
                 LE GRAND SIÈCLE: Vauban, 1633 •   Bossuet,
                 FRENCH CLASSICISM   F R A N C E   1627
                        Bay of   A
                                   Pascal, 1623 •   Lyon
                                            Academy of Lyon,
                 Bordeaux   1676
                 Academy of Bordeaux,1691
                        Biscay   • Fénelon, 1651
                        J. J. Scaliger,   Montaigne, 1533   G. D. Cas
                        1540   1625
                        St. Vincent
                        de Paul   Fermat, 1601
                        1576   CORSICA
                        • Bayle,
                        1647
                        P Y R E N E E S
SIGLO DE ORO
(Golden Age)
Before and after 1600
                 Duero
                 40°
The Escorial,
1563-84
Mariana, 1536 •   o Cervantes, 1547
                 Tagus   Madrid
Zurbaran, 1598 •   Lope de Vega, 1562   BALEARIC ISLANDS   SARDINIA
Lisbon   Calderón, 1601
Camöens, 1524
                 Guadiana   S P A I N   *Medit*
Cordova
Góngora, 1561
                 Guadalquivir
o Seville
Velasquez, 1599
Murillo, 1618   o Granada
                 Suárez, 1548

P O R T U G A L

Loire

Garonne

Rhone

Ebro

A

istiania

S W E D E N

20°   30°

Stockholm

RUSSIA

Volga

Riga

B

Dvina

openhagen • Tycho Brahe, 1546

Baltic Sea

Niemen

Königsberg

Elbe

Berlin

Odr

C

P O L A N D

50°

Vistula

Warsaw

Dnieper

OLY

Leipzig

A ERUDITORUM
1682-1776
eibniz, 1646
homasius, 1655

Böhme, 1575

Opitz, 1597

Lemberg

Dniester

D

Pufendorf,
1632

OMAN

o Nuremberg
LEOPOLDINE ACADEMY
1687

Comenius,
1591

C A R P A T H I A N S

Danube

1571

Danube

Vienna
LEOPOLDINE
ACADEMY
1652

H U N G A R Y

Buda

EMPIRE

Black Sea

E

ladio, 1518

Cremona   Venice
everdi, 1567
ivari, 1644   Malpighi, 1628

Danube

Torricelli, 1608

Adriatic Sea

O T T O M A N

40°

Florence
• Academy della Crusca -1582
ACADEMY DEL CIMENTO -1657
lileo,   Lully, 1633
1564
Bellarmine, 1542

Tiber

Constantinople

E M P I R E

F

Rome
ench Academy at Rome -1666
cademy degli Arcadi -1690
ACADEMY DEI LINCEI -1603
t. Peters Church,
1506-1667

I T A L Y

Naples
ACADEMY ROSSANO
1695
Tasso, 1544
Bruno, 1548
Bernini, 1598
Scarlatti, 1659

Aegean Sea

G

Tyrrhenian Sea

*Ionian
Sea*

Campanella, 1568

SICILY

ranean   *Sea*

RHODES

El Greco, 1542

H

CRETE

20°   30°

6   7   8   9   10

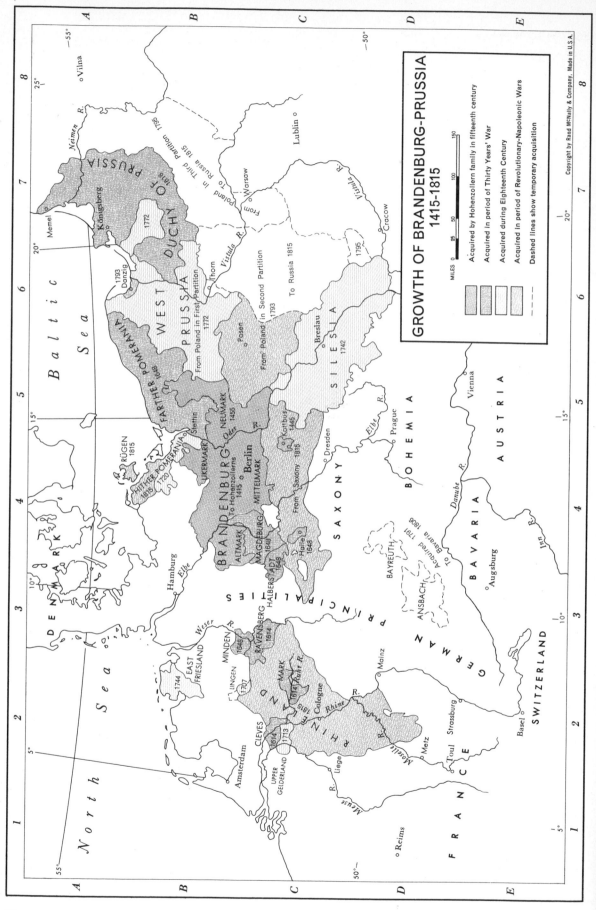

GROWTH OF BRANDENBURG-PRUSSIA
1415-1815

Acquired by Hohenzollern family in fifteenth century

Acquired in period of Thirty Years' War

Acquired during Eighteenth Century

Acquired in period of Revolutionary-Napoleonic Wars

Dashed lines show temporary acquisition

MILES 0 25 50 100 150

Copyright by Rand McNally & Company, Made in U.S.A.

EUROPE IN THE SEVENTEENTH CENTURY

▶ MAPS ON PAGES 72, 74–75, AND 76

POLITICALLY, THE GREAT DEVELOPMENTS of the seventeenth century were the decline of the Hapsburg supremacy and rise of France on the international scene, the continuing disorganization of Germany, and the development of monarchy in France and of constitutional government in England. These were all deeply affected by the Thirty Years' War (1618–48) and ensuing Peace of Westphalia, which in general represented the victory of France, Sweden, the Dutch, Protestantism, and German particularism over attempts of the Hapsburg dynasty—Spanish and Austrian—to Catholicize and dominate the central European region of the Holy Roman Empire.

The Empire and the Peace of Westphalia
▶ MAP ON PAGES 74–75

Pages 74–75 show the Holy Roman Empire after the Thirty Years' War. Note the extreme subdivision of territory. There were about three hundred states in the Empire, of which only about a quarter are indicated on the map. These states had existed for centuries, and had increased their local powers during the Reformation a century before; now, by the treaties of Münster and Osnabrück, known together as the Peace of Westphalia, they obtained the right to conclude alliances and act as sovereign units in international affairs. The king of Sweden, which was then at the height of its power, annexed the archbishopric of Bremen (but not the free city), the bishopric of Verden, and Hither Pomerania, thereby obtaining three seats in the imperial diet. France obtained sovereignty over the Three Bishoprics, Metz, Toul, and Verdun, which it had in fact occupied since 1552, and certain ambiguously defined rights of lordship in Alsace. The Dutch and Swiss were declared fully independent of the Empire. The Dutch were confirmed in a boundary that partitioned the province of Brabant and gave them control of the mouth of the Scheldt River, which was closed to ocean-going vessels by international law, so that the port of Antwerp declined while Amsterdam flourished. The Spanish Hapsburgs failed in their attempt to reconquer the Dutch, join Franche Comté and the Netherlands, and so build up a continuous Spanish zone. The Austrian Hapsburgs failed in their attempt to turn the Empire into a more unified and Catholic state. Not only were member states now considered sovereign in foreign affairs, but in religion they could be either Catholic, Lutheran, or Calvinist. In their own territories, however, notably in Austria and Bohemia, the Hapsburgs were able virtually to extirpate Protestantism; and Bavaria annexed and Catholicized the Upper Palatinate. The Peace of Westphalia marked the end of the long process of the disintegration of Germany. From 1648 to its final dissolution in 1806 the Holy Roman Empire was a nullity in the power politics of Europe.

The Rise of Prussia
▶ MAP ON PAGE 72

Meanwhile, the new power of Prussia grew up in north Germany. Its nucleus was the old march of Brandenburg, set up in the Middle Ages as a German outpost against the Slavs. The Hohenzollern family came into possession of Brandenburg in 1415; but the rapid rise of their dynasty began two hundred years later at the time of the Thirty Years' War. They then inherited Cleves, Mark, and Ravensberg in western Germany, and the duchy of Prussia in the east, well beyond the borders of the Holy Roman Empire and until 1656 feudally dependent on Poland. At the Peace of Westphalia Brandenburg was favored by France and Sweden, which saw in its growth a means of offsetting the Hapsburgs in Germany; it was thus allowed to divide Pomerania with Sweden, and to annex the archbishopric of Magdeburg and bishoprics of Halberstadt and Minden. By a policy of balance of power between France and the Hapsburgs, the elector of Brandenburg was able, during the War of the Spanish Succession, to annex Lingen and Upper Gelderland and to win the royal title of king. The new kingdom was named after Prussia, rather than Brandenburg, because Prussia lay outside the Empire. By conquering Silesia in 1742 Prussia became one of the great military powers of Europe. By agreement with Russia it shared in the partition of Poland. By being finally on the winning side in the wars against Revolutionary and Napoleonic France it was able to keep part of Poland, to annex part of Saxony, and to absorb the former small German states of the Rhineland. The power of Prussia after 1648 rested to a unique degree upon its army, but its growth to 1815, with the one great exception of the attack on Silesia, came from the processes of inheritance and calculated diplomacy rather than crude aggression.

England and France
▶ MAPS ON PAGE 76

It was also in the Thirty Years' War that France began to surpass the Hapsburgs. Its growth is shown on page 76. Roussillon, Franche Comté, large parts of Alsace, and the territories on the northeastern frontier all belonged to the Hapsburgs when annexed in the reign of Louis XIV. Lorraine was taken in 1738 from the husband of the Hapsburg Maria Theresa and given to the father of the French queen; with his death in 1766 it became definitely French. French territorial unity was completed only with the Revolution, when certain enclaves, of which papal Avignon was the largest, were absorbed.

The growth of constitutional government in England does not lend itself to representation on a map. The map on page 76 merely indicates some of the sites of the English Civil Wars of 1642–48, the "invasion" by William of Orange in 1688 upon invitation from the English parliamentary leaders, and associated battles and other disturbances in Ireland and Scotland. For a short time, under Cromwell, Ireland, Scotland, and England were united. The kingdom of Great Britain was created in 1707 by the union of England and Scotland, mainly to keep the Stuart monarchy out of Scotland.

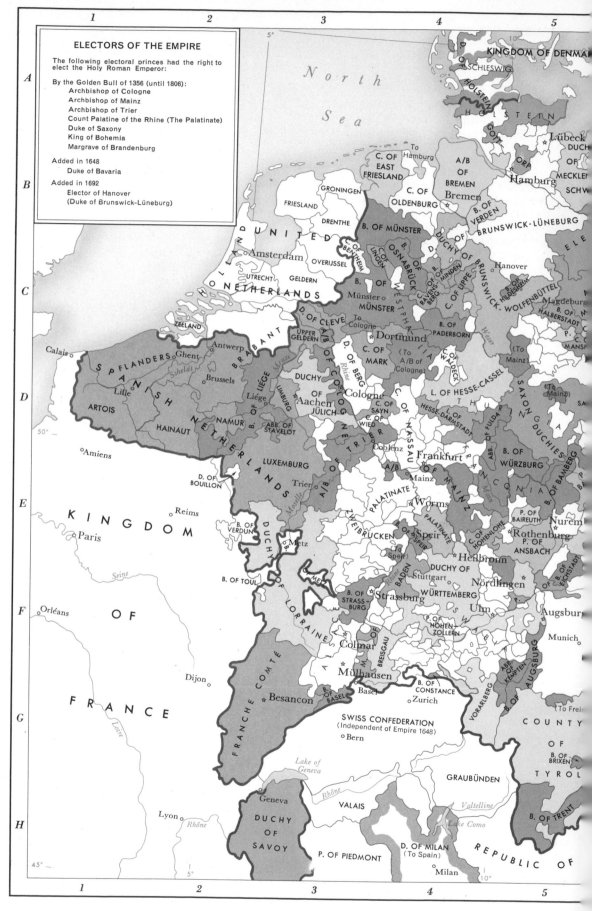

ELECTORS OF THE EMPIRE

The following electoral princes had the right to elect the Holy Roman Emperor:

By the Golden Bull of 1356 (until 1806):
Archbishop of Cologne
Archbishop of Mainz
Archbishop of Trier
Count Palatine of the Rhine (The Palatinate)
Duke of Saxony
King of Bohemia
Margrave of Brandenburg

Added in 1648
Duke of Bavaria

Added in 1692
Elector of Hanover
(Duke of Brunswick-Lüneburg)

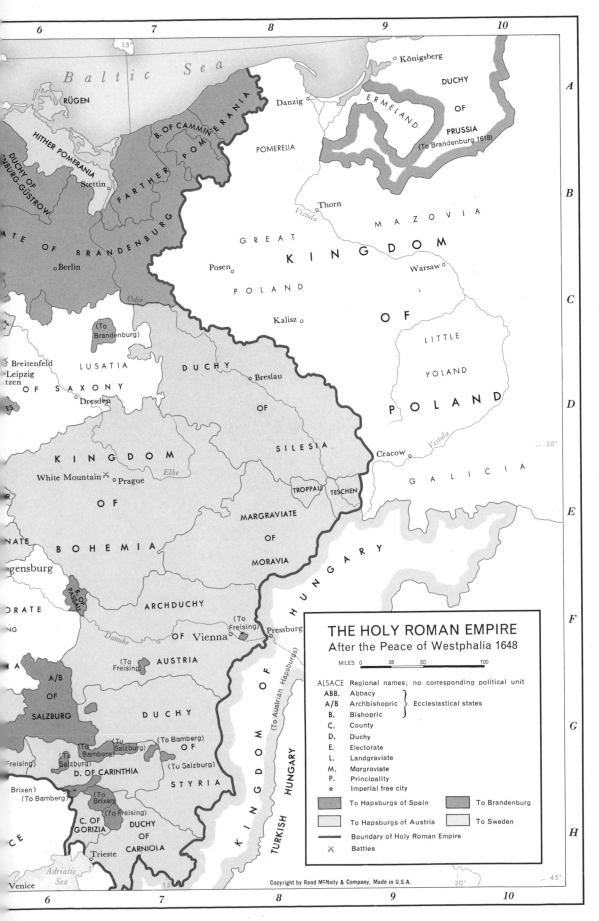

THE HOLY ROMAN EMPIRE
After the Peace of Westphalia 1648

MILES 0   25   50   100

ALSACE Regional names; no corresponding political unit
ABB.   Abbacy
A/B   Archbishopric } Ecclesiastical states
B.   Bishopric
C.   County
D.   Duchy
E.   Electorate
L.   Landgraviate
M.   Margraviate
P.   Principality
☆   Imperial free city

▨ To Hapsburgs of Spain   ▨ To Brandenburg
☐ To Hapsburgs of Austria   ☐ To Sweden
── Boundary of Holy Roman Empire
✕ Battles

Copyright by Rand McNally & Company, Made in U.S.A.

75

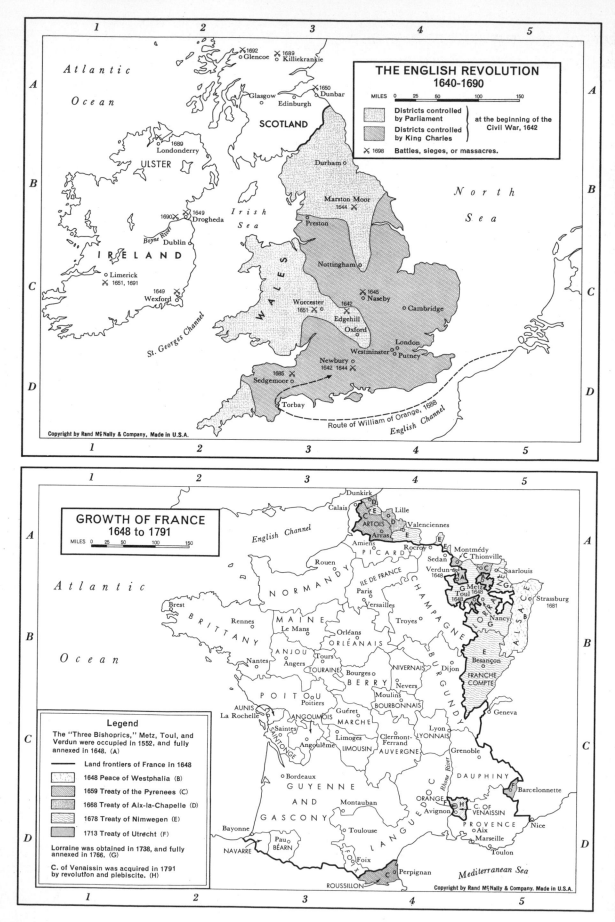

THE ENGLISH REVOLUTION
1640-1690

MILES 0 25 50 100 150

Districts controlled by Parliament — at the beginning of the Civil War, 1642

Districts controlled by King Charles

✕ 1698 Battles, sieges, or massacres.

Atlantic Ocean

1692 Glencoe   1689 Killiekrankie

Glasgow   1650 Dunbar
Edinburgh

SCOTLAND

1689 Londonderry

ULSTER

Irish Sea

1690   1649 Drogheda
Boyne River   Dublin

IRELAND

Limerick 1651, 1691

1649
Wexford

St. Georges Channel

Durham

Marston Moor 1644

North Sea

Preston

WALES

Nottingham

Worcester 1651   1645 Naseby

1642   Cambridge

Edgehill
Oxford

London
Westminster   Putney

Newbury 1642 1644

1685
Sedgemoor

Torbay

Route of William of Orange, 1688

English Channel

Copyright by Rand McNally & Company. Made in U.S.A.

GROWTH OF FRANCE
1648 to 1791

MILES 0 25 50 100 150

English Channel

Dunkirk   Calais   Lille
ARTOIS   Valenciennes
Arras

Amiens   PICARDY   Rocroy   Montmédy
Sedan   Thionville

Atlantic Ocean

Brest

NORMANDY

Rouen

Verdun 1648   Saarlouis

Metz 1648   Strasbourg 1681
Toul 1648

Paris   Nancy
Versailles
Troyes   ALSACE

BRITTANY

Rennes   MAINE   CHAMPAGNE
Le Mans

Nantes   ANJOU
Angers   ORLÉANAIS

Orléans

Tours   Bourges
TOURAINE   NIVERNAIS   Dijon

BERRY   Nevers   BURGUNDY   Besançon
FRANCHE COMPTE

POITOU   Moulins
Poitiers   BOURBONNAIS   Geneva

AUNIS   ANGOUMOIS   MARCHE
La Rochelle   Guéret   Lyon
Saintes   LYONNAIS
SAINTONGE   Limoges   Clermont-Ferrand   Grenoble
Angoulême   LIMOUSIN   AUVERGNE

DAUPHINY

Bordeaux   Rhone River   Barcelonnette

GUYENNE   ORANGE
AND   Montauban   C. OF
Avignon   VENAISSIN

GASCONY   PROVENCE
Bayonne   Aix   Nice
Pau BÉARN   Toulouse   Marseille
NAVARRE   Toulon

LANGUEDOC   *Mediterranean Sea*

Foix   Perpignan
ROUSSILLON

Legend

The "Three Bishoprics," Metz, Toul, and Verdun were occupied in 1552, and fully annexed in 1648. (A)

—— Land frontiers of France in 1648

1648 Peace of Westphalia (B)

1659 Treaty of the Pyrenees (C)

1668 Treaty of Aix-la-Chapelle (D)

1678 Treaty of Nimwegen (E)

1713 Treaty of Utrecht (F)

Lorraine was obtained in 1738, and fully annexed in 1766. (G)

C. of Venaissin was acquired in 1791 by revolution and plebiscite. (H)

Copyright by Rand McNally & Company. Made in U.S.A.

76

EUROPE AND THE EUROPEAN WORLD IN THE EIGHTEENTH CENTURY

▶ MAPS ON PAGES 78–79 AND 80

BY 1721 THERE WAS IN EVIDENCE that circle of European "powers" whose affairs made up much of European history for the next two hundred years—a maritime Britain, a strong but not dominant France, a Danubian Austria, a westernized Russia, with Prussia and Savoy-Sardinia still small but now raised to the status of kingdoms. The conflicts of these powers at the beginning of the eighteenth century have been called the first "world" war. The War of the Spanish Succession was terminated by the treaties of Utrecht (1713) and Rastatt (1714); the Northern War by the treaties of Stockholm (1720) and Nystadt (1721); the Austro-Turkish War by the Treaty of Passarowitz (1718). The following map shows Europe after these treaties.

Western Europe about 1721

▶ MAP ON PAGES 78–79

In western Europe the great issue, continuing from the Thirty Years' War, was the rise of France and the decline of Spain. France under Louis XIV threatened to subordinate all other European states to itself. With the death of the last Spanish Hapsburg king in 1700, France threatened virtually to annex Spain and Spanish America. If Spanish America and the Spanish Netherlands passed to the more active hands of the French, the whole colonial and commercial position of England and Holland would be undermined. Nor was Bourbon control of Spain and its European possessions acceptable to the Hapsburgs of Austria. England, Holland, and Austria thus led a coalition against Louis XIV.

France managed to place the Bourbon Philip V on the Spanish throne, but the Spanish empire was divided. Spain kept Spanish America; but Gibraltar and Minorca went to Britain, Sicily to Savoy, and Naples, Milan, and the Spanish Netherlands to Austria, except that Upper Gelderland, a small part of the Spanish Netherlands, went to Prussia (see page 72). In 1720, by an exchange, Austria took Sicily and Savoy took Sardinia.

England, which had united with Scotland to form the kingdom of Great Britain in 1707, was the great victor at the Peace of Utrecht. Louis XIV, who had continued to support the exiled Stuarts, was obliged to accept the English revolution of 1688. By defeating the French at Cape La Hogue in 1692 the British had taken a long step toward naval supremacy. They received Nova Scotia and Newfoundland from France at Utrecht, as well as Gibraltar and Minorca from Spain, thus establishing their sea power in the north Atlantic and western Mediterranean. France ceded its claims in the Hudson Bay territory to Britain, and Spain granted the British the *asiento*, or right to sell African slaves in Spanish America. It was at the wish of the British and Dutch that Austria acquired the Spanish (henceforth Austrian) Netherlands, where the port of Antwerp remained closed. The Dutch received the right to maintain "barrier forts" against France in Austrian-Netherland territory. The growth of Hanover at the expense of Sweden, France's ally (see below), was also beneficial to England, whose king was now the elector of Hanover.

Eastern Europe about 1721

▶ MAP ON PAGES 78–79

In eastern Europe, in 1700, Sweden was at the height of its Baltic empire, Poland still seemed strong, and Russia lay outside the European system. Peter the Great of Russia, after a severe defeat by Sweden at Narva in 1700, proceeded to "westernize" his army and government. He was thus able to repel a Swedish invasion in 1709 at Poltava (see page 114). By the treaties of Stockholm and Nystadt Russia emerged the victor. It annexed Livonia, Estonia, Ingria, and part of Karelia from Sweden; Sweden also ceded the bishoprics of Bremen-Verden to Hanover, and Stettin and part of Swedish Pomerania to Prussia. Sweden ceased to be a leading power. Russia had reached "warm water" or its "window on the West," where St. Petersburg was meanwhile built.

In southeastern Europe these were the great days of Austrian expansion under Prince Eugene of Savoy. The Turks had occupied most of Hungary since 1526; in 1683 they again besieged Vienna. The Austrians drove them away with Polish assistance, won back Hungary at the Peace of Karlowitz in 1699, crossed the Danube and occupied Serbia. By the Peace of Passarowitz (1718) Austria reached its farthest southern limits. It annexed most of Serbia and the western part of Wallachia, which, however, it had to return to the Ottoman Empire in 1739.

The World after 1763

▶ MAP ON PAGE 80

The map on page 80 shows the world after the Peace of Paris of 1763, at the close of the Seven Years' War. The great event here is the triumph of Britain over France. France ceded all its North American territories east of the Mississippi to Britain, and those west of it to Spain. France kept its fishing islands off the Newfoundland coast, and all its West Indies sugar islands. It was ejected from India as a military power, but retained trading stations at Pondichéry and elsewhere. The British conquered Bengal, the basis of their subsequent Indian empire. British sea power and colonial empire were now predominant.

The map on page 80 also shows certain cities founded in the latter half of the eighteenth century to suggest the directions in which growth was taking place. At Sydney the first Europeans settled in Australia. The Russian empire was growing at both ends: it opened the steppes by building modern Odessa, while at the same time moving into Alaska. Latin America was also growing at both ends: the Spanish missions were moving into upper California, where San Francisco was established, while development of the La Plata region led to its organization as a separate viceroyalty. The Dutch were pushing as far east as Graaff Reinet in South Africa. The founding of Pittsburgh and Cincinnati marks the beginning of migration into the American Middle West.

EUROPE IN 1721
After the treaty of Utrecht, 1713,
and Associated Treaties

Miles 0   50   100   200   300

——— Boundary of Holy Roman Empire
× × Dutch Barrier Forts

20°

10°

0°

SHETLAND ISLANDS

ORKNEY ISLANDS

HEBRIDES

Bergen

Stavanger

K

North

Sea

D

SCOTLAND   Aberdeen

KINGDOM

Glasgow   Edinburgh

Belfast

OF

GREAT   BRITAIN

IRELAND

Dublin

York

Cork

Liverpool

Nottingham

WALES   ENGLAND

Norwich

Cambridge

Bristol   Oxford

Plymouth   Portsmouth   London

BEACHY HEAD

Dunkirk

To Hanover 17

NETHERLANDS

THE UNITED

Amsterdam

Utrecht

Ryswick

The Hague

Br

Mü

Posse

Antwerp   Neerwinden   Co

THE   AUSTRIAN   Aachen

Oudenarde   Ramillies

Lille   Fontenoy   Ma

Malplaquet   NETHERLANDS   R

1714

English Channel

LA
HOGUE

Rouen

Reims

Brest   St. Malo

Paris

Seine

Nancy

LORRAINE   Strassburg

Lorient

Orléans

Nantes   Tours

Besançon   Basel

E

Bay

Rochefort

Limoges

Lyon   Geneva   Br

SW

of

Angoulême   SAVOY   Turin

Biscay   Bordeaux   Garonne

FRANCE   PIED

REP

CAPE FINISTERRE

Bayonne   Toulouse   Montpellier

PYRENEES

Avignon   To the
Pope

Marseille   Toulon

CORS
To Ge

Oporto   Valladolid   Burgos   CATALONIA

40°

Duero   Ebro

Saragossa   Barcelona

Madrid

SPAIN

SARDINIA
To Hapsburgs 17
To Savoy 1720

PORTUGAL

Tagus

Lisbon   Alcantara   Toledo

To Bourbons, 1713   Valencia

Guadiana

BALEARIC ISLANDS

MINORCA
To Great Britain 1713

MAJORCA

Guadalquivir

Seville

CAPE ST. VINCENT

Granada   Cartagena

Medit

Cadiz

CAPE TRAFALGAR

Gibraltar
To Great Britain
1713

Algiers

10°

KINGDOM OF **SWEDEN**

FINLAND

Nystad o Abo Helsingfors Viborg L. Ladoga KARELIA

Uppsala o

Stockholm o

GOTLAND

o Novgorod

St. Petersburg

INGRIA

Narva o

ESTONIA

LIVONIA
To Russia
1721

o Riga

COURLAND

Baltic

Sea

Calmar o

Copenhagen o
o Lund

ARK

o Memel

LITHUANIA

Dvina

Vitebsk o

o Smolensk

o Moscow

RUSSIAN

EMPIRE

Hamburg

Stettin

BRANDENBURG

*To Prussia
1720*

Königsberg o

Danzig o

o Thorn

PRUSSIA

o Posen

Warsaw o

POLAND

o Vilna

Grodno o

o Minsk

o Kiev

o Kharkov

King of the

OVER

Hanover

Cassel

ossbach

SAXONY Glogau o

Leipzig o

Dresden o

Breslau o

SILESIA

Vistula

o Lublin

o Lemberg

o Bar

o Targovitza

o Poltava

nkfurt

ürnberg

HOLY

ROMAN

EMPIRE

Prague o

BOHEMIA MORAVIA

AUSTRIA

BAVARIA

Munich o

heim

Innsbruck o

TYROL

Cracow o

o Czernowitz

Dniester

o Cherson

CRIMEA

KINGDOM

OF

HUNGARY

MOLDAVIA

Prut

BESSARABIA

Black

Sea

Vienna o

Salzburg o

Danube

Theiss

Buda o

Pest o

TRANSYLVANIA

WALLACHIA

o Bucharest

Laibach o

Zenta o

Temesvar o

BANAT
To Hapsburgs
1718

ria

Verona o

Venice

ma

Modena

oa

o Bologna

REPUBLIC OF VENICE

Po

Trieste o

Agram o

CROATIA

SLAVONIA

Karlowitz o

Belgrade o Passarowitz 1718-1739

To Hapsburgs 1718-1739

Danube

o Silistria

orn

TUSCANY

o Florence

Tolentino o

PAPAL
STATES

Tiber

Rome o

KINGDOM
OF
NAPLES
To Hapsburgs
1714-1735

o Bari

Adriatic

Sea

BOSNIA

Ragusa o

MONTENEGRO

SERBIA

Sarajevo o

o Nish

o Sofia

BULGARIA

o Adrianople

OTTOMAN

o Constantinople

EMPIRE

o Salonika

Tyrrhenian

Sea

Naples o

Palermo o

o Reggio

Otranto o

CORFU
(CORCYRA)

Aegean *Sea*

o Athens

o Smyrna

G

MOREA
To
Ottoman
Empire
1718

Syracuse o

SICILY
To Savoy 1714
To Hapsburgs 720-35

enis

n *e* *a* *n* *S* *e* *a*

CRETE

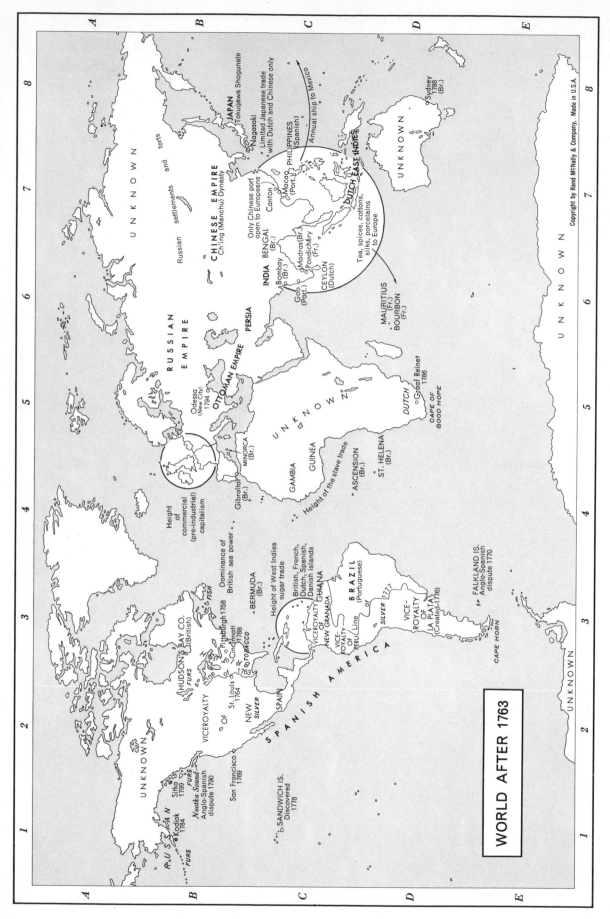

WORLD AFTER 1763

UNKNOWN

RUSSIAN EMPIRE

CHINESE EMPIRE
Ch'ing (Manchu) Dynasty

JAPAN
Tokugawa Shogunate

Nagasaki
Limited Japanese trade with Dutch and Chinese only

Only Chinese port open to Europeans
Canton

Macao (Port.)

PHILIPPINES (Spanish)

Annual ship to Mexico

DUTCH EAST INDIES

Tea, spices, cottons, silks, porcelains to Europe

INDIA
BENGAL
Bombay (Br.)
Goa (Port.)
Madras (Br.)
Pondichéry (Fr.)
CEYLON (Dutch)

PERSIA

OTTOMAN EMPIRE

Odessa (New City) 1794

Russian settlements and forts

MAURITIUS (Fr.)
BOURBON (Fr.)

Height of commercial (pre-industrial) capitalism

Gibraltar (Br.)
MINORCA (Br.)

Dominance of British sea power

GAMBIA
GUINEA

Height of the slave trade

ASCENSION (Br.)
ST. HELENA (Br.)

DUTCH
Graaf Reinet 1786
CAPE OF GOOD HOPE

UNKNOWN

Sydney 1788 (Br.)

UNKNOWN

HUDSON'S BAY CO. (British)
FURS

RUSSIAN
FURS
Kodiak 1784
Sitka 1799
Nootka Sound Anglo-Spanish dispute 1790
San Francisco 1769

Line of 1763
Pittsburgh 1768
St. Louis 1764
Cincinnati 1788
TOBACCO

VICEROYALTY OF NEW SPAIN
SILVER

SANDWICH IS. Discovered 1778

BERMUDA (Br.)

Height of West Indies sugar trade

British, French, Dutch, Spanish, Danish islands

VICEROYALTY OF NEW GRANADA

VICEROYALTY OF PERU
Line

SPANISH AMERICA

BRAZIL (Portuguese)
SILVER 1777

VICEROYALTY OF LA PLATA (Created 1776)

FALKLAND IS. Anglo-Spanish dispute 1770

CAPE HORN

UNKNOWN

Copyright by Rand McNally & Company, Made in U.S.A.

EUROPEAN CIVILIZATION
DURING THE ENLIGHTENMENT

▶ MAP ON PAGES 82–83

THE SCIENTIFIC, ARTISTIC, and literary achievements of Europe in the seventeenth century (see pages 70–71) became more widely diffused in the eighteenth, both socially and geographically— socially, by reaching new classes of society through popularization, and geographically, by extending with increasing effect into northern and eastern Europe. It was an age very conscious of its intellectual emancipation, and intent upon the benefits that might follow if new ideas were applied in practice. Variously known as the *siècle des lumières* in France, the *Aufklärung* in Germany, the *illuminismo* in Italy, or Age of Reason in England, it is commonly called the Enlightenment.

Arts and Letters

France was widely looked to for cultural leadership, though the French were themselves greatly influenced by England, especially by its parliamentary government and religious toleration. France under Louis XIV had become the paragon of aristocratic elegance and royal grandeur, as symbolized by the palace and city of Versailles. The ascendancy of France was shown by the imitations of Versailles built by rulers all over Europe, as at Queluz near Lisbon, at Caserta near Naples, and at Tsarskoe Selo near St. Petersburg. Many individual palaces showed the same French influence—Schönbrunn in Vienna, Drottningholm in Stockholm, the Loo in the Netherlands, and even Hampton Court in England, built in 1515, but now adorned with formal gardens on the French model. Many painters depicted an often idealized aristocratic existence, such as Watteau and Fragonard in France, or the great portraitists Gainsborough and Romney in England. Others, like Chardin, turned more to middle-class scenes.

Literature, with the growth of the press and of a wider reading public, freed itself from clerical, royal, and aristocratic patronage, increasingly reflected middle-class attitudes, and offered a profitable career to successful men of letters. The thought of the period became increasingly critical of aristocratic, monarchical, and ecclesiastical institutions. Writers of this bent, though differing widely among themselves, were called "philosophers" or *philosophes* in France, where they included the great names of Voltaire, Montesquieu, Rousseau, Diderot, and many others. Of essentially the same kind were Gibbon and Priestley in England, Hume and Adam Smith in Scotland, Beccaria and Galiani in Italy, Jovellanos in Spain. German literature came into its own with the generation from Lessing to Goethe and Schiller; but the eighteenth century in Germany is memorable chiefly for its musicians, Bach, Haydn, Mozart, and Beethoven having all lived at this time.

The Growth of the Press

Newspapers and magazines became common, reflecting and producing a great growth of communications and of public opinion. Not only pure literature flourished, but also scientific writing, popular science, encyclopedias, reference books, and works of public discussion. The *Times* of London, founded in 1785, was by no means the first daily newspaper, but it became one of the greatest. The Paris *Moniteur*, a daily founded in 1789, suggests the great stimulus to journalism given by the French Revolution. The *Almanach de Gotha*, founded in 1778, was an early and long-lived yearbook of political and statistical information. The *Encyclopédie*, edited by Diderot and d'Alembert, was a great compendium of scientific information and liberal opinion. The first edition of the *Encyclopaedia Britannica* appeared at Edinburgh in 1771. Museums making scientific knowledge and works of art accessible to the public were also characteristic of the period: the British Museum was founded in 1757, and various French institutions, such as the royal botanical gardens and the Louvre, partly open to the public before, became fully so after the Revolution, which was in fact a turning point in the history of museums, as it was of much else.

The Spread of the Enlightenment

The eighteenth century was notable also for the geographic spread of ideas and institutions mainly originating in western Europe. London and Paris were the two great centers; they were also by far the largest cities west of Constantinople. But scientific and literary academies, of the kind that had arisen from Italy to England in the preceding century, now were established along the perimeter of European civilization, as the map shows: at Edinburgh, Dublin, Lisbon, Madrid, Berlin, Copenhagen, Stockholm, and St. Petersburg—and at Philadelphia in America with the American Philosophical Society, founded in 1734. The incidence of birthplaces of notable men, if compared with what is shown on preceding maps (pages 54–55, 58–59, 70–71), suggests how Ireland, Scotland, and even the north of England were entering more fully into a sphere of British and hence of European civilization. In Russia, Lomonosov and Radischev figure among the founders of Russian literature and thought, and offer evidence, along with the Academy of St. Petersburg and the new royal residences of the tsars, of the Westernization that was occurring among the Russian upper classes.

National literatures were beginning in eastern Europe, and German literature was coming into its classic age. But the tone of the time was international or cosmopolitan; French was the language of international relations and the second language of all educated persons. In central and eastern Europe the upper classes often preferred French to their native tongues; King Frederick the Great wrote his literary works in French; the *Almanach de Gotha* was printed in French; and French was the official language of the academies of Berlin and St. Petersburg until after 1800.

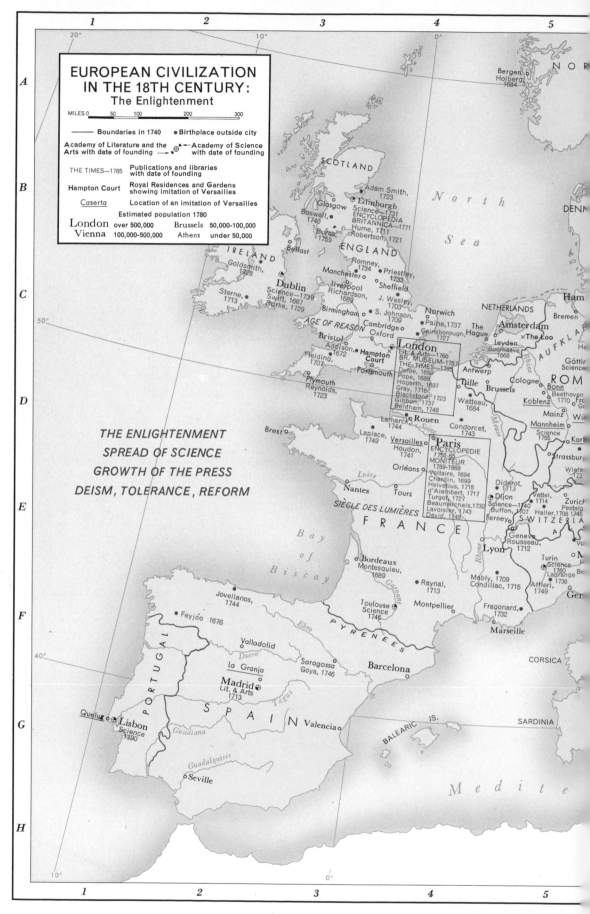

EUROPEAN CIVILIZATION IN THE 18TH CENTURY:
The Enlightenment

MILES 0   50   100   200   300

——— Boundaries in 1740   • Birthplace outside city

Academy of Literature and the   ← Academy of Science
Arts with date of founding   with date of founding

THE TIMES—1785   Publications and libraries with date of founding

Hampton Court   Royal Residences and Gardens showing imitation of Versailles

<u>Caserta</u>   Location of an imitation of Versailles

Estimated population 1780

London   over 500,000   Brussels   50,000-100,000
Vienna   100,000-500,000   Athens   under 50,000

THE ENLIGHTENMENT
SPREAD OF SCIENCE
GROWTH OF THE PRESS
DEISM, TOLERANCE, REFORM

SCOTLAND

Adam Smith, 1723
Glasgow   Edinburgh
Boswell, 1740   Science—1731
Burns, 1759   ENCYCLOPEDIA BRITANNICA—1771
Hume, 1711
Robertson, 1721

ENGLAND

IRELAND
Goldsmith, 1728
Belfast
Romney, 1734   Priestley, 1733
Manchester   Sheffield
Dublin   Liverpool
Science—1739   Richardson, 1689
Sterne, 1713   Swift, 1667
Burke, 1729   J. Wesley, 1703
Birmingham   S. Johnson, 1709
AGE OF REASON   Cambridge
Bristol   Oxford
Addison, 1672   Hampton Court
Fielding, 1707
Plymouth   Portsmouth
Reynolds, 1723

Norwich
Paine, 1737
Gainsborough, 1727
The Hague
NETHERLANDS
Amsterdam
Leyden
Boerhaave, 1668

London
LIT. & ARTS—1766
BR. MUSEUM-1757
THE TIMES—1785
Defoe, 1659
Pope, 1688
Hogarth, 1697
Gray, 1716
Blackstone, 1723
Gibbon, 1737
Bentham, 1748

Lamarck, 1744   Rouen
Laplace, 1749   Condorcet, 1743
Versailles   Paris
Houdon, 1741   ENCYCLOPEDIE 1751-65
Orléans   MONITEUR 1789-1868
Voltaire, 1694
Chardin, 1699
Helvetius, 1715
d'Alembert, 1717
Turgot, 1727
Beaumarchais, 1732
Lavoisier, 1743
David, 1748

Brest

Nantes   Tours

SIÈCLE DES LUMIÈRES

FRANCE

Lille
Brussels
Watteau, 1684
Antwerp
Cologne
Koblenz
Mainz
Mannheim
Science 1755

Diderot, 1713
Dijon
Science—1740
Buffon, 1707
Ferney
Geneva
Rousseau, 1712

Lyon

Vattel, 1714
Zurich
Haller, 1708 1746
SWITZERLA

Turin
Science 1760
Lagrange, 1736
Alfieri, 1749

Mably, 1709
Condillac, 1715

Fragonard, 1732

Marseille

Bay of Biscay

Bordeaux
Montesquieu, 1689

Raynal, 1713

Toulouse
Science 1746

Montpellier

PYRENEES

CORSICA

Jovellanos, 1744

Feyjoo 1676

Valladolid
Duero
La Granja

Saragossa
Goya, 1746

Barcelona

Ebro

PORTUGAL

Madrid
Lit. & Arts 1713

Tagus

Quelus   Lisbon
Science 1790

SPAIN   Valencia

Guadiana

BALEARIC IS.

SARDINIA

Guadalquivir

Seville

Mediterra

North Sea

DENM

Bergen Holberg, 1684

NOR

Bremen
Ham
Göttin
Science
ROM
Bonn
Beethoven 1770
Mainz
Wü
Karl
Strassbur
Wieła 173
Pesta
Kar
Ве
Gen
×The Loo
AUFKLÄR

SWEDEN

St. Petersburg
Science—1725
Peterhof Tsarskoe Selo
Slutsk

Lomonosov, 1711
(Near the White Sea)

ristiania

Upsala
Science
1728

Stockholm
Science—1741
Drottningholm
Swedenborg, 1688

Volga

Moscow
Radischev,
1749

Linnaeus,
1707

RUSSIA

Copenhagen
Science—1743

Dvina

Baltic Sea

Niemen

Königsberg
Kant, 1724

POLAND

Herder, 1744

Vistula

50°

Winckelmann,
1717
Berlin
Science
1700
Lit. & Arts
1703
Charlottenburg

Warsaw

Dnieper

LY

Potsdam

tock

Handel, 1685

Oder

Weimar

Lessing,
1729

Breslau
Wolff,
1679

Erfurt
Science
1754

Dresden

Cracow

CARPATHIANS

Dniester

ALMANACH DE
GOTHA—1778

Prague

Gluck, 1714

Nuremberg

AUSTRIA

PIRE

Nymphenburg

Danube

Vienna
Lit. & Arts
1704
Schönbrunn

Haydn,
1732

Buda Pest

Munich
Science
1759

HUNGARY

Salzburg
Mozart,
1756

Canova,
1757

80

ona

Black
Sea

Venice
Tiepolo, 1696
Goldoni, 1707

Adriatic Sea

Danube

ologna
Science
1712

lorence

40°

LUMINISMO

Galiani,
1728

ITALY

Constantinople

ome

OTTOMAN

Caserta

Naples Pompeii
Vico, 1668 Ruins discovered
Filangieri, 1748
1752

EMPIRE

yrrhenian

Sea

Ionian

Sea

Aegean

Sea

Palermo

Athens

SICILY

CRETE

PARTITIONS OF POLAND

▶ MAP BELOW

B‌Y 1795 THE POLISH STATE, once one of the great powers of Europe with territories stretching from the Baltic almost to the Black Sea, had disappeared from the map of Europe. Although its demise was brought on by its neighbors' ambitions, its internal condition rendered it helpless before foreign intrigue. With an impoverished peasantry and a government in a virtual state of anarchy, Poland was unable to compete with the modern, efficient "enlightened despotisms" of Austria, Russia, and Prussia. Their action in partitioning Poland is the classic case of eighteenth-century balance of power.

The chief architect of the partitions was Catherine the Great, who sought to enlarge Russia at the expense of both Poland and the Ottoman Empire. Exploiting the advantages following upon internal dissension in Poland, she was able by 1763 to gain paramount influence there, and even to place a former lover on the throne. In 1768 Russia became involved in a war with the Ottoman Empire which proved to be highly successful. Russian gains against Turkey threatened to upset the whole balance of power in eastern Europe. Frederick the Great suggested the partition of Poland as the means of avoiding this danger. He

would thereby not only gain the coveted West Prussia but also check the possibility that Russia might absorb all of Poland. He also feared Russo-Austrian aggrandizement at the expense of Turkey without adequate compensation to Prussia. When Catherine and Maria Theresa acquiesced, the first partition of Poland took place in 1772.

The Poles thereupon attempted to reform and strengthen their country, but were only partly successful, and were in any case stopped by their neighbors. In 1791 they adopted the Constitution of the Third of May, but Russia and Prussia interfered, and, taking advantage of the international confusion caused by the French Revolution, effected the second partition in 1793. In 1794 they put down the national uprising led by Kosciusko, and in 1795, joined by Austria, carried through the third partition.

Partly restored by Napoleon, Poland was again partitioned in 1815 (see pages 90–91). Poland was not restored to full independence until 1918, when the First World War destroyed the three empires that had partitioned it. It was again partitioned at the time of the Soviet-Nazi pact of 1939 (see pages 178–79), and again became an independent state, within the Soviet orbit, after the Second World War. Poland at this time received formerly German territories in East Prussia, Silesia, and east of the Oder River. Amid all these changes the region having a majority of Polish-speaking inhabitants was as shown on pages 94–95.

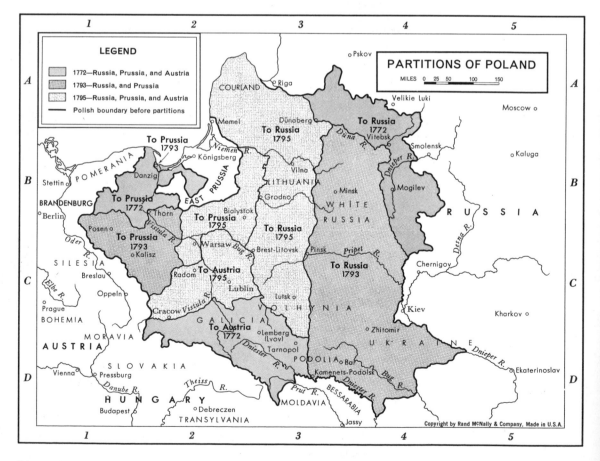

FRANCE BEFORE THE REVOLUTION

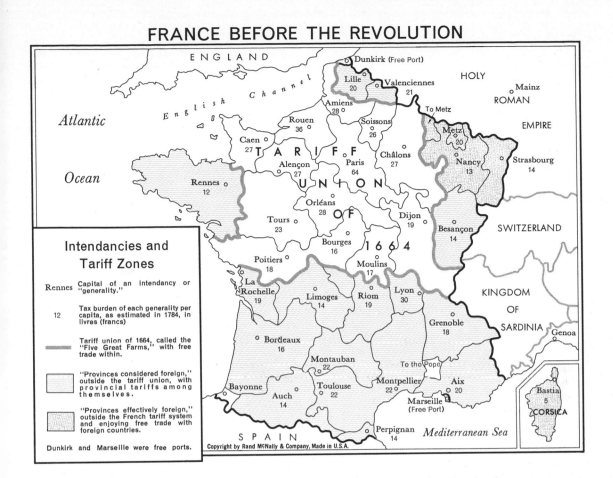

Intendancies and Tariff Zones

Rennes   Capital of an intendancy or "generality."

12   Tax burden of each generality per capita, as estimated in 1784, in livres (francs).

   Tariff union of 1664, called the "Five Great Farms," with free trade within.

   "Provinces considered foreign," outside the tariff union, with provincial tariffs among themselves.

   "Provinces effectively foreign," outside the French tariff system and enjoying free trade with foreign countries.

Dunkirk and Marseille were free ports.

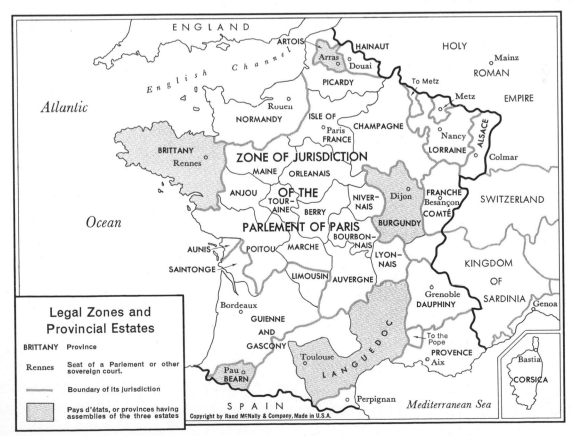

Legal Zones and Provincial Estates

BRITTANY   Province

Rennes   Seat of a Parlement or other sovereign court.

   Boundary of its jurisdiction

   Pays d'états, or provinces having assemblies of the three estates

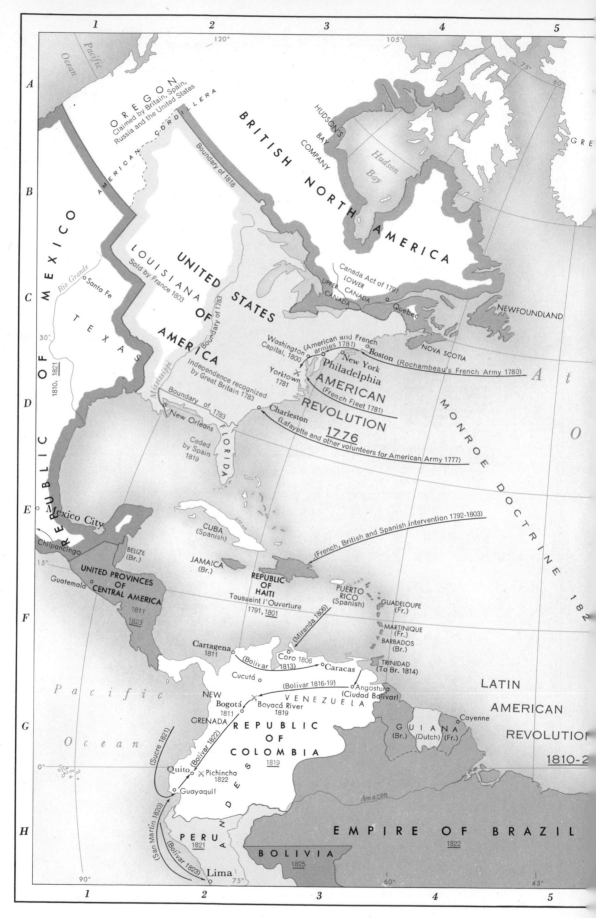

OREGON
Claimed by Britain, Spain,
Russia and the United States

BRITISH NORTH AMERICA

AMERICAN CORDILLERA

Boundary of 1818

HUDSON'S
BAY
COMPANY

Hudson
Bay

GRE

Pacific
Ocean

REPUBLIC OF MEXICO

LOUISIANA
Sold by France 1803

UNITED STATES OF AMERICA

Canada Act of 1791
LOWER
CANADA

UPPER
CANADA

Quebec

NEWFOUNDLAND

Rio Grande

Santa Fe

TEXAS

30°

1810, 1821

Mississippi

Boundary of 1783

Independence recognized
by Great Britain 1783

Washington
Capital, 1800

(American and French
armies 1781)

Boston (Rochambeau's French Army 1780)

New York

AMERICAN

Yorktown
1781

Philadelphia

REVOLUTION

(French Fleet 1781)

1776

MONROE DOCTRINE 182

At

O

Boundary of 1783

New Orleans

Ceded
by Spain
1819

FLORIDA

Charleston

(Lafayette and other volunteers for American Army 1777)

Mexico City

CUBA
(Spanish)

(French, British and Spanish intervention 1792-1803)

Chilpancingo

BELIZE
(Br.)

JAMAICA
(Br.)

UNITED PROVINCES
OF
CENTRAL AMERICA

15°

Guatemala

1811
1823

REPUBLIC
OF
HAITI
Toussaint l'Ouverture
1791, 1801

PUERTO
RICO
(Spanish)

GUADELOUPE
(Fr.)

LATIN

Cartagena
1811

(Bolivar)

Coro 1806
1813

(Miranda 1806)

MARTINIQUE
(Fr.)

BARBADOS
(Br.)

AMERICAN

Cucutá

Caracas

TRINIDAD
(To Br. 1814)

Pacific

NEW

Bogotá
1811

(Bolivar 1816-19)

VENEZUELA

Angostura
(Ciudad Bolivar)

GUIANA

REVOLUTION

Cayenne

Boyacá River
1819

(Br.) (Dutch) (Fr.)

1810-2

GRENADA

REPUBLIC
OF
COLOMBIA
1819

Ocean

(Sucre 1821)

(Bolivar 1822)

0°

Quito

Pichincha
1822

A N D E S

Guayaquil

Amazon

EMPIRE OF BRAZIL

(San Martín 1820)

PERU
1821

1822

(Bolivar 1823)

BOLIVIA
1825

Lima

90°

75°

60°

45°

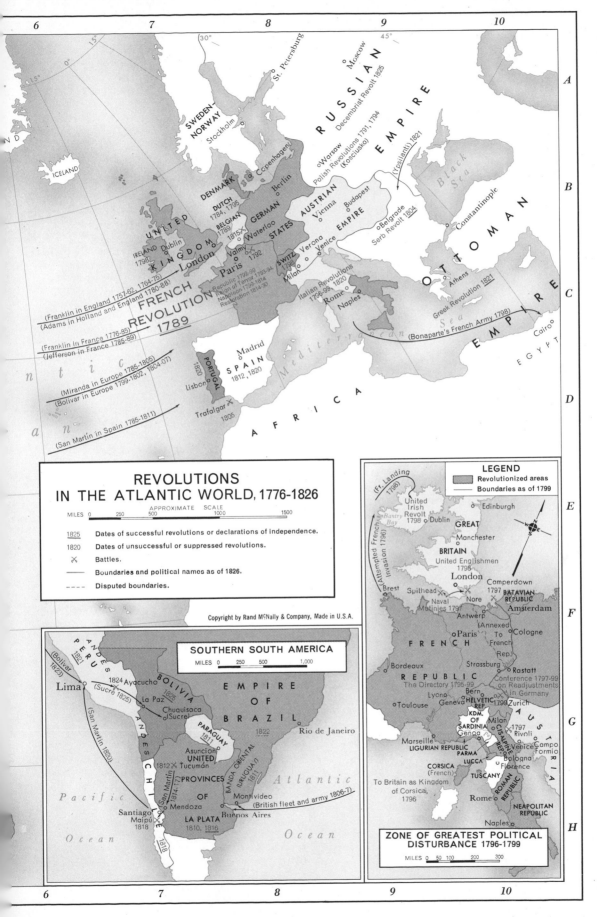

REVOLUTIONS
IN THE ATLANTIC WORLD, 1776-1826

MILES 0   250   APPROXIMATE   SCALE   1000   1500
                        500

<u>1825</u>   Dates of successful revolutions or declarations of independence.

1820   Dates of unsuccessful or suppressed revolutions.

✕   Battles.

———   Boundaries and political names as of 1826.

- - - -   Disputed boundaries.

Copyright by Rand McNally & Company, Made in U.S.A.

LEGEND

▓▓▓   Revolutionized areas
———   Boundaries as of 1799

SOUTHERN SOUTH AMERICA

MILES 0   250   500   1,000

ZONE OF GREATEST POLITICAL
DISTURBANCE 1796-1799

MILES 0   50 100   200   300

Map labels (main map):

RUSSIAN EMPIRE

Moscow
Decembrist Revolt 1825
St. Petersburg

SWEDEN-NORWAY
Stockholm

ICELAND

oWarsaw
Polish Revolutions 1791, 1794
(Kosciusko)

(Ypsilanti) 1821

Black Sea

DENMARK
Copenhagen
Berlin

DUTCH
1784, 1795
BELGIAN
1789
GERMAN
STATES
Waterloo
1815✕
Valmy
1792

AUSTRIAN
EMPIRE
Vienna
Budapest

oBelgrade
Serb Revolt 1804

Constantinople

UNITED
KINGDOM

IRELAND Dublin
1798?
London

SWITZ.
1798
Paris
Verona
Venice
Milan

Rome
Naples

Italian Revolutions
1796-99, 1820

Athens

Greek Revolution 1821

OTTOMAN EMPIRE

(Bonaparte's French Army 1798)

(Franklin in England 1757-62, 1764-75)
(Adams in Holland and England 1780-88)

FRENCH
REVOLUTION
1789

Republic 1792-99
Reign of Terror 1793-94
Napoleon 1799-1814
Restoration 1814-30

(Franklin in France 1776-85)
(Jefferson in France 1785-89)

Madrid

SPAIN
1812, 1820

PORTUGAL
1820
Lisbon

(Miranda in Europe 1785-1805)
(Bolivar in Europe 1799-1802, 1804-07)

Trafalgar ✕
1805

(San Martin in Spain 1785-1811)

Mediterranean Sea

AFRICA

Cairo
EGYPT

Atlantic Ocean

Southern South America inset:

PERU
(Bolivar 1824)
Lima
1824 Ayacucho
(Sucre 1825)
La Paz
1825
Chuquisaca
(Sucre)

ANDES
BOLIVIA

EMPIRE
OF
BRAZIL

PARAGUAY
1811

Asuncion

1812 ✕ Tucumán

UNITED
PROVINCES
OF
LA PLATA
1810, 1816

BANDA ORIENTAL
(URUGUAY)
1811

Montevideo

Rio de Janeiro

Atlantic Ocean

CHILE

San Martin
1814-17
Mendoza

Santiago
Maipú
1818

(San Martin 1820)

(Bolivar 1821)

1818

Buenos Aires

(British fleet and army 1806-7)

Pacific Ocean

Zone of Greatest Political Disturbance inset:

(Fr. Landing 1798)

United
Irish
Revolt
1798
Dublin

Bantry Bay

(Attempted French Invasion 1796)

Brest

GREAT
BRITAIN
Edinburgh

Manchester

United Englishmen
1798

London

Camperdown
1797

Spithead
Naval
Mutinies 1797
Nore ✕

BATAVIAN
REPUBLIC
Amsterdam

Antwerp
(Annexed to
French Rep.)
Cologne

FRENCH

Paris

Bordeaux

Strassburg

Rastatt
Conference 1797-99
on Readjustments
in Germany

REPUBLIC
The Directory 1795-99

Lyons
Toulouse

Bern
Geneva
HELVETIC
REP.
1799 Zurich

KDM.
OF
SARDINIA
Genoa

Milan
CISALPINE
REP.
Venice
1797 Rivoli
Campo
Formio

AUSTRIA

Marseille
LIGURIAN REPUBLIC

PARMA
LUCCA

Bologna
ROMAN
REPUBLIC
Florence

Rome

TUSCANY

CORSICA
(French)

To Britain as Kingdom
of Corsica,
1796

NEAPOLITAN
REPUBLIC

Naples

87

REVOLUTIONS IN
THE ATLANTIC WORLD

▶ MAPS ON PAGES 85 AND 86–87

THE HALF-CENTURY beginning with the American Revolution was a period of revolutionary disturbance on both sides of the Atlantic. It is of this period, indeed, that one may speak most especially of an "Atlantic Civilization." Europeans and Americans shared the ideas of the Enlightenment; they were politically much influenced by each other; communications by sea were easier than those by land. In purpose and ideals the revolutionary movements in Europe and the Americas were much alike. Both aimed at political liberty, individual rights, national sovereignty, legal equality, a modern conception of law and citizenship, a state favorable to economic expansion and orderly government through written constitutions. The practical outcome was different in different countries because of the difference in conditions.

France before the Revolution
▶ MAPS ON PAGE 85

The maps on page 85 show France of the Old Regime. In the process of uniting France, ever since the Middle Ages, many local liberties and privileges had been allowed to remain. These especially favored certain provinces, or the nobility as a class, or local economic interests protected by local tariffs or local laws. The one great centralizing feature was the institution of the intendants, administrators sent out from Paris, whose districts are shown. Note how the tax burden varied between the intendancies, partly because some regions were wealthier than others and hence paid more taxes, and partly because some were privileged and others discriminated against in taxation. Internal free trade existed only in the north. Brittany, the south, and the recently annexed regions of the northeast frontier had not yet been fully incorporated into a national trading area. Different regions had their different laws and their respective supreme courts. In a few provinces the old "estates" still met, with clergy, nobility, and Third Estate considered as separate "orders"; they were dominated by the nobility or by churchmen who were nobles. It will be seen that local tariffs, separate legal zones, the meeting of estates, and lower taxation were most often found in places farthest from Paris, or those annexed since the time of Louis XIV (cf. page 76). One aim of the French Revolution was to equalize all these anomalies.

America and the Atlantic
▶ MAP ON PAGES 86–87

On pages 86–87 we see the "Atlantic" world as a whole—although in Spanish South America, with its high mountains, communications were by the Pacific. Boundaries and political names show the situation at the end of the period, in 1826.

The American Revolution had a great immediate influence in Europe, and in Latin America a little later. It was the most successful revolution of the period in achieving its objectives. While objectives in a general way were the same everywhere, they were already the most fully realized in the Thirteen Colonies, even before the Revolution, so that there was less resistance and civil struggle in North America than elsewhere. In that sense the American Revolution was less revolutionary than the European. Nevertheless, it was French aid, with the French army and fleet combining with Washington's army at Yorktown, that effected American independence, and it was Napoleon's political difficulties later that enabled the United States to acquire Louisiana (see pages 150 and 154).

The French government entered the War of American Independence (as did the Spanish) in order to weaken Great Britain. Its aim was to redress the unfavorable peace treaties of 1713 and 1763 (see page 77). In befriending the American insurgents, however, the Bourbon monarchy gave encouragement to a great wave of public opinion in France, where the political liberty, constitutional government and degree of social equality enjoyed in America were much admired. The Americans Franklin and Jefferson, the first two United States ministers to France, while they neither foresaw nor desired revolution in that country, were of importance in the spread of liberal and pro-American ideas. John Adams played a similar role in Holland, where he was closely associated with the Dutch Patriots, as those desiring a change in the Dutch forms of government were called. The American state constitutions and bills of rights were translated into French and Dutch, and there was much excited discussion of the American Revolution in many parts of Europe.

War and Revolution in Europe

The French Revolution of 1789 was in some ways unique among revolutions of the period, especially in the degree of popular upheaval with which it began; for only in France and America did the general run of the rural population join in revolt, and in France this involved a transformation of property and social relationships that had no counterpart in America. In other respects conditions in France were like those in the rest of Europe. In all countries, even the Italian, Swiss, and Dutch republics and constitutional Great Britain, full political rights depended on membership in the established church (see page 68), and government was in the hands of patriciates or aristocracies which had become largely hereditary. There were revolutionary disturbances in Holland, Belgium, and Ireland, and at Geneva in Switzerland, even before 1789.

Revolutionary France and the conservative European governments went to war in 1792. France, meanwhile turning into a republic and passing through the Reign of Terror, proceeded to crush its adversaries in the territories it occupied, by driving away the old governments, confiscating church properties, abolishing feudal and manorial institutions, appealing for local popular support, or setting up local sympathizers in office. Thus revolution spread to neighboring countries under the aegis of the French armies. Hapsburg Belgium and the German left bank of the Rhine were annexed to France. The Batavian Republic was set up in Holland; the Helvetic Republic in Switzerland; the

Cisalpine, Ligurian, Roman, and Neapolitan (called in Paris the "Parthenopean") republics in Italy. Most of these republics received constitutions modeled on the French, embodying the new conceptions of citizenship, political rights, and popular sovereignty. Disillusionment soon set in between the French and their supporters in the new republics, and the revolutions there are shown as "unsuccessful" on the map; but many of the changes then made were retained permanently, especially in Holland. By a kind of inverse analogy to what happened on the Italian mainland the British occupied Corsica in 1796. With the aid of sympathetic Corsicans they proclaimed a "Kingdom of Corsica," which favored large landowners and the church, and of which the king of England was king. But the British were soon forced to withdraw.

The French tried also to assist Irish revolutionaries in the creation of an Irish republic, and did effect a small landing in 1798; but the Irish uprising was put down by the British. In England and Scotland pro-French sentiment was strongest before 1795; but the years 1796–99, shown in the inset on page 86, were marked by the agitation of "United Englishmen" at Manchester and by mutinies in the British Fleet, which, though nonpolitical, caused great alarm. Farther east in Europe, in the 1790's, there were disturbances in Germany and Hungary too small to record on the map, and revolution in Poland. The Polish constitutional movement of 1791 and the armed attempt led by Kosciusko in 1794 were suppressed by Russia, Prussia, and Austria, which carried through the third partition in 1795 (see page 84). Bonaparte's famous expedition to Egypt brought revolutionary ideas to the Near East. The French Revolution was the first European development to have a great influence on Islam, largely because it was not specifically Christian.

Haiti, Canada, and Latin America

In Haiti, where the western part of the island belonged to France, the French revolutionary government first gave civic rights to free Negroes and then, after a slave revolt, abolished slavery in 1793. After a decade of trouble Haiti in 1801 declared its independence, with the whole island for a time united.

The Canada Act, passed by the British Parliament in 1791 (in effect until 1840), set up the two provinces of Upper and Lower Canada and provided them with political institutions like those of the Thirteen Colonies before 1776. Lower Canada was French-speaking; Upper Canada was peopled by English-speaking refugees from the American Revolution (see page 166).

When Napoleon occupied Spain in 1808 groups formed in various Spanish American cities to oppose his rule and subsequently to assert independence. After Miranda's abortive attempt of 1806 and a wave of temporarily suppressed revolutions in 1810 and 1811, Spanish American independence was established by 1825. Some of the leaders had spent years in Europe; Miranda had also visited the United States. They were inspired, in any case,

by both the American and the French revolutions. To win independence in Spanish America required difficult military campaigns across the high Andes against royalist forces. The routes of the chief "liberators"—Bolívar, San Martín, and Sucre—are shown. Spanish American independence was favored both by the United States and by Great Britain, which had sent a substantial army to the La Plata estuary in 1807. Many individual Britons volunteered in Latin American revolutionary forces, as Lafayette and Kosciusko had done in the United States. The most famous was Admiral Cochrane, who commanded fleets for Chile and Brazil. The liberator of Chile, O'Higgins, was a Chilean of Irish parentage.

In Portuguese Brazil the regent of Portugal found refuge and set up his court during the Napoleonic wars at home. The Brazilians, unwilling to go back under Portugal, declared an independent empire in 1822, under an emperor of the Portuguese royal family. Brazil did not become a republic until 1889. (For Latin America see pages 142–43 and 146–47.)

Napoleon and After

Meanwhile, in Europe, during the years when it was dominated by Napoleon (see page 90), a revolt of the Serbs against the Ottoman Empire laid the way for Serbian autonomy and opened the Balkan revolutionary movement of the following century. In Spain in 1812 a group of liberals opposing Napoleon proclaimed a constitution, which they could not put into effect but which became famous in the following years as the "Spanish Constitution of 1812." It was modeled on the French revolutionary constitution of 1789–91. Napoleon's defeat signalized the triumph of the conservative interests in Europe (see page 91). Faced with continuing revolutionary agitation they became more repressive. Revolutionary outbreaks in Portugal, Spain, Sardinia, and Naples in 1820 were put down. The Greek revolution of the following year, launched both by Ypsilanti operating from Russia and by Greeks in the region of Greece itself, was successful after a decade of struggle, with support from Russia, Britain, and France.

In 1825 even tsarist Russia had an attempted revolution, the Decembrist Revolt, led by army officers who had seen Europe during the Napoleonic wars. It was immediately suppressed, but is considered the beginning of the modern revolutionary movement in Russia.

The European powers met in 1822 at Verona to discuss the problem of revolution. They approved a French expedition which crushed the revolution of 1820 in Spain, and also urged intervention in Spanish America to stop revolution there. The British fleet, however, was necessary for this purpose; and the British favored Spanish American independence. It was in answer to the Congress of Verona that the United States, in 1823, announced the Monroe Doctrine. This held that any further European intervention or colonialism in the Americas was contrary to the interests of the United States.

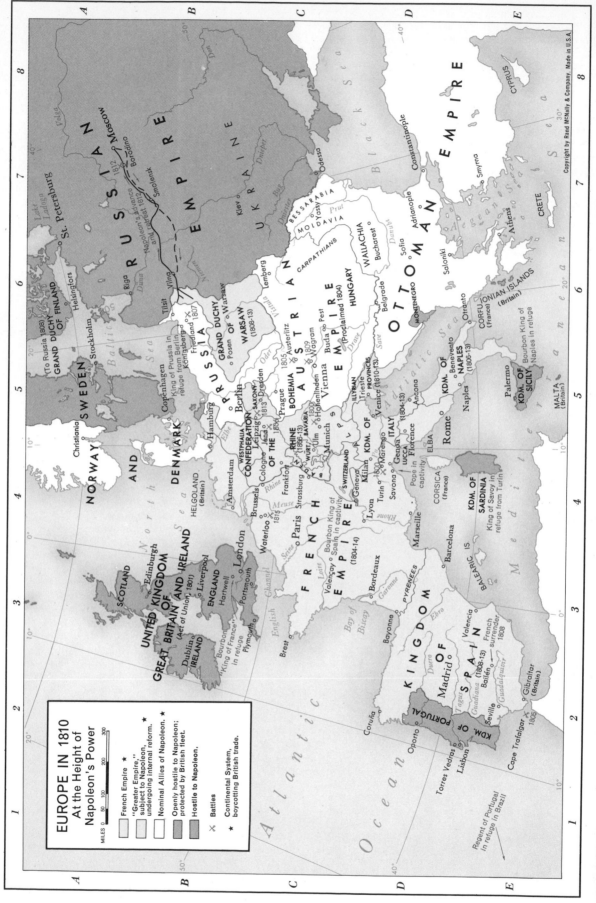

EUROPE IN 1810
At the Height of Napoleon's Power

MILES 0 50 100 200 300

★ French Empire

★ "Greater Empire," subject to Napoleon, undergoing internal reform.

★ Nominal Allies of Napoleon.

Openly hostile to Napoleon; protected by British fleet.

Hostile to Napoleon.

✕ Battles

★ Continental System, boycotting British trade.

Copyright by Rand McNally & Company. Made in U.S.A.

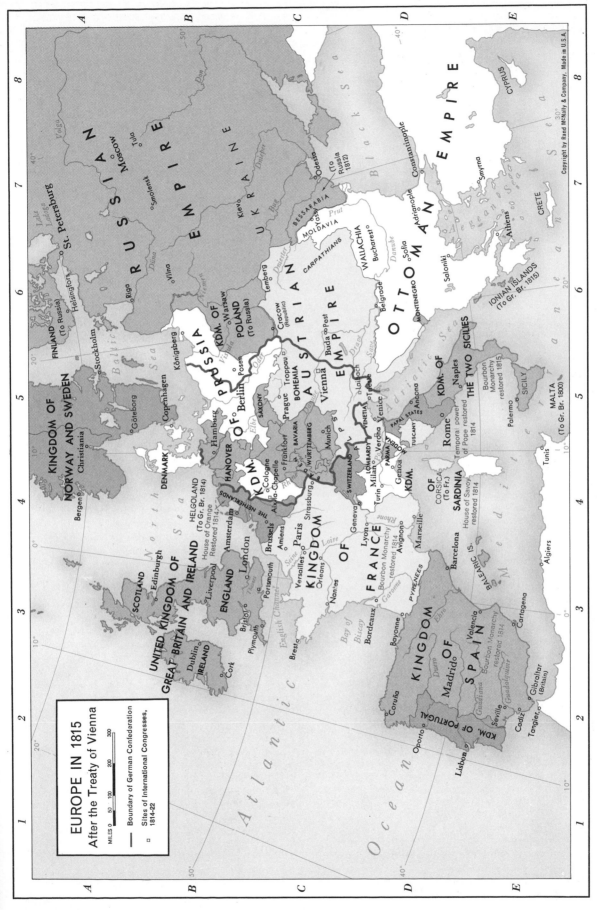

EUROPE IN 1815
After the Treaty of Vienna

Boundary of German Confederation

□ Sites of International Congresses,
1814–22

MILES 0 50 100 200 300

A B C D E

RUSSIAN EMPIRE

Volga
Moscow
Tula
St. Petersburg
Lake Ladoga
Don
Helsingfors (To Russia)
FINLAND (To Russia)
Riga
Dvina
Smolensk
Kiev
UKRAINE
Dnieper
Bug
Vilna
Niemen
Odessa
(To Russia 1812)
Bessarabia
Prut
Dniester
MOLDAVIA
Bucharest
WALLACHIA
Danube
Sofia
Adrianople
Constantinople

OTTOMAN EMPIRE

Black Sea
Smyrna
Saloniki
Athens
Aegean Sea
CRETE
CYPRUS

MONTENEGRO
Belgrade
CARPATHIANS
Buda
Pest
Drave
Save

AUSTRIAN EMPIRE

Vienna
Prague
BOHEMIA
Troppau
Laibach
Trieste
VENETIA
Venice
Verona
LOMBARDY
Milan
Turin
PARMA
MODENA
Genoa
Adriatic Sea
Ancona
PAPAL STATES
TUSCANY
Rome
Temporal power of Pope restored 1814

KINGDOM OF NORWAY AND SWEDEN
Bergen
Christiania
Stockholm
Göteborg
Copenhagen
DENMARK
Baltic Sea
Königsberg
Posen
Warsaw
KDM. OF POLAND (To Russia)
Vistula
Cracow (Republic)
Oder
SAXONY
Dresden
Elbe
Frankfort
BAVARIA
Munich
WÜRTTEMBERG
Strassburg
SWITZERLAND
Geneva
Lyons
Rhône

KINGDOM OF PRUSSIA
Berlin
Hamburg
HANOVER
KDM.
Cologne
Aix-la-Chapelle
THE NETHERLANDS
House of Orange Restored 1814
Amsterdam
Brussels
Rhine

HELGOLAND (To Gr. Br. 1814)
North Sea

SCOTLAND
Edinburgh
UNITED KINGDOM OF GREAT BRITAIN AND IRELAND
Dublin
IRELAND
Cork
ENGLAND
Liverpool
London
Bristol
Portsmouth
Plymouth
Thames
English Channel
Amiens
Paris
Versailles
Orleans
Nantes
Loire
Seine

KINGDOM OF FRANCE
Bourbon Monarchy restored 1814
Avignon
Marseille
Bordeaux
Bayonne
Garonne
PYRENEES
Bay of Biscay

KINGDOM OF SPAIN
Bourbon Monarchy restored 1814
Madrid
Valencia
Barcelona
BALEARIC IS.
Ebro
Duero
Guadiana
Guadalquivir
Seville
Cadiz
Gibraltar (Britain)
Cartagena
Coruña
Oporto
Lisbon
KDM. OF PORTUGAL
Tangier
Atlantic Ocean

CORSICA (To Fr.)
SARDINIA
House of Savoy, restored 1814
KDM. OF SARDINIA

KDM. OF THE TWO SICILIES
Naples
Bourbon Monarchy restored 1815
SICILY
Palermo
MALTA (To Gr. Br. 1800)
Tunis
Algiers
Mediterranean Sea

IONIAN ISLANDS (To Gr. Br. 1815)

Copyright by Rand McNally & Company, Made in U.S.A.

91

THE NAPOLEONIC ERA
AND THE CONGRESS OF VIENNA

▶ MAPS ON PAGES 90 AND 91

TENSION BETWEEN REVOLUTIONARY France and the European monarchies and aristocracies led in 1792 to war, which lasted until 1814. The First French Republic defeated a First Coalition in 1797, extended its boundaries to the Rhine, and brought similar republics into being in Holland, Switzerland, and Italy, as shown in the inset on page 87. A republican general, Napoleon Bonaparte, seized control in 1799 and defeated a Second Coalition at the battle of Marengo in 1800. He assumed the title of Emperor of the French in 1804, and with the defeat of a Third Coalition at Austerlitz (1805), Jena (1806), and Friedland (1807), created a "Greater Empire" (le grand empire) in central Europe, Italy, and Spain, and forced the Scandinavian and east European powers into reluctant alliance with him. He tried to bring them all, along with France, into his Continental System to ruin the exports of Great Britain, which had meanwhile confirmed its control of the sea by its victory at Trafalgar (1805). To enforce the boycott of British goods, Napoleon by 1810 had annexed the papal states, Holland, the German seaports of Bremen, Hamburg, and Lübeck, and the Illyrian Provinces directly to France.

Europe under Napoleon
▶ MAP ON PAGE 90

Napoleon carried on some of the principles of the French Revolution, which he digested into the Civil Code or Code Napoleon. He imposed reforms in all countries of his Greater Empire, with the co-operation of native reformers and by his military power. He did away with survivals of feudalism, introduced the Civil Code with its principle of equality before the law, enforced toleration and put persons of all religions, including Jews, on the same basis with respect to government, abolished church courts (such as the Inquisition in the case of Spain), and modernized the tax structure, financial administration, civil service, property law, and judicial system. He made his brother Joseph king of Spain, his brother-in-law king of Naples, and his stepson viceroy of Italy. In Germany he put various territories of minor rulers, of Prussia west of the Elbe, and of the king of England (in Hanover) into a newly created kingdom of Westphalia, of which he made his brother Jerome the king. In Saxony, Bavaria, Württemberg, and Baden the rulers willingly collaborated with Napoleon, in order to round out and modernize their states; the first three were made kings. In Poland, with the aid of Polish patriots, Napoleon undid the partitions of 1793 and 1795 by creating a Grand Duchy of Warsaw.

The reforms provoked opposition, were accompanied by continuing war, and involved subservience to France and deprivation of British and overseas products. Hence resistance rose. Russia, counting on this resistance and on British aid, repudiated the Continental System at the end of 1810. In 1812 Napoleon invaded Russia with an army of 600,000 men of many nationalities. It was the greatest single military operation before the First World War, and a colossal failure.

After Napoleon's defeat in Russia the British, who had fought the Peninsular War in Spain since 1808, were able to cross the Pyrenees and invade France from the south; Prussia and Austria joined Russia and Britain; and revolts against the French broke out in Italy and elsewhere. Napoleon was forced to abdicate in 1814.

The Restoration and the Peace of 1814-15
▶ MAP ON PAGE 91

With the defeat of Napoleon, the Bourbon monarchies were restored in France, Spain, and Naples, the king of Sardinia returned to the mainland, the House of Orange was converted for the first time into a monarchy, and the pope re-established the papal states. The British, who during the wars had penetrated all the other European colonial empires, returned the East Indies to the Dutch, but kept Malta, Helgoland, the Ionian Islands, Trinidad, St. Lucia, Mauritius, Ceylon, and the Cape of Good Hope. Russia retained its recent conquests in Finland and Bessarabia.

Other matters were arranged at the Congress of Vienna of 1814–15. Its main problems were to take precautions against a resurgent France, and to check the advance of Russia into Europe. To create points of strength against France, Belgium and Holland were united, the king of Sardinia obtained Genoa, Austria received Lombardy and Venetia, and Prussia was given the Rhineland. Poland was again partitioned to prevent the whole of it from going to Russia. Russian Poland now reached farther west than in the third partition of 1795. Prussia annexed part of Saxony, in compensation for yielding some of its Polish territories to Russia The Napoleonic kingdom of Westphalia was abolished, its territories going mainly to Prussia and to the restored state of Hanover, which was raised to the rank of kingdom. (The connection of Hanover with England ended in 1837.) In Bavaria, Württemberg, and Baden the rulers were allowed to keep the new titles and enlarged territories that they owed to Napoleon. The Holy Roman Empire was not restored. Germany was now gathered into a mere thirty-eight states (in place of the three hundred of the old Empire) and loosely organized in a confederation. Sweden was allowed to annex Norway in compensation for its loss of Finland to Russia.

The peace of Vienna was made with a minimum of ideological feeling. Constitutional charters were issued in France and Poland. The main principle of the treaty was to preserve peace through diplomatic compensation and balance of power. Poland lost its autonomous constitution in 1830, Belgium became independent in 1831, Germany and Italy were unified in a series of short wars from 1859 to 1870, Norway and Sweden separated peaceably in 1905. In general, however, the settlement of 1814 was a durable one, and there was no general European war for exactly a century after 1814.

LANGUAGES AND NATIONALITIES
OF EUROPE

▶ MAP ON PAGES 94–95

ONE OF THE CHIEF MOVEMENTS of the nineteenth century was nationalism, which involved an increasing consciousness of nationality, a desire to develop or revive distinct national cultures, and a belief that each nationality should possess an independent state of its own. Nationality was mainly determined by language. There were a few exceptions: the Swiss formed a single nationality while speaking different languages; the Dutch and Flemish felt nationally distinct, though their language was almost the same; the Irish spoke mainly English, but felt themselves to be a separate nationality.

The map on pages 94–95 shows the distribution of European languages in the nineteenth century. In some places, especially eastern Europe, local mixture and interpenetration of languages was greater than the map can show. In general outline these language areas had not changed for hundreds of years. The language border between French and German (or Flemish), for example, running through Belgium, Alsace, and Switzerland, has not changed materially since the early Middle Ages, despite recurrent shifts of political boundaries.

The map gives political boundaries for 1922, at which time, after the First World War, the principle of national self-determination had been incorporated into the European political structure, though still leaving certain linguistic minorities within various political frontiers. The map may be contrasted with political maps for other dates, most easily with the double-page map for 1721 (see pages 78–79), to show how little correspondence there had formerly been between linguistic and political frontiers, particularly in central and eastern Europe. The effects of nationalism in the century before 1922 were to unify the Germans and the Italians, replacing small states with large ones, and to break up the multinational Russian, Hapsburg, and Ottoman empires, replacing these large states with a zone of small states from Finland to Greece.

Origins of Language Groups

Most European languages are of the Indo-European family; that is, they have common features of structure and vocabulary that reveal a common origin. Although Armenian, Persian, and the ancient Sanskrit of India are also Indo-European, it is believed that the Indo-European languages originated somewhere in Europe. Basque, a unique language, apparently antedates the Indo-European expansion. Celtic languages, now confined to the western rim of Europe, were once spoken over a much wider area. The spread of the Roman Empire has left its mark in the modern Romance or Latin languages of the Iberian peninsula, France, and Rumania, in addition to Italy. The Germanic migrations of the fifth century planted Germanic languages west of the Rhine and in England and Lowland Scotland, although English has been incorporating French and Latin elements since the Norman Con-quest. In the later Middle Ages Germans also colonized east of the Elbe, and settled in towns or small pockets in parts of Poland, the east Baltic coast, Hungary, and Transylvania. In the eighteenth century, while some Germans migrated to America, others went to Russia; hence came the Volga Germans. Medieval movements also distributed the Slavic languages in the Balkans and central Europe as shown. Finnish tribes, and the related Karelians, Mordvinians, etc., whose linguistic affiliations are with northern Asia, once peopled the wilderness of northern Russia; the Slavic and Indo-European Great Russians colonized and conquered in these regions in historic times. The Magyars, related in origin to the Finns, represent an incursion into southeast Europe in the ninth century.

Declining and Reviving Languages

In the early modern period, from the sixteenth through the eighteenth century, there was a tendency for some languages to die out, or to be arrested in their development, remaining unwritten peasant or folk languages only. Thus English encroached on native Irish, French on Breton; the official and literary language of Norway became Danish; Finns wrote in Swedish, and Czechs in German. Poles and Hungarians used Latin as a political language. In some places the languages of town and country were different, because the towns represented an earlier movement of colonization: thus the towns of Finland were mostly Swedish; Riga and other east Baltic towns were German; in Poland the towns-people often spoke German or Yiddish, an east-European Jewish language derived from medieval German.

After 1800, with the romantic and nationalist movements, there was a revival of literary interest in Irish, Norwegian, Czech, Catalan, Provençal, and other hitherto subordinate languages; the Poles and Magyars gave up the official employment of Latin; and some languages, such as Finnish and Serbo-Croatian, were put to literary use almost for the first time. Journalism and universal schooling favored standard languages at the expense of dialect. The rapid growth of cities, by drawing country people into the towns, in some cases revolutionized their ethnic composition. Helsinki, Riga, and Prague grew tenfold from 1800 to 1900, becoming respectively more Finnish, Latvian, and Czech in their population.

Twentieth-Century Changes

Mass removal of peoples in the twentieth century has made changes whose effects are in some cases not clearly known. After the First World War over a million Greeks were transported from Turkey to Greece, in exchange for Turks sent to Turkey. The Baltic Germans were brought to Germany by Adolf Hitler. After the Second World War, and the moving of the Polish political frontier to the Oder River, millions of Germans of eastern Germany were driven out. The Volga Germans disappeared during the Second World War. It would be difficult to show the nationalities of eastern Europe for the mid-twentieth century with as much accuracy as the following map shows it for the nineteenth.

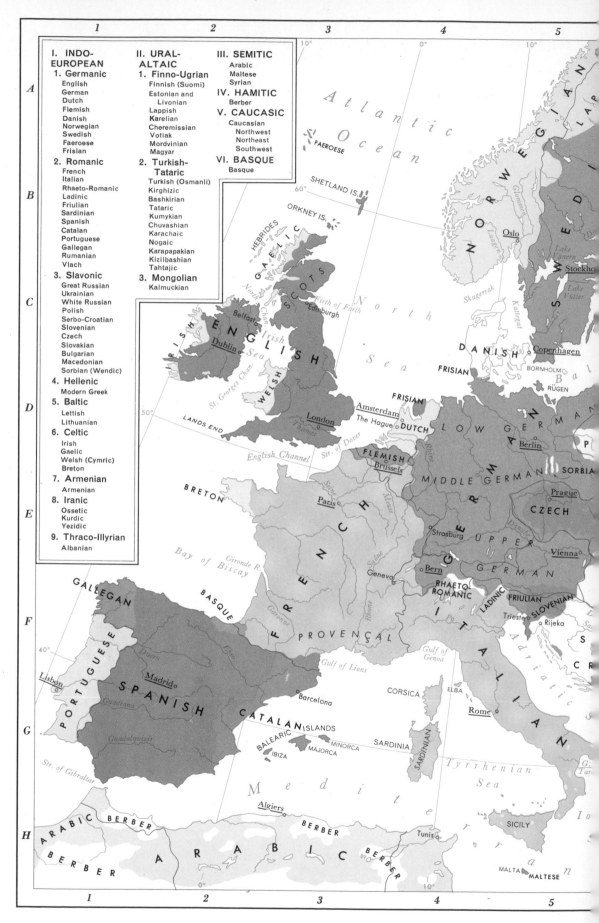

I. INDO-EUROPEAN

1. Germanic
English
German
Dutch
Flemish
Danish
Norwegian
Swedish
Faeroese
Frisian

2. Romanic
French
Italian
Rhaeto-Romanic
Ladinic
Friulian
Sardinian
Spanish
Catalan
Portuguese
Gallegan
Rumanian
Vlach

3. Slavonic
Great Russian
Ukrainian
White Russian
Polish
Serbo-Croatian
Slovenian
Czech
Slovakian
Bulgarian
Macedonian
Sorbian (Wendic)

4. Hellenic
Modern Greek

5. Baltic
Lettish
Lithuanian

6. Celtic
Irish
Gaelic
Welsh (Cymric)
Breton

7. Armenian
Armenian

8. Iranic
Ossetic
Kurdic
Yezidic

9. Thraco-Illyrian
Albanian

II. URAL-ALTAIC

1. Finno-Ugrian
Finnish (Suomi)
Estonian and Livonian
Lappish
Karelian
Cheremissian
Votiak
Mordvinian
Magyar

2. Turkish-Tataric
Turkish (Osmanli)
Kirghizic
Bashkirian
Tataric
Kumykian
Chuvashian
Karachaic
Nogaic
Karapapakian
Kizilbashian
Tahtajic

3. Mongolian
Kalmuckian

III. SEMITIC
Arabic
Maltese
Syrian

IV. HAMITIC
Berber

V. CAUCASIC
Caucasian
Northwest
Northeast
Southwest

VI. BASQUE
Basque

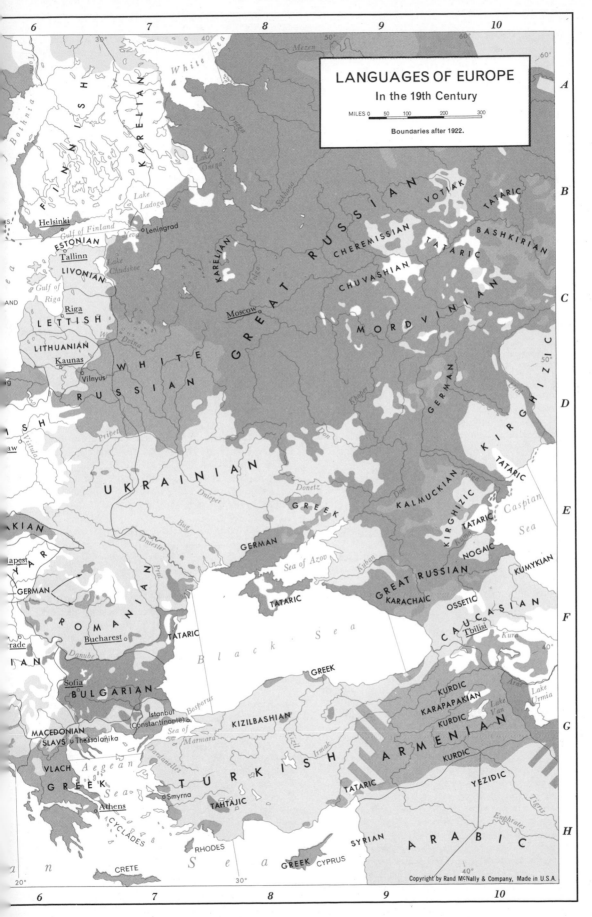

LANGUAGES OF EUROPE
In the 19th Century

MILES 0   50   100   200   300

Boundaries after 1922.

GERMANY, ITALY,
AND ENGLAND TO 1870

▶ MAPS ON PAGES 97, 98, AND 99

THE NINETEENTH CENTURY in Europe was a period of national consolidation, generally accompanied by the growth of representative government. These developments came with the increasing consciousness of nationality as defined by language, the improvement of overland communications by railway and telegraph, and the desire for an enlarged state as a vehicle of political rights (see pages 94–95 and 102). The maps on pages 98 and 99 show the German and Italian states as they existed after 1815 and were respectively combined a half-century later.

The Unification of Italy

▶ MAP ON PAGE 99

Cavour, minister to the king of Sardinia, backed by the France of Napoleon III, went to war with Austria in 1859 to drive Austria and its influence out of all Italy. Victories were won at Magenta and Solferino, but the French withdrew, so that Cavour was at first able only to annex Lombardy to Sardinia, and had to leave Venetia to the Austrians. His success encouraged liberals and revolutionaries all over the peninsula. In the Two Sicilies native revolutionaries were assisted by Garibaldi and his armed band who embarked from Genoa. All governments south of the Po collapsed, except that the pope, protected by France, was able to maintain his temporal power in the city of Rome and its environs until 1870. Plebiscites in 1860 in all the revolutionized areas expressed a wish for union with Sardinia. In 1861 representatives from all Italy except Rome and Venetia proclaimed the Kingdom of Italy under the House of Savoy. In return, however, for French recognition, Savoy proper (a French-speaking area) and the city and county of Nice were ceded to France. Italy annexed Venetia in 1866 and Rome in 1870, when Austria and France were weakened by war with Prussia.

The Unification of Germany

▶ MAP ON PAGE 98

Bismarck, minister to the king of Prussia, in alliance with Austria, went to war with Denmark in 1864 over Schleswig-Holstein. Disputes arising over these two duchies, Bismarck threw the blame on Austria. In 1866 Prussia fought the Seven Weeks' War against Austria and the other German states. Prussia won at the battle of Sadowa (Königgrätz); Bismarck dethroned the rulers of Hanover, Hesse-Kassel, and Nassau, annexing their territories to Prussia. He also annexed Schleswig, Holstein, Lauenburg, and the free city of Frankfurt. With Prussia, now much enlarged, he joined the surviving states north of the Main River in a North German Confederation. Bavaria, Württemberg, Baden, and the southern part of Hesse-Darmstadt remained outside this confederation. Bismarck played upon their fears of France, which now took belated steps to prevent German unification. Prussia easily won

the ensuing War of 1870 (the Franco-Prussian War); the south German states joined the North German Confederation to form the German empire. Alsace and part of Lorraine were taken from France and annexed.

Bismarck's empire, which lasted until 1918, was essentially a federation of crowned heads, with the king of Prussia as hereditary emperor; there were no popular plebiscites, as in Italy, by which the people themselves were deemed to have established their form of government. Cavour's Italy was a unitary kingdom, not a federal one, since all governments except that of Sardinia had been wiped out by revolution. In the German empire the chief minister was responsible to the emperor, not to parliament, but there was universal suffrage for the federal lower house. Italy was a parliamentary monarchy with a responsible ministry, but with very limited suffrage until the First World War.

The Magyars of Hungary also profited from the Austrian defeats of 1859 and 1866. In 1867 the Austrian empire converted itself into the Dual Monarchy of Austria-Hungary (see page 174), a compromise by which the Austrian Germans recognized the Magyars as equals, each ruling over subordinate nationalities within their frontiers.

The English Reform Bill of 1832

▶ MAP ON PAGE 97

The map shows the counties or shires of England, which have not changed appreciably since the tenth century. It also reduces to simple terms the great Reform Bill of 1832. From the origins of Parliament in the thirteenth century down to 1832 there had never been any general rearrangement of representation in the House of Commons. Each English county sent two members to the House. Towns having the right to be represented were called boroughs; most boroughs sent two members each. Many old boroughs had declined or failed to grow since the Middle Ages. Many rapidly growing towns, like Manchester, were not boroughs, and hence were represented only through their county members. Population had also grown substantially in the north, where before the eighteenth century it had always been very thin.

The map shows the net effect of the Reform Bill. The figure within each county shows the number of seats in the House of Commons (both county and borough seats) gained or lost by that county. Note that almost all losses were in the south, and that almost all gains were in the Midlands and in the north, where population was accumulating in the course of the Industrial Revolution (see page 101). The abolition of decayed boroughs made seats available for redistribution without increasing the size of the House.

The Reform Bill of 1832 marked a great social transformation, not because it enlarged the electorate, which it did only slightly, but because by its redistribution of seats it shared political power between the landed aristocracy and the new business interests of Lancashire and the Midlands. Democratization began with the Reform Bill of 1867, by which about a third of adult males in the United Kingdom received the vote.

ENGLISH REFORM BILL 1832

MILES 0 — 25 — 50 — 100

Counties gaining six or more county and borough members of the House of Commons in 1832

Counties gaining five or less

Counties sustaining a net loss through reduction of boroughs and those sustaining no net change are unshaded.

SCOTLAND

NORTHUMBERLAND +3

CUMBERLAND +3

DURHAM +6

WEST-MORLAND -1

NORTH RIDING 0

Y O R K

EAST RIDING -1

WEST RIDING +6

LANCASHIRE +11

CHESHIRE +7

DERBY +2

NOTTING-HAM +2

LINCOLN +1

STAFFORD +8

W A L E S

SHROPSHIRE 0

LEICESTER +2

RUT-LAND 0

NORFOLK 0

HEREFORD -1

WOR-CESTER +2

WARWICK +4

NORTH-HAMPTON -1

HUNTING-DON 0

CAM-BRIDGE +1

SUFFOLK -5

MON-MOUTH 0

GLOUCESTER +5

OXFORD 0

BUCKING-HAM -3

BEDFORD 0

HERTFORD +1

ESSEX +4

MIDDLE-SEX +4

BERKSHIRE 0

WILTSHIRE -15

SURREY -3

KENT 0

SOMERSET -4

HAMPSHIRE -7

SUSSEX -10

DEVON -4

DORSET -6

CORNWALL -28

FRANCE

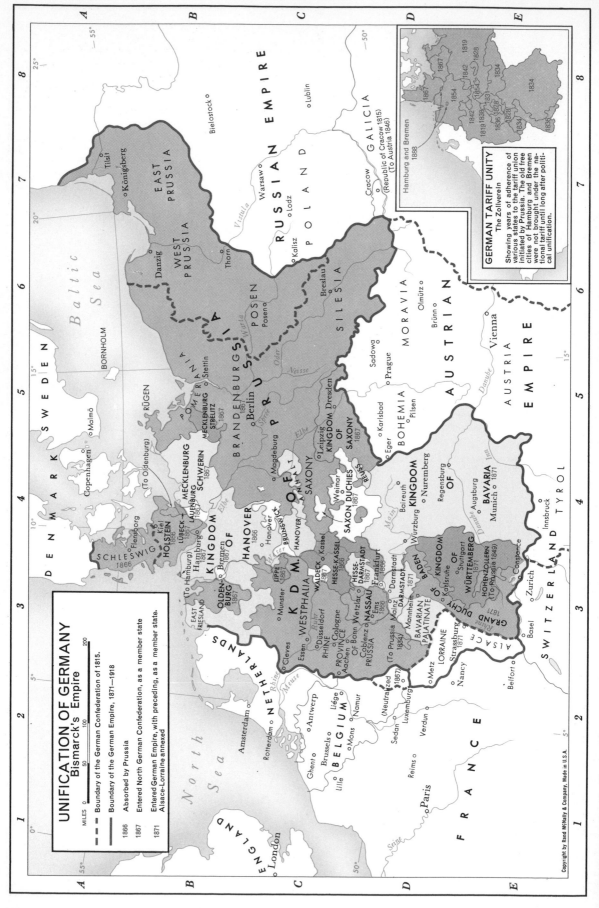

UNIFICATION OF GERMANY
Bismarck's Empire

MILES 0   50   100   200

- - - - Boundary of the German Confederation of 1815.
———— Boundary of the German Empire, 1871—1918

1866 Absorbed by Prussia
1867 Entered North German Confederation, as a member state.
1871 Entered German Empire, with preceding, as a member state.
Alsace-Lorraine annexed

GERMAN TARIFF UNITY
The Zollverein

Showing years of adherence of
various states to the tariff union
initiated by Prussia. The old free
cities of Hamburg and Bremen
were not brought under the national tariff until long after political unification.

Republic of Cracow (1815)
(To Austria 1846)

Hamburg and Bremen
1888

Copyright by Rand McNally & Company, Made in U.S.A.

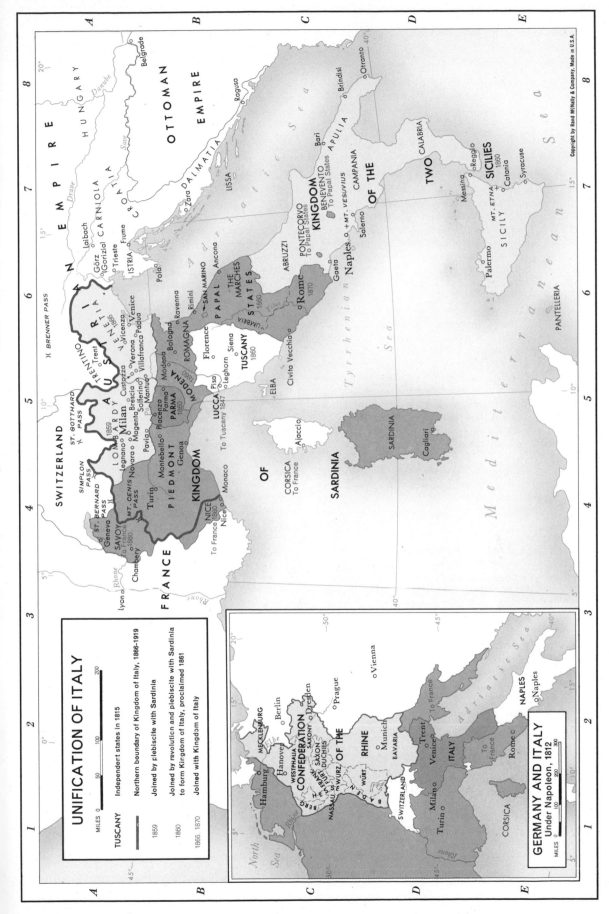

UNIFICATION OF ITALY

MILES 0   50   100   200

Independent states in 1815

Northern boundary of Kingdom of Italy, 1866-1919

TUSCANY
1859   Joined by plebiscite with Sardinia

1860   Joined by revolution and plebiscite with Sardinia to form Kingdom of Italy, proclaimed 1861

1866 1870   Joined with Kingdom of Italy

GERMANY AND ITALY
Under Napoleon, 1812

MILES 0 100 200 300

Copyright by Rand McNally & Company, Made in U.S.A.

INDUSTRIAL REVOLUTION IN ENGLAND

▶ MAP ON PAGE 101

ENGLAND WAS THE FIRST COUNTRY to be industrialized. Although the propriety of the term Industrial Revolution has often been questioned, some of the changes between 1750 and 1850 were so sweeping that no other term seems to describe them.

England in 1750

In 1750 the population of England, without Wales or Scotland, was less than 6,000,000. The largest single industry was the production of woolen cloth. It was organized by capitalistic methods, but carried on by spinners and weavers using handicraft methods mainly in their own homes. Hence the woolen industry was widely dispersed throughout agricultural districts, though with areas of concentration as shown on the map for 1750. The smelting and working of iron was carried on at small forges in many parts of the country. Cotton goods, originally imported from India, were only beginning to be produced. The west of England was a hive of industry and population; the north was still undeveloped. Since industrial processes, such as spinning, weaving, and metalworking, took place mostly in the country, there was no correlation between industrial activity and urbanization. Outside of London, no English city had as many as 50,000 inhabitants. Many Continental states, industrially less advanced than England, had great urban agglomerations. Seville and Barcelona, Naples and Milan, Prague and Warsaw, half-a-dozen cities in France and another half-dozen in Germany, were larger than any city in England—excepting always London (for size of cities, see the Appendix).

England had, however, in 1750, an accumulation of capital from commerce and agriculture seeking profitable investment, extensive markets built up by colonial and naval successes, and a merchant marine which already numbered, with the Scotch, about 8,000 ships. These conditions created an incentive to increase production for sale in the markets of the world. A series of inventions in spinning, weaving, mining, and metalworking, together with the improvement of the steam engine as a source of power, made this increase possible. Steam was first used to pump the water from coal mines; it was then applied to spinning machinery in the 1780's, and successfully used in "locomotive" engines after 1800.

England in 1850

The use of power-driven machinery required the assembling of workers in factories, or "mills" as they were called. This was accomplished most easily in the new cotton trade, where there were no established routines and interests to overcome. The cotton industry, as measured by the import of raw cotton, grew two hundred fold in the years from 1750 to 1850. Concentration into factories was more difficult in the old woolen industry, and

was accomplished with great suffering to workers whose handicrafts were destroyed. By 1850 woolens as well as cottons were produced in factories, and the textile factories were highly localized in Lancashire and the West Riding of Yorkshire (for counties, see page 97), since they were dependent for power upon coal. The iron industry, also, as it grew in scale and turned increasingly to mechanization, became concentrated near the coal fields. To facilitate internal transportation of coal, iron ore, raw materials, manufactures, and food, many canals were built after 1750 (see page 15), and railways after 1830. The west country became a byway, as population became concentrated in the Midlands, where large factory towns arose. Manchester and Liverpool in 1850 were among the largest cities in Europe, and were the most purely industrial. The total population of England, without Wales or Scotland, jumped threefold to 17,000,000 in 1850. England in 1850 was by far the most highly urbanized country of Europe (see page 102).

The Agricultural Revolution

These changes could not have occurred without corresponding changes in agriculture, by which more food was produced with fewer people laboring in the fields. By the "enclosure movement," which reached its height about 1800, old common fields were converted to private property and small private holdings were merged into larger ones. The unit of agricultural enterprise was thus enlarged, more land was brought under cultivation, and well-to-do landowners were able to invest capital and introduce new methods in farming. Meat animals became heavier; crop yields were increased. The map shows the area where enclosure of common fields was most significant. It will be seen that this region, which became one of England's richest farming districts, complements and adjoins the industrial district to the west. Even with these changes, however, England became habitually dependent on the importation of food shortly before 1800.

Political Changes

The agricultural revolution strengthened and enriched the old landowning aristocracy. Industrial growth did the same for the business class. Political conflict between these two groups was resolved by the Reform Bill of 1832 (see page 97), which by enfranchising the new manufacturing towns sent more spokesmen for modern industry to the House of Commons. In 1846, by the repeal of the Corn Laws, or protective tariff on agriculture, the business class scored another victory over the landowners. England entered upon a program of free trade, committing itself to a way of life in which, as the "workshop of the world," it depended for its existence on food and new materials from overseas. England in 1850 was the one truly industrialized country (see page 102), and so enjoyed the unique advantages of its great Victorian era.

Southwestern Scotland and the city of Glasgow also became highly industrialized before 1850. The south Wales industrial area reached its full development a little later.

INDUSTRIAL REVOLUTION IN ENGLAND 1750-1850

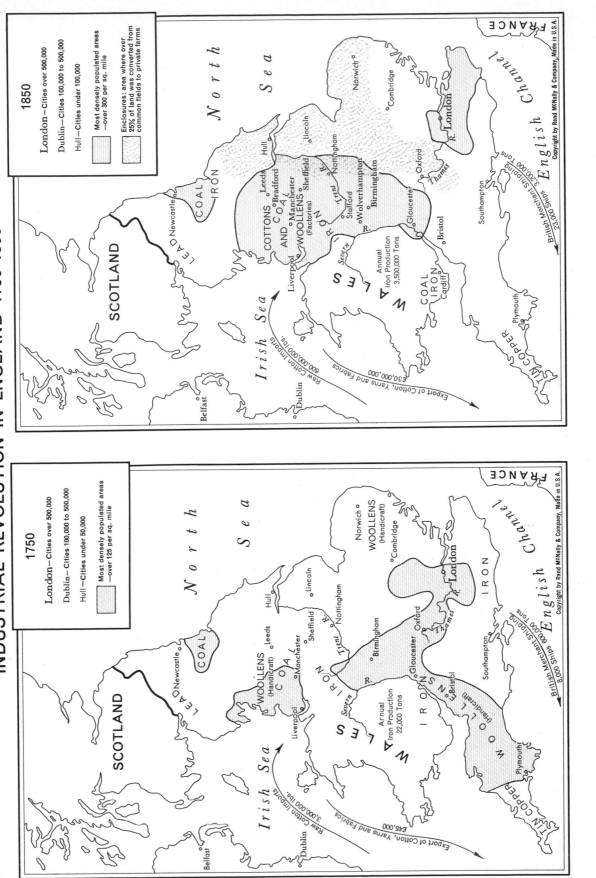

1850

London—Cities over 500,000
Dublin—Cities 100,000 to 500,000
Hull—Cities under 100,000

Most densely populated areas
—over 300 per sq. mile

Enclosures: area where over
25% of land was converted from
common fields to private farms

1750

London—Cities over 500,000
Dublin— Cities 100,000 to 500,000
Hull—Cities under 50,000

Most densely populated areas
—over 125 per sq. mile

101

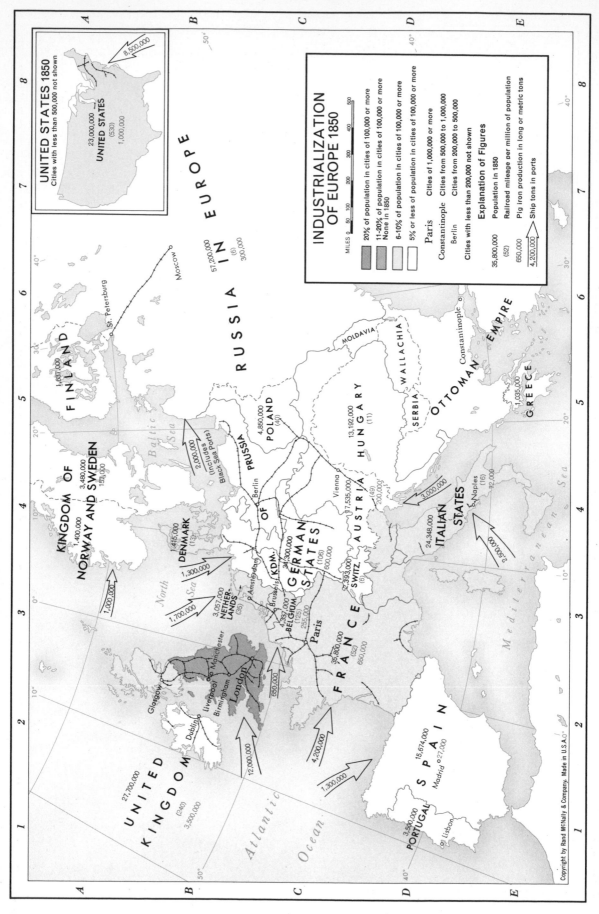

INDUSTRIALIZATION OF EUROPE 1850

UNITED STATES 1850
Cities with less than 500,000 not shown

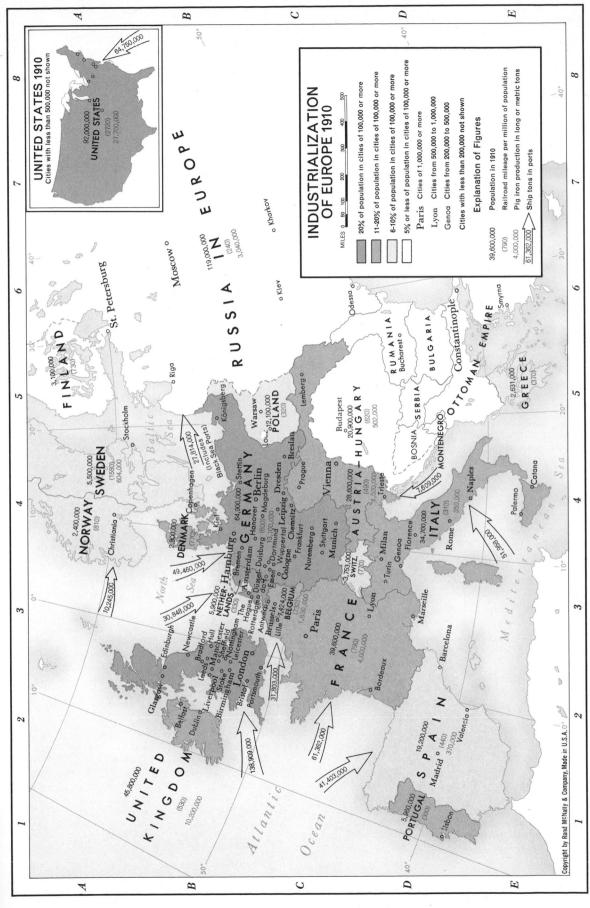

UNITED STATES 1910
Cities with less than 500,000 not shown

64,750,000

UNITED STATES
92,000,000
(2720)
27,700,000

INDUSTRIALIZATION
OF EUROPE 1910

MILES 0 50 100 200 300 400 500

20% of population in cities of 100,000 or more
11-20% of population in cities of 100,000 or more
6-10% of population in cities of 100,000 or more
5% or less of population in cities of 100,000 or more

Paris Cities of 1,000,000 or more
Lyon Cities from 500,000 to 1,000,000
Genoa Cities from 200,000 to 500,000
Cities with less than 200,000 not shown

Explanation of Figures

39,600,000 Population in 1910
(790) Railroad mileage per million of population
4,000,000 Pig iron production in long or metric tons
61,362,000 Ship tons in ports

EUROPE

IN

RUSSIA

Moscow 119,000,000
(240)
3,040,000

Kharkov

Kiev

St. Petersburg

FINLAND
3,100,000
(730)

Riga

Odessa

RUMANIA
Bucharest

BULGARIA

SERBIA

BOSNIA

MONTENEGRO

Constantinople

OTTOMAN EMPIRE

Smyrna

GREECE
2,631,000
(370)

SWEDEN
5,500,000
(1680)
604,000

Stockholm

Baltic Sea

Königsberg

Warsaw
POLAND
(320)

Breslau

Lodz 12,100,000

Budapest
20,900,000
(620)
502,000

AUSTRIA—HUNGARY
28,600,000
(490)
4,500,000

Vienna

Prague

7,609,000

Trieste

Lemberg

27,814,000
(Includes Black Sea Ports)

Copenhagen
DENMARK
(770)

Kiel

2,800,000

Stettin

GERMANY
64,900,000
(600)
13,100,000

Berlin
Hamburg
Bremen Hanover Magdeburg
Dresden
Leipzig
Dortmund Wuppertal Chemnitz
Essen Cologne
Düsseldorf Frankfurt
Duisburg
Nuremberg
Stuttgart
Munich

NORWAY
2,400,000
(810)

Christiania

NETHER-
LANDS
5,900,000
(330)

Amsterdam
The
Hague
Rotterdam
Antwerp
Brussels
Lille
BELGIUM
7,424,000
(1330)

Strasbourg

SWITZ.
3,753,000
(770)

Milan
Turin
Genoa
Florence

ITALY
34,700,000
(310)
330,000

Rome

Naples

Palermo

Catana

10,245,000

30,848,000

49,460,000

31,803,000

Edinburgh
Glasgow
Belfast
Dublin
Newcastle
Bradford
Leeds
Liverpool Hull
Manchester
Sheffield
Stoke
Birmingham Nottingham
Leicester
London
Bristol
Portsmouth

UNITED
KINGDOM
45,800,000
(530)
10,200,000

138,909,000

FRANCE
39,600,000
(790)
4,000,000

Paris
1,566,000

Lyon

Bordeaux

Marseille

61,362,000

41,403,000

SPAIN
19,200,000
(440)
370,000

Madrid

Valencia

Barcelona

PORTUGAL
5,960,000
(330)

Lisbon

North Sea

Atlantic Ocean

Mediterranean Sea

THE INDUSTRIALIZATION OF EUROPE: THE RAILROAD AGE, 1850–1910

▶ MAPS ON PAGES 102 AND 103

THE WESTERN WORLD as recently as the middle of the nineteenth century, except for England, was still basically preindustrial. Although modern capitalism, science, and technology had been developing for centuries, most countries were still predominantly rural. Cities with more than 200,000 people were rare. Two generations, the brief period of about sixty years preceding the First World War, saw the momentous transformation of industrialism and urbanization. The changes are shown in the two maps of Europe on pages 102 and 103, which should be read in comparison with each other.

Indices of Industrialization

Urbanization, or the degree to which people live in large cities, is widely regarded as one index to a modern or industrial society. Hence the color scheme on these two maps shows degree of urbanization, here defined as the proportion of a country's population living in cities of 100,000 or more inhabitants. Total population of each country, at both dates, is shown in the figure appearing above the country's name. Another index to "modernity," especially for this period, is mileage of railway track; this mileage, in proportion to population, is shown for various countries in parentheses below their names. Railway lines are shown on the 1850 map; in 1910 they were so dense that they are not shown at all. Production of iron is likewise indicated; in 1910 it was steel production that gave a country industrial power, but the figures given for 1910 are for pig iron, to maintain comparability with those for 1850. Volume of maritime tonnage, ships and cargoes combined, moving annually in and out of the ports of various countries, is also shown.

Europe in 1850

The first thing to strike the eye is the unique position of England in 1850. At this time England was the only country to have over 20 per cent of its people in large cities; no other had more than 10 per cent. It produced half the world's iron. It already had a railway network, with over twice as much mileage in proportion to population as any other European country. Its ports cleared more ocean tonnage than those of France, Germany, Italy, and the Low Countries combined. Its population had trebled in a hundred years. On such facts were based the international leadership of England at the time, the growth of the British Empire and the world market centering about British free trade.

France in 1850, as ever since the Middle Ages, was still the most populous country under a single government west of Russia. It still produced more iron than all the German states without Austria. Germany, however, was taking more initiative in railway development than France. Though still divided politically, it had the most complete railway net outside of England and Belgium. With continuous track from the Atlantic to Warsaw and from south of Vienna to Hamburg, Germany in 1850 could benefit from its central position and stood on the eve of sudden and enormous growth. As for railways in other countries about 1850, note that Moscow and St. Petersburg were connected with each other, but not yet with western Europe; that in France Paris was not yet connected with the Mediterranean; that railway building had barely begun in Italy; and that in the United States the Middle West still had no uninterrupted rail communication with the East.

As railroads were built, land transportation became for the first time in history as easy as transportation by water. Bulky foods, coal, and heavy raw materials could now be moved in great volume, quickly, over long distances. Manufacturing and population concentrated increasingly in cities, which could expand indefinitely because they drew food, fuel, and raw materials from distant points. Goods could be moved between the interior and the seaports in far greater quantities than ever before. Hence maritime commerce greatly expanded. Ships after 1850, like railroads, were moved by coal and made of iron, which, in turn, they could themselves transport. Railway networks and shipping lanes merged into an interlocking transportation system, with its nucleus in western Europe but reaching into all parts of the world. Europeans were increasingly fed from the American Middle West, the Argentine, or the steppes of south Russia, all of which were developed and brought into the world market by the railroad and the steamship. To obtain such imports, Europe exported its manufactures, which it often financed by loans and investments, that is, by the export of capital. It was also the age of mass emigration from Europe.

Expansion from 1850 to 1910

The profound changes made in sixty years are apparent when the two maps are compared. First to be noticed is the extraordinary expansion; second, the changes in urbanization; third, the changed relative position of various countries.

As for expansion, population grew rapidly everywhere, though less in countries like England and France which had seen their greatest rate of increase before 1850. Iron production multiplied threefold in England, sixfold in France, twenty-six fold in Germany. Ocean tonnage expanded almost twelvefold for the United Kingdom, and even more for the Continent (because of the railroads)—fifteen times for France and Russia, twenty times for Italy, over thirty times for Germany, and almost as much for Holland and Belgium, the gateways to Germany and the Continent. When it is considered that Europe was not a new country, like the United States, that it was receiving no immigrants but was supplying them instead, its economic growth in these years is even more astounding than that of the United States.

The Cities

The cities of Europe in 1850 stood in much the same relation, in size, to each other as in the eighteenth century (for city populations see the

Appendix). London was the giant, with more than 2,000,000 inhabitants; Paris had 1,000,000; but no other city, even in England, had as many as 500,000. Paris was over five times bigger than the next largest French city, a fact which helps to explain its influence in the revolutionary movements of 1830 and 1848. Such excessive predominance of a single super city marks an early phase of modern urbanization (sociologists have observed the same phenomenon in the mid-twentieth century in southeast Asia). On our map of Europe in 1850, which shows only cities of 200,000 or more, no French city except Paris appears, no Italian city except Naples, no German cities except Vienna and Berlin, all, it should be noted, political capitals as well as economic centers. The coloring for 1850 shows Germany as no more urbanized than Russia; this is misleading, since Germany had many busy small towns, but the truth is that Germany, like Russia, had less than 5 per cent of its population in cities of more than 100,000 in 1850.

By 1910 the whole urban picture of Europe was different. London still led, and Paris came second, but Berlin and Vienna also had 2,000,000 people, and secondary cities of considerable size were numerous in all economically developed countries, notably England and Germany. They were particularly close together in the coal and iron districts of the English Midlands (from Birmingham to Leeds on the map) and the Ruhr valley in Germany, the area running about fifty miles east of Düsseldorf.

Geographical Distribution

The 1910 map reveals a highly urbanized industrial nucleus about the North Sea, surrounded very roughly by concentric rings in declining order of urbanization.

England in 1910 no longer enjoyed its unique position of 1850. Germany and the Netherlands now had, like England, over 20 per cent of their people in cities of more than 100,000. All countries of western and northern Europe, except the maritime Netherlands, now had more railway track per capita than Great Britain. British ocean tonnage was still vast, and still more than double that of any other country, but its predominance was less inordinate than in 1850. Germany now, in 1910, produced more iron and steel than England, and over three times as much as France. This was due chiefly to the development of the Ruhr valley, and in lesser degree to the fact that Germany between 1871 and 1918 possessed the valuable iron fields of Lorraine.

The 1910 map also shows the difference between western and eastern Europe. Every country west of Russia and Hungary was more highly urbanized in 1910 than in 1850, as may be seen by differences in color on the two maps. Russia, before the Revolution of 1917, had made great strides in industrialization; it had built many railroads, it took active part in maritime commerce, and it produced ten times as much iron in 1910 as in 1850. Nevertheless, by comparison with western Europe at the time, or with the Soviet Union some decades later, Russia was still undeveloped.

Consequences of Industrialization

Industrialism and urbanism produced serious social problems, to which solutions were proposed in this period by the growing socialist parties and the beginnings of the welfare state. The economic primacy of Europe, never greater than in these sixty years, made possible the imperialism by which much of Asia and Africa was reduced to a colonial status. Even Russia, and to a lesser degree the United States, were dependent at this time on European capital and technology. An enormous emigration from Europe in these years, often called the greatest migration in history, helped to build up the United States, Canada, Latin America, Australia, New Zealand, and Asiatic Russia (see the Appendix). The radically altered position of Germany, where economic revolution reinforced the effects of political unification, was one cause of the First World War. This war, for reasons that the two maps make clear, was the first war of modern type fought between industrial countries. In general, the sense of insecurity that came from dependence on world markets, and the continuing political division among sovereign national states at a time when modern transportation had created an international economy, were among the deepest causes of the war of 1914–18 and of subsequent world problems not yet solved.

Despite the disasters that befell it after 1910, Europe continued to enjoy certain advantages of industrialization. One advantage was a high level of income in proportion to population, a figure which unfortunately cannot be computed for dates prior to the mid-twentieth century. Even after the Second World War, however, the countries of western and northern Europe enjoyed the highest income per capita in the world—except only the United States, Canada, Australia, and New Zealand.

The United States

For comparison, insets in the two maps show the United States in 1850 and in 1910. In 1850 the United States had a smaller population than France. Only 6 per cent of its people lived in towns of more than 100,000. Nevertheless, even in 1850 signs of future growth were apparent. New York, with over 600,000 people, was already larger than any European city except London and Paris. The United States already produced more iron than any country except England. Its tonnage of foreign trade was enormous, largely consisting of raw cotton in exchange for loans and manufactures. It was busily building railroads, having far more mileage per capita in 1850 than any country in the world. It was the chief beneficiary of European emigration. Results were apparent in 1910, when the United States had more people than any European country except Russia, entered along with England and Germany into the category of the most highly urbanized, still had far more railroads per capita than any other country, and produced as much iron as Germany, England, and France combined. Whereas in 1850 England produced half the world's iron, almost half (about 42 per cent) was produced in 1910 by the United States.

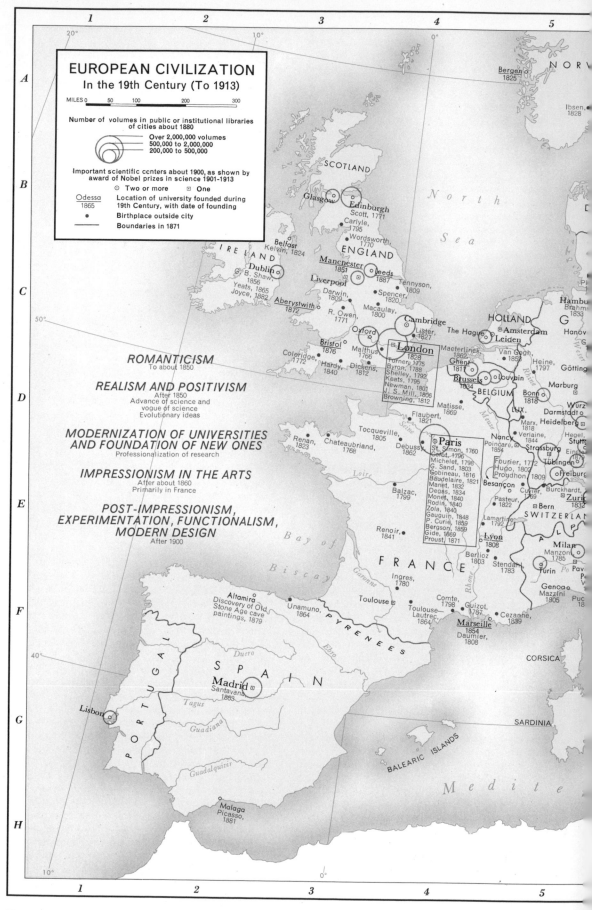

EUROPEAN CIVILIZATION
In the 19th Century (To 1913)

MILES 0 — 50 — 100 — 200 — 300

Number of volumes in public or institutional libraries
of cities about 1880

Over 2,000,000 volumes
500,000 to 2,000,000
200,000 to 500,000

Important scientific centers about 1900, as shown by
award of Nobel prizes in science 1901-1913

⊙ Two or more   ⊡ One

Odessa   Location of university founded during
1865   19th Century, with date of founding

•   Birthplace outside city

——   Boundaries in 1871

ROMANTICISM
To about 1850

REALISM AND POSITIVISM
After 1850
Advance of science and
vogue of science
Evolutionary ideas

*MODERNIZATION OF UNIVERSITIES
AND FOUNDATION OF NEW ONES*
Professionalization of research

IMPRESSIONISM IN THE ARTS
After about 1860
Primarily in France

*POST-IMPRESSIONISM,
EXPERIMENTATION, FUNCTIONALISM,
MODERN DESIGN*
After 1900

NORWAY

Bergen
1825

Ibsen,
1828

SCOTLAND

Glasgow   Edinburgh
Scott, 1771
Carlyle,
1795
Wordsworth,
1770

North
Sea

IRELAND   ENGLAND

Belfast
Kelvin, 1824
Dublin
G. B. Shaw,
1856   Manchester   Leeds
Yeats, 1865   1851   1887   Tennyson,
Joyce, 1882   Liverpool   1809
Aberystwith   Darwin,   Spencer,
1872   1809   1820
R. Owen,   Macaulay,
1771   1800
Cambridge
Oxford   Lister,
Coleridge,   1627
1772   Malthus,   London
Bristol   1766   1828
1876   Hardy,   Dickens,   Turner, 1775
1840   1812   Byron, 1788
Shelley, 1792
Keats, 1795
Newman, 1801
J. S. Mill, 1806
Browning, 1812

HOLLAND
The Hague   Amsterdam
Leiden
Maeterlinck,
1862   Van Gogh,
Ghent   1853   Heine,
1817   1797
Brussels   Louvain
1834   BELGIUM   Bonn
LUX.   1818
Marx,
1818   Heidelberg
Verlaine,
1844   Hegel,
Nancy   Strassburg
Poincaré,   1854
Matisse,   Tübingen
1869   Fourier, 1772
Flaubert,   Hugo, 1802   Freiburg
1821   Proudhon, 1809
Tocqueville,   Besançon
1805   Paris   Cuvier,   Burckhardt,
Renan,   Debussy,   St. Simon, 1760   1769   Zurich
1823   Chateaubriand,   1862   Corot, 1796   1832
1768   Michelet, 1798   Pasteur,
G. Sand, 1803   1822   Bern
Gobineau, 1816   SWITZERLAND
Baudelaire, 1821
Balzac,   Manet, 1832
1799   Degas, 1834   Lamartine   Milan
Monet, 1840   1792   1785
Rodin, 1840   Lyon   Turin
Renoir,   Zola, 1840   1808   Genoa
1841   Gauguin, 1848   Berlioz   Mazzini
P. Curie, 1859   1803   Stendhal   1805
Bergson, 1859   1783
Gide, 1869   FRANCE
Proust, 1871
Ingres,
1780   Comte,
Toulouse   1798   Guizot,
Toulouse-   1787   Cezanne,
Altamira   Lautrec,   1839
Discovery of Old   1864   Marseille
Stone Age cave   Unamuno,   PYRENEES   1854
paintings, 1879   1864   Daumier,
1808
CORSICA

PORTUGAL   SPAIN
Duero   Madrid
Santavana,
Tagus   1863
Lisbon   SARDINIA
Guadiana

Guadalquivir
BALEARIC ISLANDS

Malaga   Mediterranean
Picasso,
1881

Hamburg
Brahms,
1833
Hanover
Göttingen
Marburg
Würzburg
Darmstadt
Stuttgart
Einstein

Po
Pavia
Puccini,
1858

Bay of
Biscay

Loire

Seine

Meuse

Rhine

Garonne

Rhone

6   7   8   9   10

20°

Sibelius,
1865

Björnson,
1832

Helsinki
1828

30°

St. Petersburg

A

Upsala

SWEDEN

Stockholm
1878

Strindberg,
1849

Stravinsky,
1882

Rimsky Korsakov,
1844

Dorpat
1802

Mussorgsky,
1835

Bakunin,
1814

Gorki,
1868

Moscow
Pushkin, 1799
Dostoievsky, 1821
Kropotkin, 1842

Baltic Sea

K

Copenhagen
Kierkegaard,
1813

Dvina

R U S S I A

Tolstoy,
1828

Lenin,
1870
(200 miles
east)

B

Danzig
Schopenhauer,
1788

Niemen

Mickiewicz,
1798

Turgeniev,
1818

Tchaikovsky,
1840
(In the Urals)

C

M A N Y

Berlin
1809

Oder

Tieck,
1773

Vistula

Warsaw
Chopin, 1810
Mme. Curie,
1867

50°

Volga

enbuttel

Halle

Fichte,
1762,

Leipzig
Wagner,
1813

Dresden

Breslau

Freytag,
1816

Hauptmann,
1862

Cracow

C A R P A T H I A N S

Dniester

Gogol,
1809

Kharkov
1804

Dnieper

D

Prague

Freud,
1856

A U S T R I A

Dvorak,
1841

ch

Vienna
Schubert, 1797
J. Strauss, 1825

Budapest

Cluj
1872

Jassy
1860

Odessa
1865

E

H U N G A R Y

R U M A N I A

Black
Sea

nice

Belgrade
1863

Danube

Bologna

Rossini,
1792

S E R B I A

lorence

Leopardi,
1798

Adriatic Sea

Sofia
1888

O T T O M A N

F

d'Annunzio,
1863

Croce,
1866

40°

Rome

I T A L Y

Tiber

Constantinople
Robert College
(American)
1863

rrhenian
Sea

Naples

Excavations at
Troy, 1871 ff.

E M P I R E

G

Ionian
Sea

GREECE

Palermo

SICILY

Athens
1837
Schools of Classical
Archeology:
French, 1846
German, 1874
American, 1881
British, 1886
Italian, 1910

H

CRETE

Sea

30°

20°

6   7   8   9   10

EUROPEAN CIVILIZATION
IN THE NINETEENTH CENTURY

▶ MAP ON PAGES 106–07

THE MAP ON PAGES 106–07 attempts to illustrate the geography of European civilization in the century before the First World War. The zone of common culture—that is the area within which people were engaged in activities, intellectual or other, which aroused a sympathetic understanding among other people throughout the area—had now become coterminous with virtually the whole continent, including Russia (compare pages 54–55, 58–59, 70–71, 82–83). The higher culture of Russia had become Europeanized, as is suggested by the names of Russian writers and musicians well known in Europe, so that Russia is colored on this map in the same way as the rest of Europe. A musician, a scientist, and a poet appear also for Poland. On the other hand, the map exhibits the same clustering about the region of the North Sea as the map of European industrialization on page 103.

Books, Libraries, and Nobel Prizes

Books are a common feature of most civilized undertakings—literary, journalistic, scientific, or technical—and the concentration of books, in libraries available to the public, has been chosen as a significant fact of the kind that can readily be indicated on a map. Quality and extension of scientific work can hardly be plotted, but are reflected in the Nobel prizes instituted in 1901; the location of Nobel prize winners in science and medicine, at the time of winning the prize, can also be shown on a map. The number of books and of Nobel prize winners may serve as an index to intensity and distribution of civilization.

By this standard London and Paris were still the main centers of European civilization in the nineteenth century. Each city (and no other) had over 2,000,000 volumes in its libraries in 1880. Germany, with its numerous old capitals and university towns, was full of libraries of middling and smaller size, as was Italy to a lesser degree. Germany, Italy, France, Britain, Belgium, and Holland were still the regions where civilization was, so to speak, most dense—as in the Middle Ages (see pages 54–55). East of Germany and south of the Pyrenees one had to travel a good many miles to find a large collection of books, or to meet anyone who had received a Nobel prize.

The extraordinary centralization that had become characteristic of France is apparent. Almost half the literary and artistic notables shown for France were born in Paris, to which those born in the provinces were attracted also. No other country showed so great a concentration. Paris could boast of over 2,000,000 volumes in libraries, but no other French city had as many as 200,000. Paris had nine Nobel prize winners from 1901 to 1913, more than any other city of Europe; but there were only two others in all France, one at Nancy

and one at Toulouse. Germany, on the other hand, revealed its scientific strength in thirteen Nobel prize winners (to France's eleven), of whom five were in Berlin, the others distributed throughout the country. Holland with five Nobel prizes had more than any other country in proportion to population. In England Cambridge could claim two Nobel prizes by 1913; London, Manchester, and Liverpool, one each; Oxford, a stronghold of the older learning, none.

Universities

The modernization and spread of universities were also significant items. Older universities were modernized, as at Cambridge, to accommodate the new sciences. New ones were founded either to encourage newer scientific and social studies, as at the University of London, or to make higher education more easily available to the people, as at the universities of Manchester, Liverpool, or Marseille; or, in addition to these reasons, to stimulate national culture and civilization themselves, as in eastern Europe, at Helsinki, Dorpat, Kharkov, Odessa, Jassy, Cluj, Belgrade, Sofia, and Athens. The University of Berlin was founded in 1809 both to promote modern studies and to contribute to the national revival of Germany during the period of the Napoleonic empire. For the most part, outside of England, the older countries of European civilization felt little need to establish new universities after 1800.

The founding of the American Robert College at Constantinople was of some importance in the spread of Western ideas in Turkey.

The Course of Ideas

The century began with the general reaction against the Enlightenment known as romanticism, whose chief spokesmen, such as Coleridge or Victor Hugo, can be identified on the map. The nineteenth century differed also from the eighteenth in the new kind of meaning found in historical and evolutionary ideas, represented, in various ways, by the names of Hegel, Ranke, Darwin, Spencer, or the Swiss Burckhardt. It was in the nineteenth century that the ancient past, beyond what had long been known from the Bible and the Greco-Roman classics, was brought to the knowledge of Europeans; this development is suggested by the excavations at Troy and the discovery of Old Stone Age paintings in Spain. Classical archaeology flourished with the new schools at Athens.

The mid-century was characterized by "realism" in thought and the arts, itself soon followed by a variety of movements. The great impressionists revolutionized painting in France. The physical sciences were transformed by the work of Max Planck, the Curies, and Albert Einstein, to name only those shown on the map. Psychology by the end of the period had felt the influence of Freud. The industrialized, middle-class or "bourgeois" society of the day was criticized, from various points of view, by such otherwise wholly diverse personages as Thomas Carlyle, Bernard Shaw, Baudelaire, Ibsen, Karl Marx, and Friedrich Nietzsche.

RUSSIA IN THE KIEVAN
AND
MONGOL PERIODS

MILES 0 50 100   200   300   400

Russian lands lost in 10th and 11th Centuries

Kievan Russia in 1237

Western boundary of Mongol Empire

Principality of Moscow in 1462

Russia in 1533

Copyright by Rand McNally & Company, Made in U.S.A.

109

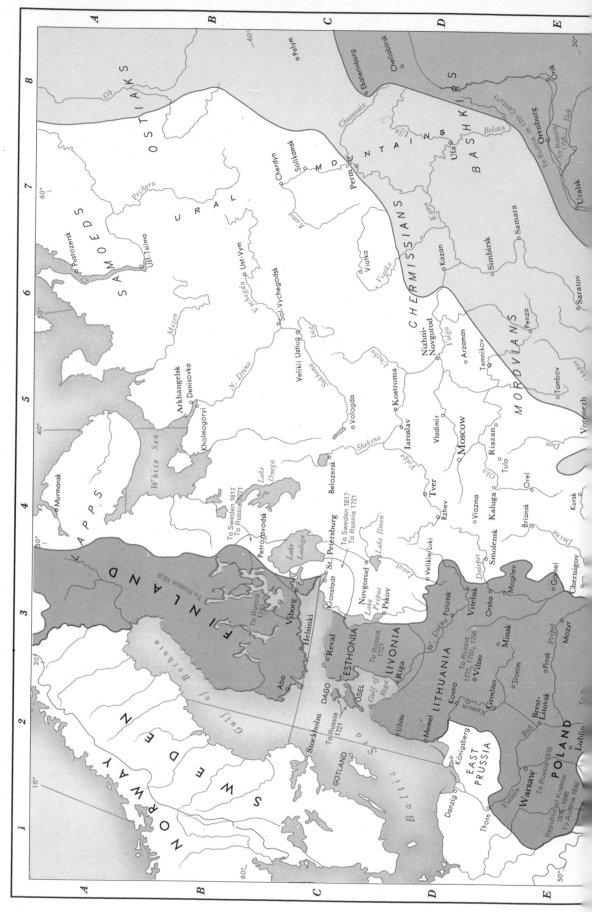

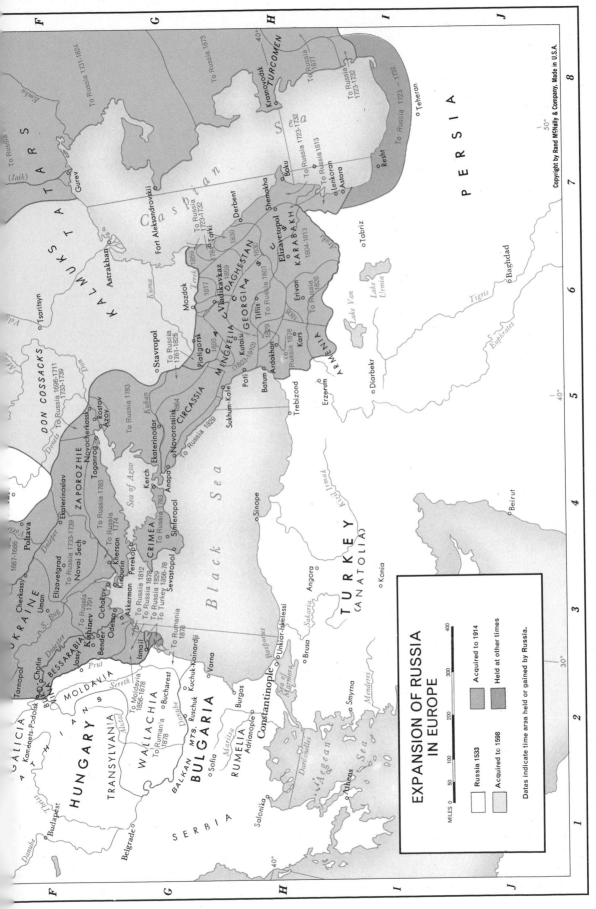

EXPANSION OF RUSSIA
IN EUROPE

| MILES 0 | 50 | 100 | 200 | 300 | 400 |

Russia 1533

Acquired to 1598

Acquired to 1914

Held at other times

Dates indicate time area held or gained by Russia.

Copyright by Rand McNally & Company, Made in U.S.A.

111

RUSSIA AND THE RUSSIAN EMPIRE

▶ MAPS ON PAGES 109, 110–11, 114, AND 115

RUSSIAN HISTORY is a story of colonization and expansion, during which the Russian people, from an original base along the Dnieper River, came to occupy or control the whole north Eurasian plain from the borders of Prussia to the Pacific Ocean. As early as the seventeenth century their state was already the largest empire in the world, reaching a third of the way around the globe at the sixtieth parallel of north latitude. Facing both Europe and Asia, yet distinct from both, the Russians were obliged to deal with the events of two continents. Until the sixteenth century their problems came mainly from Asia; thereafter, the rivalries of Europe engaged their strength and attention.

Over 150 languages are spoken within the borders of what came to be the Russian empire. Linguistic groups west of the Urals and the Caspian Sea are shown on page 95. The largest is the Slavic, composed of Great Russians, White Russians, and Ukrainians.

The Kievan Period
▶ MAP ON PAGE 109

Russian Slavs first appear in reliable historical records about the third century A.D., at which time they were living in what is now west-central European Russia. Much later, in the ninth century, at the time of the great expansion of the Northmen (page 45), the Viking Rurik began to unify the tribes along the Dnieper. His son Oleg, about 875, captured Kiev, which became the capital of the first Russian state. Kiev lay along the main artery of trade which ran from Constantinople and the Near East to the Baltic and northwestern Europe (page 53), so that these early Russians came into contact with Constantinople, then by far the greatest city of all Europe. From Constantinople the Russians were converted to Christianity in 988. But where Russia's neighbors—the Swedes, Poles, and Germans—embraced the Latin Christianity of Rome, Russia adopted the Greek Christianity of Constantinople. The growing separation or schism between Rome and Constantinople, usually dated from 1054, kept Russia out of touch with western Europe. New inroads of barbarians had the same effect. In the tenth and eleventh centuries the Pechenegs and the Polovtsians overran the lands north of the Black Sea, broke Russian communications with Constantinople, and forced the Russian peoples, who had moved into the steppes, back into the more northerly forest zone. Then in 1237–38 the Mongol Batu Khan, at the head of the Golden Horde, dealt the final blow to the state of Kiev.

The Mongol Period

For over two centuries, from 1238 to about 1480, Russia lay within the far-flung Mongol empire (see pages 126–27). Russia was therefore excluded from the developments in Europe during the later Middle Ages and Renaissance. On the other hand, subordination to the Mongols was fairly loose, for the Golden Horde remained essentially nomadic in political organization, so that there was little intermarriage between the Mongols and the more settled Slavs; nor did the Mongols attempt to interfere with the Christian church. The Mongols were satisfied with the payment of tribute, whose collection they eventually put in the hands of Russian princes. One of these was the prince of Moscow, who grew rich as taxgatherer for the conquerors, and emerged as the strongest political force in Russia. In 1480, by refusing further payment of tribute, Ivan III of Moscow ended the period of Mongol domination.

Muscovy

The princes of Moscow now began to build a second Russian state, replacing the older Kievan Russia destroyed by the Mongols. The wife of Ivan III was Zoë, niece of the last Byzantine emperor; and after the fall of Constantinople to the Turks, in 1453, Ivan claimed, on the basis of this relationship, the leadership of the whole Orthodox Christian world. In 1471 he subjugated Novgorod, which had built up a trading empire of its own. In 1485 he conquered Tver. Expansion continued in the next century under Ivan IV, the "Terrible." Although the Golden Horde no longer existed as a political unit, three important khanates remained —Kazan, Astrakhan, and the Crimea. Kazan fell to Ivan IV in 1552, Astrakhan four years later.

The Russian Empire in Europe
▶ MAP ON PAGES 110–11

The Time of Troubles, 1604–13, was followed by the establishment of the Romanov dynasty, which ruled until the Revolution of 1917. Russian expansion in Europe under the Romanovs is shown on the map in pink. The first step was to drive away the Poles and Swedes who had invaded Russia during the Time of Troubles. By 1667 this was accomplished, and the Russians were even able, by exploiting Ukrainian hostility to the Poles, to annex a small part of the Ukraine, including historic Kiev.

Peter the Great ascended the throne in 1689. Russia still had no access to the Black or Baltic seas, and was still harassed by stronger western neighbors. Peter began the process of conscious and deliberate Westernization, by which he aimed at the adoption of Western technical, military, and administrative methods to strengthen his state and advance his foreign policy. In foreign policy his great desire was to reach the sea. Badly defeated by the Swedish Charles XII in 1700 at Narva, he was able to destroy the Swedish invaders in 1709 at Poltava in the Ukraine. By the peace of Nystadt, in 1721, he obtained Estonia, Livonia, and the head of the Gulf of Finland, where in 1703 he founded the city of St. Petersburg, his "window to Europe." Meanwhile, he also enjoyed successes on the side toward Persia, where he occupied the western and southern shores of the Caspian; but he was unable to make headway against the Turks, for though he took Azov in 1696 he had to yield it in 1711. After his death, however, in the interval between his reign and Catherine's, Russia annexed the strategic Zaporozhie area, which gave an outlet to Azov.

Catherine the Great (1762–1796) renewed the expansion to the west and south. First, she went to war with Turkey for control of the north coast of the Black Sea. She was so successful in this war that her neighbor, Frederick of Prussia, thought the time ripe to take territory from Poland, lest Russia overturn the balance of power. Austria being also brought in, the first partition of Poland ensued in 1772 (see page 84), after which Catherine resumed her war with Turkey, concluded by the epochal Treaty of Kuchuk-Kainardji of 1774. She thereby obtained Kherson and a permanent post on the Black Sea, as well as rights to pass through the Straits (the Bosporus and Dardenelles) and to intercede with the Turkish government for Orthodox Christians in the Ottoman Empire (see page 65). In 1783 Catherine took the Crimea, and in 1791, by the Treaty of Jassy, obtained the Black Sea coast as far as the river Dniester, where the city of Odessa was modernized and rebuilt.

In the wars against the French Revolution and Napoleon, from 1792 to 1814, Russia made important gains. Catherine carried through the second and third partitions of Poland; Alexander I acquired Finland from Sweden in 1809, and Bessarabia from Turkey in 1812. Alexander also made a strong attempt to acquire the whole of the former Poland; he was obliged at the Congress of Vienna to accept a compromise, obtaining "Congress Poland," whose borders, however, carried the Russian power further west than the third partition of 1795 had done.

After 1815, and down to the First World War and the Russian Revolution, Russia annexed Circassia, Georgia, parts of Armenia, and other places in the Caucasus, but it expanded no further in the direction of western Europe, except that from 1829 to 1856 and again from 1878 to the First World War it held a small area controlling the northern mouth of the Danube.

The Russian Empire in Asia
▶ MAP ON PAGE 115

Russian expansion had always gone on simultaneously eastward and westward. Europeans, as they became familiar with Russia in the eighteenth century, found it hard to imagine what Russia was like on the "other" side; and even today it is not always realized that the Russians reached the Pacific Ocean in the years when the English were founding New England.

Sibir, the capital of the Siberian khanate, another leftover from the Mongol empire, was subjugated by the Russians in 1581. Government officials, private merchants and adventurers pushed across the Urals. In northern Asia—that is, Siberia—the main incentive was economic, to find the rich sables which commanded princely prices in European markets. In the eighty years following 1581 expansion across Siberia was very rapid. It followed the four great river systems—the Ob-Irtysh, the Enisei, the Lena, and their tributaries—which were separated only by low rolling hills. As early as 1598 the Russians were well beyond the Ob. Tomsk was founded in 1604, Yakutsk in 1632, Okhotsk on the Pacific in 1649. It was not until the eighteenth century, however, that the Pacific region was assimilated into the empire, Kamchatka being annexed by 1732, the eastern tip of Eurasia by 1800. Meanwhile Bering had conducted his explorations, which are shown on page 132. Soon after 1800 the Russian American Company carried the search for furs to Alaska, and reached as far south as Fort Ross on the California coast.

In their rapid crossing of northern Asia the Russians very early collided with China. In Siberia they had met only with weak and primitive tribes. In the Amur valley they entered territory claimed by the Chinese empire, with its old culture and tightly-knit organization. By the treaty of Nerchinsk of 1689 the Russians had to give up their stations in the Amur region to China. Not until the nineteenth century, when China had been weakened by war with Britain and France and by internal disorder, were the Russians able to make advances in this direction. They then annexed the areas north of the Amur and east of the Ussuri. In 1860 they founded Vladivostok. By 1900 Russian influence was strong in Manchuria and Korea, where it led to the Russo-Japanese War (see page 135). Meanwhile, the completion of the Trans-Siberian Railroad after 1900 gave continuous communication by rail across the Eurasian continent.

Central Asia presented different problems. Although the Russians had commercial relations with this area as early as the sixteenth century, there were no such economic allurements as the furs of the north; rivers were scanty or nonexistent, and the climate repelled Russian immigration, at least until the Soviet period. In the eighteenth century, by fortifications from Orenburg to Omsk, the government sought to hold off nomadic encroachment on the Siberian settlements. Active military operations began in the nineteenth century. The Russians took Tashkent in 1865, Bukhara in 1868, Khiva in 1873, Geok-Tepe in 1881, Merv in 1884. These thrusts greatly alarmed the British in India.

European Invasions of Russia
▶ MAP ON PAGE 114

Russia has been invaded six times by Europeans since 1700. The first invasion was that of Charles XII of Sweden, who at first won an easy victory at Narva in 1700, but was then drawn on to destruction in 1709 at Poltava, between Kiev and Kharkov. This Swedish assault hastened Peter's policy of Westernization. The second invasion of Russia was Napoleon's disastrous expedition to Moscow in 1812. The third was the Anglo-French assault in the Crimean War of 1854–56. This was dwarfed by the fourth, the German invasion during the First World War. The fifth invasion was that of the Allied powers intervening against the communist revolution: the Anglo-French-American intervention at Archangel and the Anglo-French intervention in the Black Sea region are shown on the map. American and Japanese forces at the same time landed at Vladivostok. As part of these same operations may be considered the Polish offensive of 1920 against the communist government, by which the Poles hoped to acquire for their restored Poland some of the White Russian territories that had belonged to Poland before 1793. The sixth invasion, and by far the most formidable, was that of the Germans in the Second World War. It carried them in 1942 to the gates of Moscow, to Stalingrad, and almost to the Caspian Sea.

EUROPEAN INVASIONS
OF RUSSIA

MILES 0 50 100   200   300   400

- – – – 1815 Boundaries
——— 1920 Boundaries

States colored as of 1920

INVASIONS OF RUSSIA

INVASION ROUTES
– · – · – Swedish invasions by Charles XII 1700-1709
——— Napoleon's invasion and retreat from Moscow 1812
- - - - Crimean War—Allied invasion of Evpatorlia and battle of Sevastopol

WORLD WAR I
—·—·— British, French, and U.S. intervention in Russia
▭▭▭ Deepest penetrations: (1) German 1918; (2) Polish 1920; and (3) Allied

WORLD WAR II
——— German advance to Dec. 1941
⊓⊓⊓⊓ German advance in 1942
—○—○— Russian front Dec. 1943
—●—●— Eastern front Dec. 1944

CRIMEAN WAR
✕ Allied assaults on Russian Coastal areas

Copyright by Rand McNally & Company. Made in U.S.A.

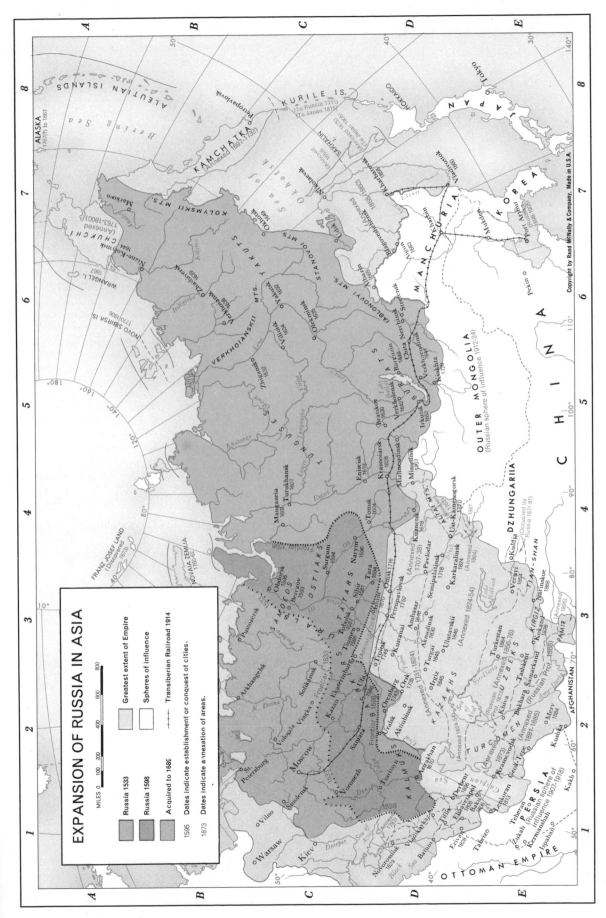

EXPANSION OF RUSSIA IN ASIA

MILES 0 100 200 400 600 800

Russia 1533	Greatest extent of Empire
Russia 1598	Spheres of influence
Acquired to 168€	

+-+-+ Transiberian Railroad 1914

1595 Dates indicate establishment or conquest of cities.

1873 Dates indicate annexation of areas.

Copyright by Rand McNally & Company, Made in U.S.A.

ANCIENT INDIA AND CHINA

▶ MAPS ON PAGES 118 AND 119

IN THE FERTILE VALLEYS of the Indus and Huang rivers, as in Mesopotamia and along the Nile, men of the Stone Age developed agriculture and a settled village life, from which in time arose cities, systems of writing, division of labor, social classes, and government (see pages 18–19). Thus these areas were independent centers of civilization, like the Near East—or Near West, as Asians might prefer to call it—in that their civilization at first grew up locally, not by transmission or diffusion from older civilized areas. The civilization generated in the two river valleys spread respectively to the regions that became the India and China of history. From India and China other parts of eastern, southern, and central Asia received their civilization until the intrusion of the more aggressive civilization of modern Europe and the West.

Indian civilization first appeared in the Indus valley in the third millennium before Christ (see page 21). It spread first into the broad valley of the Ganges, then through the rest of the Indian subcontinent, and ultimately to Ceylon, the Indo-Chinese peninsula and the principal Indonesian islands. Chinese civilization originated in the second millennium B.C. in the lower valley of the Yellow River (the Huang Ho). It spread over what is now China, and eventually into Korea, Japan, Annam in northeastern Indo-China, Mongolia, Tibet, and Turkestan. Great mountain ranges separate China from India, which have even been said to be as different from each other as either is from Europe. Nevertheless, there has been some cultural exchange between them since early times, the most important being the Buddhism which made its way from India to China by way of central Asia during the early centuries of the Christian era. India, being closer to Mesopotamia and the Mediterranean, has been influenced from that direction throughout its history. The most significant import into India from the Near East was undoubtedly Islam. The less advanced peoples of southern, central, and eastern Asia have always admired and freely borrowed from Indian and Chinese civilization, and it is significant that India and China are again reasserting their influence after a period of eclipse by the West.

A word of caution is in order on the following series of maps. Boundary indications for Asia before the modern period are not to be too literally understood, for the boundaries were often vague at the time, and the sources of our knowledge are highly uncertain.

Ancient India

▶ MAPS ON PAGE 118

The Indus valley civilization of the third millennium B.C., first revealed by archaeological excavation in the 1920's, had its main centers in the large cities of Mohenjo–daro and Harappa and was clearly ancestral to later Indian civilization. The second millennium B.C. was a period of migration of uncivilized tribes speaking Indo-European languages, who moved in upon the older civilized

centers. They included the Persians, the Greeks, and the ancestors of most Europeans (see page 93). Those who crossed the mountains into northwest India are known as Aryans. The Aryan invaders combined their own culture with that of the lands they conquered to form the Indo-Aryan civilization of the Vedic period, which expressed itself in the great poetic and philosophical literature in Sanskrit, and came to extend over the Indus River system and the Gangetic plain. Here, in the contact between alien races and cultures, were to be found the early beginnings of caste and other characteristics of later Hindu civilization.

The first millennium B.C. saw three developments in northern India of great importance. Strong kingdoms, such as Magadha and Kosala, gradually absorbed numerous small independent states. Second, two great religions appeared, beginning as movements of emancipation from, or fulfillment of, the older Hindu religion; one was Jainism, founded by Vardhamana Mahavira (540?–468? B.C.); the other was Buddhism, founded by Gautama the Buddha (563?–486? B.C.). Third, in 516 B.C. the Persians under Darius invaded the Indus valley, thus establishing channels of communication through which Persian and Greek influences came into India in the following centuries (see pages 27 and 31). In 327 B.C. Alexander the Great, having conquered the Persian Empire, led his Macedonian army into the Indus valley from the northwest, and established control over Gandhara and the territories now called the Punjab and Sind. Although Alexander's empire began to break up immediately after his death, Greek cultural influence persisted for centuries in Gandhara, as in other outposts now located in Iran and Afghanistan. Probably Alexander's main contribution to India was the welding together of loose political units, by which the way was prepared for the first great Indian empire, the Mauryan empire.

Based on Magadha in the Ganges valley, the Mauryan empire flourished from 322 B.C., when its founder Chandragupta seized the capital city of Pataliputra, to 185 B.C., when the last ruler of the dynasty died. Chandragupta united north India from the mouths of the Ganges to the watershed west of the Indus. He then took over, from a satrap of the Alexandrian empire, the regions of Arachosia and Gandhara up to the Hindu Kush mountains. His son Bindusara extended the empire to about the fifteenth parallel of latitude, except for Kalinga on the east coast, which was later annexed by Asoka. The reign of Asoka (273–232 B.C.) saw the height of the Mauryan empire, and is one of the great periods of Indian history. Shortly after the conquest of Kalinga Asoka was converted to Buddhism, whereupon, forswearing militarism, he devoted himself to the welfare of his people and the propagation of Buddhism. His missionaries brought Buddhism and Indian civilization to Ceylon and elsewhere.

The breakup of the Mauryan empire, which may have been hastened by Asoka's rejection of military force, was followed by a long period of division in India. Through the invasion routes of the northwest frontier came Greeks from Bactria, Sakas or Scythians, and Kushans, pushed in turn by the expanding Huns of inner Asia. A Kushan empire, at its height, reached from north of the Oxus River through Gandhara and the upper Indus valley into the Gangetic plain. Meanwhile, south India, the Deccan, was dominated by the Andhras, a people from its southeastern edge.

The fourth and fifth centuries of the Christian era saw the ascendancy of the Gupta empire, which occupied the whole Gangetic plain, reached west to the sea, and exercised a suzerainty over Nepal and other regions to the north and east. This was a period of great development of Hindu philosophy and of artistic and literary achievement. The Gupta empire, however, declined rapidly at the end of the fifth century after invasion by the Huns, who at this time assaulted India, as they did Europe, from their homelands in central Asia.

Ancient China

▶ MAP ON PAGE 119

Chinese civilization appears to have originated some centuries later than that of the Indus valley. There is some historical and archaeological evidence of a fairly advanced Hsia period (the so-called Black Pottery culture) in the lower Huang River valley toward the middle of the second millennium B.C. The much richer Shang (Yin) culture of the thirteenth and twelfth centuries B.C. is abundantly authenticated. The Shang possessed many of the basic elements of later Chinese civilization, including a fully developed written language and a sophisticated system of ancestor worship; and they produced bronze, sculpture, and handicrafts of the highest artistic and technical quality. Toward the end of the second millennium B.C. the city state of Shang (see inset, page 119) was conquered by the less civilized Chou people of the Wei valley. There thus occurred a phenomenon many times repeated in later Chinese history, as partly Chinified barbarians took advantage of weakness in the Middle Kingdom to occupy its rich cities and farmlands, and to become in turn the patrons and defenders of Chinese civilization.

The Chous, conquering much of the present provinces of Hupeh, Honan, Hopei, Shansi, and Shantung (for provinces see pages 123 and 131), governed through a feudal system which lasted two or three hundred years. In 771 B.C. the Chou king lost control of his feudatories. By the fifth century traditional relationships had broken down, and there followed a time of anarchy known as the Period of Warring States. This troubled era inspired the great philosophical movement of which the outstanding thinkers were K'ung Ch'iu (Confucius), Meng K'o (Mencius), Mo Ti, Chuang Chou, and Shang Yang. In the third century the virtually independent states were conquered by a relentless ruler of the semibarbaric Ch'in, located in the Wei valley, the ancient home of the Chous. Unifying China in 221 B.C., he took to himself the title of Shih Huang-ti, or First Emperor.

The Ch'in dynasty was a brief one, lasting only from 221 to 206 B.C., but it organized a strong central government, standardized weights, measures, laws, and language, and extended political control into south Manchuria and the central section of south China as far as the present Canton. It also combined and strengthened various early walls to form the Great Wall, to shield China from the Hsiung Nu, or Huns.

The Ch'in rule was severe, and shortly after the death of Shih Huang-ti the dynasty was overthrown. A crude soldier, Liu Pang, was then able to found the Han dynasty, which lasted for over four hundred years, with a brief interregnum (202 B.C.–9 A.D., 25–220 A.D.). The period before the interregnum, called the Former Han Dynasty, reached a high point under Emperor Wu (140–87 B.C.). Chinese control now extended (see page 119) not only over what we call China proper and Manchuria, but over half of Korea, Tongking, and the Tarim basin in Chinese Turkestan. Confucianism was given official preferment, scholarship flourished, and the centralized bureaucratic state, built on the Ch'in pattern, was humanized by Confucian ethics. The last century or more of the Han dynasty saw a renewal of struggle between officials, eunuchs, and consort families, with growing anarchy and oppression, which dominated Chinese life after the fall of the Han.

Since Chinese history is customarily periodized by dynasties, a list of the principal dynasties for all periods is given here for convenience. The Shang and Chou periods, though often called dynasties, were not such in the later sense; many lesser dynasties, sometimes ruling simultaneously in various parts of the country, maintained themselves in periods between the principal ones.

Ch'in—221–206 B.C.
Han—202 B.C.–9 A.D., 25–220 A.D.
T'ang—618–907.
Sung—960–1279.
Yüan (Mongol)—1279–1368.
Ming—1368–1644.
Ch'ing (Manchu)—1644–1912.

Eurasia about 200 A.D.

At the end of the Han period in China, roughly contemporary with the Roman Empire in the West, the area of civilization was as shown on pages 18–19. Between the Chinese and Roman worlds lay India and Hellenized Iran. The great civilizations remained essentially unknown to one another; but there was some communication by sea between India and the Mediterranean, and by land between China and both India and central Asia. There was enough contact for Buddhism to spread in China, and for Ptolemy of Alexandria, about 150 A.D., to devise the map of the habitable world shown on page 10. Beyond the Roman and Chinese military frontiers northern Eurasia was still barbarous, occupied by a multitude of peoples including the Huns, whose movements after 200 A.D. were to disturb all the great civilizations, as explained above and on page 41.

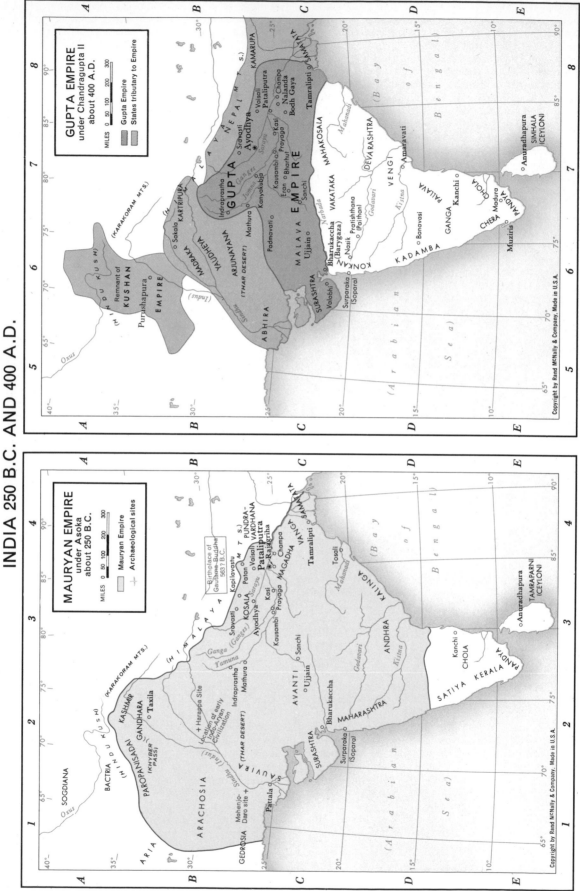

INDIA 250 B.C. AND 400 A.D.

MAURYAN EMPIRE
under Asoka
about 250 B.C.

MILES 0 50 100 200 300

Mauryan Empire
Archaeological sites

SOGDIANA
Oxus
ARIA
BACTRIA
(HINDU KUSH)
PAROPANISADAI
GANDHARA
KASHMIR
(KHYBER PASS)
Taxila
(KARAKORAM MTS.)
ARACHOSIA
Location of early
Indo-Aryan
Civilization
Harappa Site
Indraprastha
(THAR DESERT)
Mathura
Mohenjo-
Daro site
GEDROSIA
Pattala
MAURVA
Sindhu (Indus)
SURASHTRA
Surparaka
(Soparai)
Bharukaccha
MAHARASHTRA
Ujjain
AVANTI
SATIYA
KERALA
PANDYA
CHOLA
Kanchi
(H I M A L A Y A)
Ganga (Ganges)
Yamuna
Sravasti
KOSALA
Ayodhya
Kausambi
Kasi
Prayaga
Sanchi
Godavari
Krisna
ANDHRA
Birthplace of
Gautama-Buddha
563? B.C.
Kapilavastu
Patan
Vaisali
PUNDRA–
VARDHANA
MAGADHA
Pataliputra
Rajagriha
Champa
VANGA
Tamralipti
Mahanadi
Tosali
KALINGA
SAMATATA
(B a y   o f   B e n g a l)
Anuradhapura
TAMRAPARNI
(CEYLON)
(A r a b i a n   S e a)

Copyright by Rand McNally & Company. Made in U.S.A.

GUPTA EMPIRE
under Chandragupta II
about 400 A.D.

MILES 0 50 100 200 300

Gupta Empire
States tributary to Empire

(HINDU KUSH)
Remnant of
KUSHAN
Purushapura
EMPIRE
(KARAKORAM MTS.)
Sakala
KARTRIPURA
MADRAKA
YAUDHEYA
ARJUNAYANA
ABHIRA
(THAR DESERT)
(Indus)
Sindhu
SURASHTRA
Valabhi
Surparaka
(Soparai)
KONKAN
Bharukaccha
(Barygaza)
Nasik
Ujjain
MALAVA
Padmavati
Mathura
Indraprastha
Kanyakubja
Jumna
Ganges
Eran
Bharhut
Kausambi
Prayaga
Sanchi
Narbada
Nasik
Prathishthana
(Paithan)
VAKATAKA
MAHAKOSALA
Mahanadi
Godavari
Krisna
KADAMBA
Banovasi
VENGI
DEVARASHTRA
Amaravati
PALLAVA
GANGA
Kanchi
CHOLA
CHERA
Madura
PANDYA
Muziris
NEPAL
Srawasti
Ayodhya
Kasi
Vaisali
Pataliputra
Champa
Nalanda
Bodh Gaya
Tamralipti
SAMATATA
KAMARUPA
(H I M A L A Y A   M T S.)
GUPTA EMPIRE
Saryu
(B a y   o f   B e n g a l)
Anuradhapura
SIMHALA
(CEYLON)
(A r a b i a n   S e a)

Copyright by Rand McNally & Company. Made in U.S.A.

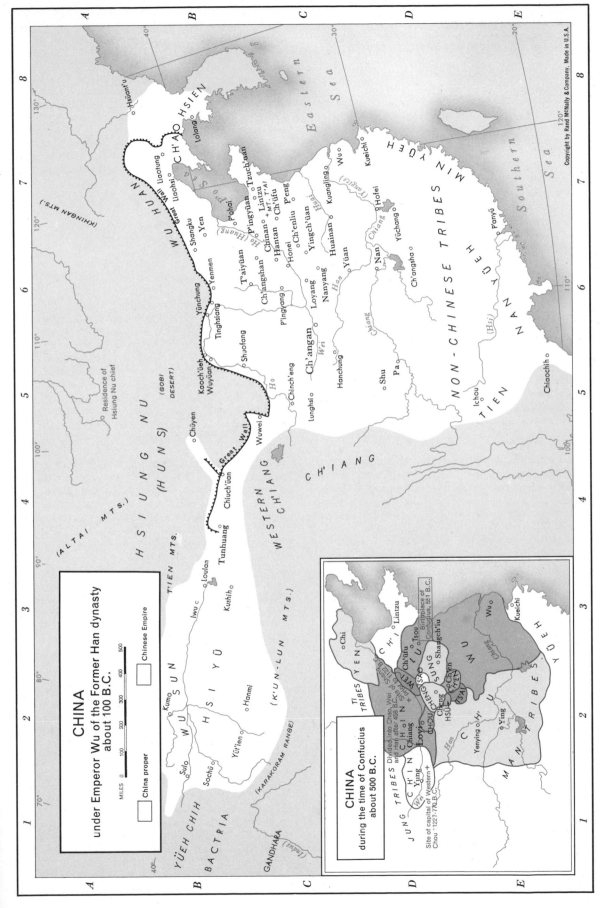

SOUTH AND EAST ASIA:
THIRD TO THIRTEENTH CENTURIES

MAPS ON PAGES 122–23 AND 124

ABOUT A MILLENNIUM PASSED from the weakening of the Han and Gupta empires, in China and India respectively, to the rise of the Mongols. Europe in this same millennium saw the general decay of ancient civilization, then a long Dark Age in which a new culture was gestated, then the birth of medieval Christian civilization (see pages 42–43, 46–47, 54–55). Asia experienced no such dramatic breakdown or new departure; indeed, during this millennium Hinduism evolved into its modern form, and the T'ang and Sung periods are still regarded as the great age of Chinese culture. In some respects, however, the developments of East and West were analogous. As civilization was extended to central, northern, and eastern Europe in the Middle Ages, so it was extended at this time to the Indo-Chinese peninsula, the Indonesian islands, and Japan. Moreover as Christianity spread to all Europe (see page 53), so Buddhism spread through east Asia; and Islam, while occupying part of Europe and being expelled from it, spread to India, central Asia, western China, and, ultimately, Indonesia. Indeed, Islam and Christianity reached the Philippine Islands about the same time, in the sixteenth century (see page 124).

India after the Gupta Empire

After the disappearance of the Gupta empire in the fifth century India remained fragmented for over a thousand years. Harsha, ruling in Kanauj from 606 to 647, controlled about the same area as the Guptas, provided a good administration, sponsored Buddhism and Hindu Brahmanism, and is counted as one of the great rulers of India; but he was murdered and his empire collapsed. Gauda, under the Pala dynasty, was a prosperous kingdom in the eighth and ninth centuries, and Kanauj was again important in the ninth and tenth; Kashmir seems to have flourished also. Moslem raids began, however, about the year 1000. By 1200, after a determined invasion by Muhammad of Ghur, the Hindu states of north India were extinguished and the foundation was laid for Moslem control. In south India the Chalukyas rose to power, and crushed the Pallavas in 740, but were in turn overcome by the Rashtrakutas, who dominated the Deccan for two hundred years. In the tenth and eleventh centuries the Cholas ruled southeastern India and Ceylon, and dominated the trade with southeast Asia. The whole first Christian millennium was in fact a great period of cultural diffusion from India to Sumatra, Java, Malaya, and what are now Siam (Thailand) and Cambodia.

Jainism and Buddhism flourished in India in the early centuries after the fall of the Guptas, but gradually lost out to the older Hinduism, until by 1200 Jainism had little influence and Buddhism had almost disappeared from its native land. Hinduism developed its characteristic beliefs and practices. Buddhism meanwhile was carried to China by way of central Asia, and Buddhism and other features of Indian civilization passed into southeast Asia.

China: The T'ang and Sung Dynasties

The fall of the Han dynasty in China was followed by disunion and barbarian invasion, as in Europe; but the barbarians, or non-Chinese, were quickly assimilated, and since civilization did not decline, but even advanced in some ways, the period, though turbulent and distressing, is not considered a Dark Age. A short-lived Sui dynasty reunited the country in 581 (like the Ch'in in 221 B.C.), but was soon followed by the T'ang (618–907). Under the T'ang, for a time, Chinese control extended farther west than ever before, but about 750 the Moslems and Tibetans drove out the Chinese, who were not to return to central Asia for another thousand years.

In the T'ang period the bureaucratic system was perfected, to operate virtually unchanged until the twentieth century. It was an age of great poetry, and of painting and sculpture, mostly Buddhist. There was extensive trade with India and with west Asia, both by the old caravan routes and by newer sea routes from Kwangchow (Canton). Foreigners from far and near poured into the T'ang capital at Ch'angan, influencing many aspects of Chinese life. It was at this time that Chinese civilization moved into Korea and Japan.

The T'ang dynasty met with increasing difficulties and was followed in the tenth century by the Sung. Harassed by non-Chinese neighbors—the Juchens and Mongols from the north, the T'ais of Nan Chao from the south—the Chinese increasingly turned in upon themselves, though maintaining overseas trade with southeast Asia and Japan. They concentrated on their own native ideas, motifs, and institutions; landscape painting was perfected, beautiful work was done in porcelain, and the invention of printing stimulated a lasting revival of neo-Confucian scholarship.

Korea

Invaded by the Chinese emperor Wu about 100 B.C., then by tribes from the north, and then by the Japanese from the fourth to the seventh centuries A.D., and divided meanwhile among several states within itself, Korea was a land of dissension and turmoil until one of the Korean states, Silla, united the country in 670. The record of these centuries is so confused that it is hard even to be sure of the names of certain cities at given dates; on the following map, therefore, the capitals of Silla and the neighboring P'o Hai, as of 750 A.D., are simply indicated as "capitals," without names. The Korean peninsula remained united under Silla until 935. The first hundred years of this period were particularly fruitful in literary and artistic development, in which Buddhism, which had come to the area as early as 372, played a particularly important role. Early in the tenth century a new state, Koryo (whence our name Korea), arose and again united the country. Thereafter Korean civilization flourished for more than two hundred years, especially at the capital city, Kaesong (see page 127).

Japan

The earliest reliable historical knowledge of Japan relates to the second and third centuries of the Christian era. At that time the powerful Yamato clan extended military control over the central and western part of the islands. The Japanese from the fourth to the seventh centuries were very active in Korea, where they first came under the direct influence of Chinese civilization, taking from it their written language, the Buddhist religion, and certain political and economic concepts. Many Koreans also migrated to Japan, bringing with them an advanced artisanship and other achievements of a Chinified culture. During the Suiko period (593–628) Buddhism became firmly established in Japan, and foundations were laid for a form of government, influenced by China, that was to prevail for several centuries. For the next hundred and fifty years the Japanese devoted themselves to the absorption of Chinese civilization and its adaptation to the conditions of Japanese life. They sent missions to China to study and bring back whatever might be of use. This is the classical period of Japanese civilization, when the first national histories and much of the greatest Japanese architecture, painting, sculpture, and poetry were produced.

The first capital, built at Nara in 710, was laid out like Ch'angan, the capital of T'ang China. In 784 the capital was moved to Nagaoka, and ten years later a magnificent new and permanent capital, again on the model of Ch'angan, was built at Heian, the modern Kyoto. The Heian period (794–1185) saw a decline in contacts with China, and the evolution of a rich and more distinctively Japanese civilization, marked by the growth of powerful Buddhist sects and the emergence of a new military class that was to play a leading role in Japanese life down to modern times. In 858 the Fujiwara clan assumed a regency over the emperor which it continued to exercise until 1160, establishing a system of hereditary dictatorship (called the Bakufu after 1185) that was exercised by one noble family or another until 1868. The chief of this form of government came to be called the shogun.

Southeast Asia

Civilization was brought to southeast Asia by Indian princes, who as early as the first and second centuries A.D. crossed by sea from Chola and Pallava in southern India to what are now Cambodia, Cochin China, and Malaya. The first state thus to be created by Indian rulers was Funan, established in the first century of the Christian era in the region of Cambodia and Cochin China. Funan extended its control up the Mekong and Menam rivers and into the Malay peninsula, where Kedah and Langkasuka date from the second century.

After five hundred years Funan was conquered in the sixth century by Chenla, an Indianized kingdom of the Khmer peoples to the north. In the eighth century Chenla seems to have come under the influence of the Sailendras of Java, but in 802 the Khmers were liberated by the founder of the Angkor dynasty, which flourished until the end of the twelfth century, and left spectacular buildings whose ruins have recently been uncovered. The reduced Khmer empire of the thirteenth century appears on page 127.

Farther south rose the Srivijayan empire centered in eastern Sumatra. About 850 it seems to have been taken over by the Sailendras, who had created a flourishing Buddhist kingdom in Java a century earlier. Under the Sailendras the Srivijayan power, wealth, and prestige were supreme in the region until the thirteenth century.

All these kingdoms derived Buddhism, Brahmanism, a written language, and artistic styles from India, mainly from its southern tip, with which they continued to maintain trade and cultural relations.

Burma and Tibet

Indian civilization, including Buddhism, reached the Mon peoples of lower Burma in the fifth and sixth centuries. Burman invaders from the north, establishing their capital at Pagan about the middle of the eleventh century, united Burma for more than two centuries.

Tibet or T'ufan received its civilization from both India and China, becoming Buddhist in the seventh century. For Tibet the period of its greatest eminence was from the eighth to the twelfth centuries, when it exercised control over Nepal and large areas of central Asia. The Tibetans on one occasion even invaded the Chinese capital at Ch'angan.

Buddhism and Islam

In summary, the most important intercultural force in east and southeast Asia during the first millennium of the Christian era was Buddhism. It first appeared in China in the later Han period, and spread during the troubles that followed the Han collapse. Providing intellectual challenge for the educated, solace for the suffering, and salvation for all, it had won almost universal acceptance in China by the sixth century; by the ninth, it had passed the peak of its influence and had begun to decay. Many Buddhist missionaries made their way from India and central Asia to China; and many Chinese Buddhists made the long pilgrimage to India to visit Buddhist shrines, study with Buddhist teachers, and bring back Buddhist writings and relics. A Chinese form of Buddhism was adopted in Korea and Japan; a more purely Indian form in Ceylon and southeast Asia. Meanwhile, as already noted, Buddhism virtually disappeared in India itself, where Hinduism prevailed.

Islam appeared in India at the beginning of the second Christian millennium, and in the following centuries spread to Indonesia, parts of China, and farther into central Asia.

In Asia there did not develop, as in Europe, the idea that all persons living in the same locality should have the same religion, nor even, except among the Moslems, the idea that an individual person should adhere to only one religious faith. Various religions and cultural elements could be mixed in various ways, and Asia became diversified at a time when spiritual unity was accepted as a desirable goal in Europe.

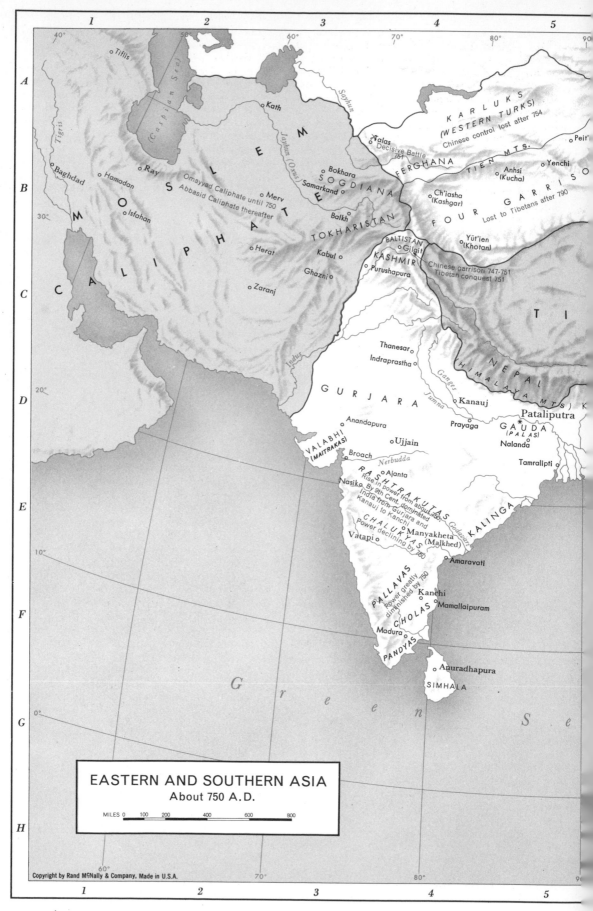

EASTERN AND SOUTHERN ASIA
About 750 A.D.

MILES 0   100   200   400   600   800

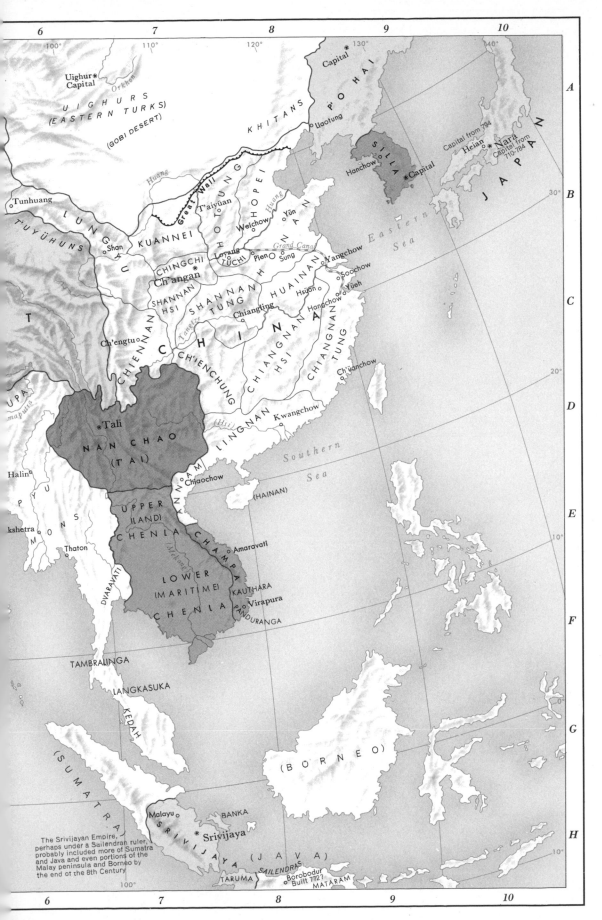

6　　　　　7　　　　　8　　　　　9　　　　　10

*Uighur
Capital

U I G H U R S
(E A S T E R N   T U R K S)

(G O B I   D E S E R T)

Orkhon

KHITANS

Capital

P'
O
H
A
I

Huang

Great Wall

Liaotung

SILLA

Capital from 794

Heian

Nara
Capital from
710–784

J
A
P
A
N

A

o Tunhuang

T'aiyüan

T'U-YÜHUNS

Huang

L U N G Y U

KUANNEI

HOTUNG

HOPEI

Weichow

Yün

Eastern

B

30°

Hanchow

Capital

o Shan

CHINGCHI

Loyang

TUCH'I

Pien

Sung

N A N

Sea

Ch'angan

SHANNAN

HUAINAN

Yangchow

T

SHANNAN
HSI

SHANNAN
TUNG

Chiangling

Hsiton o

Soochow

o Yüeh

C

20°

Ch'engtu o

C H I N A

Hangchow o

C H'I E N C H U N G

CHIANGNAN
HSI

CHIANGNAN
TUNG

Ch'üanchow

U P A

mapuna

CHIENNAN

Tali

N A N   C H A O
(T'A I)

L I N G N A N

(Hsi)

Kwangchow

Southern

D

Halin o

P
Y
U

A
N
N
A
M

Chiaochow

Sea

E

10°

kshetra o

M
O
N
S

Thaton o

UPPER
(LAND)

C H E N L A

C H A M P A

Amaravati

(HAINAN)

DVARAVATI

Mekong

LOWER
(MARITIME)

KAUTHARA

Virapura

CHENLA

PANDURANGA

F

TAMBRALINGA

LANGKASUKA

G

0°

KEDAH

(B O R N E O)

(S U M A T R A)

S
R
I
V
I
J
A
Y
A

Malayu o

BANKA

H

The Srivijayan Empire,
perhaps under a Sailendran ruler,
probably included more of Sumatra
and Java and even portions of the
Malay peninsula and Borneo by
the end of the 8th Century

Srivijaya

(J A V A)

10°

TARUMA

SAILENDRAS

Borobodur
Built 712?

MATARAM

100°

6　　　　　7　　　　　8　　　　　9　　　　　10

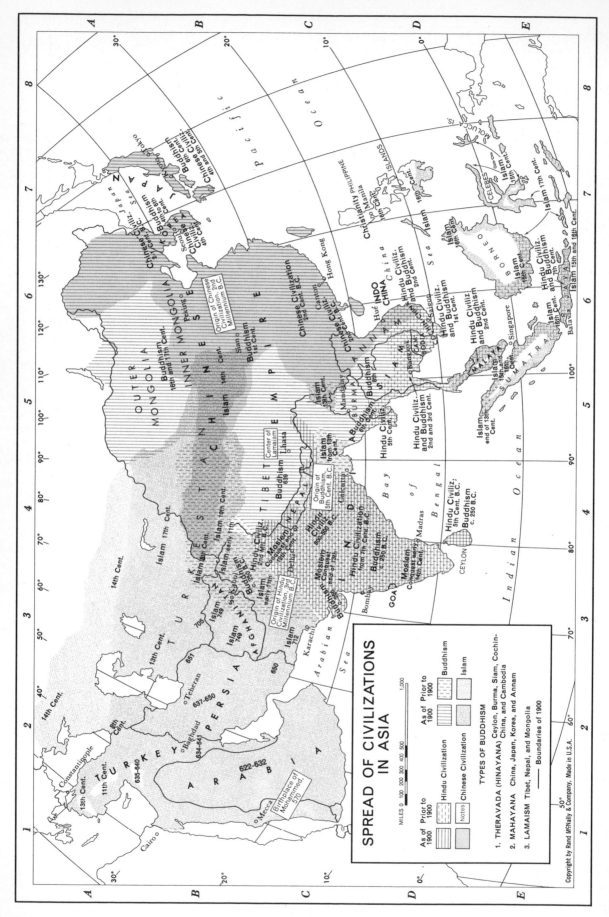

SPREAD OF CIVILIZATIONS IN ASIA

MILES 0 100 200 300 400 500   1,000

TYPES OF CIVILIZATION

| As of Prior to | |
| Prior to 1900 | 1900 | |

| | Hindu Civilization |
| | | Notes | Chinese Civilization |

TYPES OF BUDDHISM

| As of Prior to | | |
| Prior to 1900 | 1900 | |

| | | Buddhism |
| | | Islam |

1. THERAVADA (HINAYANA) Ceylon, Burma, Siam, Cochin-
   China, and Cambodia.

2. MAHAYANA China, Japan, Korea, and Annam.

3. LAMAISM Tibet, Nepal, and Mongolia.

―――― Boundaries of 1900

Copyright by Rand McNally & Company, Made in U.S.A.

124

ASIA IN THE MONGOL PERIOD

▶ MAP ON PAGES 126–27

THE MAP ON PAGES 126–27 shows Asia at the death of Kublai Khan in 1294, at which time the Mongol empire was at its height. In area it was the largest in world history, consisting of four coordinate empires, shown in shades of yellow, all of which recognized the headship of the Great Khan, and which together reached from the Black Sea and the Persian Gulf to the Pacific Ocean.

Rise of the Mongols

Certain Mongol tribes of nomadic horsemen, living south of Lake Baikal, were united by one of their hereditary chiefs, who in 1206, after extending control over various neighboring peoples, was proclaimed "universal emperor" or Jenghis Khan. They then launched upon a rapid and ruthless conquest that carried them over most of Asia and eastern Europe. Before Jenghis' death in 1227 they had destroyed the Hsi Hsia kingdom, driven the Juchen Chin dynasty in north China south to the Huang River, conquered the Kara Khitai kingdom in Turkestan, and made destructive raids into Persia and southern Russia. Jenghis' successor, Ogadai, subjugated Korea, the remaining Chin territory in north China, and crushed the Persian sultanate of Khwarezm, the kingdoms of Azerbaijan and Georgia, and Kievan Russia (see page 109). Mongol armies even pushed as far as Liegnitz in Silesia, where in 1241 they overthrew a combined Polish and German army. Latin Europe thus stood open before them, but the Mongols at this time received news of the death of Ogadai, and their leaders returned to the Far East.

Soon renewing their depredations on various fronts, they destroyed the Thai (or T'ai) kingdom of Nan Chao in southwest China in 1253, the Abbasid caliphate of Baghdad in 1258, and the Sung dynasty in central and south China in 1279; and they sent raiding forces into Syria, Anatolia, the Balkans, India, Annam and Burma, and across the sea to Java and Japan.

This extraordinary achievement of a few small tribes is to be explained by the organizing genius of Jenghis Khan and his successors, the Mongol reputation for efficiency and ferocity which paralyzed most resistance, and the fact that most of their victims happened to be weak and disorganized when attacked.

The Mongol Empire

Under Kublai Khan, a grandson of Jenghis, Asia was more unified than at any time before or since. Routes of travel were relatively safe and filled with numerous travelers between East and West. Merchants and even missionaries passed from western Europe into east Asia. The best known in later ages has always been the Venetian merchant Marco Polo, since he wrote a history of his travels and observations; but there were also other Europeans in China at this time, including some religious emissaries from the pope in Rome.

Unified by the primacy of the Great Khan, which was recognized until after the death of Kublai, the Mongol empire was at the same time divided into four parts. The empire of the Great Khan was essentially China, plus Korea and the old Mongol homelands. The empire of Jagatai, second son of Jenghis, was in central Asia. The Ilkhan empire of Hulagu, who like Kublai was a grandson of Jenghis, consisted of Persia and Mesopotamia. The empire of Batu comprised central and south Russia and the region east of the Urals; it is known also as the empire of Kipchak or the Golden Horde.

Even before Kublai's death the various Mongol ruling groups began to be assimilated to their subject peoples, who in most cases were more civilized than they were. Kublai Khan was himself almost completely Chinese in education and outlook. He proclaimed a new Chinese dynasty, the Yüan, and undertook to rule in accordance with Confucian tradition. He was followed by weak successors, who not only lost control over other Mongol khans to the west but were increasingly unable to cope with governmental problems in China. Finally in 1368 Chinese rebels drove the Mongols outside the Great Wall and established the Ming dynasty.

India and South Asia

India was raided but never ruled by the Mongols. It did see at this time, however, the beginning of a series of Moslem dynasties which were long to rule portions of north India from Delhi. Many of these sultans of Delhi patronized art and literature, but they tended to be intolerant of Hinduism, and the period was one of continuing turmoil in India. A Moslem kingdom of Bahmani dominated central India from 1347 to 1484, and a Hindu kingdom of Vijayanagar dominated the south from 1336 to 1565.

Under Mongol blows, the Thais of Nan Chao (called Shans in Burma) migrated southward, and established a new state of Sukhothai or Syam. During the fourteenth and fifteenth centuries Sukhothai conquered the Khmer kingdom, and exerted influence in parts of Burma and the Malay peninsula. The Shans, related to the Thais, dominated Burma for three hundred years.

Another brief Mongol-like terror occurred at the end of the fourteenth century, when Timur (or Tamerlane), vizier to the last Jagatai Khan, overthrew his master and ravaged Persia, Azerbaijan, Mesopotamia, and India as far as Delhi. His empire, whose capital was at Samarkand, did not long outlast his death in 1405, though his descendants ruled Transoxiana and eastern Persia until 1500.

One consequence of the decline of the Mongols, insignificant from the Asian point of view, was the interruption of European contacts with east Asia. Europeans knew less of China in the sixteenth century than in the thirteenth (see page 61). The rise of Muscovy in the east European plain was another consequence of Mongol recession, but "khans" continued to rule in south Russia until the days of Catherine the Great (see pages 66, 110–11).

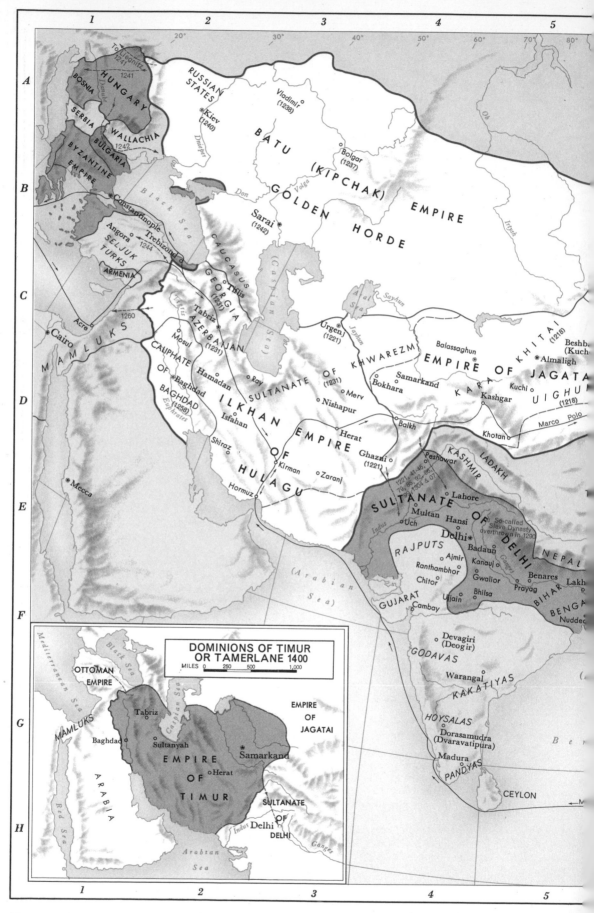

A

BOSNIA
HUNGARY
To Liegnitz
1241
1241
SERBIA
WALLACHIA
1242
BULGARIA
BYZANTINE
EMPIRE

RUSSIAN
STATES
*Kiev
(1240)
Vladimir
(1238)

BATU
(KIPCHAK)
GOLDEN
HORDE
EMPIRE

Bolgar
(1237)

B

Constantinople
Trebizond
Angora
1244
SELJUK
TURKS
ARMENIA

Black Sea

Sarai
(1242) *

Dnieper
Don
Volga
Irtysh
Ob

C

Acre
1260

CAUCASUS
Tiflis
(1231)
GEORGIA
Tabriz
(1231)
AZERBAIJAN

Tigris

Aral
Sea
Sayhun

Urgenj
(1221)
KHWAREZM

Balassaghun

EMPIRE OF JAGATAI

KARA KHITAI
(1218)
Beshba
(Kuch

D

*Cairo
MAMLUKS

Mosul
CALIPHATE
Hamadan
OF
*Baghdad
BAGHDAD
(1258)
Isfahan
Euphrates

Ray
SULTANATE
OF
(1231)
Nishapur
Merv
Samarkand
Bokhara
Balkh
Herat

Caspian Sea
Jayhun

Almaligh
Kuchi
Kashgar
UIGHU
(1218)
Khotan
Marco Polo

E

*Mecca
Shiraz
Kirman
Zaranj
Hormuz
ILKHAN EMPIRE OF HULAGU
Ghazni
(1221)

1221 41 45
79 85 92 96
1304 & 07
Peshawar
KASHMIR
LADAKH
Multan Hansi
Uch
Lahore
So-called
Slave Dynasty
overthrown in 1290
SULTANATE OF DELHI
Delhi*
RAJPUTS
Badaun
Ajmir
Ranthambhor
Kanauj
Gwalior
Benares
Chitor
Prayag
NEPAL
Lakh
BIHAR
Ujjain
Bhilsa
BENGA
Cambay
Nuddec

Indus
Ganges

F

GUJARAT

(Arabian
Sea)

Devagiri
(Deogir)
GODAVAS

Warangal
KAKATIYAS

G

**DOMINIONS OF TIMUR
OR TAMERLANE 1400**
MILES 0 250 500 1,000

Mediterranean Sea
Black Sea
OTTOMAN
EMPIRE
MAMLUKS
Tabriz
Caspian Sea
EMPIRE
OF
JAGATAI
Baghdad
Sultanyah
*Samarkand
EMPIRE
OF
TIMUR
Herat

ARABIA
Red Sea

SULTANATE
OF
Delhi
DELHI

Indus
Ganger

HOYSALAS
Dorasamudra
(Dvaravatipura)
Madura
PANDYAS
CEYLON
Ber

H

Arabian
Sea

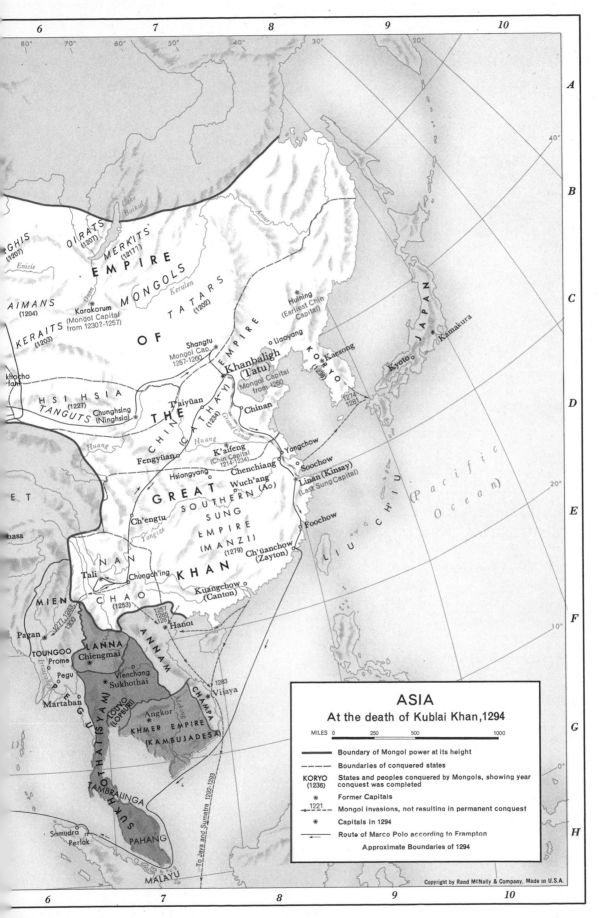

ASIA
At the death of Kublai Khan, 1294

MILES 0   250   500   1000

——— Boundary of Mongol power at its height

- - - Boundaries of conquered states

KORYO
(1236)   States and peoples conquered by Mongols, showing year
           conquest was completed

⊛   Former Capitals

1221   Mongol invasions, not resulting in permanent conquest

⊛   Capitals in 1294

——— Route of Marco Polo according to Frampton

          Approximate Boundaries of 1294

Copyright by Rand M°Nally & Company, Made in U.S.A.

127

SOUTH AND EAST ASIA: SIXTEENTH TO EIGHTEENTH CENTURIES

▶ MAPS BELOW AND ON PAGES 130–31 AND 132

IN THESE CENTURIES India and China reached new heights of political organization, and all Asia felt the first impact of the modern West.

The Mogul Empire in India
▶ MAP ON PAGE 130

The Mogul (or Mughul) empire, the most extensive known in India since the time of Asoka almost two thousand years before, was established early in the sixteenth century by the Moslem Babur, a Jagatai Turk descended from Timur. Akbar (1556–1605), the greatest of the Mogul emperors, added Bengal and other parts of north India. He reorganized the administration, and encouraged toleration between Moslems and Hindus. His successors, Shah Jahan (1628–1658) and Aurangzeb (1659–1707), while they enlarged the Mogul empire to its greatest extent (see inset, page 130) and sponsored such wonders of architecture as the Taj Mahal, also tried to make all India Moslem, destroyed Hindu temples, and enforced conversion by economic pressure and by arms. Hinduism nevertheless remained the religion of most Indians, probably strengthened by the ordeal. During these internal disturbances the Portuguese, Dutch, French, and British established trading stations in the ports. By 1775, as shown on the map, the Mogul empire had shrunk to the region of the upper Ganges, various Indian states had emerged as independent, and the British had begun to build their Indian empire in Bengal.

China, Burma, Siam, Japan
▶ MAPS BELOW AND ON PAGES 130–31

In China, Manchu descendants of the Juchens, who had ruled north China as the Chin dynasty before the Mongol conquest, took advantage of the fall of the Mings, in 1644, to set up their own Ch'ing (or Manchu) dynasty, which lasted until 1912. Chinese civilization flourished under the two great emperors, K'ang-hsi (1662–1722) and Ch'ien-lung (1736–1795), who attempted to live up to Confucian standards of rule. Under Ch'ien-lung the Chinese empire attained its greatest extent since the T'ang period, reaching far into inner Asia. Chinese suzerainty was also recognized by Korea, Liuch'iu (Ryukyu), Annam, Siam, and Nepal.

Burma, divided for a century and a half, was reunited in 1753 by fierce Burmans from the upper Irriwaddy. They invaded Siam, and destroyed Ayuthia in 1767. Rama I freed Siam from Burmese control, and established a new Siamese dynasty with a new capital at Bangkok in the 1780's.

In Japan a feudalism that had been developing for centuries reached its height in 1600, when the Tokugawa shogunate, ruling in the name of the

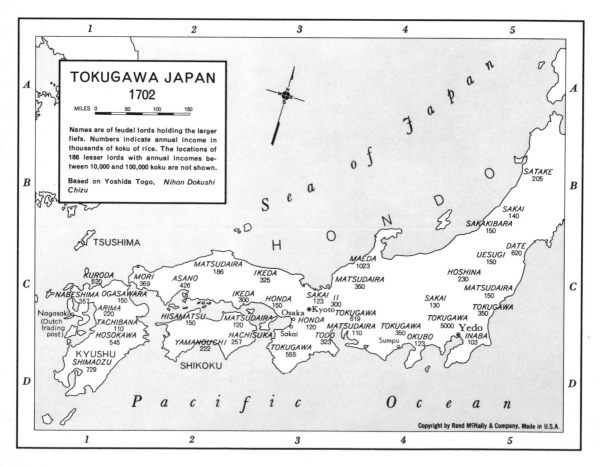

TOKUGAWA JAPAN
1702

MILES 0 50 100 150

Names are of feudal lords holding the larger fiefs. Numbers indicate annual income in thousands of koku of rice. The locations of 186 lesser lords with annual incomes between 10,000 and 100,000 koku are not shown.

Based on Yoshida Togo, *Nihon Dokushi Chizu*

Copyright by Rand McNally & Company. Made in U.S.A.

Japanese emperor, assumed a control which it maintained until 1868. The location and relative wealth of the great feudatories of Tokugawa Japan are shown on page 128. The Tokugawa shogunate undertook to freeze Japanese society and isolate it from the rest of the world.

Europeans in Asia
▶ MAP ON PAGES 130–31

The Portuguese had reached India in 1498, and the East Indies, China, and Japan in the next half-century (see pages 62–63). They dominated Asian trade for over a hundred years. By 1775 they had been virtually eliminated from Ceylon and the East Indies by the Dutch, and from India by the English and French. The Dutch were well established in Java, but held only disconnected posts through the rest of the East Indian archipelago. They alone of the Europeans were allowed to trade with Japan. They retained their superiority in the south Asian trading zone until surpassed by the British at the end of the eighteenth century.

The first British post in India was at Surat in 1612; by 1700 the main British centers were at Bombay, Madras, and Calcutta. The chief French establishments were at Pondichéry and Chandernagore. As the Mogul empire weakened, leaving India more divided, and as European military and organizational methods improved, the British and French East India companies, though essentially commercial concerns, were able to maintain their own armed forces and conduct their own diplomacy among the Indian states. The Anglo-French duel for empire was largely settled in the Seven Years' War, ending in 1763, so that by 1775, as shown on pages 130–31, the French had been eliminated from the political contest in India, and the British proceeded to the occupation of Bengal which grew into the British Indian empire. The French retained control, however, of their trading stations at Pondichéry, Chandernagore, and elsewhere. The British again gained advantages in Asia from the Revolutionary and Napoleonic wars in Europe, during which they took Ceylon and Malacca from the Dutch. Near Malacca they founded Singapore in 1819.

In China and Japan the authorities had sufficient strength to keep Europeans under control, and in both countries the fear that European merchants and missionaries would disrupt the political system led to measures of isolation. In the seventeenth century the Tokugawa shoguns tried to extirpate Japanese Christian converts, prohibited foreign trade except to the Chinese and Dutch at Nagasaki, and forbade Japanese to go overseas. In China in the seventeenth century there was a good deal of activity by Christian missionaries, notably the Jesuits, who introduced Western learning into China and made China better known to the West. Early in the eighteenth century, however, the Chinese expelled foreign missionaries and confined trade with Europeans to the port of Canton. China was still strong enough to hold the Russians north of the Amur valley, negotiating the Treaty of Nerchinsk in 1689. At Nerchinsk a French Jesuit in Chinese service interpreted in Latin between the Russians and Chinese.

Chinese and Japanese attempts to immunize themselves from Western influence broke down in the nineteenth century, when the Western nations became militarily too powerful for the older Eastern societies to resist.

Exploration of the Pacific Ocean
▶ MAP ON PAGE 132

The Pacific Ocean was first crossed by Magellan in 1520, but was not fully explored until two and a half centuries later. In 1565 a Spanish expedition from Mexico captured Manila. A deserter from this expedition, Alonzo de Arellano, seeking to get back to Mexico, made the first eastward crossing, hotly pursued by a more authorized navigator, the elderly Augustinian friar, Andrés de Urdaneta. Mendaña discovered the Solomon Islands in 1567. Spanish galleons made an annual commercial voyage between Mexico and Manila for the next two centuries without making any significant discoveries, since they followed routes standardized to catch the winds. The famous expedition of Francis Drake in the Pacific in 1578–79 was meant more as a plundering raid than as a contribution to knowledge, but Drake may have sailed farther north along the American coast than anyone before him.

After 1600 the Dutch became active in the Pacific. They rounded Cape Horn in 1616 (see page 61). In 1642–43 Abel Tasman, on orders from the Dutch governor of Java, van Diemen, sailed from Mauritius in the Indian Ocean in the direction of Australia. Tasman never sighted Australia, but he did discover Tasmania, New Zealand, and the Fiji Islands. The Dutch van Roggeveen in 1722 discovered Easter Island and Samoa.

A Dane, Vitus Bering, in Russian service and on orders from Peter the Great, discovered Bering Strait in 1728, and thus at last proved Asia and America to be separate continents. On a later voyage he explored Alaska and the Aleutian Islands. The French Bougainville made a number of minor discoveries in 1768.

The greatest of Pacific explorers was the Englishman James Cook, who made three voyages. Sent by the British Admiralty and the Royal Society to observe the transit of Venus at Tahiti in 1769, he completed this mission, then thoroughly examined the New Zealand coasts, satisfying himself that they did not protrude from a great southern continent, as had been thought possible since Tasman's day. He then sailed to Botany Bay, which he named, and charted the eastern coast of Australia. His second voyage, begun in 1772, was largely in the Antarctic, and so cannot be traced on the present map. He dispelled one of the oldest geographical myths by proving that no great southern continent existed, at least within latitudes significant for human habitation. On his third voyage, begun in 1776, Cook discovered the Hawaiian (or Sandwich) Islands, probed the North American coast from Oregon to Alaska, passed through Bering Strait, and returned to Hawaii, where he met his death at the hands of the natives. Though a few discoveries remained to be made, Cook's voyages brought the great era of Pacific exploration to a close.

For Arctic explorations, see pages 170–71.

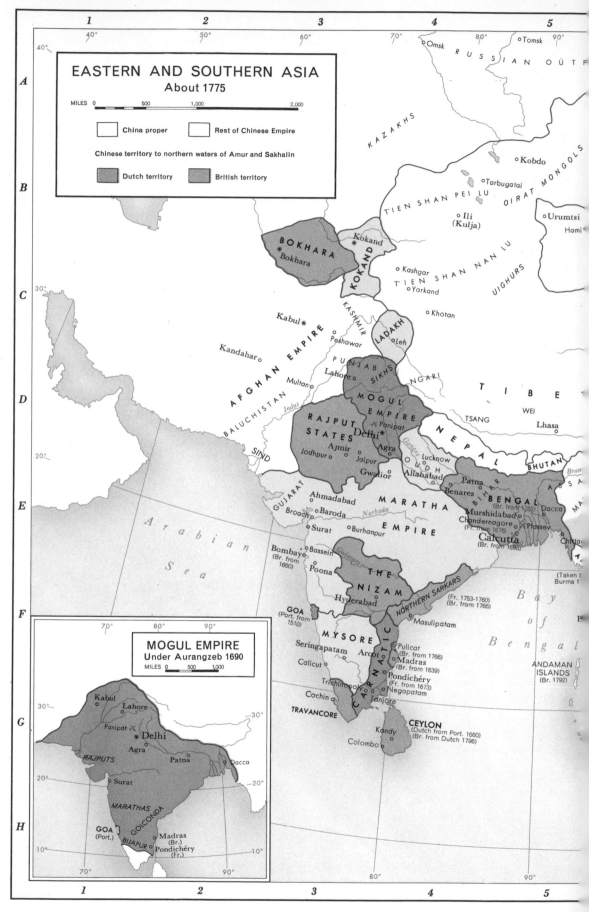

EASTERN AND SOUTHERN ASIA
About 1775

MILES 0   500   1,000   2,000

China proper   Rest of Chinese Empire

Chinese territory to northern waters of Amur and Sakhalin

Dutch territory   British territory

RUSSIAN OUT[P]

o Omsk

o Tomsk

K A Z A K H S

o Kobdo

o Tarbugatai

T'IEN SHAN PEI LU   OIRAT MONGOLS

o Ili
(Kulja)

o Urumtsi

Hami

BOKHARA
* Bokhara

KOKAND
* Kokand

T'IEN SHAN NAN LU

o Kashgar

UIGHURS

o Yarkand

o Khotan

Kabul *

KASHMIR

Peshawar o

LADAKH
o Leh

AFGHAN EMPIRE

Kandahar o

PUNJAB

Lahore o

SIKHS

NGARI

T I B E [T]

WEI

TSANG

o Lhasa

BALUCHISTAN

Multan o

Indus

MOGUL
EMPIRE

* Panipat

RAJPUT
STATES

Delhi *

Agra

Ganges

N E P A L

BHUTAN

SIND

Jodhpur o

Ajmir

Jaipur o

Gwalior o

Lucknow o

O U D H

Allahabad o

Benares o

Patna o

BIHAR

BENGAL
(Br. from 1765)

Bram

ASSA[M]

Dacca o

GUJARAT

Ahmadabad o

M A R A T H A

Narbada

Murshidabad o

Chandernagore
(Fr. from 1676)

Plassey o

MA[

Broach o

Baroda o

E M P I R E

Burhanpur o

Calcutta
(Br. from 1698)

Chitta[

Surat o

A r a b i a n

Bombay
(Br. from
1660)

Bassein o

Poona o

Godavari

THE
NIZAM

Hyderabad o

NORTHERN SARKARS

(Taken b[
Burma 1[

B a y

S e a

GOA
(Port. from
1510)

Masulipatam o

(Fr. 1753-1760)
(Br. from 1766)

o f

MYSORE

Arcot o

Seringapatam o

Calicut o

Pulicat
(Br. from 1766)

Madras
(Br. from 1639)

C A R N A T I C

Trichinopoly o

Pondichéry
(Fr. from 1673)

Negapatam o

B e n g a l

ANDAMAN
ISLANDS
(Br. 1792)

P

Cochin o

Tanjore o

TRAVANCORE

CEYLON
(Dutch from Port. 1660)
(Br. from Dutch 1796)

o Kandy

Colombo o

MOGUL EMPIRE
Under Aurangzeb 1690

MILES 0   500   1,000

Kabul o

Lahore o

Panipat

Delhi *

Agra

Patna o

RAJPUTS

Dacca o

Surat o

MARATHAS

GOLCONDA

GOA
(Port.)

BIJAPUR o

Madras
(Br.)

Pondichéry
(Fr.)

6 7 8 9 10

BURIAT MONGOLS
Irkutsk
Kiakhta
Nerchinsk
assutai
Urga
TER MONGOLIA
OUTER MONGOLIA
KHALKHA MONGOLS
Tsitsihar
MANCHURIA
Amur
Kirin
MANCHUS
FORTY NINE MONGOL
BANNERS OF INNER MONGOLIA
CHAHAR MONGOLS
Jehol
Shengching (Mukden)
YEZO
40°
A
KANSU
TORGUT MONGOLS
DAM GOLS
ONOR MONGOLS
Kalgan
Great Wall
Paoting
Peking
CHIHLI
JAPAN
HONSHU
KOREA
Seoul
Yedo
B
30°
Lanchow
Huang
Taiyüan
SHANSI
Sian
SHENSI
Kaifeng
HONAN
ANWEI
SHANTUNG
Tsinan
Grand Canal
Changning
Kyoto
Sakai Osaka
SHIKOKU
KYUSHU
Chengtu
SZECHWAN
Yangtze
HUPEH
Wuchang
Nanchang
KIANGSI
Anking
CHEKIANG
Hangchow
Nanking
Nagasaki
(Dutch trading post of Deshima from 1641)
LIUCHIU
Pacific
Ocean
C
Changshao
HUNAN
Foochow
FUKIEN
D
20°
Kweiyang
KWEICHOW
Kweilin
KWANGSI
KWANGTUNG
Kwangchow (Canton)
Macao
(Port. trading post from 1557)
Zelandia Castel
(Dutch, 1624-1662)
FORMOSA
Yünnan
YUNNAN
Bhamo
Hsi (West)
Hanoi
TONGKING
E
10°
Chiengsen
Luang Prabang
Thanh Hoa
Tongking, Annam and Cochin-China formed Vietnam Empire 1802
ANNAM
Mekong
China Sea
Manila
PHILIPPINE
ISLANDS
(Spain)
Chiengmai
Sukhotai
Vientiane
(Laos states of Luang Prabang and Vientiane, under Siamese Suzerainty from 1778)
Hué
F
Martaban
Lopburi
Ayuthia
(Destroyed by Burmese in 1767)
Bangkok
(Built 1780's)
Siemreap
COCHIN-CHINA
CAMBODIA
Phnom Penh
Saigon
(Taken by Annam 1776)
G
0°
ligor
Patani
KEDAH
Penang
(Br. from 1786)
PERAK PAHANG
SELANGOR
BRUNEI
Menado
HALMAHERA
MOLUCCAS
CERAM
SUMATRA
Malacca
JOHORE
(Dutch 1641-1795, 1818-1824) (Br. 1795-1818, since 1824)
RIAU ARCH
(Center of Bugis power)
Siak
BORNEO
CELEBES
Amboina
H
Padang
MINANGKABAU
Jambi
Palembang
BANGKA
BILLITON
Succadana
Banjermassin
Macassar
130°

Copyright by Rand McNally & Company, Made in U.S.A.

6 7 8 9 10

131

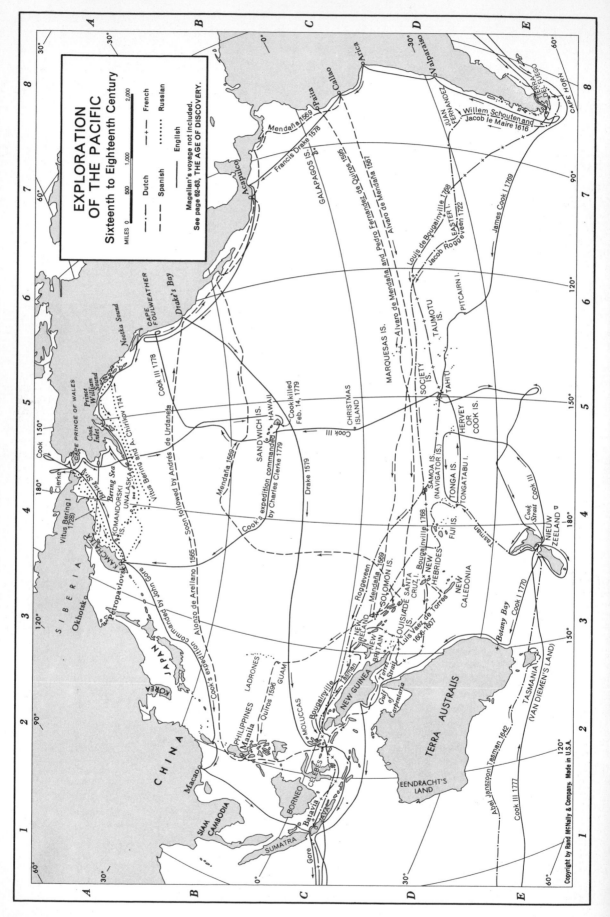

EXPLORATION OF THE PACIFIC
Sixteenth to Eighteenth Century

MILES 0   500   1,000   2,000

— ·— Dutch   —+— French
                  ···+··· Russian
— — Spanish   ········· English

Magellan's voyage not included.
See page 62-63, THE AGE OF DISCOVERY.

CHINA

SIBERIA

JAPAN

KOREA

SIAM
CAMBODIA

Okhotsk

Petropavlovsk

Vitus Bering I.
1728)

Bering Sea

KAMCHATKA

KOMANDORSKI
IS.

UNALASKA

Vitus Bering and A. Chirikov 1741

Cook 150°

CAPE PRINCE OF WALES

Cook
Inlet

Prince
William
Sound

Nootka Sound

CAPE
FOULWEATHER

Drake's Bay

Cook III 1778

Clerke

Soon followed by Andrés de Urdaneta

Alonzo de Arellano 1565

Gore commanded by John Gore

Cook's expedition commanded

Mendaña 1569

Drake 1579

SANDWICH IS.

HAWAII

Cook killed
Feb. 14, 1779

Cook's expedition commanded
by Charles Clerke 1779

Cook III

CHRISTMAS
ISLAND

MARQUESAS IS.

SOCIETY
IS.

TAHITI

TAUMOTU
IS.

PITCAIRN I.

HERVEY
OR
COOK IS.

SAMOA IS.
(NAVIGATOR IS.)

TONGA IS.

TONGATABU I.

FIJI IS.

NEW
HEBRIDES

NEW
CALEDONIA

Macao

PHILIPPINES

Manila

LADRONES

GUAM

MOLUCCAS

BORNEO

CELEBES

Batavia

JAVA

SUMATRA

Quiros 1596

Gore

Roggeveen

Mendaña 1569

SOLOMON IS.

NEW
IRELAND

NEW
BRITAIN

NEW GUINEA

Bougainville

Tasman

Torres
Strait

Gulf of
Carpentaria

LOUISIADE
IS.

SANTA
CRUZ I.

Bougainville 1768

Luis Vaez de Torres
1606, 1607

Roggeveen

TERRA AUSTRALIS

EENDRACHT'S
LAND

Botany Bay

Cook 1770

NIEUW
ZEELAND

Cook
Strait Cook III

Tasman

Cook III

TASMANIA
(VAN DIEMEN'S LAND)

Abel Janszoon Tasman 1642

Cook III 1777

Acapulco

Mendaña 1569

Paita

Callao

Francis Drake 1578

GALAPAGOS IS.

Arica

Valparaiso

JUAN FERNANDEZ

Willem Schouten and
Jacob le Maire 1616

TIERRA
DEL FUEGO

CAPE HORN

Alvaro de Mendaña and Pedro Fernandez de Quiros 1567

Alvaro de Mendaña 1567

Louis de Bougainville 1768

EASTER I.

Jacob Roggeveen 1722

James Cook I 1769

Copyright by Rand McNally & Company. Made in U.S.A.

132

ASIA IN 1900

▶ MAP ON PAGES 134–35

THE INDUSTRIALIZATION OF EUROPE (see pages 102–3) enabled the chief European states to exercise a much greater political domination over the old civilizations of Asia than they had formerly achieved, or had even wished to acquire. It gave them also more extensive economic interests in Asia, involving the investment of capital, the building of railroads, and the setting up of new plantations and industries, which penetrated Asian life more deeply than the more purely commercial contacts of earlier centuries had done. European control in Asia reached its highest point at the close of the nineteenth century and in the first decade of the twentieth.

European Empires in Asia

India was the heart of the British Empire. By the 1890's all India, except for a few minor ports left in the hands of Portugal and France, belonged to the British, much of it annexed directly to the British crown, the rest left as dependent princely states such as Hyderabad or Kashmir. Burma, annexed in several instalments in 1826, 1853, and 1886, was administered by the government of India. Ceylon had been taken from the Dutch in 1795; it was a separate crown colony. Farther east, the British, having occupied Malacca from 1795 to 1818 during the Revolutionary-Napoleonic wars in Europe, obtained its formal cession by Holland in 1824. Malacca, however, lost its old importance as a commercial and strategic center with the establishment of Singapore by the British in 1819. The neighboring Malay states accepted British protection in the 1870's and 1880's, except for four along the Siamese border that still acknowledged Siamese suzerainty. Sarawak, Brunei, and North Borneo also became British protectorates in the 1880's. Hong Kong, ceded by China to Britain in 1842, had become the great British naval and commercial center in east Asia. The British "lifeline" into this region passed through the Suez Canal.

The Dutch during the nineteenth century extended political control over the whole East Indies (except north Borneo and the Portuguese half of Timor), which they had long exploited economically through arrangements with local rulers. Among the last steps were the final pacification of northwestern Sumatra in 1907 and the establishment of direct Dutch rule over Bali in 1908.

France, having begun by annexing Cochin China in 1862 and 1867, and obtaining a protectorate over Cambodia in 1863, proceeded in the last two decades of the century to acquire protectorates over Annam, Tongking, and Laos, and organized the whole into an Indo-Chinese Union, ruled from Saigon. Russia during the second half of the nineteenth century completed the annexation of all territory north of the Amur and east of the Ussuri rivers, west of Chinese Turkestan and north of Afghanistan (except that the small sultanates of Khiva and Bokhara became protectorates), and northern Persian territories down to the present Iranian boundary (see page 115; for German and United States acquisitions in the Pacific islands see pages 170–71).

Independent States in Asia

In 1900 only the Ottoman Empire, Persia, Afghanistan, Nepal, Bhutan, Siam, China, Korea, and Japan retained a formal independence. The Ottoman Empire was only half Asian, and in any case declining (see page 174). Persia was encroached upon increasingly by Russia. Nepal and Bhutan were small inaccessible mountain states. Afghanistan was preserved as a buffer between Britain and Russia, Siam as a buffer between Britain and France. China and Korea seemed in grave danger of partition. Only Japan showed strength and genuine independence. It had come out of its isolation under pressure of Commodore Perry in 1854, and had rapidly adjusted to the modern world, becoming an industrial and expansionist power itself (see page 181).

Even in the formally independent states Europeans won political and economic privileges incompatible with true independence. Foreigners living or traveling in one of these countries were subject only to their own laws and courts, not the laws and courts of the Asian country in which they lived or traveled. They paid favorable duties and tariffs which could not be changed without the consent of all the Western treaty powers. In China, Korea, and Japan, as shown on the map, there were "treaty ports" where foreigners lived. In the principal treaty ports there were "extraterritorial" settlements governed by European consuls. Japan, having shown its proficiency by defeating China in the war of 1895, was able to get rid of these foreign encumbrances.

The Crisis of the Turn of the Century

The Japanese victory over China in 1895, by disclosing both the weakness of China and the rising strength of Japan, set the European powers into motion to obtain further concessions in China. In 1898 they took "leases" to establish naval and economic centers: Russia in the Liaotung Peninsula, Germany at Kiaochow Bay, Britain at Weihaiwei, France at Kwangchowwan. These powers at the same time obtained "spheres of interest" in China: Russia in Manchuria, Germany in Shantung, Britain in the Yangtze valley, France on the Indo-China border. Russian advances in Korea led to the Russo-Japanese War, after which Japan took over control of that country and also the Russian leases and other rights in southern Manchuria. In 1907 Britain and France agreed to spheres of influence in Siam, and Britain and Russia to similar spheres in Persia.

The map also shows the state of railway development in 1900. British India had the most elaborate railway system in Asia. Construction of the "Berlin to Baghdad" railroad had begun in the Ottoman Empire. The Trans-Siberian was nearing completion. Its main line was to run from Chita to Vladivostok via the north bank of the Amur River, so as to remain within Russian territory; but since this route was indirect, a shorter line, the Chinese Eastern Railway, was built across Manchuria after 1900.

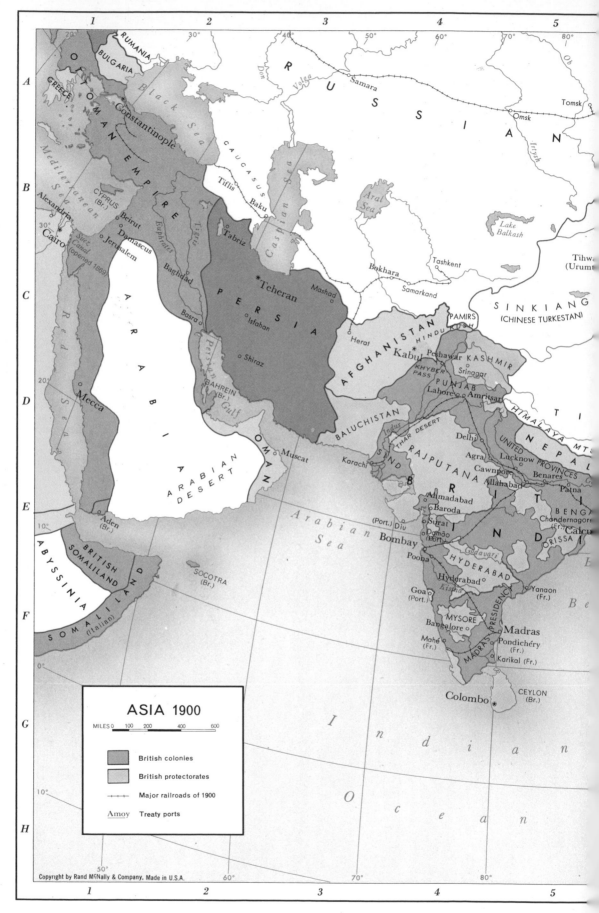

ASIA 1900

MILES 0   100   200   400   600

British colonies

British protectorates

Major railroads of 1900

Amoy Treaty ports

Map labels:

RUMANIA
BULGARIA
GREECE
OTTOMAN EMPIRE
Constantinople
Black Sea
CAUCASUS
RUSSIAN
Don
Volga
Samara
Omsk
Tomsk
Irtysh
Ob
CYPRUS (Br.)
Beirut
Damascus
Jerusalem
Tiflis
Baku
Caspian Sea
Aral Sea
Lake Balkash
Tashkent
Tihwa (Urum...
Alexandria
Cairo
Suez Canal (opened 1869)
Mediterranean Sea
Euphrates
Tigris
Baghdad
Tabriz
Mashad
Bokhara
Samarkand
SINKIANG (CHINESE TURKESTAN)
Red Sea
ARABIA
Basra
PERSIA
Teheran
Isfahan
Herat
AFGHANISTAN
Kabul
Peshawar
PAMIRS
HINDU KUSH
KASHMIR
Srinagar
Mecca
Shiraz
BAHREIN (Br.)
Persian Gulf
OMAN
Muscat
BALUCHISTAN
Karachi
Indus
SIND
KHYBER PASS
PUNJAB
Lahore
Amritsar
HIMALAYA MTS.
NEPAL
TIB...
ARABIAN DESERT
THAR DESERT
RAJPUTANA
Delhi
Agra
Lucknow
Cawnpore
Allahabad
Benares
Patna
UNITED PROVINCES
BRITISH
INDIA
BENGAL
Chandernagore (Fr.)
Calcutta
Aden (Br.)
Ahmadabad
Baroda
(Port.) Diu
Surat
Damão (Port.)
Bombay
Poona
HYDERABAD
Godavari
ORISSA
BRITISH SOMALILAND
ABYSSINIA
SOMALILAND (Italian)
SOCOTRA (Br.)
Arabian Sea
Goa (Port.)
Hyderabad
Krishna
Yanaon (Fr.)
MYSORE
Bangalore
Mahé (Fr.)
MADRAS PRESIDENCY
Madras
Pondichéry (Fr.)
Karikal (Fr.)
Colombo
CEYLON (Br.)
Indian Ocean

R   U   S   S   I   A   N

E   M   P   I   R   E

Heilung (Amur)

Lake
Baikal

Irkutsk   Chita

SAKHALIN
(Russ.)
(Southern half
to Japan 1905)

CHISHIMA
(KURILS)
(Jap.)

HOKKAIDO

Hakodate

M   O   N   G   O   L   I   A

Urga

MANCHURIA

Kirin

Vladivostok

Sea
of
Japan

GOBI DESERT

(Liaotung Peninsula
Russ. lease 1898,
transferred to Japan 1905)

Mukden

Newchwang

Pyongyang   Wonsan

KOREA
(Annexed by
Japan
1910)

H   O   N   S   H   U

Niigata

Tokyo

(Treaty port status
abolished in Japan 1899)

C   H   I   N   E   S   E

E   M   P   I   R   E

Peking

Chinwangtao

Tientsin

Dalny
(Dairen)
Port
Arthur

Chefoo

Seoul

Chemulpo

Weihaiwei
(Br. lease 1898)

Kiaochow Bay
(Ger. lease 1898,
Japan 1914)

Pusan

Kyoto
Kobe
Osaka

Yokohama
Nagoya

OGASAWARA
(BONINS)
(Jap.)

Lanchow

Tsinan

Tsingtao

Nagasaki

SHIKOKU

KYUSHU

J   A   P   A   N

Sian

Kaifeng

C   H   I   N   A

Napking

Chinkiang

Soochow

Shanghai

Chengtu

Ichang

Hankow   Wuhu

Wuchang

Hangchow

Ningpo

RYUKYU IS.
(Japan)

P   a   c   i   f   i   c

Lhasa

Chungking

Shasi

Yochow

Kiukiang

Nanchang

Wenchow

Changsha

Santuao

Foochow

ASSAM

Brahmaputra

BHUTAN

H

(Br. from 1885)

Yünnanfu

Mengtze

Szemao

Amoy

Swatow

Taihoku

TAIWAN
(FORMOSA)
(Japan)
(from China 1895)

Hsi (West)   Canton

Wuchow   Samshui

Lungchow

Pakhoi

Hong Kong
(Br. 1842, Suppl.
lease 1898)

Macao
(Port.)

Kwangchowwan
(Fr. lease 1898)

Kiungchow

Mandalay

BURMA
(Br. from 1852)

Prome

TONGKING
(Fr. prot.
from 1884)

Hanoi

Luang Prabang

LAOS
(Fr. prot. 1893)

A
N
N
A
M

(To
Fr. 1907)

Hué

FRENCH
INDO-
CHINA

HAINAN

LUZON

Manila

PHILIPPINE

CAROLINE IS.
(Ger.)
(Purchased from
Spain 1898)

PALAU IS.
(Ger.)
(Purchased from
Spain 1898)

Rangoon

SIAM

Bangkok

Mekong

CAMBODIA
(Fr. prot. from 1863)

Phnom
Penh

COCHIN-
CHINA
(Fr. prot.
1862-67)

Saigon

South
China
Sea

Iloilo   Cebu

ISLANDS

MINDANAO

P   a   c   i   f   i   c

ANDAMAN
IS.
(Br.)

Gulf
of
Siam

Zamboanga

Finally subdued
the Dutch, 1899

ACHEH

Penang

NICOBAR
IS.
(Br.)

FEDERATED
MALAY STATES
(from 1895)

Malacca

JOHORE

(To Br. prot. 1907-09)

S   U   M   A   T   R   A

Singapore

BANKA

NORTH
BORNEO

BRUNEI

SARAWAK

B   O   R   N   E   O

CELEBES

MOLUCCAS

Amboina

NEW
GUINEA

Palembang

BILLITON

Batavia

Semarang

Surabaya

J   A   V   A

Solo

BALI

TIMOR
(Port.)

Jokjakarta

135

AFRICA IN THE NINETEENTH CENTURY

▶ MAPS ON PAGES 137 AND 138–39

AFRICA AT THE BEGINNING of the nineteenth century was still the "dark" continent (see page 137), unknown to Europeans except for its coasts, and with native Africans themselves aware of little beyond their own tribal lands. The Niger was thought to flow westward to the sea through the Senegal and Gambia rivers, supposedly its branches. Nomenclature was different: the Congo was more often called the Zaire; what is now the Sudan was called Nubia; and the "Soudan" was the southern Sahara. There were a number of African kingdoms of some importance, such as the Tukulor (often misnamed the Fulah) empire, the kingdom of Uganda, and the Zulu kingdom in the south, recently established by the Zulus in a great wave of internal migration. Abyssinia was an ancient Christian kingdom; Liberia did not yet exist. The British had recently taken Cape Colony from the Dutch, who had been there since 1652. British settlement had not begun. The Dutch inhabitants were on the eve of their great trek of 1836, by which they were to establish the Transvaal and the Orange Free State. The Mediterranean coast was better known to Europe, but quite independent of it; indeed, Europeans looked with trepidation on the "Barbary pirates" of Algiers and Tunis.

The travels of Mungo Park and James Bruce, shown on the map, had begun to penetrate the African mysteries. Tombouctu had enjoyed a fabulous repute in Europe since the Middle Ages, but an illiterate American sailor, who claimed to have been taken there as a slave in 1810, may have been the first Westerner to see it in modern times.

European possessions in Africa in 1815, except for the Dutch nucleus at the Cape Colony, were limited to disconnected trading posts and old slave stations on the coasts.

Exploration of the Interior

▶ MAP ON PAGES 138–39

All was changed before the end of the century, as may be seen on pages 138–39, which show Africa in 1898. The Frenchman Caillé and the German Barth crossed the Sahara. The greatest of African explorers, David Livingstone, setting out from Capetown, explored the Kalahari Desert, crossed the continent from Angola to Mozambique (Portuguese East Africa), traced the Zambezi River, and discovered lakes Nyassa and Tanganyika, near which he was found by H. M. Stanley in 1871. Stanley then explored the course of the Congo River. In the 1860's the German Nachtigal crossed the Sudan to Lake Chad, and the Englishman Baker proceeded up the Nile to Lake Albert Nyanza.

The Partition of Africa

By the 1880's what is usually known as the scramble for Africa was at its height, as British, French, Germans, Italians, and Portuguese—along with King Leopold II of Belgium, aided by Stanley —sought to stake out zones of domination in the interior. There were attempts at international regu-

lation: a conference at Berlin laid down rules for occupation, and set up the Congo as a "free state" with Leopold as its sovereign; and a later conference at Brussels undertook to suppress African slavery and to control the importation of firearms and liquors. By 1898 all Africa had been parcelled out among the several European powers, except Morocco and Tripoli (which were to lose their independence in 1911), Liberia, founded by ex-slaves from the United States and vaguely under its protection, and Abyssinia, which the Italians tried and failed to conquer in 1896.

The African Colonial Empires

France acquired the largest area, which, however, was largely desert. The French worked inland from Algeria, the Senegal, the Ivory Coast, and the right bank of the lower Congo, from which J. B. Marchand started out in 1897 on a west-to-east continental crossing, only to be stopped by the British at Fashoda. The French also at this time subjugated Madagascar, where they had commercial interests of much older date.

There was a substantial British emigration to Cape Colony and Natal during the nineteenth century. British expansionists, notably the great empire builder Cecil Rhodes, outflanked the two Boer republics, the Transvaal and Orange Free State, by moving up into Bechuanaland. Next, the "Chartered Company"—mainly Rhodes' creation—pushed north into what is now Rhodesia, conquering Matabeleland in 1893, and thwarting the Portuguese dream of a coast-to-coast empire. Since meanwhile Britain had occupied Egypt, Rhodes and others aspired to a continuous British territory from north to south, and even dreamed of a Cape to Cairo railway. This ambition was checked by the growth of German East Africa, which, however, passed to British hands after World War I. The British also assumed a protectorate over Zanzibar, and developed the Niger area and Gold Coast in the west.

German explorers paved the way for colonial rule in east Africa, much of which was dependent on the Moslem sultan of Zanzibar, who in 1885 was forced to yield his mainland territories to Germany. In the Kamerun, the explorer Nachtigal outmaneuvered a British consul in 1884 by persuading a local ruler to sign a treaty with Germany. Much the same happened in Togo. German Southwest Africa was mostly wasteland.

The Italians, having initiated colonial rule in Eritrea and Somaliland, attempted to invade and conquer Abyssinia, but were defeated in 1896 at Aduwa, the one battle of the period in which Europeans were worsted by native African fighters. Portugal greatly extended its territories in Angola and Mozambique, but was unable to connect them. Spain emerged from the partition with its old holdings at Fernando Pó and Río Muni, and staked out boundaries for the barren Río de Oro on the west coast.

The century ended with the Boer War, in which the British, after troubles arising with discoveries of gold in the Transvaal, subdued the two Boer republics and forced them into the British Empire, though with much local autonomy.

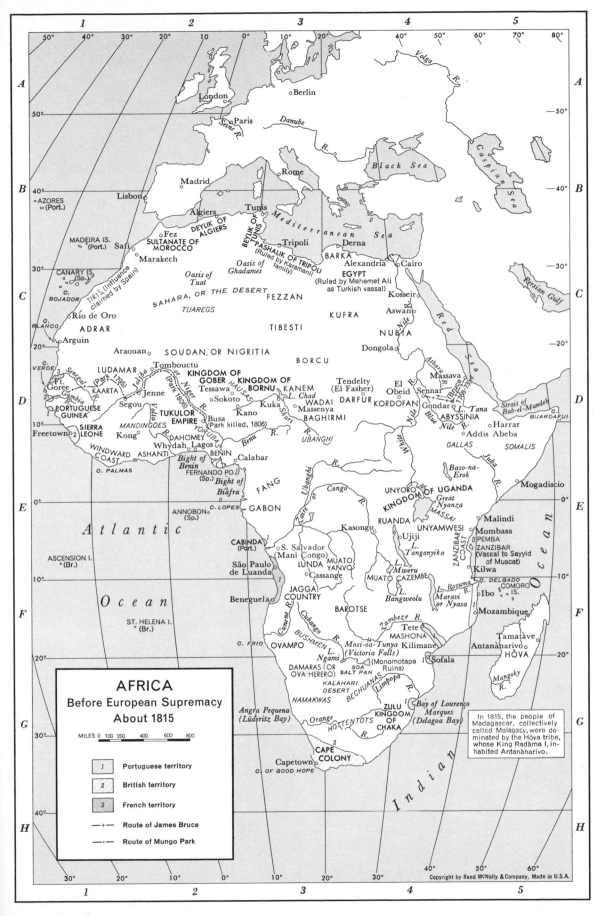

AFRICA
Before European Supremacy
About 1815

MILES 0 100 200 400 600 800

1	Portuguese territory
2	British territory
3	French territory
—+—	Route of James Bruce
—·—	Route of Mungo Park

In 1815, the people of
Madagascar, collectively
called Malagasy, were do
minated by the Hòva tribe,
whose King Radàma I, in
habited Antanànarivo.

Copyright by Rand McNally & Company, Made in U.S.A.

London
Berlin
Paris
Seine R.
Danube
Madrid
Rome
Black Sea
Volga R.
Caspian Sea
Lisbon
AZORES (Port.)
Algiers
Tunis
Mediterranean Sea
BEYLIK OF TUNIS
DEYLIK OF ALGIERS
PASHALIK OF TRIPOLI (Ruled by Karamanli family)
Tripoli
BARKA
Derna
Alexandria
Cairo
Fez
SULTANATE OF MOROCCO
Safi
Marakech
MADEIRA IS. (Port.)
Oasis of Tuat
Oasis of Ghadames
EGYPT (Ruled by Mehemet Ali as Turkish vassal)
Kosseir
Persian Gulf
CANARY IS. (Sp.)
C. BOJADOR
TIRIS (Influence claimed by Spain)
SAHARA, OR THE DESERT
FEZZAN
Aswan
Nile
Red Sea
Río de Oro
ADRAR
TUAREGS
TIBESTI
KUFRA
NUBIA
Dongola
C. BLANCO
Arguin
Araouan
SOUDAN, OR NIGRITIA
BORCU
C. VERDE
Senegal R.
Gambia R.
LUDAMAR (Park 1795)
Tombouctu
Niger R.
(Park 1806)
Joliba R.
HAUSAS
KINGDOM OF GOBER
Tessawa
KINGDOM OF BORNU
KANEM
L. Chad
Tendelty (El Fasher)
El Obeid
Massava
Atbara R.
Gondar
L. Tana
ABYSSINIA
Strait of Bab-el-Mandeb
C. GUARDAFUI
Ft. Gorée
KAARTA
Jenne
Sokoto
Kano
Kuka
WADAI
Massenya
DARFUR
KORDOFAN
Sennar
Blue Nile R.
Harrar
Addis Abeba
PORTUGUESE GUINEA
Segou
TUKULOR EMPIRE
Busa (Park killed, 1806)
BAGHIRMI
Shari R.
White Nile
SIERRA LEONE
Freetown
MANDINGOES
Kong
DAHOMEY
YORUBA
Benu R.
UBANGHI
GALLAS
SOMALIS
WINDWARD COAST
ASHANTI
Whydah, Lagos
BENIN
Calabar
Bight of Benin
FERNANDO PO (Sp.)
Bight of Biafra
FANG
Ubanghi R.
Congo R.
Baso-na-Erok
Juba R.
Mogadiscio
C. PALMAS
ANNOBON (Sp.)
C. LOPES
GABON
Zaire R.
UNYORO
KINGDOM OF UGANDA
Great Nyanza
MASSAI
Malindi
Atlantic Ocean
ASCENSION I. (Br.)
CABINDA (Port.)
S. Salvador (Mani Congo)
Kasongo
RUANDA
UNYAMWESI
Ujiji
L. Tanganyika
ZANZIBAR COAST
Mombasa
PEMBA
ZANZIBAR (Vassal to Sayyid of Muscat)
Kilwa
São Paulo de Luanda
LUNDA
MUATO YANVO
Cassange
L. Mweru
MUATO CAZEMBE
Indian Ocean
ST. HELENA I. (Br.)
JAGGA COUNTRY
Beneguela
L. Bangweolu
L. Maravi or Nyasa
Rovuma R.
C. DELGADO
COMORO IS.
Ibo
Mozambique
BAROTSE
Zambeze R.
Tete
MASHONA
Kilimane
Sofala
Tamatáve
Antanànarivo
HÒVA
C. FRIO
Cunena R.
Cubango R.
OVAMPO
Mosi-oa-Tunya (Victoria Falls)
(Monomotapa Ruins)
Mangoky R.
BUSHMEN
L. Ngami
DAMARAS (OR OVA-HERERO)
SOA SALT PAN
KALAHARI DESERT
BECHUANAS
Limpopo R.
Angra Pequena (Lüderitz Bay)
NAMAKWAS
ZULU KINGDOM OF CHAKA
Bay of Lourenço Marques (Delagoa Bay)
Orange R.
HOTTENTOTS
CAPE COLONY
Capetown
C. OF GOOD HOPE

137

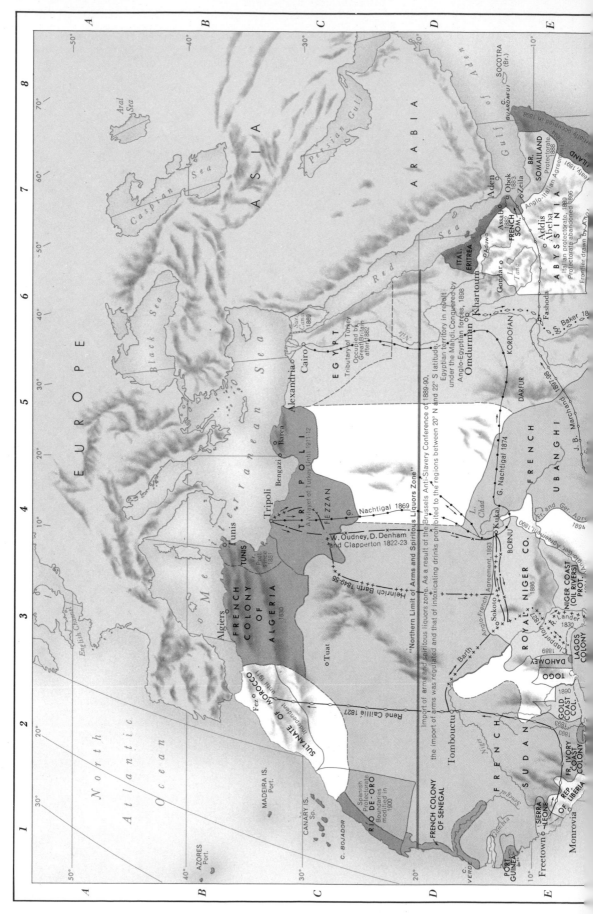

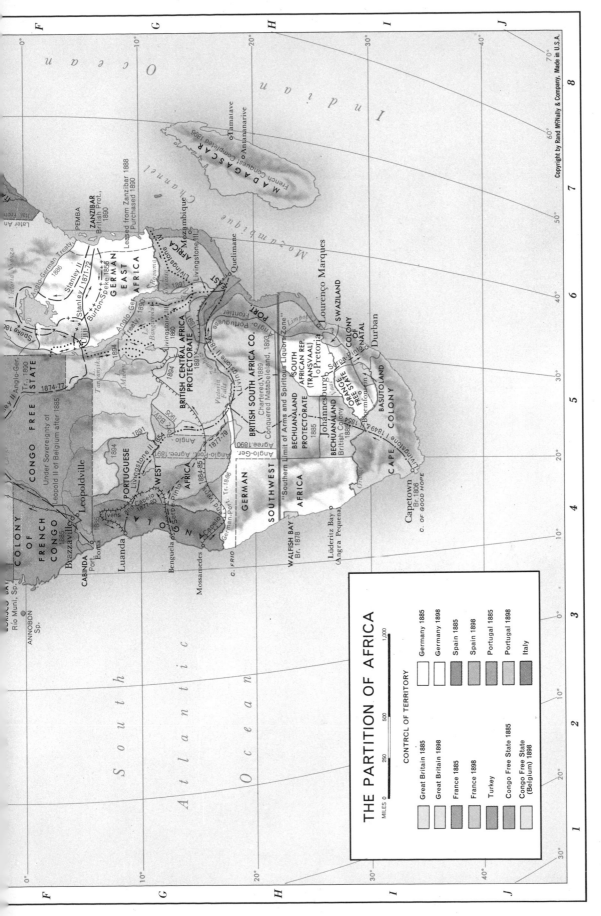

INDIAN AMERICA
AND COLONIAL AMERICA

▶ MAPS ON PAGES 140, 142–43, AND 144

THIS GROUP OF MAPS illustrates the history of the Americas before the wars of independence. For the West Indies and the territory that became the United States see also pages 148, 149, and 150.

The American Indians
▶ MAP ON PAGE 140

It is agreed that the American aborigines were not native to America, but came to it at an unknown date, perhaps as recently as the last ice age, when a land bridge existed between America and Asia. In America they developed very unevenly. Four higher cultures appeared: the Nahua (Aztec) of south central Mexico; the Mayan of Yucatan; the Chibcha of highland Colombia; and the Quechua (Inca) of Peru and Bolivia. These peoples all practised an intelligent agriculture, worked gold and silver but not iron, and built handsome stone temples and sizable cities. They had complex priesthoods and diverse forms of government. On the other hand, they had no writing but the crudest, and the Incas and Chibchas had none at all; and the absence of beasts of burden, except for the small llama and alpaca (confined to the Andes), made for difficulties all the greater since they never invented the wheel.

The Indians north of Mexico were mainly hunters and fishers, though some were agricultural, like the Choctaws, Creeks, and Seminoles. The anthropophagical habits of the Caribs in the West Indies (called "Caribals" or "Canibals" in Columbus' time) gave a new noun to the Europeans. Indian tribes are shown on the map in places where Europeans first met them; many later moved.

Latin America to 1790
▶ MAP ON PAGES 142–43

The Spanish and Portuguese empires in three hundred years developed to the point shown on pages 142–43. The Spanish empire began with Columbus' second voyage and conquest of the Greater Antilles. Spanish colonization of the mainland began in 1509 at the isthmus of Darien. Explorations in the next half-century staked out the area that Spain was to claim (see page 62). By conquest, missionary enterprise, emigration, and agricultural and mining activities the Spanish American empire grew steadily until the close of the eighteenth century.

Its fundamental unit was the viceroyalty, governed by a high-born Spaniard in the name of the king. The first viceroyalty, that of New Spain, founded at Mexico in 1535, came to include everything from what is now the western United States to Central America. The viceroyalty of Peru, set up in 1542 at Lima, long embraced the whole of Spanish South America. A third viceroyalty, New Granada, was established in 1740 to strengthen defenses against the rising menace of foreigners, mainly British, from the Caribbean. The fourth and last

viceroyalty, La Plata, was created in 1776 at Buenos Aires, largely to resist Portuguese pressure from Brazil. These viceroyalties lasted until the beginning of the movement for independence in 1810. They were so large, and transport and communications within them were so difficult, that captaincy generals and presidencies were partly detached from them and governed in effect by officials of their own. Each viceroyalty was also divided into audiencias, or areas governed by royally appointed judges. In the eighteenth century the Spanish Bourbons, imitating the more efficient French administrative system, introduced intendancies for fiscal affairs; those for New Spain are shown on the map.

Brazil, discovered by the Portuguese Cabral in 1500, was not colonized by the Portuguese until 1530. They then divided the coast east of the meridian established by the Treaty of Tordesillas (see page 61) into fifteen captaincies which were turned over to private proprietors to colonize. These grants gradually reverted to the Portuguese crown. In the 1550's a French group, largely Huguenot, attempted to found a colony at Guanabara Bay (Rio de Janeiro), but they were driven away. The Dutch in the seventeenth century captured numerous settlements in northeastern Brazil, and came near to permanent occupation (see page 144), but the Brazilian Portuguese, with some help from the home country, finally managed to expel them. The interior was explored by bandeirantes (banner companies of São Paulo) in search of gold, jewels, plunder, and slaves. The latter two were often appropriated from the Spanish Jesuit missions in Paraguay. The bandeirantes became so formidable that the Spanish government, giving up the effort to maintain the obsolete Tordesillas line, surrendered enough territorial claims to Portugal in the eighteenth century to bring Brazil to approximately its present size. Brazil was made permanently a viceroyalty in 1714.

Northern Europeans in the Americas
▶ MAP ON PAGE 144

The huge reaches of America which Spain and Portugal divided between them were soon infiltrated by northern Europeans. The Dutch hoped to take Brazil and the sister colony of Angola in Africa from Portugal. They failed. Many Dutch fleeing from Brazil withdrew to New Amsterdam, until then very secondary in Dutch calculations. Other byproducts of the south Atlantic venture were Dutch settlements at Curaçao and Surinam (Dutch Guiana), which today comprise nearly all that is left of the once great Netherlands colonial empire.

Early French efforts at colonization in Brazil and Florida were annihilated by Portugal and Spain. French enterprise developed in the St. Lawrence and Mississippi valleys, which the French were the first fully to explore and to colonize. By 1752 the French had a post as remote as Fort La Jonquière at what is now Calgary. British ventures in North America are well known; the British colonies appear in more detail on page 150.

In the eighteenth century the most profitable of all north European colonies in America were the West Indian sugar islands (see page 148).

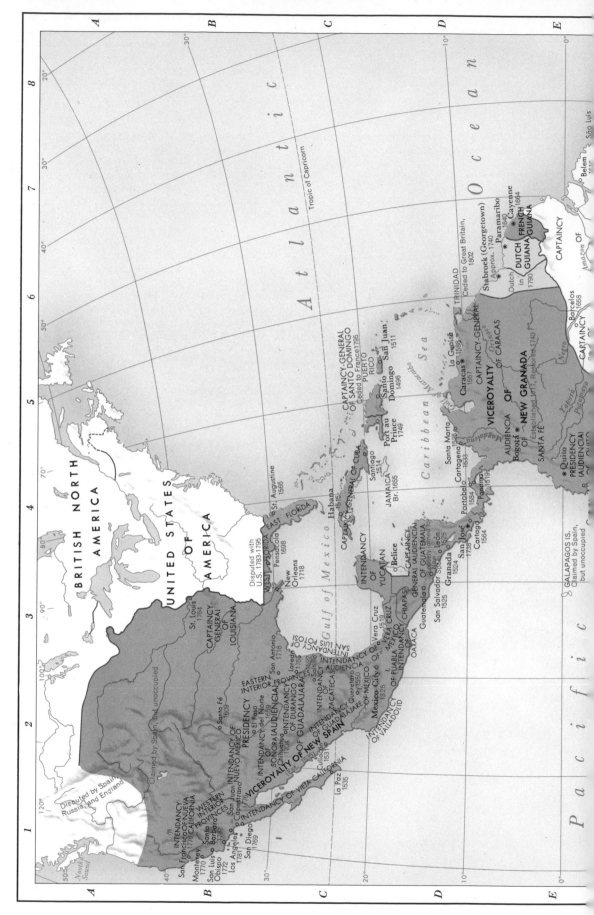

A   B   C   D   E

BRITISH NORTH AMERICA

UNITED STATES OF AMERICA

Disputed by Spain, Russia, and England

Claimed by Spain, but unoccupied

INTENDANCY OF NUEVA CALIFORNIA
San Francisco 1776
Monterey 1770
San Luis Obispo 1772
Santa Barbara 1786
Los Angeles 1781
San Diego 1769
San Juan Capistrano 1776

WESTERN INTERIOR PROVINCES
PRESIDENCY OF NUEVO MEXICO
Santa Fé 1609
El Paso 1659
Chihuahua 1704

SONORA (AUDIENCIA) OF DURANGO

St. Louis 1764

CAPTAINCY-GENERAL OF LOUISIANA

EASTERN INTERIOR PROVINCES
San Antonio 1718
Laredo 1755
Saltillo

INTENDANCY OF ZACATECAS

INTENDANCY OF GUADALAJARA
Querétaro 1531
Guadalajare 1531
Culiacán 1531

VICEROYALTY OF NEW SPAIN

INTENDANCY OF VIEJA CALIFORNIA
La Paz 1535

INTENDANCY OF SAN LUIS POTOSI

INTENDANCY OF VALLADOLID

INTENDANCY OF MEXICO
Mexico City 1325

INTENDANCY OF PUEBLA
INTENDANCY OF CHIAPAS

INTENDANCY OF OAXACA

INTENDANCY OF VERA CRUZ
Vera Cruz 1519

West Florida
Pensacola 1698
New Orleans 1718

EAST FLORIDA
St. Augustine 1565

Habana 1515

CAPTAINCY-GENERAL OF CUBA

Santiago 1514

JAMAICA Br. 1655

Port au Prince 1749

CAPTAINCY-GENERAL OF SANTO DOMINGO
Ceded to France 1795

PUERTO RICO
San Juan 1511

Santo Domingo 1496

INTENDANCY OF YUCATAN
Belice

CAPTAINCY-GENERAL OF GUATEMALA (AUDIENCIA)
Guatemala 1524
San Salvador 1528
León 1524
Granada 1524
San José 1738
Cartago 1564

Gulf of Mexico

Caribbean Sea

TRINIDAD Ceded to Great Britain, Approx. 1740

Stabroek (Georgetown) 1640
Paramaribo 1640
Cayenne 1664

DUTCH in GUIANA 1790
DUTCH GUIANA
FRENCH GUIANA

La Guira 1588
Caracas 1567
Santa Marta 1525/0
Cartagena 1533
Portobelo 1584
Panamá 1519

CAPTAINCY-GENERAL OF CARACAS

VICEROYALTY OF NEW GRANADA
AUDIENCIA OF NEW GRANADA
Bogotá 1538
SANTA FÉ

Quito 1534
PRESIDENCY (AUDIENCIA) OF QUITO

Established 1717, Restored 1740

GALAPAGOS IS.
Claimed by Spain, but unoccupied

Barcelos 1668
CAPTAINCY OF

Belem 1616
São Luis

Amazon

CAPTAINCY OF

A t l a n t i c   O c e a n

Tropic of Capricorn

P a c i f i c

Nootka Sound

A   B   C   D   E

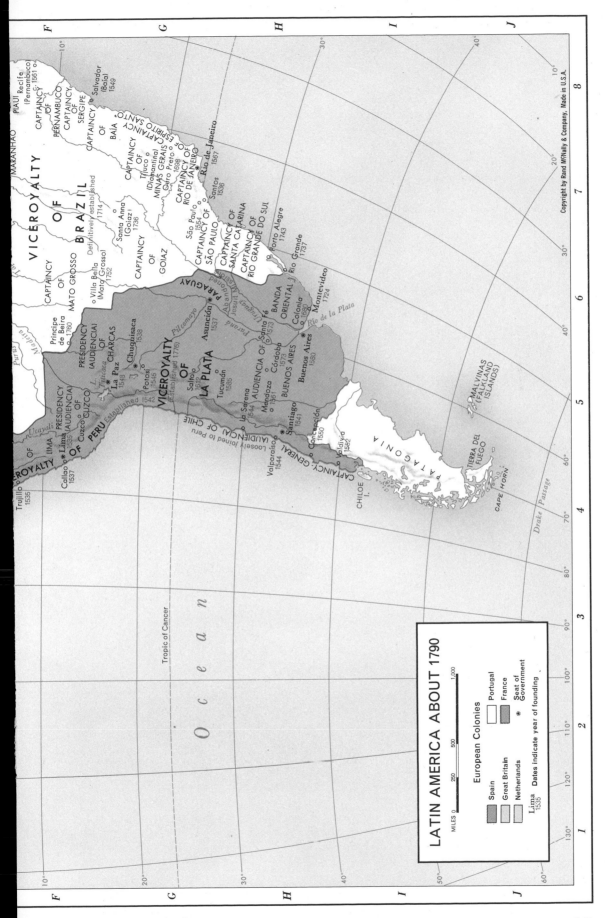

MARANHÃO

VICEROYALTY

OF

BRAZIL

PIAUI
CAPTAINCY
OF
PERNAMBUCO

Recife
(Pernambuco) 1561

CAPTAINCY
OF
SERGIPE

Salvador
(Baía)
1549

CAPTAINCY
OF
BAIA

CAPTAINCY
OF ESPIRITO SANTO

CAPTAINCY
OF
MATO GROSSO

CAPTAINCY
OF
MINAS GERAIS
1698

Tijuco
(Diamantina)

Ouro
Preto

Rio de Janeiro
1567

o Villa Bella
(Mato Grosso)
1752

Definitively established
1714

Santa Anna
(Goiaz)
1736

CAPTAINCY
OF RIO DE JANEIRO

Santos
1536

Príncipe
de Beira
1760

CAPTAINCY
OF
GOIAZ

São Paulo
1554

CAPTAINCY OF
SÃO PAULO

CAPTAINCY OF
SANTA CATARINA

CAPTAINCY OF
RIO GRANDE DO SUL

Porto Alegre
1743

Rio Grande
1737

PRESIDENCY
(AUDIENCIA)
OF
CHARCAS

PARAGUAY

DISTRICT OF PARAGUAY

Asunción
1537

BANDA
ORIENTAL

Montevideo
1724

Colonia
1680

Rio de la Plata

VICEROYALTY
OF
LA PLATA

(Established 1776)

Chuquisaca
1538

La Paz
1548

Potosi
1545

AUDIENCIA OF
Santa Fe
1573

Córdoba
1573

AUDIENCIA OF
BUENOS AIRES

Buenos Aires
1580

PRESIDENCY
(AUDIENCIA)
OF
CUZCO

Cuzco
1532

Salta
1582

Tucumán
1565

Mendoza
1561

PERU Established 1542

VICEROYALTY

OF

PERU

PRESIDENCY
(AUDIENCIA)
OF LIMA

Lima
1535

Callao
1537

Trujillo
1535

La Serena
1544

Santiago
1541

Concepción
1550

CAPTAINCY-GENERAL (AUDIENCIA) OF CHILE

Loosely joined to Peru

Valparaíso
1544

Valdivia
1562

CHILOE I.

MALVINAS
(FALKLAND
ISLANDS)

PATAGONIA

TIERRA DEL
FUEGO

CAPE HORN

Drake Passage

O c e a n

Tropic of Cancer

Copyright by Rand McNally & Company. Made in U.S.A.

Ucayali

Purus

Madeira

Paraná

Uruguay

Paraguay

Pilcomayo

L. Titicaca

LATIN AMERICA ABOUT 1790

European Colonies

- Spain
- Great Britain
- Netherlands
- Portugal
- France
- * Seat of Government

Lima
1535   Dates indicate year of founding

MILES 0   250   500   1,000

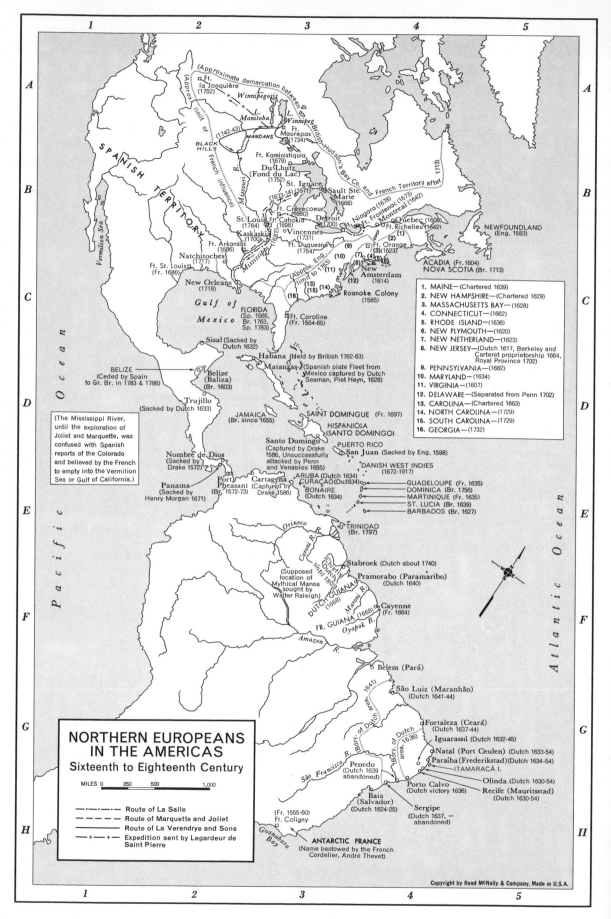

NORTHERN EUROPEANS
IN THE AMERICAS
Sixteenth to Eighteenth Century

MILES 0   250   500   1,000

.—..—..—..— Route of La Salle
— — — — — Route of Marquette and Joliet
————— Route of La Verendrye and Sons
—+—+—+— Expedition sent by Legardeur de Saint Pierre

1. MAINE—(Chartered 1639)
2. NEW HAMPSHIRE—(Chartered 1629)
3. MASSACHUSETTS BAY—(1628)
4. CONNECTICUT—(1662)
5. RHODE ISLAND—(1636)
6. NEW PLYMOUTH—(1620)
7. NEW NETHERLAND—(1623)
8. NEW JERSEY—(Dutch 1617, Berkeley and Carteret proprietorship 1664, Royal Province 1702)
9. PENNSYLVANIA—(1682)
10. MARYLAND—(1634)
11. VIRGINIA—(1607)
12. DELAWARE—(Separated from Penn 1702)
13. CAROLINA—(Chartered 1663)
14. NORTH CAROLINA—(1729)
15. SOUTH CAROLINA—(1729)
16. GEORGIA—(1732)

(The Mississippi River, until the exploration of Joliet and Marquette, was confused with Spanish reports of the Colorado and believed by the French to empty into the Vermilion Sea or Gulf of California.)

Ft. la Jonquière (1752)
(Approx. limit of French influence)
L. Winnipegosis
L. Manitoba
L. Winnipeg
Ft. Maurepas (1734)
(1742-43)
(Approximate demarcation between)
SPANISH TERRITORY
BLACK HILLS
MANDANS
Vermilion Sea
Missouri R.
Ft. Kaministiquia (1679)
Du Lhutz (Fond du Lac) (1752)
St. Ignace (1671)
(1673-74)
Sault Ste. Marie (1668)
British Hudson's Bay Co. and French Territory after (1713)
NEWFOUNDLAND (Eng. 1583)
Niagara (1678)
Ft. Frontenac (1673)
Montreal (1642)
Ft. Richelieu (1642)
Québec (1608)
Ft. Crèvecoeur (1680)
St. Louis (1764)
Ft. Cahokia (1698)
Detroit (1700)
Vincennes (1731)
Kaskaskia (1700)
Ft. Duquesne (1754)
Ft. Arkansas (1686)
Natchitoches (1717)
Ft. St. Louis (Fr. 1686)
New Orleans (1718)
Mississippi R.
(Approx. Eng. limit to 1763)
Ft. Orange (1623)
New Amsterdam (1614)
ACADIA (Fr. 1604)
NOVA SCOTIA (Br. 1713)
Roanoke Colony (1585)
Gulf of Mexico
FLORIDA (Sp. 1565, Br. 1763, Sp. 1783)
Ft. Caroline (Fr. 1564-65)
Sisal (Sacked by Dutch 1632)
Habana (Held by British 1762-63)
Matanzas (Spanish plate Fleet from Mexico captured by Dutch Seaman, Piet Heyn, 1628)
BELIZE (Ceded by Spain to Gr. Br. in 1783 & 1786)
Belize (Baliza) (Br. 1603)
Trujillo (Sacked by Dutch 1633)
JAMAICA (Br. since 1655)
SAINT DOMINGUE (Fr. 1697)
HISPANIOLA (SANTO DOMINGO)
Santo Domingo (Captured by Drake 1586, Unsuccessfully attacked by Penn and Venables 1655)
PUERTO RICO
San Juan (Sacked by Eng. 1598)
DANISH WEST INDIES (1672-1917)
Nombre de Dios (Sacked by Drake 1572)
Port Pheasant (Br. 1572-73)
Cartagena (Captured by Drake 1586)
Panama (Sacked by Henry Morgan 1671)
ARUBA (Dutch 1634)
CURAÇAO (Du 1634)
BONAIRE (Dutch 1634)
GUADELOUPE (Fr. 1635)
DOMINICA (Br. 1756)
MARTINIQUE (Fr. 1635)
ST. LUCIA (Br. 1639)
BARBADOS (Br. 1627)
TRINIDAD (Br. 1797)
Orinoco R.
Caroni R.
(Supposed location of Mythical Manoa sought by Walter Raleigh)
Stabroek (Dutch about 1740)
Pramorabo (Paramaribo) (Dutch 1640)
(Chiefly Dutch until 1803)
DUTCH GUIANA (1668)
FR. GUIANA
Maroni R.
Cayenne (Fr. 1664)
(1668)
Oyapok R.
Amazon R.
Belem (Pará)
São Luiz (Maranhão) (Dutch 1641-44)
(1641)
(bdry. of Dutch area)
Fortaleza (Ceará) (Dutch 1637-44)
(1636)
Iguarassú (Dutch 1632-45)
Natal (Port Ceulen) (Dutch 1633-54)
Paraíba (Frederikstad) (Dutch 1634-54)
ITAMARACÁ I.
Olinda (Dutch 1630-54)
Recife (Mauritsstad) (Dutch 1630-54)
Porto Calvo (Dutch victory 1636)
Penedo (Dutch 1639 abandoned)
São Francisco R.
Sergipe (Dutch 1637, — abandoned)
Baia (Salvador) (Dutch 1624-25)
(Fr. 1555-60)
Ft. Coligny
Guanabara Bay
ANTARCTIC FRANCE (Name bestowed by the French Cordelier, André Thevet)

Pacific Ocean

Atlantic Ocean

LATIN AMERICA
AFTER INDEPENDENCE

▶ MAP ON PAGES 146–47

THE EUROPEAN colonial systems, as they had grown up since the Age of Discovery (see pages 62–63), were liquidated or transformed during the half-century of revolution in the Atlantic world (see pages 86–87). The independence of the United States amputated a large portion of the older British Empire; the French in losing Haiti lost the most lucrative of their eighteenth-century colonies; the Dutch empire, with the loss of the Cape of Good Hope and Ceylon, was virtually confined to the East Indies. In addition, Spanish and Portuguese America became independent—except for Cuba and Puerto Rico, which remained Spanish until 1898.

A few details of the Latin American revolutions are shown on pages 86–87. The map on pages 146–147 shows Latin America in the decades following independence.

The Spanish American Republics

In a general way the new republics followed jurisdictional lines of the former Spanish empire (see pages 142–43), but in no case did one of the great viceroyalties hold together. Localist aspirations and needs, arising from the great distances and diversity of conditions and fomented by regional chieftains or dictators called *caudillos*, tended to pull apart the larger units. When Mexico, for example, became independent in 1821, at first as a monarchy under Agustín de Iturbide, the Central Americans were persuaded to remain united with it as in the former viceroyalty of New Spain. When Iturbide was overthrown in 1823, Central America separated from Mexico. At first it was an independent confederation, but in 1838 it broke into the five small republics of Guatemala, El Salvador, Honduras, Nicaragua, and Costa Rica. Subsequent attempts to revive the confederation have been in vain.

Northern South America, liberated by Bolívar, at first held together as the Republic of Colombia, called Great Colombia by historians to distinguish it from the reduced Colombia of later times. At Bolívar's death in 1830 it had already broken up, because of mutual jealousies, into New Granada (the present Colombia), Venezuela, and Ecuador. Panama remained with Colombia until its secession over the canal issue in 1903.

Bolivia was separated from the viceroyalty of La Plata (in effect Argentina) during the wars of independence. During these same wars Argentina also lost the provinces known as Paraguay and Uruguay. Chile, shut off by the Andes, had developed a separate identity long before.

Spanish America, since its independence, has receded at its northern extremity and expanded in the south. Mexico, having unwisely permitted a large English-speaking immigration from the United States into Texas, faced a Texan revolt in 1836. Texas became an independent republic, and was annexed in 1845 to the United States. After the ensuing war with the United States, Mexico lost its northern territories from Texas to upper California. In 1853 the inept dictator, Santa Anna, consented to part with the Mesilla Strip (Gadsden Purchase) for cash. The far south, below about 40° south latitude, was wild Indian country when the Chilean and Argentine republics were established. Not until the last quarter of the nineteenth century did these two states bring these regions under their authority. The southern part of the Argentine-Chilean boundary was long disputed, since the crest of the Andes, accepted in principle as the boundary, was difficult to locate. In 1898 the two republics came close to war over Tierra del Fuego and the Strait of Magellan, but in 1902, through British arbitration, they accepted the southern boundary which still exists. Argentina still claims the Falkland Islands

Nineteenth-Century Wars

There were three principal Latin American wars in the nineteenth century, in addition to the war between Mexico and the United States. In 1836 the Bolivian dictator, Santa Cruz, sought to form a federation between Bolivia and Peru. Chile, feeling itself threatened for balance-of-power reasons, sent its troops into Peru. Aided by Peruvians hostile to Santa Cruz, the Chileans broke up the confederation; Santa Cruz went into exile, and Peru and Bolivia resumed their separate existence.

The War of the Pacific, begun in 1879, with Chile again opposed to Peru and Bolivia, arose both from balance-of-power considerations and from rivalries over the nitrate-producing provinces of Tacna, Arica, Tarapacá, and Atacama. The first three were part of Peru; Atacama was Bolivian; but Chilean companies were most active in exploitation of the nitrate. Chile went to war when Peru and Bolivia seemed about to tax the companies out of existence. Easily winning, Chile annexed all four provinces. The loss was especially serious for Bolivia, which was left without a seacoast. Chile returned Tacna to Peru in 1929.

The third war was that of the Triple Alliance against Paraguay. The unbalanced Paraguayan dictator, López, dreaming of carving out a South American empire for himself, recklessly attacked both Argentina and Brazil, which were joined by Uruguay. The war ended in 1870 with López dead, Paraguay invaded, devastated, and almost depopulated, and cessions made to Brazil and Argentina as shown on the map. Paraguay recouped its losses to some extent in the twentieth century, by making good its claims against Bolivia in the Chaco.

Brazil

Portuguese-speaking Brazil, though independent in 1822, remained a monarchy until 1889 (see page 89). The stablest of the Latin American states in the nineteenth century, and able to deal with its problems in a constructive way before embarking on its own republican experiment, Brazil also conducted a successful diplomacy with its neighbors. Indeed, Brazilian contributions to international law have obtained a world-wide recognition. The map shows territorial cessions to Brazil by half-a-dozen other states. Brazil accomplished this expansion with a minimum of violence, except in the case of the Paraguayan war.

A t l a n t i c   O c e a n

Tropic of Cancer

UNITED STATES

Ohio

Mississippi

Missouri

Arkansas

Red

Sabine

Rio Grande

New
Orleans

Gulf of Mexico

Habana

CUBA
Sp. until 1898

DOMINICAN REPUBLIC
United with Haiti
until 1844

Santiago HAITI

Port au
Prince Santo
Domingo

VIRGIN
ISLANDS
(Den.)

PUERTO
RICO
Sp. until 1898

JAMAICA
(British)

Caribbean   Sea

TRINIDAD
(British)

CURACAO (Dutch)

La Guaira

Caracas

VENEZUELA
(1830)

Orinoco

BRITISH
GUIANA

DUTCH
GUIANA

FRENCH
GUIANA

MARAJO I.

Belem

Amazon

Ceded by Ecuador
to Brazil 1904

Ceded by
Venezuela to
Brazil 1859

New Granada 1831
Granadine Confederation 1858
United States of Colombia 1863
Republic of Colombia 1886

GREAT
COLOMBIA
(1819-1830)

Bogotá

Ceded by
Colombia to
Brazil 1907

Quito
ECUADOR
State of the Equator 1830
o Rest of the Equator 1835

Panama

PANAMA ISTHMUS
To Colombia 1821-1903

Santa Marta

Gulf of
Maracaibo

MOSQUITO COAST
British Protectorate
1841-50

BRITISH
HONDURAS

Belice

HONDURAS

Tegucigalpa

NICARAGUA

Managua

San José
COSTA RICA

GALAPAGOS IS
Ecuador since 1832

Pacific   Ocean

MEXICO

TEXAS
Independent 1836
Annexed to U.S. 1845
Republic 1824
Monarchy 1822-23

Santa Fé

Chihuahua o

Monterrey

Mesilla Strip
Sold to U.S.
1853

Tampico

Jalapa
Vera Cruz

Mexico
City

Puebla

Acapulco

YUCATAN
Independent
1839-48

CHIAPAS
To Mexico 1824

Guatemala
GUATEMALA

San Salvador
SALVADOR

CENTRAL AMERICA
Independent 1821
United with Mexico 1821
Independent Confederation 1823
Divided into five states 1838

LOWER

CALIFORNIA

Ceded to U.S.
1848

42nd
Parallel

San Francisco
Monterey

San Diego

Columbia

Gila

San Pedro

Colorado

San Juan

146

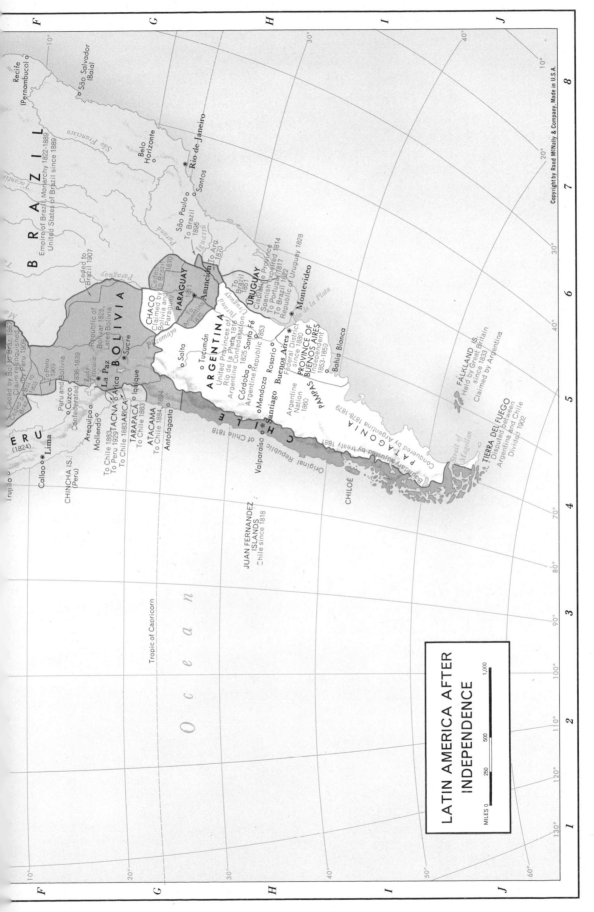

LATIN AMERICA AFTER
INDEPENDENCE

MILES 0   250   500   1,000

Copyright by Rand McNally & Company, Made in U.S.A.

147

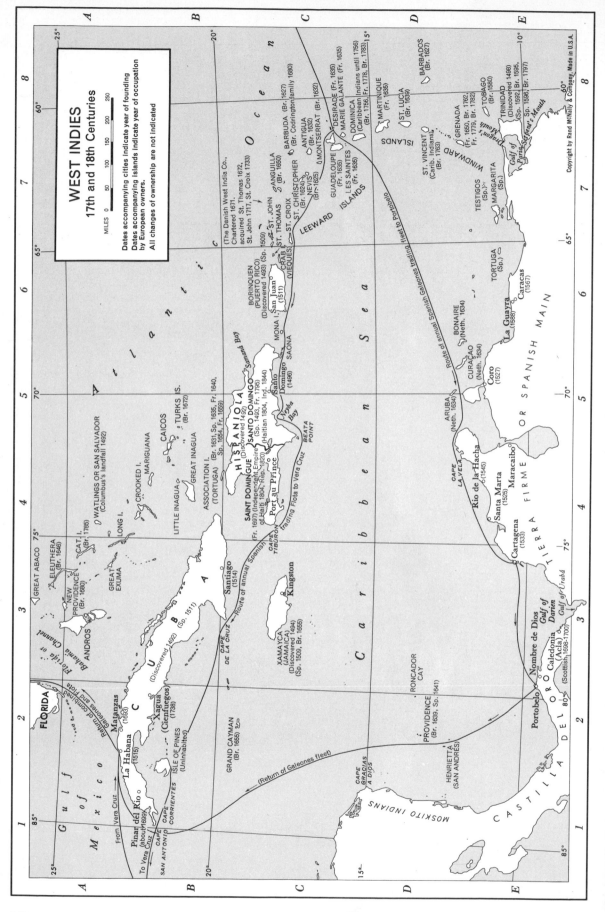

WEST INDIES
17th and 18th Centuries

MILES
0 50 100 150 200 250

Dates accompanying cities indicate year of founding
Dates accompanying islands indicate year of occupation
by European owners.
All changes of ownership are not indicated

(The Danish West India Co.,
Chartered 1671.
acquired St. Thomas 1672,
St. John 1717, St. Croix 1733)

Copyright by Rand McNally & Company, Made in U.S.A.

A t l a n t i c   O c e a n

BARBUDA (Br. 1627)
ANGUILLA (Br. 1650)
ST. CHRISTOPHER (Br. 1624)
ANTIGUA (Br. 1632)
BARBADOS (Br. 1627)
DESIRADE (Fr. 1635)
MARIE GALANTE (Fr. 1635)
MONTSERRAT (Br. 1632)
NEVIS (Br. 1625)
MARTINIQUE (Fr. 1635)
ST. LUCIA (Br. 1639)
DOMINICA (Caribbean Indians until 1756) (Br. 1756, Fr. 1778, Fr. 1783, Br. 1783)
GUADELOUPE (Fr. 1635)
LES SAINTES (Fr. 1635)
TRINIDAD (Discovered 1498) (Sp. 1592, Br. 1595, Sp. 1596, Br. 1797)
TOBAGO (Br. 1580)
GRENADA (Fr. 1650, Br. 1762, Fr. 1779, Br. 1782)
ST. VINCENT (Carib. Indians) (Br. 1763)

ST. JOHN
ST. THOMAS
ST. CROIX
ANTIGUA (Br. Codrington family 1680)

L E E W A R D   I S L A N D S

W I N D W A R D   I S L A N D S

Dragon's Mouth
Gulf of Paria
Serpent's Mouth

CRAB I. or
VIEQUES

BORINQUEN
(PUERTO RICO)
(Discovered 1493) (Sp.)
San Juan (1511)

MONA I.
SAONA (1496)

Route of annual Spanish Galeones trading fleet to Portobelo

TESTIGOS (Sp.)
MARGARITA (Sp.)
TORTUGA (Sp.)
BONAIRE (Neth. 1634)
CURAÇAO (Neth. 1634)
Caracas (1567)
La Guayra (1588)
Coro (1527)
ARUBA (Neth. 1634)

O R   S P A N I S H   M A I N

HISPANIOLA (Discovered 1492)
SANTO DOMINGO
(Sp. 1493, Fr. 1795)
(Haitian 1804, Ind. 1844)
Santo Domingo
SAINT DOMINGUE
(Fr. 1697) (Independent Empire
of Haiti 1804, Rep. 1820)
Port au Prince
Neyba Bay
Samaná Bay
BEATA POINT
CAPE TIBURON

C a r i b b e a n   S e a

Trading Flota to Vera Cruz

CAPE LA VELA
Río de la Hacha (1545)
Santa Marta (1525)
Maracaibo
Cartagena (1533)
TIERRA FIRME

A t l a n t i c

TURKS IS. (Br. 1672)
ASSOCIATION I. (TORTUGA) (Br. 1631, Sp. 1635, Fr. 1640, Sp. 1654, Fr. 1659)
CAICOS
GREAT INAGUA
LITTLE INAGUA
MARIGUANA
CROOKED I.
LONG I.
WATLINGS OR SAN SALVADOR (Columbus's landfall 1492)
GREAT EXUMA
CAT. I. (Br. 1785)
ELEUTHERA (Br. 1646)
GREAT ABACO

Florida or Bahama Channel

NEW PROVIDENCE (Br. 1680)
ANDROS

FLORIDA

G u l f   o f   M e x i c o

From Vera Cruz
To Vera Cruz
Return of combined
Galeones and Flota
(about 1699)

CAPE SAN ANTONIO
CAPE CORRIENTES
Pinar del Río
Matanzas (1693)
La Habana (1515)
Xagua (Cienfuegos) (1738)
ISLE OF PINES (Uninhabited)
Santiago (1514)
CAPE DE LA CRUZ
Route of annual Spanish

C U B A
(Discovered 1492) (Sp. 1511)

XAMAYCA (JAMAICA)
(Discovered 1494)
(Sp. 1509, Br. 1655)
Kingston

GRAND CAYMAN (Br. 1655)

RONCADOR CAY
PROVIDENCE (Br. 1639, Sp. 1641)
HENRIETTA (SAN ANDRÉS)
CAPE GRACIAS A DIOS
(Return of Galeones fleet)

MOSKITO INDIANS

Nombre de Dios
Portobelo
Caledonia (Acla)
(Scottish, 1698-1700)
Gulf of Darien
Gulf of Urabá
CASTILLA DEL ORO
TIERRA FIRME
CASTILLA

148

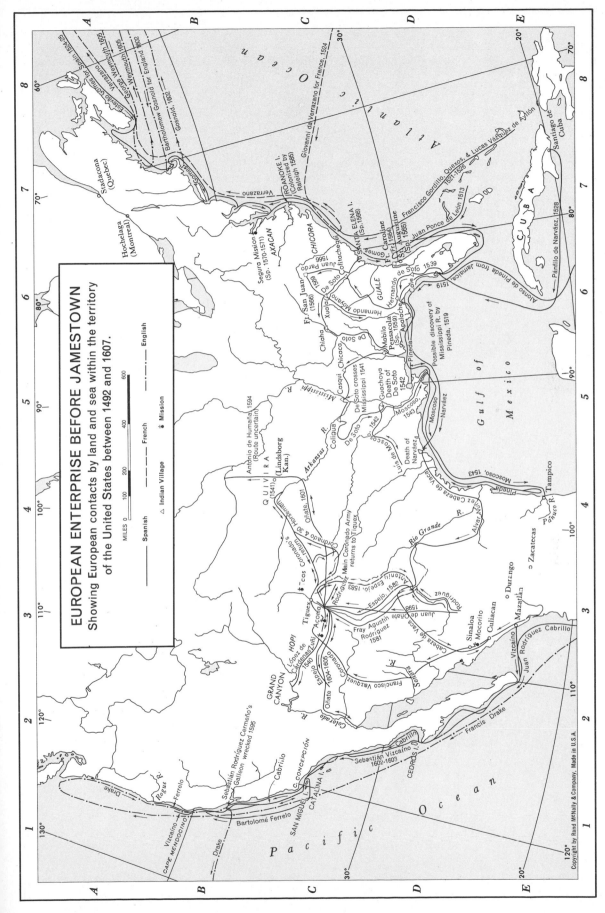

EUROPEAN ENTERPRISE BEFORE JAMESTOWN

Showing European contacts by land and sea within the territory
of the United States between 1492 and 1607.

MILES 0 100 200 400 600

△ Indian Village   ꙮ Mission

————— Spanish
—·—·— French
—··—··— English

149

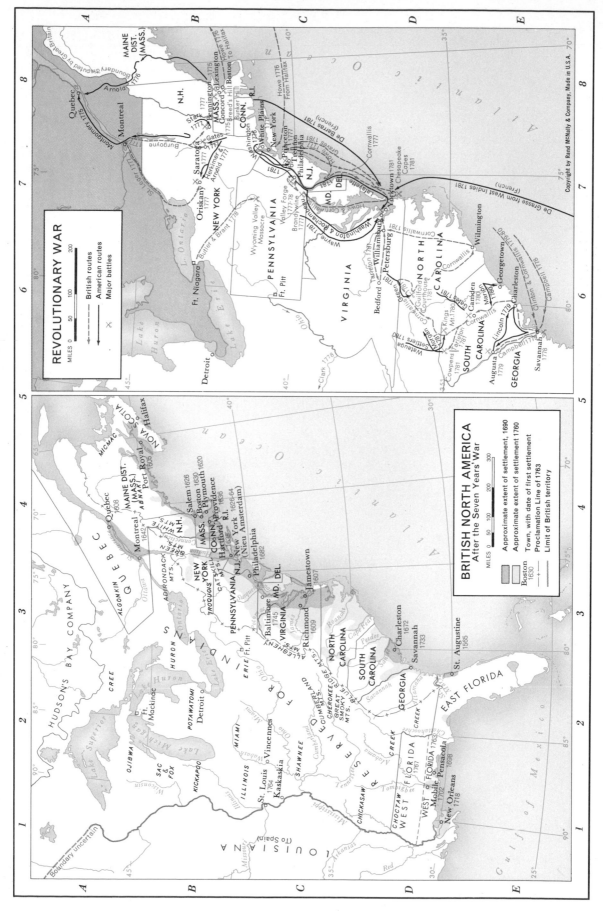

REVOLUTIONARY WAR

MILES 0 50 100 200

— — British routes
- - - - American routes
✕ Major battles

BRITISH NORTH AMERICA
After the Seven Years' War

MILES 0 50 100 200 300

Approximate extent of settlement, 1690
Approximate extent of settlement 1760

Boston — Town, with date of first settlement
1630

Proclamation Line of 1763
Limit of British territory

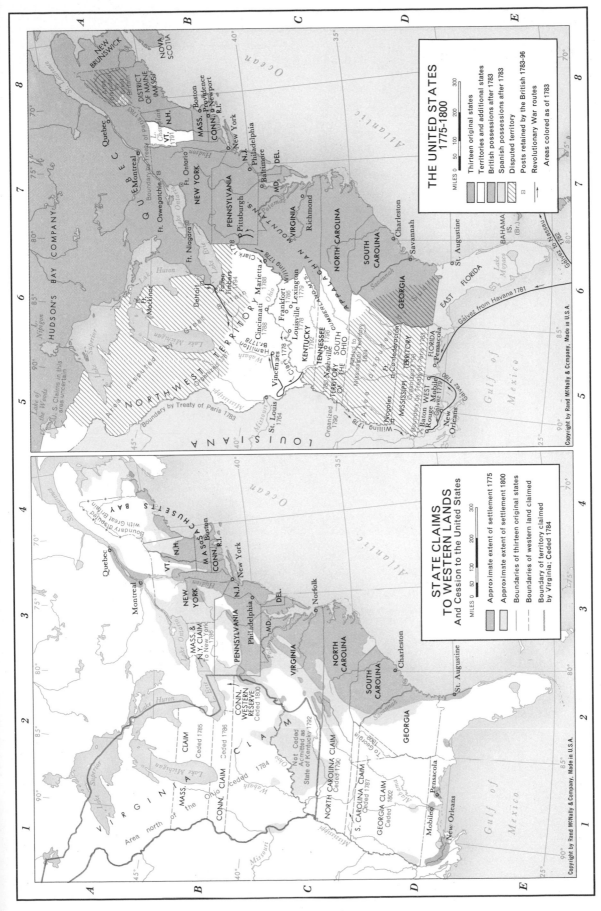

THE UNITED STATES
1775-1800

MILES 0   50   100   200   300

- Thirteen original states
- Territories and additional states
- British possessions after 1783
- Spanish possessions after 1783
- Disputed territory
- ⊡ Posts retained by the British 1783-96
- ← Revolutionary War routes
- Areas colored as of 1783

Copyright by Rand McNally & Company, Made in U.S.A.

NORTHWEST TERRITORY

LOUISIANA

STATE CLAIMS
TO WESTERN LANDS
And Cession to the United States

MILES 0   50   100   200   300

- Approximate extent of settlement 1775
- Approximate extent of settlement 1800
- Boundaries of thirteen original states
- Boundaries of western land claimed
- Boundary of territory claimed by Virginia; Ceded 1784

Copyright by Rand McNally & Company, Made in U.S.A.

VIRGINIA CLAIM

MASS. CLAIM   Ceded 1785

CONN. CLAIM   Ceded 1786

CONN. WESTERN RESERVE Ceded 1800

Ceded 1784

Not Ceded Admitted as State of Kentucky 1792

NORTH CAROLINA CLAIM   Ceded 1790

To Georgia

S. CAROLINA CLAIM   Ceded 1787

GEORGIA CLAIM   Ceded 1802

To Georgia 1802

ORIGIN AND GROWTH
OF THE UNITED STATES

▶ MAPS ON PAGES 148, 149, 150, 151, AND 154–55

THIS GROUP OF MAPS illustrates the territory which, except for the West Indies, eventually became the United States. The story begins in the days of Columbus, for though Columbus himself never laid eyes on any point now in the continental United States, his contemporary Vespucci cruised extensively along its shores (see page 62). Both coasts and much of the interior had been examined by Europeans before the English settled at Jamestown or Captain John Smith ever saw Pocahontas.

Explorations before 1607

▶ MAP ON PAGE 149

The early Spanish explorations were a byproduct of activities in the West Indies and Mexico. Ponce de León in 1513 discovered Florida from Puerto Rico. Gomes, Pineda, and Cabrillo sought a water passage through the continent, searching respectively along the Atlantic, Gulf, and Pacific coasts. Next came the quest for treasure and fabled cities of the interior. Such was the expedition of Narváez; its only survivors were Cabeza de Vaca and a few companions who walked from the Texas coast to Culiacán on the Pacific. De Soto found not treasure but the Mississippi River in 1541. Greatest of these overland adventurers was Coronado, who set out from Mexico in 1540, looking for the Seven Cities of Cibola and Golden Quivira. What he found was the Grand Canyon and the flatlands of Kansas. In 1609 Oñate established the city of Santa Fe, which is thus of almost exactly the same age as Jamestown or Quebec. The oldest surviving city within the present limits of the United States is, however, St. Augustine, where the Spanish set up a garrison in 1565, after destroying the neighboring French settlement at Fort Caroline.

The coasts were further explored by Verrazano, a Florentine in French service on the usual search for a passage; by Francis Drake, who may have reached as far north as the state of Washington; and by Gosnold and Weymouth, who soon after 1600 made the New England coast better known to the English.

The West Indies

▶ MAP ON PAGE 148

In the seventeenth century, though they founded the United States and Canada, Europeans were much more interested in the regions farther south (see page 144). Dutch, French, and English were established in the Lesser Antilles before 1640. The Spanish lost Jamaica to England in 1655, and western Hispaniola to France in 1697. The map shows the route of the famous Spanish galleons (*galeones*),which came from Spain by the southern route, and returned by the northern, to catch the favorable winds. The wealth of the Spaniards made piracy a long recognized occupation in the West Indies. It went through various stages: first, the

gentlemen sea rovers of Elizabeth's day who served their queen by plundering Spanish towns and shipping; then the "buccaneers," of somewhat lower social status, who in the seventeenth century still combined their depredations with some pretension of public service; then, in the eighteenth century, the entirely unauthorized cutthroats and outlaws made famous in *Treasure Island*.

The later seventeenth and the eighteenth centuries were the great period of international economic importance for the West Indies. Immense numbers of Negro slaves were brought in to raise sugar and other subtropical products. The islands were so valuable that many of them changed hands, during the wars, more frequently than the map can show. The West Indies lost their old importance in the nineteenth century, after the rebellion and ensuing independence of the Haitian Negroes during the French Revolution, and the subsequent abolition of slavery by the European powers.

Spain lost Cuba and Puerto Rico, the last vestiges of its great American empire, in the war of 1898 with the United States. Denmark sold its islands (the Virgin Islands) to the United States in 1917. There have been no other changes of ownership in the West Indies since the time of Napoleon. The Dutch have been in Curaçao, the French in Martinique, the British in Barbados—to name only the more considerable of the smaller islands—for more than three hundred years, that is, since the wave of expansion which founded Virginia and New England.

The English Mainland Colonies
and the American Revolution

▶ MAPS ON PAGE 150

The first permanent English colony in America (or indeed anywhere) was planted at Jamestown in Virginia in 1607. All the future Thirteen Colonies of the American Revolution, except Georgia, were established before 1700, and Dutch and Swedish settlements along the Hudson and the Delaware (the "North" and "South" rivers) had been taken over by the English. There were no great viceroyalties as in Spanish America; each colony was separately attached to the mother country, and the attempt in 1686 to combine the northern colonies into a Dominion of New England came to nothing. Colonies originated in grants of land and governmental organization by the king. Some original grants were made to proprietors, some to companies, some to groups of actual settlers; the later trend was to convert them all to the pattern of the royal colony with a governor appointed by the British crown. In all the English colonies the settlers participated in some kind of representative body.

Grants of land under the early charters varied greatly in size. Those to Lord Baltimore for Maryland and to the New Jersey proprietors were modest; but Massachusetts, Connecticut, and the Carolinas, by their charters, extended straight west from sea to sea; and Virginia enjoyed the most grandiose domain of all, reaching both west and northwest, in principle, to the Pacific Ocean. These claims to western lands were ceded by the states to the federal union after the Revolution (see page 151).

The area of actual settlement, as of 1690, 1760, 1775, 1800, 1820, and 1850, may be traced on pages 150, 151, and the inset on page 155. From the beginning the population was of mixed national origins; not only were the small original Dutch and Swedish settlements absorbed, but there was considerable immigration of Scotch-Irish and Germans in the eighteenth century.

The English colonies, until 1763, were flanked by the Spanish in Florida and by the French in the St. Lawrence valley. Following the explorations of La Salle and others (see page 144), the French penetrated the region of the Great Lakes and the Mississippi and its tributaries, including the Ohio River, where their aspirations conflicted with those of the British colonials. In 1763, after the Seven Years' War, the British took the whole region east of the Mississippi from France, and Florida from Spain.

After 1763 the British government attempted a more centralized direction of the empire which had been thus enlarged. A new revenue policy was adopted for the colonies; assurances were given to the conquered French in the Quebec Act of 1774, by which Quebec was extended up the Lakes and into the Illinois country, and a Proclamation Line was drawn in 1763 along the crest of the Alleghenies, beyond which white settlement was temporarily halted, pending the settlement of difficulties with the Indians. These and other actions of the home government led to the American Revolution. The principal battles and campaigns are shown on page 150 (see also pages 86–87).

The United States, 1775–1800

▶ MAPS ON PAGE 151

Only some of the many problems facing the new republic can be well illustrated on a map. The treaty of 1783 gave it a boundary along the Mississippi, but Canada remained British, and Florida (which then reached to the Mississippi) became again Spanish, as before 1763. Since 1763 New Orleans and the region west of the Mississippi had also been Spanish. The British, citing certain grievances against the Americans, continued to occupy Fort Niagara, Detroit, Mackinac and other places within the borders of the United States.

Meanwhile, the area of settlement continued to expand. The cession of their old land claims by the several states to the United States was of great importance. It made it possible for the thirteen original states to agree to the new federal constitution of 1787, and to adopt the principle that new regions, when sufficiently populous, should become states of the same kind as the original thirteen. Vermont, Kentucky, and Tennessee became states in the 1790's. Eventual statehood was foreseen in the organization of the Northwest Territory in 1787, and the Mississippi Territory in 1788.

The expansion of population, while it made the disputes with Spain and Britain more troublesome, also greatly aided in their solution. But difficulties with Britain were not wholly removed until after the War of 1812 (see page 166), nor those with Spain until the acquisition of Florida by the United States.

The United States, 1800–1850

▶ MAP ON PAGES 154–55

For the United States the nineteenth century began with the extraordinary good fortune of the Louisiana Purchase. In 1819 the United States obtained Florida from Spain. In 1845 it annexed Texas with full Texan consent. After the ensuing Mexican War it took from Mexico the region shown on the map as far as the Pacific, which was supplemented by the Gadsden Purchase of 1853 (see page 146). Against Britain the United States obtained no territorial advantages in the War of 1812, but was able to negotiate favorable boundaries in the following years in the Minnesota region, in Maine, and in the Oregon country. By 1853 the United States reached its subsequent continental limits.

Population grew and spread very rapidly, both from a high rate of natural increase and from rising immigration. Large cities rose in the Northeast, with New York, Philadelphia, Baltimore, and Boston, in that order, having over 100,000 inhabitants in 1850. In the Old West—that is, trans-Appalachia—new states and cities sprang into being. Even New Orleans and Cincinnati had populations of about 115,000 at mid-century. The movement across the Alleghenies, which had begun even before the Revolution with settlements in Kentucky, was greatly facilitated after 1800 by such improvements as the National Road (Cumberland Road) and the Erie Canal. The former ran from Cumberland, Maryland, to St. Louis; the latter gave a water route from the Northeast all the way to northern Illinois and Wisconsin. Railroad building was also already extensive by 1850. At that time the population had reached 23,000,000, from less than 6,000,000 in 1800. There were thirty-one states in the Union in 1850, reaching to the first tier west of the Mississippi, and supplemented by Texas and California. Discovery of gold at Sutter's Fort brought a rush of English-speaking immigration to California, which had hitherto been preponderantly Spanish; and the adjudication of the Oregon question about the same time opened the way to the peopling of the Pacific Northwest.

From the edge of continuous settlement to the Pacific coast, as may be seen in the inset on page 155, there lay in 1850 some half the width of the continent, unoccupied except by Indians, buffalo, and a few old Spanish towns like Santa Fe, a vast region of plains, mountains, and occasional deserts, that could be crossed only in wagons or on horseback. It had been explored in former times by French fur traders (see page 144), then in 1804–06 by Lewis and Clark for the United States government, then in the 1830's and 1840's by such free-lance trappers as Kit Carson. The earliest important settlement to be made from the United States in this area was Salt Lake City, founded in 1847 by Mormons fleeing from Illinois. Probably the most famous of routes used by emigrants was the Oregon Trail, which began at St. Joseph, Missouri, and after crossing the plains and the Rocky Mountains divided, not far from Great Salt Lake, into branches of which one led on into Oregon, one to the region of San Francisco, and one to that of Los Angeles.

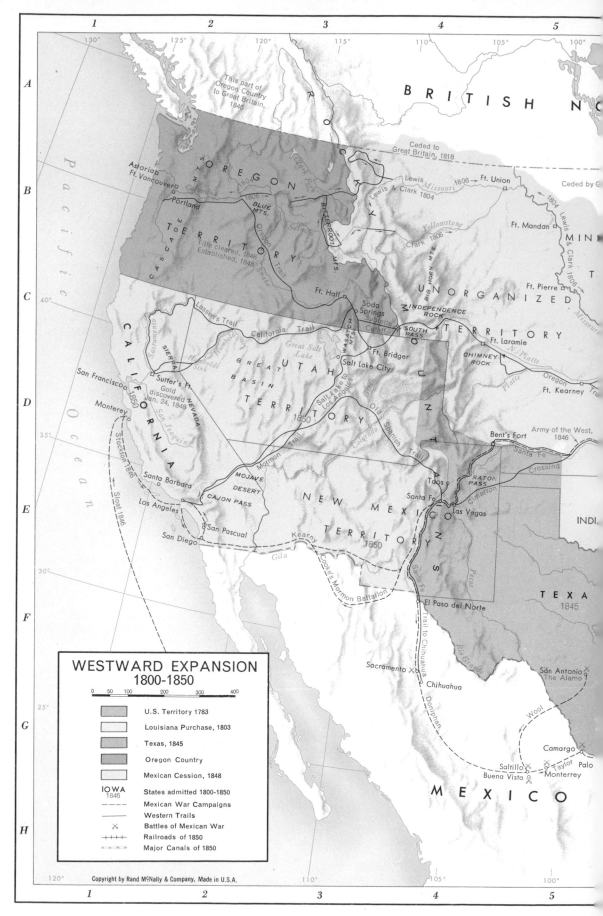

WESTWARD EXPANSION
1800-1850

Scale: 0 50 100 200 300 400

	U.S. Territory 1783
	Louisiana Purchase, 1803
	Texas, 1845
	Oregon Country
	Mexican Cession, 1848
IOWA 1846	States admitted 1800-1850
– – –	Mexican War Campaigns
———	Western Trails
✕	Battles of Mexican War
+++++	Railroads of 1850
═══	Major Canals of 1850

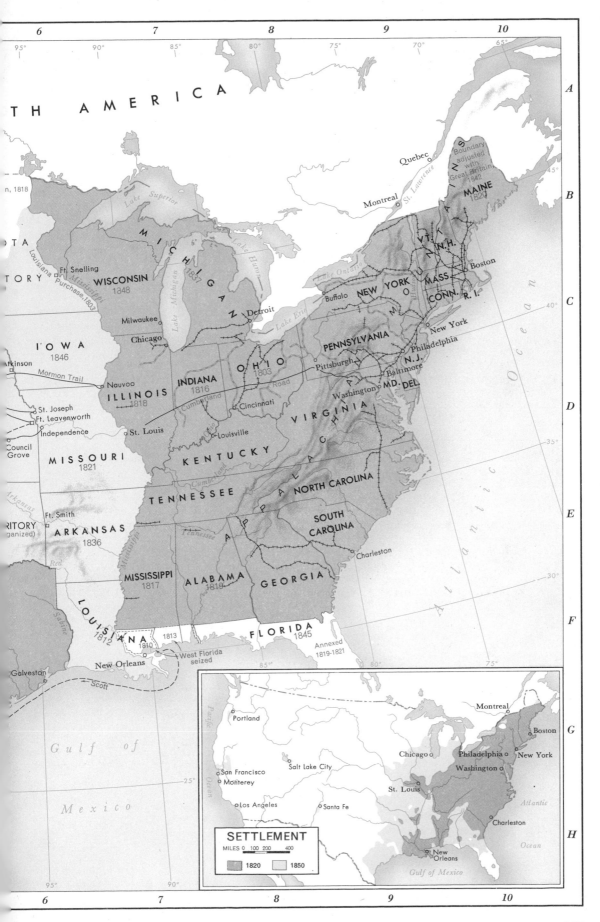

95° 90° 85° 80° 75° 70° 65°

NORTH AMERICA

Quebec

Boundary
adjusted
with
Great Britain
1842

Montreal

St. Lawrence

MOUNTAINS

MAINE
1820

VT.
N.H.
MASS.
CONN.
R.I.

Boston

Lake Superior

MICHIGAN
1837

Lake Huron

Ft. Snelling

Louisiana Purchase, 1803
Mississippi

WISCONSIN
1848

Lake Ontario

Buffalo

NEW YORK

New York

Lake Michigan

Milwaukee

Chicago

Detroit

Lake Erie

PENNSYLVANIA

Philadelphia

Pittsburgh

N.J.

I'OWA
1846

Mormon Trail

Nauvoo

ILLINOIS
1818

INDIANA
1816

OHIO
1803

Cumberland Road

Cincinnati

Washington

MD.
DEL.

Baltimore

rkinson

St. Joseph
Ft. Leavenworth
Independence

St. Louis

Louisville

VIRGINIA

Council
Grove

MISSOURI
1821

KENTUCKY

Cumberland

NORTH CAROLINA

Arkansas

RRITORY
(ganized)

Ft. Smith

ARKANSAS
1836

TENNESSEE

Tennessee

APPALACHIAN

SOUTH
CAROLINA

Charleston

Red

MISSISSIPPI
1817

ALABAMA
1819

GEORGIA

Mississippi

LOUISIANA
1812

1810

1813

West Florida
seized

FLORIDA
1845

Annexed
1819-1821

Sabine

Scott

Galveston

New Orleans

Gulf of Mexico

45°

40°

35°

30°

Atlantic Ocean

SETTLEMENT

MILES 0 100 200 400

1820	1850

Portland

Montreal

Boston

Pacific Ocean

Chicago

Philadelphia
Washington

New York

San Francisco
Monterey

Salt Lake City

St. Louis

Atlantic

Los Angeles

Santa Fe

Charleston

New Orleans

Gulf of Mexico

Ocean

25°

THE AMERICAN CIVIL WAR

▶ MAPS ON PAGES 157, 158, AND 159

As the United States expanded in the first half of the nineteenth century, there developed the situation known as sectionalism, or the tendency for different and increasingly antagonistic societies to take form in the North and South.

Sectionalism in 1860

▶ MAP ON PAGE 157

The South remained overwhelmingly rural, and after 1800 increasingly devoted to the production of cotton, particularly in the Deep South, as shown on the map, from South Carolina to Texas. The cotton planters depended on Negro slavery for their labor supply, and for their markets they looked mainly to Great Britain, where the importation of raw cotton (see page 101) multiplied two hundred times in the century before 1850.

The North became a land of cities and of family farms engaged in the production of wheat and corn. The manufacturing area, in 1860, lay in the northeast from Baltimore to the factory towns north of Boston; it was linked with the West (from Ohio to Iowa) by complementary markets as between factories and farms, by recency of emigration from the East, and, in 1860, by the railway network. Slavery was unsuited to the North, where there was growing repugnance for an institution on which the South had come tragically to depend.

When the Kansas and Nebraska territories were organized in 1854 there was much dispute over whether slavery should be allowed in them or in the future states to be set up there. By the Dred Scott Decision, in 1857, the Supreme Court protected slavery in the territories. Against the apparent menace of an extension of slavery the Republican Party grew up in the 1850's. It was a Northern party, and the first purely sectional party in the history of the United States. After its electoral victory in 1860 eleven Southern states seceded from the United States and formed the Confederate States of America. The four northernmost states in which slavery existed did not secede; they were Missouri, Kentucky, Maryland, and Delaware; western Virginia, after refusing to secede, was admitted as the state of West Virginia in 1863.

Civil war followed when President Lincoln refused to recognize the right of secession or the legal existence of the Confederate States.

The Civil War

▶ MAPS ON PAGES 158 AND 159

The Confederacy at the beginning of the war, in 1861, controlled the area south of the Potomac River and the middle of Missouri and Kentucky. The North had twice the population of the South, and virtually all the manufacturing industry in America. It nevertheless found victory difficult, for the South embraced a very large area, in which the population fought on its own ground and in its own defense. The South won a good many battles, as indicated by the Confederate symbol on page 158, but the North, year by year, as the bands of color show, encroached farther into Confederate territory.

Basic to the strategy of the war was the role of the Union navy. The Confederacy was recognized as a belligerent by Great Britain and other European states, to which it looked for imports or for actual intervention; but this advantage was nullified by the Union blockade of Southern ports, of which several were in fact occupied by Union troops in 1862.

The most dramatic theater was in the East, where the two capitals, Washington and Richmond, faced each other across a distance of only a hundred miles. But the Western theater was more fluid and decisive, for only after victories in the West, where the Confederacy was first divided by Union victories along the Mississippi, and then again divided by the Union march from Chattanooga to the Atlantic coast, could the final Union victory in Virginia be achieved.

Major land fighting began with the humiliation of the Union army at the first battle of Bull Run, near Washington, in July, 1861. In the next year Union forces invaded the Williamsburg peninsula in an attempt to capture Richmond, but they were obliged to withdraw. The armies then met repeatedly in the area west of Washington in the terrible battles at Antietam, Fredericksburg, and Chancellorsville. In 1863, facing deadlock in the East and mounting adversity in the West, the Confederacy resolved upon invasion of the North, and General Lee led his army into Pennsylvania, in the hope of cutting the North in two as Grant's successes on the lower Mississippi were dividing the South. The resulting Battle of Gettysburg, won by the Union in July, 1863, was the greatest single turning point of the war. Lee retired into Virginia.

In the West the Union forces, after taking Forts Henry and Donelson, moved on to occupy western Tennessee, where they won the Battle of Shiloh in 1862. They then moved down to besiege Vicksburg, while Union naval units moved upstream from New Orleans. The capture of Vicksburg cut off Louisiana and Texas from the other Confederate states. Union troops then concentrated in the neighborhood of Chattanooga, a key point on the main east-west railway line of the South. Defeated at Chickamauga, they won the ensuing battle of Lookout Mountain, a victory which made possible the occupation of Atlanta and Sherman's famous march through Georgia in 1864. This campaign of devastation, from Atlanta to the sea, was designed both to isolate Lee in Virginia from the Deep South and to dramatize the hopelessness of further resistance.

The organized military power of the Confederacy was thus confined to the Eastern theater, where Lee surrendered at Appomattox in April, 1865.

By the Emancipation Proclamation of 1863 President Lincoln, using the war powers of the presidency, decreed the end of slavery in areas engaged in hostilities against the United States. Constitutional amendment after the war abolished slavery everywhere in the Union. The war ended the power of slave owners as a force in American political life. It stimulated and was followed by great industrial and capitalistic expansion.

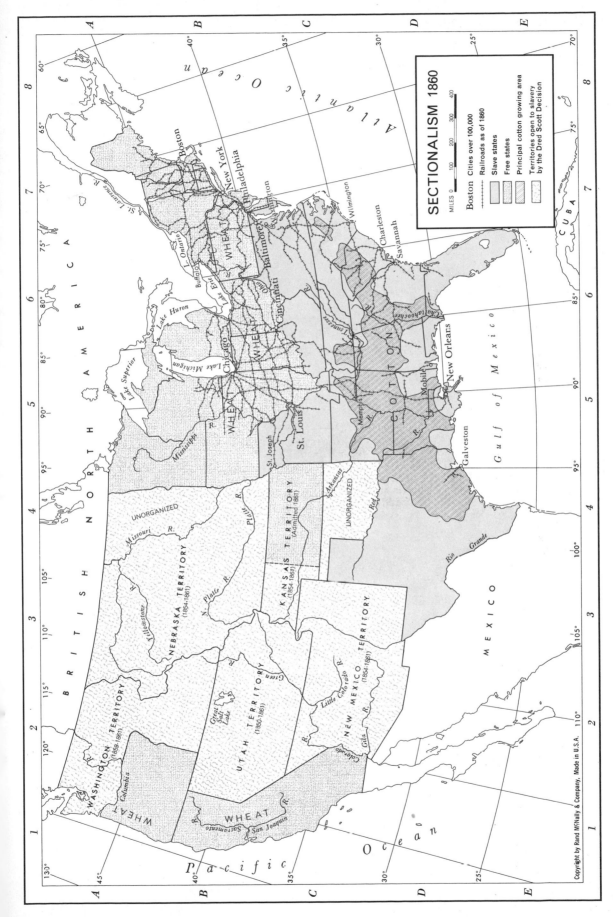

SECTIONALISM 1860

MILES 0   100   200   300   400

Boston   Cities over 100,000
+++++++ Railroads as of 1860
         Slave states
         Free states
         Principal cotton growing area
         Territories open to slavery
         by the Dred Scott Decision

Copyright by Rand McNally & Company, Made in U.S.A.

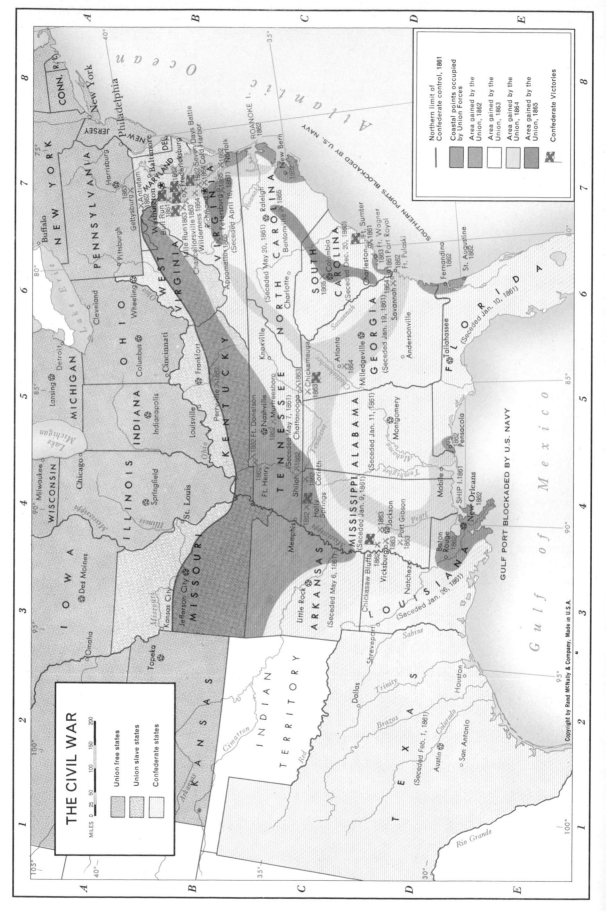

THE CIVIL WAR

MILES 0 25 50 100 150 200

- Union free states
- Union slave states
- Confederate states

Legend (upper right)

— Northern limit of Confederate control, 1861

⊗ Coastal points occupied by Union Forces

- Area gained by the Union, 1862
- Area gained by the Union, 1863
- Area gained by the Union, 1864
- Area gained by the Union, 1865

✕ Confederate Victories

SOUTHERN PORTS BLOCKADED BY U.S. NAVY

GULF PORT BLOCKADED BY U.S. NAVY

Copyright by Rand McNally & Company. Made in U.S.A.

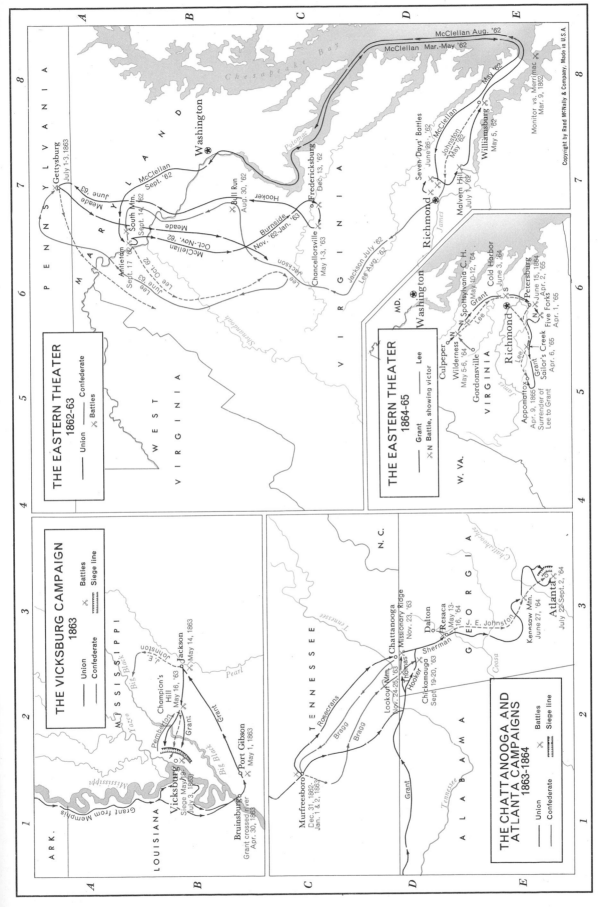

THE EASTERN THEATER
1862-63

Union
Confederate
✗ Battles

Copyright by Rand McNally & Company. Made in U.S.A.

Chesapeake Bay

Washington

McClellan Aug. '62
McClellan Mar.-May '62
Johnston
May '62
Seven Days' Battles
June 26-'62
McClellan
May '62
Williamsburg
May 5, '62
May '62
Monitor vs. Merrimac ✗
Mar. 9, 1862

Gettysburg
July 1-3, 1863
Meade June '63
McClellan Sept. '62
Meade
South Mtn.
Sept. 14, '62
Bull Run
Aug. 30, '62
Hooker
Fredericksburg
Dec. 13, '62
Burnside
Nov. '62-Jan. '63
Chancellorsville
May 1-3, '63
Antietam
Sept. 17 '62
Lee Oct. '62
McClellan
Oct.-Nov. '62
Jackson
Lee '63
Jackson July '62
Lee Aug. '62
Richmond
Malvern Hill
July 1, '62

PENNSYLVANIA
MARYLAND
WEST VIRGINIA
VIRGINIA
Potomac
Shenandoah
Rappahannock
James

THE EASTERN THEATER
1864-65

Union ——— Grant   Lee
✗ N Battle, showing victor

W. VA.
MD.
Washington
Culpeper
Wilderness
May 5-6, '64
Gordonsville
Spotsylvania C. H.
N May 10-12, '64
Grant
Lee
Cold Harbor
June 3, '64
Petersburg
June 15, 1864
Apr. 2, '65
Five Forks
Apr. 1, '65
Sailor's Creek
Apr. 6, '65
Grant
Richmond
Lee
Appomattox
Apr. 9, 1865
Surrender of
Lee to Grant
VIRGINIA
James

THE VICKSBURG CAMPAIGN
1863

Union
Confederate
✗ Battles
⋯⋯ Siege line

ARK.
MISSISSIPPI
LOUISIANA
Grant from Memphis
Vicksburg
Siege May 19-
July 3, 1863
Bruinsburg
Grant crossed river
Apr. 30, 1863
Port Gibson
✗ May 1, 1863
Champion's Hill
May 16, '63 ✗
Pemberton
Grant
Jackson
✗ May 14, 1863
J. E. Johnston
Big Black
Yazoo
Pearl

THE CHATTANOOGA AND
ATLANTA CAMPAIGNS
1863-1864

Union
Confederate
✗ Battles
⋯⋯ Siege line

N. C.
TENNESSEE
ALABAMA
GEORGIA
Murfreesboro
Dec. 31, 1862,
Jan. 1 & 2, 1863 ✗
Rosecrans
Bragg
Bragg
Chattanooga
Lookout Mtn.
Nov. 24-25, '63
Thomas
Hooker
Missionary Ridge
Nov. 23, '63
Chickamauga
Sept. 19-20, '63
Dalton
Resaca
May 13-16, '64
Sherman
J. E. Johnston
Kennesaw Mtn.
June 27, '64
Atlanta ✗
July 22-Sept. 2, '64
Grant
Tennessee
Coosa
Chattahoochee

159

DEVELOPMENT OF THE UNITED STATES

▶ MAPS ON PAGES 162-63, 164, AND 165

THE FOLLOWING MAPS are intended to represent civilization in the United States over a period of some three hundred years, and social and economic development between 1890 and 1950.

American Civilization

▶ MAP ON PAGES 162-63

The form of the five maps of European civilization in the preceding pages is here followed for American civilization, so that there may be a kind of comparability, though the form is less suited to the United States than to Europe. Political and economic matters are excluded, and civilization is taken to consist in activities, institutions, and persons of cultural or scientific importance. These are located according to their geographical whereabouts, or, for persons, their place of birth. It must be remembered that the range and influence of a great institution, such as the Library of Congress, is not fully defined by its mere location; and for the United States, especially, where movement has been the essence of national growth, place of birth of notable individuals may have little significance for their actual careers. A few exceptions have therefore been made, to show, for example, that the Hungarian born Joseph Pulitzer was identified with St. Louis, and that Brigham Young, born in Vermont, is remembered for his connection with Salt Lake City. In general, as on the maps showing European civilization, the names of persons on the present map are plotted according to their place of birth, as a uniform and determinable item for all concerned, and since in any case the first question often asked about a person is where he came from. It is to be noted, too, that the map covers three hundred years, though only the oldest parts of the country could have had any civilization for so long a time. This fact alone would be enough to give a heavy emphasis to the East. The map, with its inset, shows a concentration of cultural activity in parts of the country where greater age, wealth, and density of population have been in its favor.

Cultural Institutions and Centers

Colleges and universities are of even more importance as carriers of civilization in a new country than in an old one. Colleges established in the colonial period are shown. The oldest are Harvard, 1636; William and Mary, 1693; Yale, 1701; and Princeton, 1746. The founding of state universities began immediately after the Revolution. The oldest state-supported universities are in the seaboard South, in Georgia and the Carolinas. They were founded soon after independence because there were no private colleges south of Williamsburg. Settlers crossing the mountains often made the establishment of a college one of their first concerns. Private colleges are too numerous to show; but the state university of every state west of the Alleghenies is on the map. These public institutions, adopted more from Continental than from English models, were designed both for the education of

youth and to promote useful knowledge and civilization in the wilderness. The universities are older than the states themselves in Tennessee, Michigan, Minnesota, the Dakotas, Oklahoma, Wyoming, Utah, New Mexico, Arizona, Montana, Idaho, and Washington. They are as old as the states, or scarcely less so, in Indiana, Wisconsin, Iowa, and Colorado. State universities developed more slowly where private colleges were abundant, as in the Northeast.

The American Philosophical Society, founded at Philadelphia in 1734, was a scientific academy of the kind shown on pages 70–71 and 82–83 for Europe. The Library of Congress dates from 1800, the Pennsylvania Academy of Arts from 1805. Painting and sculpture are represented on the map by the words "art school" in different parts of the country; art schools often grew up in conjunction with galleries and museums, or with state universities, as at Iowa City. The Southwest came to have important colonies of painters. Jazz music was associated with New Orleans. New York became in the nineteenth century, and even more in the twentieth, a leading center in painting, and the chief center for musical and theatrical affairs. The publication of books, magazines, and newspapers was somewhat more decentralized; although New York also led in these fields, it did not predominate as much as London and Paris in England and France. The characteristic American art of the moving picture was concentrated in southern California. The great philanthropic foundations, which became distinctive American cultural institutions in the twentieth century, generally had their headquarters in New York.

Like the map of European civilization in the nineteenth century (see pages 106–7), the present one shows concentrations of books and of Nobel prizes. Books in large numbers give no assurance of creativeness, as may be seen from the case of Athens, where libraries followed the cultural decline (see page 27); but they are significant as a common auxiliary shared by many fields of interest. The map shows that libraries in 1950 were concentrated in the northeast quadrant of the country and in California. There were four cities with over 6,000,000 volumes in municipal, university, and other institutional libraries—with Washington and New York well in the lead, and about equal, followed by the Boston-Cambridge area and by Chicago. The incidence of Nobel prizes in science and medicine offers a rough index to the location of creative science. Thirty-two such prizes were awarded from 1901 to 1951 for work done in the United States. Seven prize winners were in New York at the time of the award; five in Berkeley; four each at the California Institute of Technology, at Washington University in St. Louis, and at Harvard; two each at the University of Chicago and the Mayo Clinic at Rochester, Minnesota; one each at Schenectady, Rochester, and Ithaca, New York, and at Bloomington, Indiana. Five Americans have received the Nobel prize for literature—Sinclair Lewis, Eugene O'Neill, Pearl Buck, William Faulkner, and Ernest Hemingway—as well as the American born T. S. Eliot.

The men and women whose names appear on

the map will be readily recognized for their contributions to American life. New England until late in the nineteenth century was a great producer of talent in many fields. It serves as a reminder of the continuing importance of immigration to observe the number of those born abroad who did important work in the United States, and the variety of countries from which they came. The list, somewhat arbitrarily, begins with Roger Williams and proceeds through men of such diverse gifts as Albert Einstein and Charles S. Chaplin. Six of the Nobel prize winners in science and medicine, mentioned above, were born in Europe, and one in South Africa. On the other hand, voluntary residence in Europe by native Americans has been a minor theme in American history, especially in some branches of literature and the arts. A list of such expatriates, from Copley to T. S. Eliot, suggests the balance of trade in such matters.

Economic and Social Development, 1890–1950

▶ MAPS ON PAGES 164 AND 165

The Civil War was followed by rapid development of the West. Gold and silver rushes hastened the settlement of California and the mountain states. The first transcontinental railroad was completed in 1869, and half-a-dozen more were operating by 1914. The Indians, many of whom had been moved from the East in earlier times and promised permanent asylum in the West, now found, by 1890, after bitter resistance, that even in the West they must submit to the ways of the white man. The plains region came under cultivation, with the wheat zone shifting after 1890 to Kansas and the Dakotas, where it adjoined the Canadian prairie provinces, opened up at this same time (see page 167). Corn and its accompanying livestock became characteristic of the older Middle West.

Transformation of the West, great as it was, was secondary to the tremendous growth of the country as a whole. Population tripled in the half-century following 1850; swollen by natural increase and by tides of immigration, it reached 75,000,000 in 1900. It doubled again between 1900 and 1950. Movement continued into cities and suburbs. Denser agricultural settlement tended to be stabilized at about the hundredth meridian, but the spread of irrigation, between 1890 and 1950, produced many thickly-peopled areas in California and all the Western states. Southern Florida also developed at this time.

Industrialization continued, with the rise of big business and ever larger corporate structures, especially in steel, meat packing, oil, railroads, farm implements, and banking. The growth of huge organizations contributed greatly to the increase of productivity of both capital and labor, but it involved also the dangers inherent in monopoly, it put small business under serious competitive pressure, and it raised difficulties in employer-employee relations, since the organization of labor lagged well behind the organization of management. There was also a sectional overtone in the stresses of the day, since the center of the new financial and industrial system lay along the axis from Boston, New York, and Philadelphia to Chicago and St. Louis. The South and West enjoyed less direct benefit, so that much of the demand for cheaper money, for trust busting, and for regulation of railroad rates came from the agrarian South and West rather than from the industrial Northeast.

By 1950, as the following maps show, the growth of manufacturing was for the most part in areas which were already the manufacturing centers of the country in 1890. There were, however, significant geographical changes: northern New England in 1950 was no longer a leading manufacturing center, and new manufacturing areas had opened up, notably in the region of Detroit, in parts of the South, and on the Pacific coast. To a great extent these new areas harbored entirely new industries of a kind that did not exist in 1890. The production of motor vehicles at Detroit is an example. The twentieth century also added airplanes, household appliances, moving pictures, radio, television, light metals, and plastics. There was a revolution in food packaging and distribution. Advertising and instalment purchasing became adjuncts of the mass market. A whole range of new service industries also appeared, in which men operated filling stations, repaired television sets, or managed motels. Women in this period also entered the labor force. Meanwhile, the farm population declined, as heightened productivity on the farm enabled fewer farmers to support the rest of the country.

The New Society

The occupational structure of the American people was thus altogether different in 1950 from what it had been in the early days of the Industrial Revolution. So were their living habits. The motor car and the paved road broke down the old isolation of the farm, revolutionized rural living, enabled city-dwellers to move to the suburbs, and helped to decentralize manufacturing by taking many lighter industries out of the great cities. Moving pictures, radio, television, the family car, and summer vacations transformed amusements and entertainment. The educational level precipitously rose.

The new economic system, the two world wars, the great depression, and the great prosperity led to many changes, one of which was the growth of government. The national government entered into forms of regulation and service that soon came to be taken for granted even by those who at first opposed them. It exercised a control over the powerful components of the economic system, it provided measures of social security, it developed projects of reclamation and conservation.

The net result may be suggested statistically by the fact that per-capita income in the United States, by the mid-twentieth century, was double that of the most prosperous countries of western Europe, and incomparably higher than in most parts of the world. Distribution of income was less unequal than in the past, thanks to high productivity, rising wages, wide stock ownership, and progressive income taxes. The United States had developed a way of life almost without historical precedent. Its wealth and economic power were also one of the main forces in the international affairs of the world as a whole in a troubled time.

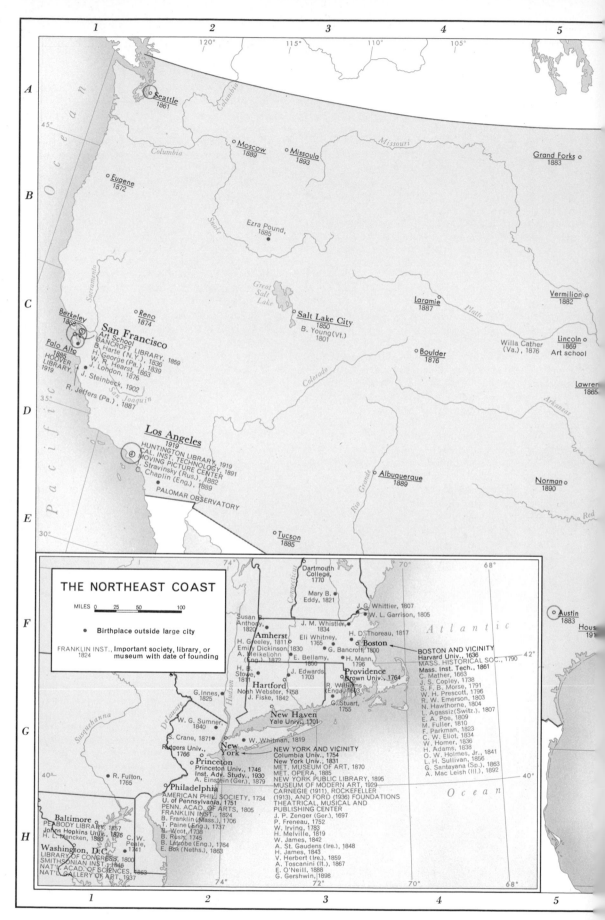

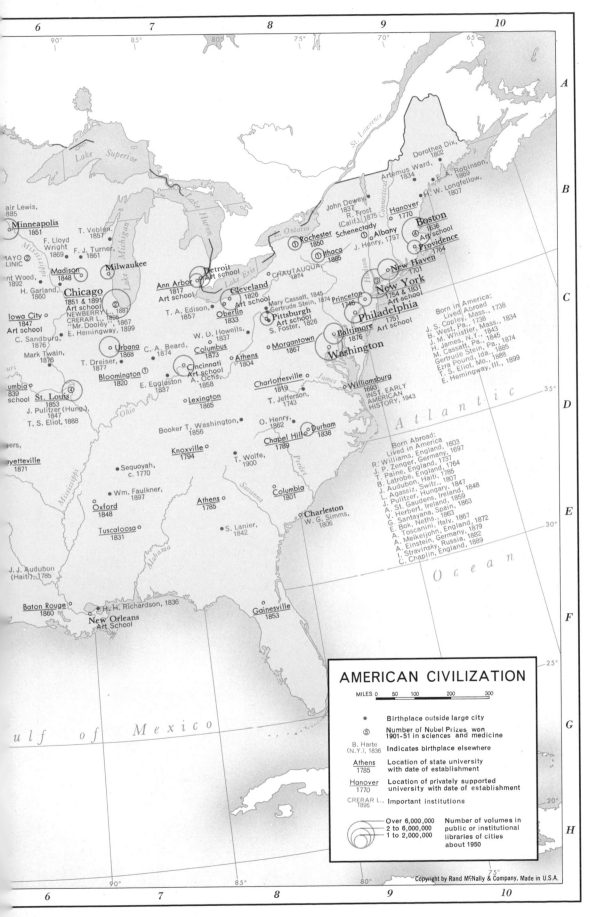

AMERICAN CIVILIZATION

MILES 0   50   100   200   300

- • Birthplace outside large city
- ⑤ Number of Nobel Prizes won 1901-51 in sciences and medicine
- B. Harte (N.Y.), 1836   Indicates birthplace elsewhere
- Athens 1785   Location of state university with date of establishment
- Hanover 1770   Location of privately supported university with date of establishment
- CRERAR L. 1895   Important institutions
- Over 6,000,000 / 2 to 6,000,000 / 1 to 2,000,000   Number of volumes in public or institutional libraries of cities about 1950

Map labels (reading across):

6   7   8   9   10

90°   85°   80°   75°   70°   65°

Lake Superior
Lake Huron
Lake Michigan
Lake Erie
Lake Ontario
St. Lawrence

Dorothea Dix, 1802
Artemus Ward, 1834
E. A. Robinson, 1869
H. W. Longfellow, 1807

nair Lewis, 1885
Minneapolis 1851
T. Veblen, 1857
F. Lloyd Wright 1869
F. J. Turner, 1861
John Dewey, 1837
R. Frost (Calif.), 1875
Hanover 1770
Boston 1636 Art school
Providence 1764

MAYO ㉒ CLINIC
nt Wood, 1892
Madison 1848
Milwaukee
Rochester 1850
Schenectady
Albany
J. Henry, 1797
Ithaca 1865

H. Garland, 1860
Chicago 1851 & 1891 Art school NEWBERRY L., 1887 CRERAR L., 1895
Detroit 1817 Art school
CHAUTAUQUA 1874
New Haven 1701

Iowa City 1847 Art school
Ann Arbor 1817 Art school
Cleveland 1826 Art school
Mary Cassatt, 1845
Gertrude Stein, 1874
Princeton 1746
New York 1754 & 1831 Art school

C. Sandburg, 1876
T. A. Edison, 1857
Oberlin 1833
Pittsburgh Art school
S. Foster, 1826
Philadelphia 1751 Art school

Mark Twain, 1876
Urbana 1868
C. A. Beard, 1874
W. D. Howells, 1837
Morgantown 1867
Baltimore 1876
Washington

T. Dreiser, 1877
Columbus 1873
Athens 1804

Bloomington 1820
E. Eggleston 1837
Cincinnati Art school A. Ochs, 1858

Born in America; Lived Abroad
J. S. Copley, Mass., 1738
B. West, Pa., 1738
J. M. Whistler, Mass., 1834
H. James, N.Y., 1843
M. Cassatt, Pa., 1845
Gertrude Stein, Pa., 1874
Ezra Pound, Ida., 1885
T. S. Eliot, Mo., 1888
E. Hemingway, Ill., 1899

umbia 839 school
St. Louis 1853
J. Pulitzer (Hung.), 1847
T. S. Eliot, 1888
Lexington 1865
Charlottesville 1819
T. Jefferson, 1743
Williamsburg 1693 INST. EARLY AMERICAN HISTORY, 1943

Booker T. Washington, 1856
O. Henry, 1862
Durham 1838

yers,
ayetteville 1871
Knoxville 1794
Chapel Hill 1789
James
Peedee

Born Abroad; Lived in America
R. Williams, England, 1603
J. P. Zenger, Germany, 1697
T. Paine, England, 1737
B. Latrobe, England, 1764
J. Audubon, Haiti, 1785
L. Agassiz, Switz., 1807
J. Pulitzer, Hungary, 1847
A. St. Gaudens, Ireland, 1848
V. Herbert, Ireland, 1859
G. Santayana, Spain, 1863
E. Bok, Neths., 1863
A. Toscanini, Italy, 1867
A. Meiklejohn, England, 1872
A. Einstein, Germany, 1879
I. Stravinsky, Russia, 1882
C. Chaplin, England, 1889

T. Wolfe, 1900
Sequoyah, c. 1770
Wm. Faulkner, 1897
Oxford 1848
Athens 1785
Columbia 1801
Charleston W. G. Simms, 1806
Tuscaloosa 1831
S. Lanier, 1842

J. J. Audubon (Haiti), 1785
Baton Rouge 1860
H. H. Richardson, 1836
New Orleans Art school
Gainesville 1853

ulf of Mexico

Atlantic Ocean

35°
30°
25°
20°

Copyright by Rand McNally & Company, Made in U.S.A.

NATIONAL DEVELOPMENT 1890

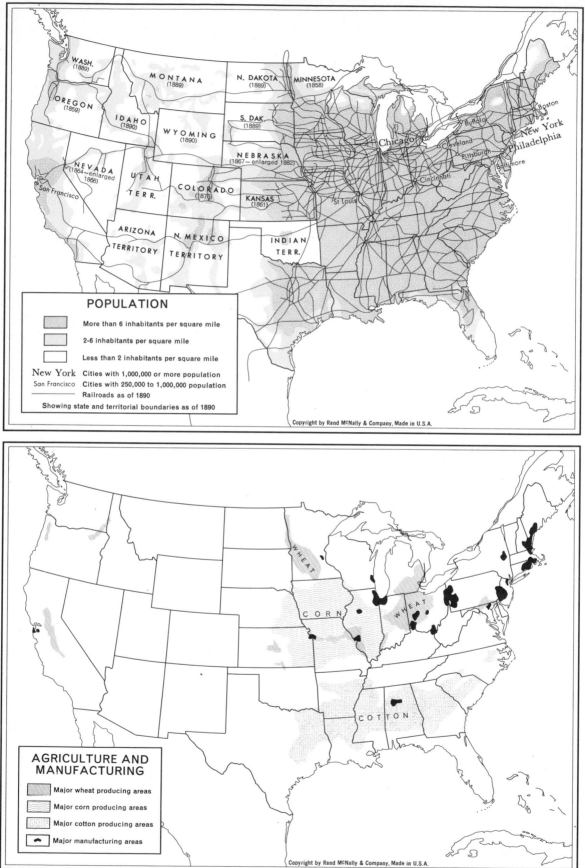

POPULATION

	More than 6 inhabitants per square mile
	2-6 inhabitants per square mile
	Less than 2 inhabitants per square mile

New York Cities with 1,000,000 or more population
San Francisco Cities with 250,000 to 1,000,000 population
—— Railroads as of 1890

Showing state and territorial boundaries as of 1890

AGRICULTURE AND
MANUFACTURING

	Major wheat producing areas
	Major corn producing areas
	Major cotton producing areas
	Major manufacturing areas

NATIONAL DEVELOPMENT 1950

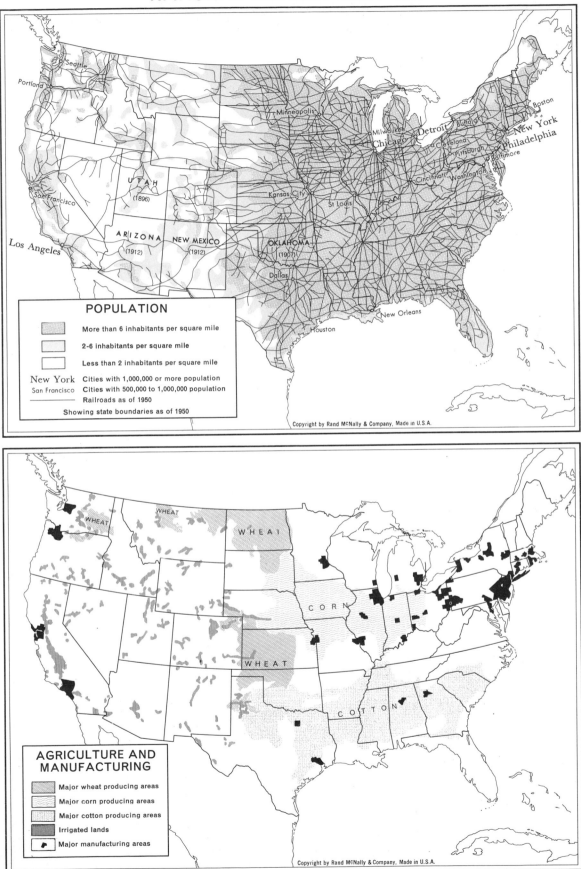

POPULATION

More than 6 inhabitants per square mile

2-6 inhabitants per square mile

Less than 2 inhabitants per square mile

New York — Cities with 1,000,000 or more population

San Francisco — Cities with 500,000 to 1,000,000 population

— Railroads as of 1950

Showing state boundaries as of 1950

Copyright by Rand McNally & Company, Made in U.S.A.

AGRICULTURE AND MANUFACTURING

Major wheat producing areas

Major corn producing areas

Major cotton producing areas

Irrigated lands

Major manufacturing areas

Copyright by Rand McNally & Company, Made in U.S.A.

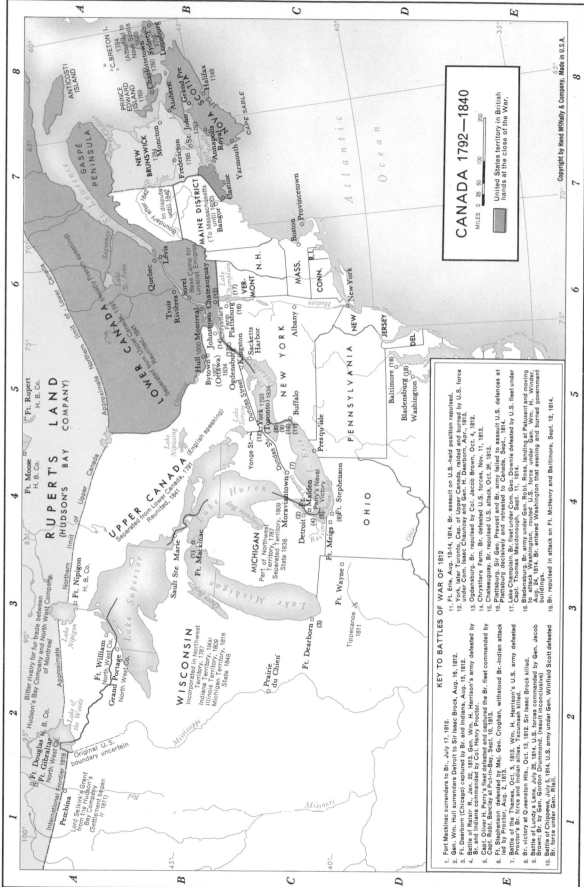

CANADA 1792—1840

MILES 0 25 50 100 200

United States territory in British hands at the close of the War.

Copyright by Rand McNally & Company, Made in U.S.A.

KEY TO BATTLES OF WAR OF 1812

1. Fort Mackinac surrenders to Br., July 17, 1812.
2. Gen. Wm. Hull surrenders Detroit to Sir Isaac Brock, Aug. 16, 1812.
3. Ft. Dearborn (Chicago) captured by Br. and Indians, Aug. 15, 1812.
4. Battle of Raisin R., Jan. 22, 1813, Gen. Wm. H. Harrison's army defeated by Br. and Indians commanded by Col. Henry Proctor.
5. Capt. Oliver H. Perry's fleet defeated and captured the Br. fleet commanded by Capt. Robt. Barclay at Put-in-Bay, Sept. 10, 1813.
6. Ft. Stephenson defended by Maj. Geo. Croghan, withstood Br.-Indian attack led by Proctor, Aug. 2, 1813.
7. Battle of the Thames, Oct. 5, 1813, Wm. H. Harrison's U.S. army defeated Proctor's Br. force and Indian allies. Tecumseh killed.
8. Br. victory at Queenston Hts., Oct. 13, 1812. Sir Isaac Brock killed.
9. Battle of Lundy's Lane, July 25, 1814. U.S. forces commanded by Gen. Jacob Brown; Br. by Gen. Gordon Drummond. (result inconclusive)
10. Battle of Chippewa, July 5, 1814. U.S. army under Gen. Winfield Scott defeated Br. force under Gen. Riall.
11. Ft. Erie, Aug. 13-14, 1814. Br. assault on U.S.-held position repulsed.
12. York, later Toronto, Apr. of Upper Canada, raided and burned by U.S. force under Com. Isaac Chauncey and Gen. H. Dearborn, Apr., 1813.
13. Ogdensburg. Br. repulsed by Col. Jacob Brown, Oct. 4, 1812.
14. Chrystler's Farm. Br. defeated U.S. forces, Nov. 11, 1813.
15. Chateauguay. Br. repulsed U.S. attack, Oct. 26, 1813.
16. Plattsburg: Sir Geo. Prevost and Br. army failed to assault U.S. defences at Plattsburg decisively and retreated to Canada, Sept., 1814.
17. Lake Champlain. Br. fleet under Com. Geo. Downie defeated by U.S. fleet under Capt. Thomas Macdonough, Sept. 11, 1814.
18. Bladensburg. Br. army under Gen. Robt. Ross, landing at Patuxent and moving to attack Washington, routed U.S. force under Gen. Wm. H. Winder, Aug. 24, 1814. Br. entered Washington that evening and burned government buildings.
19. Br. repulsed in attack on Ft. McHenry and Baltimore, Sept. 12, 1814.

166

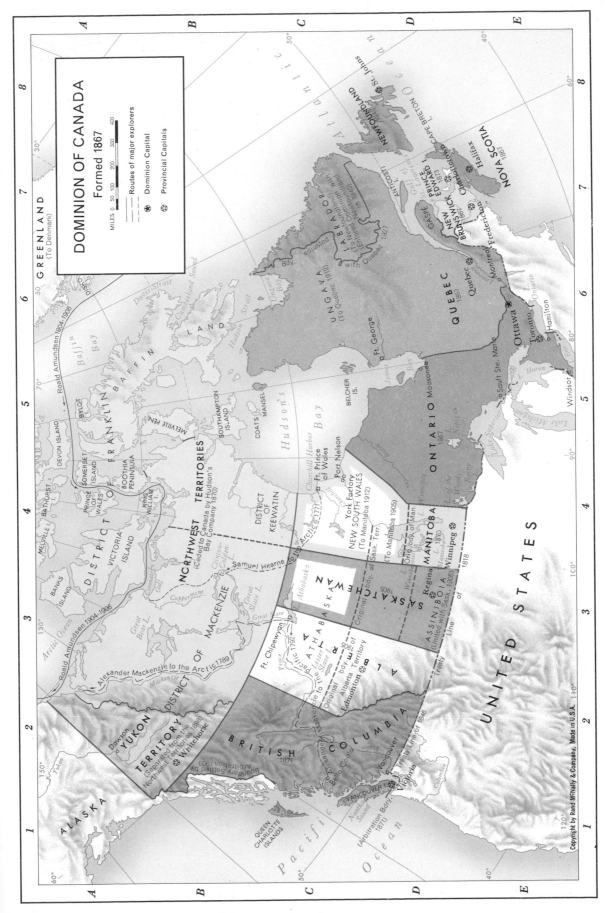

DOMINION OF CANADA

Formed 1867

MILES 0 50 100 200 300 400

- - - - Routes of major explorers
⊛ Dominion Capital
⊗ Provincial Capitals

Copyright by Rand McNally & Company, Made in U.S.A.

CANADA

▶ MAPS ON PAGES 166 AND 167

QUEBEC HAD BEEN FOUNDED as long ago as 1608, the year after Jamestown, but the modern history of Canada begins at the time of the American Revolution. On the one hand, the French settlers, who had come under the British crown as recently as 1763, refused to follow the English colonials into revolution. On the other hand, tens of thousands of Americans of the Thirteen Colonies, also refusing to accept the revolution, took refuge in other parts of British North America. These Loyalists flocked into Nova Scotia, and then on into its hinterland, where the new province of New Brunswick was created in 1784. Thousands also moved into the wilderness north of lakes Ontario and Erie. In 1791 the British government divided the former large province of Quebec into Upper Canada and Lower Canada. Upper Canada (later Ontario) was English-speaking; Lower Canada (the modern province of Quebec) was French-speaking, although even here enough Loyalists settled for the province to lose its exclusively French character.

For the Canadians the War of 1812 was a successful defense against the greater manpower and resources of an expansionist United States. It therefore strengthened Canadian national feeling. The war brought no changes of boundaries. After its close, which coincided with the close of the Napoleonic wars in Europe, another stream of immigration poured into Canada, this time from Great Britain, with Scotland heavily represented. In 1837 there were small rebellions in both the Canadas, led in Lower Canada by Louis Papineau, in Upper Canada by William Mackenzie. After the suppression of the rebellions, the government of Great Britain despatched the Earl of Durham to study the Canadian situation.

Durham's Report: Responsible Government

Durham's Report, one of the most famous political documents in the English language, emphasized that the Canadians must be allowed to govern themselves, within the Empire. His ideas thus marked an important step, not only for the two Canadas, but for the subsequent development of the British Commonwealth of Nations. Durham privately hoped that the French in Canada would eventually be assimilated to the English-speaking population; in any case he believed they must develop a common citizenship. He proposed, therefore, the reunion of Upper and Lower Canada into one province, as before 1791. This was done in 1840. Beginning in 1846 the British colonial office granted "responsible government," which meant that the existence of ministries, or executive officials, should depend on the will of Canadian legislatures, not of the British governor. Thus the essence of the British system of cabinet or parliamentary government was introduced.

Meanwhile, boundaries were adjusted with the United States. A treaty of 1818 established the present international frontier from Lake Superior to the Rocky Mountains. The Webster-Ashburton Treaty of 1842 drew the Maine boundary. In 1846 the Oregon question was settled by extension of the 1818 line to the Pacific.

The Dominion of Canada

▶ MAP ON PAGE 167

Durham's Report had foreseen, for the indefinite future, a confederation of the various British North American provinces. Various arguments in the mid-nineteenth century favored such an arrangement: the union of French and English in a single province, after 1840, did not work very well; the vast western region could not indefinitely remain under the Hudson's Bay Company; railroads were being built; the province of Manitoba could be foreseen; and some Canadians felt that the British government had not served their best interests in yielding so much to the United States in the boundary treaties. During the American Civil War British sympathy with the South antagonized the North; and some Canadians feared that the United States, if it lost the South, would make another attempt, as in 1775 and 1812, at the annexation of Canada.

Representatives of the various provinces therefore met at Quebec in 1864. Outlines of union were agreed upon, and fears allayed—as of the French who were afraid that their culture and religion would be submerged, and of the small Maritime Provinces which feared being overshadowed by the more rapidly growing provinces of the interior. The British North America Act, written in Canada by Canadians, and legally enacted by the British Parliament in 1867, founded the Dominion of Canada.

The dominion began with four provinces: Nova Scotia, New Brunswick, and Upper and Lower Canada, now renamed Ontario and Quebec. Manitoba was added in 1870, British Columbia in 1871, Prince Edward Island in 1873. Meanwhile, in 1870, the Hudson's Bay Company transferred its huge territories to the dominion. The following decades saw considerable emigration into the western prairies, much of it from the United States, so that the provinces of Alberta and Saskatchewan were created in 1905. The almost uninhabited Northwest Territories were and are governed directly from Ottawa. Athabaska and New South Wales, formerly part of the Northwest Territories, were added to the three prairie provinces as the line of settlement moved northward. In 1898, to deal with problems arising from the Klondike gold rush, the Yukon Territory was set up with a separate administration. Newfoundland was for a long time a dominion by itself; in 1949 it became a province of Canada, bringing in its dependency Labrador.

The Canadian government combines British and United States principles. The British system of cabinet government, with ministers responsible to a parliament, obtains at both the dominion and provincial levels. A federalism modeled on that of the United States holds the provinces together and assures each a measure of local independence. Until 1926 the British crown had charge of Canadian foreign policy, but in that year Canada began to send its own diplomatic representatives to Washington and other capitals. In this, as in other respects, Canadian practice became standard for other members of the Commonwealth.

THE WORLD ABOUT 1900

▶ MAP ON PAGES 170–71

THE YEAR 1900 saw the height of modern imperialism, which at this time meant the domination of other parts of the world by European or Western powers, though one non-Western state, Japan, had also begun to build a colonial empire. Most of Asia, Africa, and the Pacific islands were now under a colonial rule which was rapidly to disintegrate in the following half-century. For more detail on Asia and Africa about 1900, see pages 134–35 and 138–39.

The British Empire

By far the greatest of colonial empires was the British, upon which it was said that the sun never set. It included self-governing areas of European settlement: Canada, Australia, New Zealand, and what was to become in 1910 the Union of South Africa. It included British India, to which many autonomous Indian princely states were subordinated, and to which Baluchistan and Burma had recently been added. A good many colonies in Negro Africa belonged to it, as did the protectorates of Egypt and the Anglo-Egyptian Sudan. The older British establishment at Hong Kong was supplemented in 1898 by the acquisition of Weihaiwei; and there were British spheres of influence in the Yangtze valley and in Persia. All was held together by British trade, British capital, British islands, and a British navy whose supremacy in 1900 no one contested.

The Russian Empire

The Russian empire, unlike the others, was a land mass contiguous with its home country (see page 115). In the last third of the nineteenth century it made annexations in central Asia. The Russians and British arranged the Afghan frontier in such a way as not to adjoin each other. Russian influence was felt also in Persia and western China, and at the close of the century in Manchuria, where the Russians occupied Port Arthur in 1898.

The French Empire

France, which had lost a colonial empire in the eighteenth century, had begun to acquire another with the occupation of Algeria in 1830. Except for Algeria, most of the French empire in 1900 had been acquired within the past generation. Most of it was in Africa, very extensive in area, but largely desert. The French also held the small French Somaliland at the entrance to the Red Sea; they completed the occupation of Madagascar in 1896; they had conquered Indo-China, and had encroached on Siam, which, however, maintained its independence. Like the British, Americans, and Germans, the French had taken over various Pacific islands.

Newer Empires

Germany, Italy, Belgium, the United States, and Japan had come recently into the colonial field. The German colonial empire, which lasted only until the First World War, consisted of four segments of Africa—East Africa, Southwest Africa, Togo, and Kamerun—a foothold on the Shantung peninsula in China, and the northeastern part of New Guinea and neighboring island groups.

Italy held Eritrea and a part of Somaliland, and in 1896 attempted a conquest of Abyssinia, but was defeated by Abyssinians at the battle of Aduwa. In 1911 Italy took Tripoli from Turkey and renamed it Libya.

Belgium possessed only one colony, the Congo, which, however, was valuable for its rubber (as later for uranium), and was in area as large as the United States east of the Mississippi.

Japan had hardly emerged from its self-seclusion when it launched upon overseas annexations, taking the Kurile Islands to the north, and the Ryukyus to the south. The latter were ceded by China, as was Formosa, in 1895. The conflict of Japanese and Russian interests in Manchuria and Korea led to the Russo-Japanese War of 1904, from which Japan gained Port Arthur, southern Sakhalin, and, in effect, Korea (see page 181).

The United States, after purchasing Alaska in 1867, moved into the Pacific, where it annexed Hawaii in 1898. It went to war with Spain in the same year, obtaining the Philippines and Puerto Rico and establishing a virtual protectorate over Cuba. Guam, Wake, and part of Samoa became American territories at the same time, the Panama Canal Zone in 1903.

Older Empires

The Dutch empire, like the British, represented the continuous enterprise of three centuries, but in 1900 was limited to the East Indian islands. The Dutch took no part in the rivalries in Asia and Africa, except to consolidate their formerly disconnected holdings in their archipelago (see page 131), where they occupied their part of New Guinea only at the turn of the century, and completed the conquest of Sumatra as late as 1909.

Portugal still held Goa in India, Macao in China, Timor in the East Indies, various Atlantic islands, a small part of Guinea, and the large ill-defined African regions of Angola and Mozambique (Portuguese East Africa). For a time the Portuguese aspired to a trans-African empire joining these latter two, but British penetration from the Cape into Rhodesia kept the two Portuguese colonies apart.

Spain really ceased to be a colonial power after the Spanish-American War, but retained a useless stretch of African coast called Río de Oro.

The Turkish empire, though shown on the map, was not a colonial empire in the usual sense, and had long been losing ground to its neighbors (see pages 67 and 174).

Arctic Exploration

Although Arctic exploration had nothing to do with colonial enterprise, except insofar as both expressed the expansive vitality of the new industrial and scientific civilization, the present map offers a convenient place on which to exhibit the chief Arctic voyages. The old search for a northeast passage (see pages 62–63) now at last succeeded; the sea route along northern Siberia was opened for the first time. The American Peary reached the North Pole in 1909.

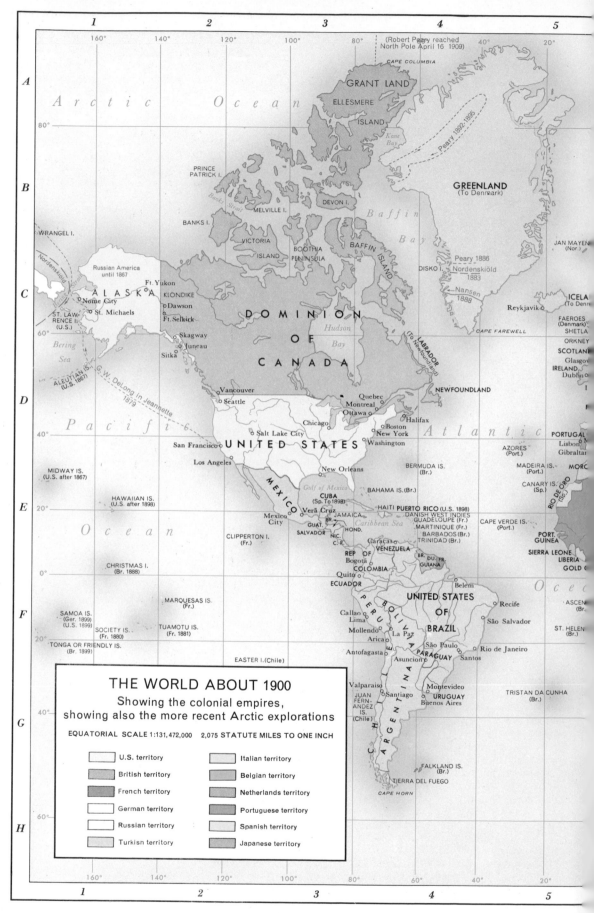

THE WORLD ABOUT 1900

Showing the colonial empires,
showing also the more recent Arctic explorations

EQUATORIAL SCALE 1:131,472,000   2,075 STATUTE MILES TO ONE INCH

U.S. territory		Italian territory
British territory		Belgian territory
French territory		Netherlands territory
German territory		Portuguese territory
Russian territory		Spanish territory
Turkish territory		Japanese territory

6   7   8   9   10

20°   40°   60°   80°   100°   120°   140°   160°

Fridtjof Nansen in Fram 1893-1896

Arctic Ocean

80°

SPITSBERGEN
(Norway 1920)

FRANZ JOSEF LAND OR
FRIDTJOF NANSEN LAND
(Russia 1928)

NORTHERN LAND
(NICHOLAS II)

NEW SIBERIAN
ISLANDS

DE LONG IS.

Baron Adolf Erik

Barents Sea

BEAR I.
(Nor.)

DeLong 1879-1881

1893 — 1896

B

TAIMYR PENINSULA

Nordenskiöld In Vega

WRANGEL
I.

Kara Sea

NOVAYA ZEMLYA

1819-1879

Hammerfest

NORTH
CAPE

Vardö

De Long Strait

KDM.
OF
SWEDEN
AND
NORWAY

Archangel

R U S S I A N   E M P I R E

Yakutsk

C

GR. DUCHY OF
FINLAND
Russian Tsar Grand
Duke since 1809

60°

Christiania

St. Petersburg

Tobolsk

Tomsk

Krasnoyarsk

Lena

*Sea of
Okhotsk*

Petropavlovsk

Stockholm

Moscow

Ufa

Kurgan

Omsk

Trans-Siberian Railway

Irkutsk

Chita

Blagovyeshchensk

SAKHALIN
(Russia 1875)

Hamburg

Samara

Volga

Irtish

Khabarovsk

KURILE IS.

GER. Berlin

Warsaw

*Aral
Sea*

*Lake
Balkash*

MONGOLIA

Urga

MANCHURIA

Harbin

Vladivostok

Nordenskiöld 1879

D

Vienna

AUS.
HUNG.

Budapest

Odessa

Don

Caspian Sea

MONGOLIA

Moukden

Port Arthur
(Russia 1898)

EMPIRE

Naples

SERB.
RUM.
BUL.

Black Sea

KULJA
(Russia 1871-1888)

E M P I R E

Peking

KOREA

OF

ITALY

TURKISH EMPIRE

Constantinople

Merv
(1885)

SINKIANG

O F

Huang Ho

Weihaiwei
(Br. 1898)

Tsing Tao
(Ger. 1897)

JAPAN

Tokyo

40°

GREECE

CRETE
(Gr. 1898)

CYPRUS
(Br. 1878)

Teheran

Kashgar

Kabul

C H I N A

Ch'ing, Manchu
Dynasty since 1644

Shanghai

Yokohama

Pacific

MALTA
(Br.)

Bagdad

AFG.

TIBET

Lhasa

CHINA PROPER

RYUKYU IS.
(Jap. 1879)

OGASAWARA IS.
(BONIN IS.)
(Jap. 1876)

MARCUS I.
(Jap. 1899)

TRIPOLI
(Turk.)

Alexandria

PERSIA

BALUCH.
(Br. 1876)

Delhi

NEPAL

BHUTAN

Macao Hong
(Port.) Kong
(Br.)

FORMOSA
(Jap. since 1895)

WAKE I.
(U.S. 1898)

20°

EGYPT

ARABIA

OMAN

Muscat

BRITISH INDIAN EMPIRE
also many semiautonomous
Indian states

BURMA

INDIA

Mandalay

Kwang-Chaw-Wan
(Fr. 1898)

MARIANAS
(Ger. 1899)

MARSHALL IS.
(Ger. 1899)

SUDAN

ERIT.

Mecca

KURIA
MURIA IS.
(Br.)

Bombay

Calcutta

Rangoon

SIAM

FR.
INDO-
CHINA

PHILIPPINE
IS.
(U.S. 1899)

GUAM
(U.S. 1898)

CAROLINES
(Ger. 1899)

E

ADEN

SOCOTRA
(Br. 1886)

GOA
(Port.)

Madras

ANDAMAN IS.
(Br.)

Bangkok

PELEW IS.
(Ger. 1899)

GILBERT IS.
(Br. 1899)

KAMERUN

ABYSSINIA

FR. SOM.
BR. SOM.

LACCADIVE IS.
(Br.)

Malié
(Fr.)

Pondichéry

CEYLON

NICOBAR IS.
(Br.)

STRAITS
SETTLEMENTS

SARAWAK
(Br.)

N.
BORNEO
(1888)

MOLUCCA

Ocean

CONGO FREE
STATE
Ruled by
Leopold II of
Belgium

E. AFR.

IT SOM

MALDIVE IS.
(Br.)

Singapore

BORNEO

NEW GUINEA
(Neth.
1901)

NEW MECKLENBURG
(Ger.
1884)

GER.
E. AFR.

ZANZIBAR
(Br. 1890)

SEYCHELLES
(Br.)

SUMATRA

CÉLEBES
(Port.)

BISMARCK IS.
(Ger. 1884)

NEW
POMERANIA
(Br.
1884)

ELLICE IS.
(Br. 1892)

ANGOLA

RHODESIA

COMORO IS.
(Fr.)

Mozambique

Indian

JAVA

COCOS IS
(Br. 1876)

TIMOR
(Neth.)

SOLOMON IS.
Div. between
Br. and Ger. 1899

FIJI IS.
(Br. 1874)

F

MADAGASCAR
(Fr. 1896)

MAURITIUS (Br.)

Darwin

NEW
HEBRIDES

GER.
S.W.
AFR.

TRANS-
VAAL

BECHUANA
LAND

PORT. E. AFR.

REUNION (Fr.)

NORTHERN
TERRITORY

C O M M O N W E A L T H
O F
A U S T R A L I A
(including Tasmania formed in 1901)

NEW
CALEDONIA
(Fr.)

LOYALTY IS.
(Fr. 1864)

ANGE
STATE

CAPE
COLONY

NATAL

Lourenço
Marques

WESTERN
AUSTRALIA

SOUTH
AUSTRALIA

QUEENSLAND

Brisbane

Capetown

Perth

Adelaide

NEW
SOUTH
WALES

VICTORIA

Sydney

Ocean

Melbourne

Wellington

G

TASMANIA

60°

NEW
ZEALAND
Organized as a
Dominion in 1907

H

20°   40°   60°   80°   100°   120°   140°   160°

Copyright by Rand McNally & Company, Made in U.S.A.

6   7   8   9   10

THE EARLY TWENTIETH CENTURY

▶ MAPS ON PAGES 174, 175, 176, 177, AND 178-79

THE FIRST WORLD WAR was one of the great turning points of European and of all modern civilization. It had many deep causes, but actually began over a dispute in the Balkans. The following maps show the Balkan Peninsula before 1914, Europe in 1914, the campaigns of 1914–18, and Europe as it was between the First World War and the Second.

The Balkan Peninsula to 1914
▶ MAP ON PAGE 174

The heavy gray line shows the boundaries of the Ottoman Empire in 1815. This once mighty power (see page 65) was now threatened both by European expansionism and by the rising nationalism of the Balkan peoples. Of the various Balkan nationalities under Turkish rule (see page 95), the Serbs were the first to take successful steps toward independence. Greece was recognized as an independent kingdom in 1833. In 1840–41 the Straits were placed under international control by an agreement following a crisis in Egypt, which also became autonomous. In the Crimean War, 1854–56, Russia was prevented by Britain and France from extending its influence in the Balkans. Meanwhile, Rumanian nationalism produced in 1858 the fusion of Moldavia and Wallachia in a common principality of Rumania.

In the 1860's the Austrian Germans, forced out of Germany by Bismarck, made a compromise with the other chief group in the Hapsburg empire, the Magyars of Hungary. In the resulting Dual Monarchy, whose internal border is shown on page 174, the Austrian Germans and the Magyars, now equals, each ruled over subordinate peoples. Austro-Hungarian expansionism turned southeast.

Balkan Slavs rose against the Turks in 1875. In Russia there was a great wave of sympathy for these fellow Orthodox Christians; the Russian government went to war with Turkey, on which in 1878 it imposed the Treaty of San Stefano. This treaty set up a large Bulgaria, shown by the dashed line on the map. Austria-Hungary and Great Britain viewed the creation of so large a Russian satellite with alarm. Peace was preserved at the Congress of Berlin of 1878, which replaced the Treaty of San Stefano with a general compromise, divided Bulgaria into three parts, recognized the full independence, with enlargement, of Serbia, Montenegro, and Rumania, returned southern Bessarabia to Russia, and allowed Austria-Hungary to "occupy and administer," though not annex, Bosnia and Herzegovina. Britain received the island of Cyprus.

The agreements of 1878 allayed great-power conflicts in the Balkans for thirty years. Native nationalist agitations meanwhile increased. In 1885 a revolution in Rumelia joined it with Bulgaria. The Greeks pushed their border to the north in 1881; Crete became autonomous in 1898. Macedonia became inflamed in the 1890's. In 1908 Bulgaria became independent, and Austria-Hungary annexed Bosnia-Herzegovina, antagonizing the South Slavs and the Russians.

In 1911–12 Italy took Tripoli and the Do-decanese Islands from the Ottoman Empire, which, thus weakened, was attacked by the small Balkan states. A settlement of 1913 ejected Turkey from Europe except for a small region adjoining Constantinople; created Albania, the last Balkan territory to be set up as independent; divided Macedonia between Greece and Serbia to the annoyance of Bulgaria; enlarged Montenegro; and turned over the southern Dobrudja to Rumania.

The Balkans in 1913 were the danger zone of Europe. Among the South Slavs—the peoples of Serbia, Bosnia, Herzegovina, Montenegro, Dalmatia, and Croatia-Slavonia, all of whom spoke the Serbo-Croatian language, plus the Slovenians to the north —the sentiment had grown that they all belonged to one Yugoslav nationality. The union and independence of this new nationality threatened the Austro-Hungarian empire with dismemberment.

Europe in 1914: The Alliances
▶ MAP ON PAGE 175

This map shows by its color scheme the two warring alliances of the First World War. These alliances had developed over the preceding quarter-century. Their existence in 1914, or the needs and fears which they represented, explains why all Europe went to war over an incident in the Balkans.

After Bismarck had defeated France, in 1871, he sought to preserve the new status quo against retaliation. In 1879 he signed the Dual Alliance with Austria-Hungary. For a time Bismarck tried also to hold Russia within his orbit, but after his retirement France and Russia came together in their alliance of 1894. Russia thus gained French support for its aims in the Balkans; France gained in Russia a partner, which the French government and investors built up by extensive loans for support against the rising power of Germany. Italy in 1882 joined with Germany and Austria-Hungary to form the Triple Alliance, which, however, Italy did not support when the war came. Great Britain by 1907 came to agreements with both France and Russia, laying to rest its disputes with these powers over African and Asian questions. Thus was formed the Triple Entente, or threefold "understanding."

In a series of international crises from 1908 to 1914 members of the two alliances tested each other's strength. War was avoided in the crisis of 1908, when Austria annexed Bosnia, and in the following crises brought on by the Italo-Turkish and Balkan wars and by rivalries in Morocco. In 1914 Francis Ferdinand, heir to the Hapsburg throne, was assassinated by a South Slav patriot at Sarajevo in Bosnia. The Austrian government determined to put an end to the South Slav agitation, which it regarded as a menace to its vital interests. The Serbs rejected an Austrian ultimatum; they were supported by Russia. Germany felt obliged to stand with its ally Austria, as did France with Russia. Britain supported France. The five powers were at war by August 4, 1914. The Ottoman Empire in November joined with Germany out of fear of Russia. In May, 1915, Italy, long tepid toward the Triple Alliance, chose to side with the Entente. In October, 1915, Bulgaria, by attacking Serbia, linked its destinies with the German Empire. Thus were formed the wartime alliances as shown on the map.

The War and the Treaties

▶ MAP ON PAGES 178–79

The first power to suffer total disaster was tsarist Russia. Military defeat, disorganization, and discontent led to revolution in March, 1917. The communists, seizing power in the following October, took Russia out of the war. This loss to the western alliance was made up by the intervention of the United States. The German and Austro-Hungarian empires collapsed in 1918; Germany became a republic, and Austria-Hungary disintegrated into its component national groups. The war was the most terrible ever waged until that time; there were over 10,000,000 dead and 20,000,000 wounded; and material cost was estimated at over $350,000,000,000.

The war was followed by the Peace of Versailles with Germany in 1919, lesser treaties with the other defeated states, and minor wars between Poland and Russia and between Greece and Turkey. These all resulted in 1922 in borders as shown on the map. Germany lost Alsace-Lorraine to France, northern Schleswig to Denmark, and a region called the Polish Corridor, by which the revived state of Poland received access to the sea. Territorially, the main principle of the postwar settlement was that of national self-determination. Various linguistic groups of eastern Europe (see page 95) emerged as sovereign national states. Finland, Estonia, Latvia, and Lithuania became independent of the now defunct Russian empire. Poland was reconstituted with territories formerly belonging to Russia, Germany, and Austria. Of formerly Austro-Hungarian territories, the old Bohemia, Moravia, and Slovakia became the republic of Czechoslovakia; the Trentino went to Italy; Slovenia, Dalmatia, Croatia, and Bosnia combined with Serbia to form Yugoslavia; Transylvania went to Rumania; and Austria and Hungary became small separate states.

Europe, 1922–40

▶ MAP ON PAGES 178–79

The map shows by color the "revisionist" and "status quo" powers of the interwar years. Germany was naturally the power chiefly interested in a revision of the treaties; Italy became revisionist under the dictator Mussolini. France, with Germany weakened, had the greatest interest in maintaining the new status quo. Obsessed by the fear of 70,-000,000 Germans in Germany and Austria, as against 40,000,000 French, France demanded and obtained at the peace conference the imposition of heavy reparations, economic disabilities, and unilateral disarmament on Germany, and a guarantee that Germany and Austria should never unite, as seemed likely in the 1920's, since Austria, with the dissolution of the Hapsburg empire, had become a small and purely German state. France also, in the 1920's, unable to resume its old alliance with a Russia now communist, reached agreements against Germany with Poland and the Little Entente, composed of Czechoslovakia, Yugoslavia, and Rumania. In effect, however, since the United States had withdrawn as a factor in the European balance, France depended for the furtherance of its aims on Great Britain, and the British were less fearful of German revival than were the French.

The great depression of the early 1930's weakened the Weimar Republic and made many Germans more receptive to Adolf Hitler and the claims of his Nazi Party. Hitler obtained control of Germany in 1933. In the following years he repudiated various clauses of the Versailles Treaty step by step. At no point did France and Britain feel sufficient faith in the Versailles Treaty to uphold it by force; a revulsion against all war, bred in the Western democracies by the losses and apparent futility of the war of 1914–18, made it difficult to conduct any decisive diplomacy or to take any risks. In 1935, by a plebiscite in the rich coal-producing area of the Saar, the voters chose reunion with Germany. In 1936 Hitler by unilateral action reoccupied the Rhineland with German troops. In the same year he announced a program of German rearmament. Both Germany and Italy tested their weapons in the Spanish Civil War which broke out in that year. Hitler then turned to the acquisition of ethnic Germans outside Germany itself; these were the Germans of Czechoslovakia, called Sudetens; the Germans of Austria, and those of Danzig, made a free city in 1919. In 1938 he carried through the *Anschluss* or annexation of Austria. Later in that year, with the consent of Britain and France obtained by his threats at Munich, he gained the Sudetenland from Czechoslovakia. He thus broke the power of the most successful of the new states created at the close of the First World War.

When Hitler, in March, 1939, went on to occupy Bohemia and Moravia, which were unquestionably Slavic, it became clear that his aims were not merely the self-determination of Germans, but were more probably the subjugation of Europe. Britain now gave a guarantee to Poland and opened belated negotiations with Russia. Russia, however, made a pact with Germany instead, the Soviet-Nazi alliance of 1939, by which the two agreed to divide Poland. Poland was invaded by the Germans, then by the Russians; Britain, having guaranteed Poland, accepted war with Germany, as did France.

Hitler's main aim may have been to exploit eastern Europe and the Russian territories for German advantage. Learning, however, in 1939, that the western powers would not consent to such a German march to the east, he embarked on what was intended as a small war in the west to precede the great war in the east. His agreement of 1939 with Russia, to divide Poland, was meant to postpone hostilities with Russia until victory had been won in the west. Having overrun Poland in 1939, the Germans in 1940, with little fighting, occupied Norway, Denmark, Belgium, and Holland, crushed France, and opened an air offensive against Britain. Mussolini meanwhile joined Germany, and opened an attack on the Balkans, with so little success that he had to appeal for German aid. In 1940, controlling the continent west of Russia, Adolf Hitler seemed to be one of the great conquerors of all time.

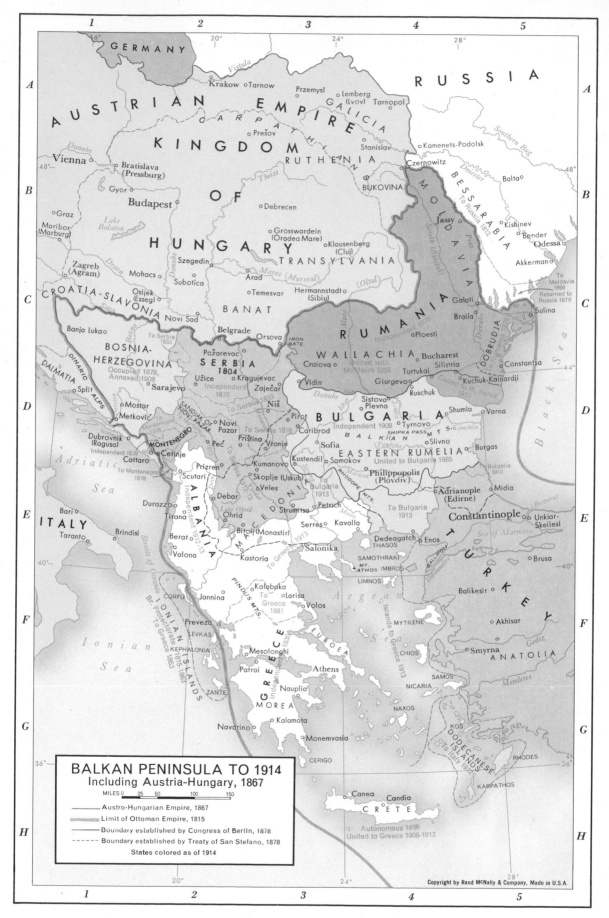

BALKAN PENINSULA TO 1914
Including Austria-Hungary, 1867

MILES 0 25 50   100   150

——— Austro-Hungarian Empire, 1867

▬▬▬ Limit of Ottoman Empire, 1815

——— Boundary established by Congress of Berlin, 1878

------- Boundary established by Treaty of San Stefano, 1878

States colored as of 1914

Copyright by Rand McNally & Company, Made in U.S.A.

GERMANY

RUSSIA

AUSTRIAN EMPIRE

KINGDOM

Vienna
Bratislava
(Pressburg)
Gyor
Graz
Maribor
(Marburg)
Budapest
Zagreb
(Agram)

Krakow Tarnow
Przemysl
Lemberg
(Lvov) Tarnopol
GALICIA
Presov
Stanislav
RUTHENIA
BUKOVINA
Czernowitz
Kamenets-Podolsk
BESSARABIA
To Russia 1812
Jassy
Kishinev
Bender
Odessa
Akkerman

OF

Debrecen
Grosswardein
(Oradea Mare)
Klausenberg
(Cluj)
TRANSYLVANIA
Szegedin
Arad
Subotica
Temesvar
Hermannstadt
(Sibiu)

HUNGARY

Lake
Balaton

M O L D A V I A

To Moldavia
1856
Returned to
Russia 1878

CROATIA-SLAVONIA
Mohacs
Novi Sad
BANAT
Belgrade
Orsova
IRON
GATE
Galati
Braila
Sulina

R U M A N I A
Independent 1878

Banja Luka
BOSNIA-HERZEGOVINA
Occupied 1878,
Annexed 1908
Sarajevo
DALMATIA
Split
Mostar
Metkovic
DINARIC ALPS
Dubrovnik
(Ragusa)
Independent 1878
Cattaro
To Montenegro
1878

SERBIA
1804
Pozarevac
Uzice Kragujevac
Zajecar
Independent
1878

WALLACHIA
United with
Moldavia 1856
Craiova
Vidin
DANUBE
Bucharest
Ploesti
Silistria
DOBRUDJA
Ceded to Rumania
1878
Constantsa
Giurgevo
Turtukai
Kuchuk-Kainardji

SANDJAK OF NOVI PAZAR
To Serbia 1833
Nis
Pirot
Caribrod
Sistova
Plevna
Ruschuk
Shumla
Varna

BULGARIA
Independent 1908
Tyrnovo
BALKAN MTS.
SHIPKA PASS
Slivno
Kamchia

MONTENEGRO
Independent 1878
Cetinje
Novi
Pazar
Pec
To Serbia 1878
Pristina
Prizren
Scutari
Durazzo
ALBANIA
Independent 1912-13
Tirana
Berat
Valona

Kumanovo
Skopje (Uskub)
To Bulgaria 1913
Veles
Debar
MACEDONIA
Strumitsa
Petrich
Ohrid
Lake Ohrid
Bitolj (Monastir)
Serres
Kavalla

Vranje
Kustendil
Sofia
Samokov
EASTERN RUMELIA
United to Bulgaria 1885
Philippopolis
(Plovdiv)
RHODOPE MTS.
Bulgaria
1913
Burgas
Bulgaria
1913
Adrianople
(Edirne)
Midia

Constantinople
Unkiar-Skelessi

ITALY
Bari
Taranto
Brindisi

Dedeagatch
Enos
THASOS
SAMOTHRAKI
MT. ATHOS IMBROS
LIMNOS
To Greece 1913
GALLIPOLI
Dardanelles
Sea of Marmora
Brusa
Balikesir

TURKEY

ANATOLIA
Smyrna
Akhisar
Gediz
Menderes

PINDUS MTS.
Kalabaka
To Greece 1881
Larisa
Volos

GREECE
Independent 1830

Jannina
Preveza
LEVKAS
IONIAN ISLANDS
Br. Protectorate
To Greece 1863
1815-1863
KEPHALONIA
CORFU
ZANTE

Mesolonghi
Patrai
MOREA
Nauplia
Navarino
Kalamata
Monemvasia
CERIGO

Athens
EUBOEA
Islands to Greece 1913
CHIOS
MYTILENE
SAMOS
NICARIA
NAXOS
DODECANESE ISLANDS
To Italy 1912
KOS
RHODES
KARPATHOS

Canea Candia
C R E T E
Autonomous 1898
United to Greece 1908-1913

Adriatic Sea

Ionian Sea

Aegean Sea

Black Sea

Vistula

Danube

Theiss

Drava

Maros (Muresul)

Danube

Southern Bug

Dniester

Pruth

Serath (Siretul)

Oltul

Timok

To Serbia 1833

174

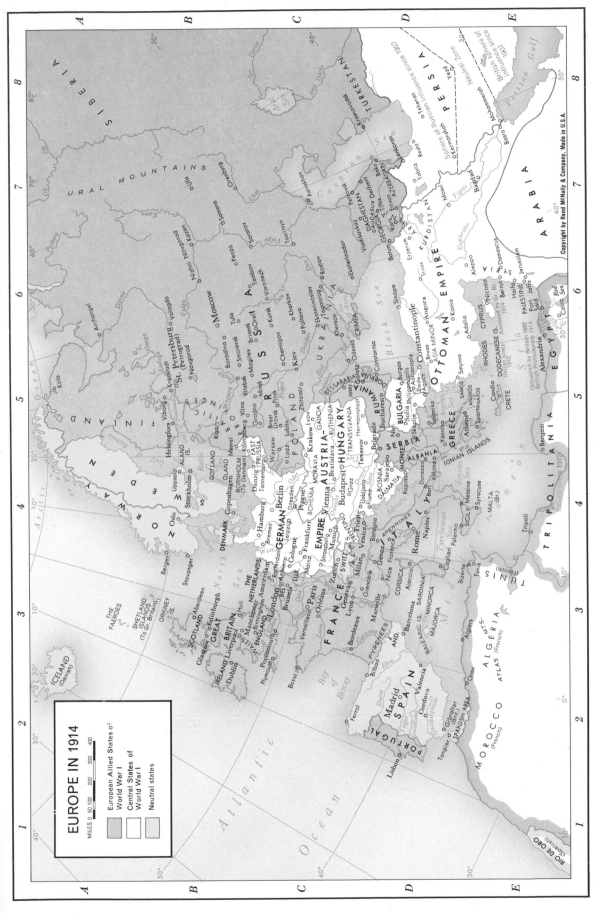

EUROPE IN 1914

MILES 0 50 100   200   300   400

European Allied States of
World War I

Central States of
World War I

Neutral states

Copyright by Rand McNally & Company, Made in U.S.A.

THE FIRST WORLD WAR

A<small>T THE OUTBREAK</small> of war in 1914 all the major powers had military plans prepared for a quick victory. All thought that the war would be short, believing that no modern and industrialized state could sustain a long war without economic disruption. The most spectacular plan was the German Schlieffen Plan, which, assuming a two-front war and anticipating that the Russians would be slower to mobilize, called for an initial concentration of forces against France. While the German left flank held French forces on the Rhine, the right flank was to sweep through Belgium, northern France, and around Paris to take the French armies in the rear, after which the German forces were to regroup against the Russians. The French strategy provided for the concentration of French troops on the center and right flanks to deliver a crushing blow on the Rhine front. Austro-Hungarian and Russian plans were less definite, but the Russians aimed at driving a wedge between the Central Powers and making a direct assault on Berlin.

All these plans met defeat in the early months of the war. The Germans weakened their right flank in the west to meet the Russian threat in East Prussia. German forces almost reached Paris, but were thrown back at the Battle of the Marne. The

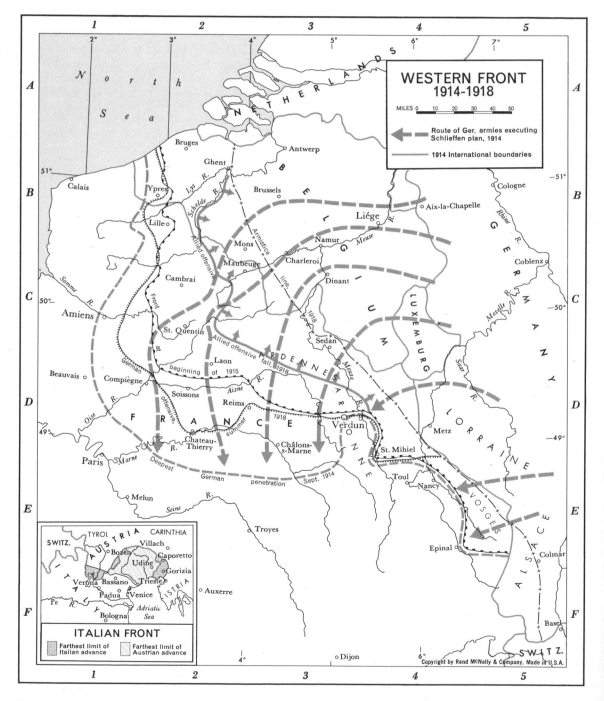

176

Russians meanwhile defeated the Austrians, but were routed by the Germans in the battle of Tannenberg. With the hope of a short war now lost, operations on the Western Front settled into the trenches. The use of the machine gun, barbed wire, and slow-moving heavy artillery gave the advantage to the defensive; hereafter the advance of armies, in the west, was measured in yards rather than miles. In a long war the British naval blockade of Germany became very important; contrariwise, the German submarine offensive came close to cutting off Britain.

In 1915 the Germans and Austrians made tremendous but futile efforts to annihilate Russia. In 1916 the main operations shifted back to France, where the Germans launched a great attack at Verdun, and the Allies in the Somme valley. Both cost hundreds of thousands of lives, but accomplished nothing. Italy joined the Allies in 1915, but the Italo-Austrian campaigns remained inconclusive. In 1918, after the Russian Revolution, the Germans swept into the Ukraine and also penetrated deeply into France. By this time American aid was arriving in force, and the Germans signed an armistice on November 11, 1918.

The First World War, though the colonial world was deeply affected, remained essentially a European struggle. United States intervention became effective only at the end. Large-scale engagement of American troops was limited to the Argonne and the St-Mihiel salient in the summer and fall of 1918.

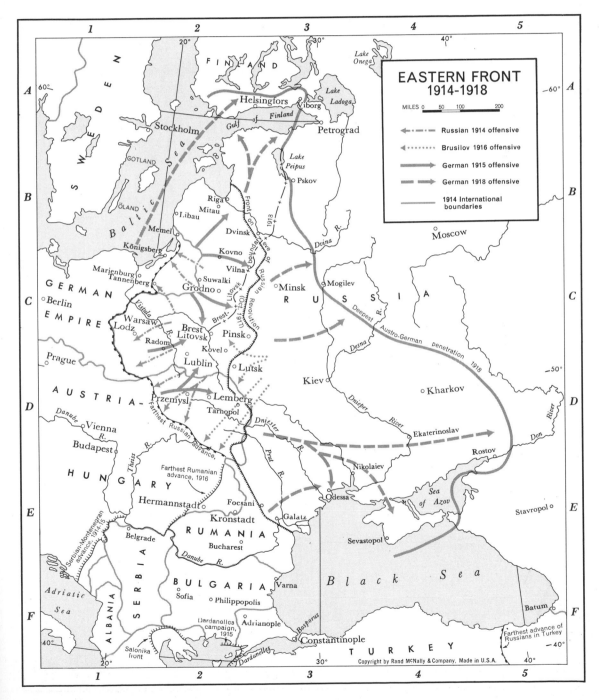

EASTERN FRONT
1914-1918

MILES 0   50   100   200

←·—·— Russian 1914 offensive

←······· Brusilov 1916 offensive

←—— German 1915 offensive

←- - - German 1918 offensive

—— 1914 International boundaries

Copyright by Rand McNally & Company. Made in U.S.A.

ICELAND

Reykjavik

A

THE FAEROES

SHETLAND ISLANDS

HEBRIDES

ORKNEY IS.

B

Bergen

Stavanger

Oslo

Uppsala

Helsingfors (Helsinki)

ALAND IS.

Tornio

Vaasa (Vasa)

SCOTLAND

Aberdeen

Glasgow

Edinburgh

North Sea

Göteborg

Stockholm

GOTLAND

EST Anne U

C

IRISH FREE STATE

Belfast

GREAT

Liverpool

Leeds

Hull

Manchester

Sheffield

Dublin

Cork

BRITAIN

WALES

ENGLAND

Cardiff

Oxford

Birmingham

London

DENMARK Occupied by Germany 1941

Aalborg

Hälsingborg

Copenhagen

Kiel

Lübeck

Hamburg

ÖLAND

Bornholm

Memel

MEMELAND

Konigsberg

Danzig

LITHUANI Annexed To Ger. 1939

Kovno (Kaunas)

Vi

Gro

D

Plymouth

Bristol

Portsmouth

CHANNEL IS.

Brest

Rennes

St. Nazaire

Havre

Caen

Amiens

Lille

Dunkirk

Dover

Brussels

BEL.

THE NETHERLANDS Occ. by

HELGOLAND

Bremen

Hanover

Stettin

EAST PRUSSIA

Tannenberg

Bialystok

Brest Litovsk

Amsterdam

Rotterdam

LUX.

Cologne

Essen

Magdeburg

Cassel

Leipzig

GERMANY

Berlin

Potsdam

Dresden

Breslau

Posen

Warsaw

POLAN

Nazi-Soviet Pact Annexed by Germany 1939

SILESIA

Cracow

Lublin

E

Amiens

Paris

Versailles

Verdun

Reims

Occupied by Germany 1940

Fontainebleau

Orleans

Dijon

La Rochelle

Bordeaux

Bay of Biscay

FRANCE

VICHY FRANCE 1940

Limoges

Lyon

Grenoble

Montpellier

Toulouse

Avignon

Nice

PYRENEES

ANDORRA

Marseille

Toulon

SAAR

LORRAINE

ALSACE

Strassburg

Basle

Zürich

Berne

SWITZERLAND

Geneva

ALPS

Munich

Innsbruck

TRENTINO

LIECH.

Milan

Verona

Turin

Parma

Genoa

San Remo

Ravenna

Bologna

Florence

Ancona

ITALY

SAN MARINO

Rome

Nürnberg

Mannheim

Stuttgart

BAVARIA

Pilsen

Prague

CZECHOSLOVAKIA

To Ger. at Munich 1938

Vienna

AUSTRIA

Anschluss 1938

Graz

Zagreb

CROATIA

Trieste

Venice

Fiume

YUGOSLAVIA

Ljubljana

Mohacs

Budapest

HUNGARY

Oradea

TRANSYLVANIA

Cluj

RUMA

Belgrade

SERBIA

Temisoara

Sibiu

WALLAC

Bucha

Rusche

Sistova

BU Anne U

RUTHENIA

Košice

Tesin

Przemysl

Lemb

Ilwo

Tarnopol

F

LISBON

PORTUGAL

Oporto

Coimbra

Madrid

Tagus

SPAIN

Toledo

Salamanca

Valladolid

Burgos

Santander

Bayonne

Corunna

Duero

Guadiana

Córdoba

Seville

Granada

Almería

Cádiz

Gibralter (To Great Britain)

Tangier

SPANISH AREA

Rabat

Oran

MOROCCO To France

ATLAS

MOUNTAINS

Algiers

BALERIC ISLANDS (To Spain)

Valencia

Barcelona

Cartagena

MINORCA

MAJORCA

Ajaccio

CORSICA (To France)

SARDINIA (To Italy)

Cagliari

Naples

Bari

Taranto

Brindisi

Palermo

Messina

SICILY

Syracuse

Tyrrhenian Sea

DALMATIA

Split

Zara

Sarajevo

BOSNIA

MONTE-NEGRO

Cattaro

LAGOSTA (To Italy)

Dubrovnik (Ragusa)

Antivari

Durazzo

ALBANIA

Valona

CORFU

Novi Pazar

Skoplje

MACEDONIA

Tirana

Yannina

CEPHALLENIA

IONIAN ISLANDS

BELGRADE

BULG

Sofia

Philippopolis

Adriano

Deds-Aga

Kavala

Salonika

GREECE

LESBOS

Messolongi

Patras

Athens

Sparta

Ionian Sea

CRETE

Ca

G

Tunis

Tripoli

MOROCCO

ALGERIA To France

TUNIS French Protectorate

MALTA (Br.)

Mediterranean

TRIPOLITANIA To Italy

Gulf of Sidra

Bengazi

CYRENAICA To Italy

LIBYA

AFRICA

H

Copyright by Rand McNally & Company, Made in U.S.A.

Europe 1922-40 map

THE SECOND WORLD WAR

▶ MAPS ON PAGES 181, 182–83, AND 184

CONTROLLING THE EUROPEAN continent west of Russia in the summer of 1940, the Germans under Hitler turned to attack the only power then at war with them, namely, Great Britain. The ensuing aerial Battle of Britain was won by the British. With Britain unreduced, Hitler invaded Russia in June, 1941 (see pages 183 and 114). The United States, aiding Britain but remaining formally nonbelligerent, was attacked in December, 1941, by Japan, which opened its operations by the bombing of Pearl Harbor and invasion of the Philippine Islands, then a possession of the United States. The United States now came into the war both with Japan and with Germany and its ally, Italy.

Expansion of Japan
▶ MAP ON PAGE 181

Japan had shown expansionist tendencies since the last decades of the nineteenth century, when it became the one independent Westernized or industrialized Asian power. It had asserted its sovereignty over the Kurile and Bonin islands by 1875, taken Formosa in 1895, obtained southern Sakhalin and rights at Port Arthur after the Russo-Japanese War, acquired control of Korea in 1910, and occupied some of the German Pacific islands during the First World War.

In 1932 the Japanese opened military operations in China. The Second World War weakened the British, French, and Dutch colonial regimes in southeast Asia; it was American resistance to Japanese designs on French Indo-China that finally impelled the Japanese into war with the United States. In 1942 Japanese expansion reached its height with naval control of the southwest Pacific and military penetration of much of China, the Philippines, Burma, the Indo-China peninsula, Singapore, and the Dutch East Indies, from which Australia was threatened.

The Height of Axis Expansion, 1942
▶ MAP ON PAGES 182–83

For all the Axis powers—Germany, Italy, and Japan—the year 1942 was the high point of their success. German submarines moved into the western Atlantic to hold off American aid to Europe. German armies occupied much of European Russia. France was in part occupied and in part left to the subservient Vichy regime, by which North Africa was rendered harmless to the Germans. German forces had moved through Italian Libya into Egypt and driven the British back upon Cairo. The grand strategy of the Axis was for the Germans, moving east via Egypt and the Caucasus, to join forces with the Japanese moving west into India. Axis control of Near Eastern oil fields and of India would ruin Britain and isolate Russia before American intervention could become effective. Germany and Japan could then reorganize the world.

But the year 1942 was also the turning point. The Russians stopped the Germans at the great Battle of Stalingrad. The British won the Battle of

El Alamein and moved west along the coast. Anglo-American forces had meanwhile landed in Morocco and Algeria; they joined with the British from Egypt to crush a German army in Tunisia, and then to invade Sicily and Italy itself in 1943. Meanwhile, the Axis tide had been turned even earlier in the Pacific: in May, 1942, the Americans won the Battle of the Coral Sea, and so preserved communications with an independent Australia, and in June the Battle of Midway, by which American supremacy in the central Pacific was reasserted. By these naval victories it became possible to maintain land forces in the Pacific islands, where the Japanese were first engaged at Guadalcanal in May, 1942.

The American strategy was, while holding Japan in the Pacific, to concentrate first on the destruction of the German war machine in Europe, after which Japan could be defeated at leisure. The American industrial system became a source of supply for British and Russian as well as American forces. It was, however, seriously blockaded by German submarines in 1942, and was in any case at a great distance from the battle fronts, as shown in days of ship travel on the map. By 1943 the Americans and British had won the Battle of the Atlantic, and were building more ship tonnage than they lost by sinkings, so that movement of American supplies, weapons, and troops in great volume became possible. A huge concentration of armed force was built up in Britain, from which the air war was launched against Germany in preparation for the land invasion of Europe.

The Defeat of Germany and Japan
▶ MAP ON PAGE 184

American and British forces landed in Normandy in June, 1944. At this time the Russians had pushed the Germans back as far as Poland. Enormous pressure was applied to the Germans from the west, south, and east; the advance of the Allied forces is shown on the map at successive periods some months apart. Adolf Hitler killed himself in his own elaborate bomb shelter on April 30, 1945. The war in Europe was over.

In the Pacific, beginning at Guadalcanal in May, 1942, the Americans, at first very slowly, moved from island to island in the direction of Japan. They retook the Philippines late in 1944. When the war ended in Europe American forces had occupied Okinawa and Iwo Jima, from which they prepared to subject the home islands of Japan to bombings of the kind used against Germany, and to shift troops from Europe for a massive invasion. This proved to be unnecessary, because on August 6, 1945, the Americans dropped an atomic bomb on Hiroshima, where 80,000 persons were killed by a single explosion. Another such bomb fell on Nagasaki. The Japanese surrendered at once.

For the Soviet Union, Germany, Japan, China, and the United States, the number of deaths of military personnel exceeded that of the First World War. Because of the bombings, and the policies of deliberate extermination on the part of Hitlerite Germany, the number of civilian deaths, though unknown, probably exceeded the number of military fatalities for the first time in many generations in the conflicts of civilized peoples.

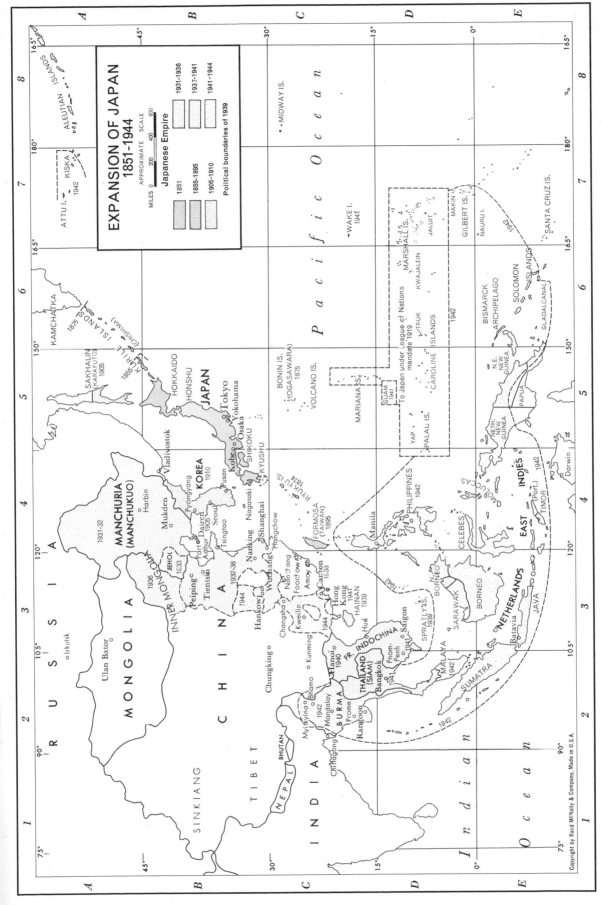

EXPANSION OF JAPAN
1851-1944

APPROXIMATE SCALE
MILES 0 200 400 600

Japanese Empire

1851
1855-1895
1905-1910

1931-1936
1937-1941
1941-1944

Political boundaries of 1939

Copyright by Rand McNally & Company, Made in U.S.A.

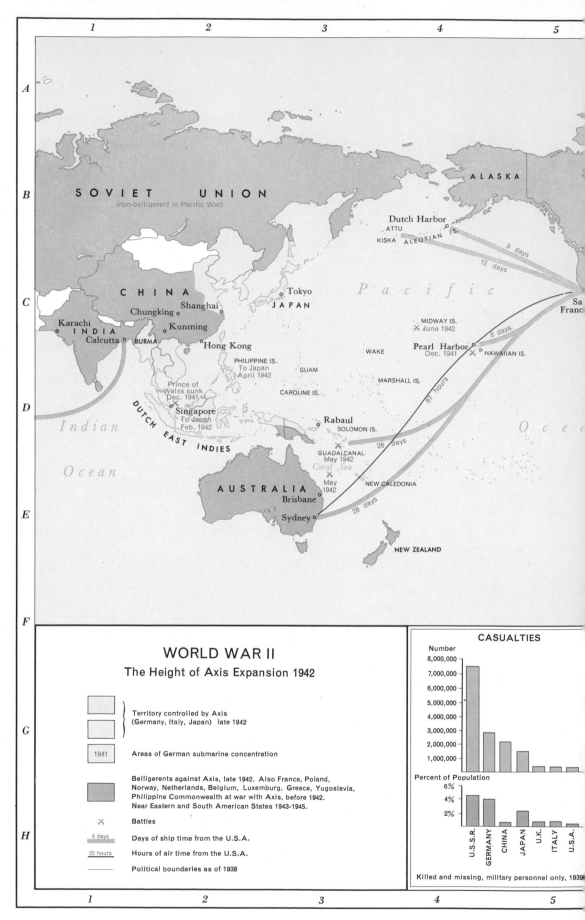

WORLD WAR II

The Height of Axis Expansion 1942

Territory controlled by Axis
(Germany, Italy, Japan) late 1942

1941   Areas of German submarine concentration

Belligerents against Axis, late 1942. Also France, Poland,
Norway, Netherlands, Belgium, Luxemburg, Greece, Yugoslavia,
Philippine Commonwealth at war with Axis, before 1942.
Near Eastern and South American States 1943-1945.

✕   Battles

9 days   Days of ship time from the U.S.A.

20 hours   Hours of air time from the U.S.A.

Political boundaries as of 1938

CASUALTIES

Number
8,000,000
7,000,000
6,000,000
5,000,000
4,000,000
3,000,000
2,000,000
1,000,000

Percent of Population
6%
4%
2%

U.S.S.R.   GERMANY   CHINA   JAPAN   U.K.   ITALY   U.S.A.

Killed and missing, military personnel only, 1939

Map labels

ALASKA

SOVIET UNION
(non-belligerent in Pacific War)

CHINA

Chungking   Shanghai

Karachi
INDIA   Kunming
Calcutta   BURMA

Tokyo
JAPAN

Hong Kong

PHILIPPINE IS.
To Japan
April 1942

GUAM

CAROLINE IS.

Prince of
Wales sunk
Dec. 1941

Singapore
To Japan
Feb. 1942

DUTCH EAST INDIES

Indian

Ocean

Rabaul
SOLOMON IS.

GUADALCANAL
May 1942

Coral Sea
May
1942

AUSTRALIA
Brisbane
Sydney

NEW ZEALAND

NEW CALEDONIA

Pacific

Ocean

Dutch Harbor
ATTU
KISKA   ALEUTIAN IS.
9 days
12 days

Sa
Franc

MIDWAY IS.
June 1942

WAKE

MARSHALL IS.

Pearl Harbor
Dec. 1941   HAWAIIAN IS.

8 days

6? hours

26 days

28 days

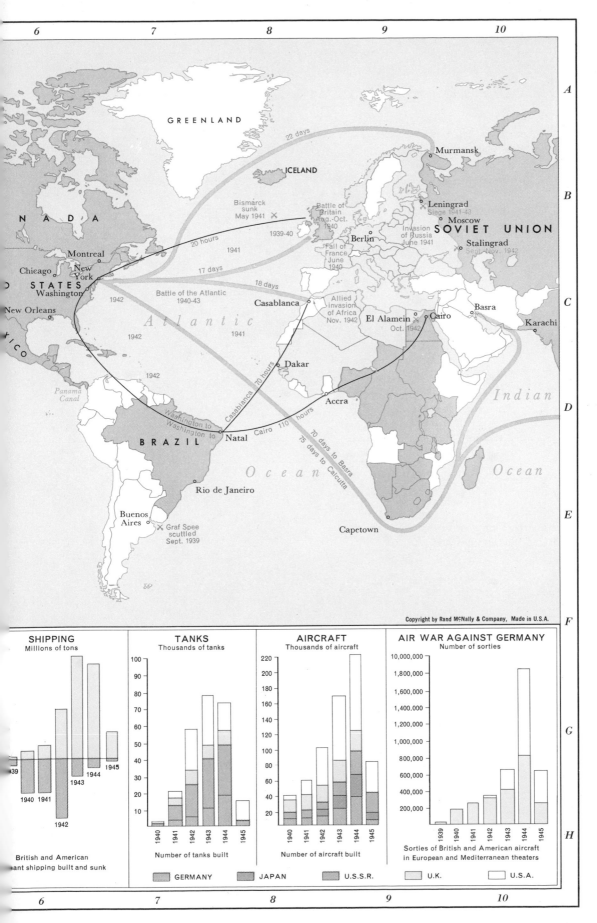

GREENLAND

ICELAND

22 days

Murmansk

Leningrad
Siege 1941-43

Moscow

SOVIET UNION

Stalingrad
Sept.-Nov. 1942

Bismarck
sunk
May 1941

Battle of
Britain
Aug.-Oct.
1940

1939-40

Invasion
of Russia
June 1941

Berlin

Fall of
France
June
1940

NADA

Montreal

Chicago

New
York

STATES

Washington

20 hours

1941

17 days

18 days

New Orleans

Battle of the Atlantic
1940-43

Casablanca

Allied
invasion
of Africa
Nov. 1942

El Alamein
Oct. 1942

Cairo

Basra

Karachi

XICO

1942

1942

1941

Atlantic

Dakar

Casablanca 70 hours

1942

Washington to

Washington to
Natal

Accra

Cairo 110 hours

70 days to Basra

Indian

BRAZIL

75 days to Calcutta

Ocean

Rio de Janeiro

Buenos
Aires

Graf Spee
scuttled
Sept. 1939

Capetown

Ocean

Panama
Canal

Copyright by Rand McNally & Company, Made in U.S.A.

SHIPPING
Millions of tons

1939
1940 1941
1942
1943
1944
1945

British and American
merchant shipping built and sunk

TANKS
Thousands of tanks

100	
90	
80	
70	
60	
50	
40	
30	
20	
10	

1940 1941 1942 1943 1944 1945

Number of tanks built

AIRCRAFT
Thousands of aircraft

220	
200	
180	
160	
140	
120	
100	
80	
60	
40	
20	

1940 1941 1942 1943 1944 1945

Number of aircraft built

AIR WAR AGAINST GERMANY
Number of sorties

10,000,000	
1,800,000	
1,600,000	
1,400,000	
1,200,000	
1,000,000	
800,000	
600,000	
400,000	
200,000	

1939 1940 1941 1942 1943 1944 1945

Sorties of British and American aircraft
in European and Mediterranean theaters

GERMANY   JAPAN   U.S.S.R.   U.K.   U.S.A.

DEFEAT OF GERMANY AND JAPAN 1943-1945

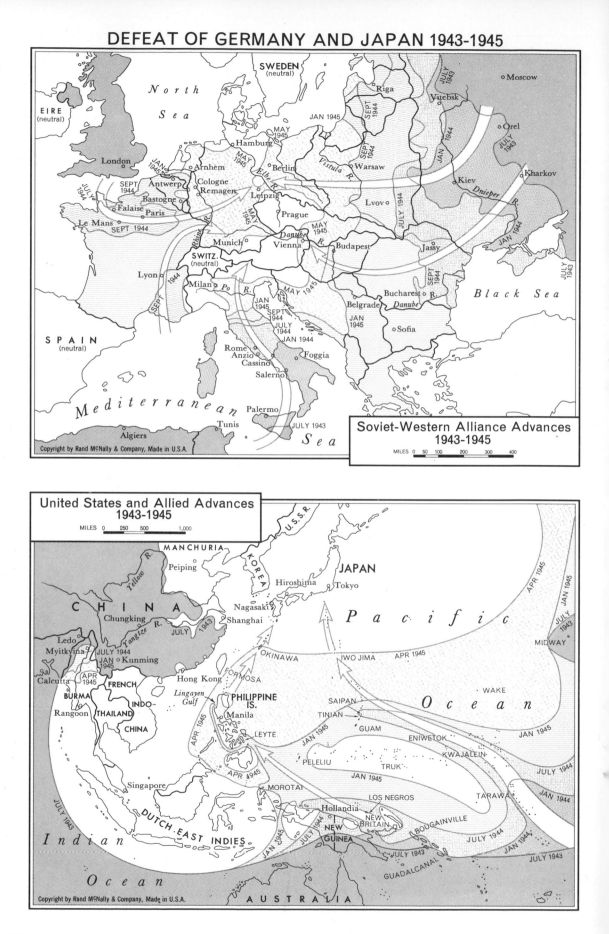

Soviet-Western Alliance Advances
1943-1945

MILES 0 50 100 200 300 400

United States and Allied Advances
1943-1945

MILES 0 250 500 1,000

Copyright by Rand McNally & Company, Made in U.S.A.

EUROPE AFTER
THE SECOND WORLD WAR

▶ MAP ON PAGE 186

THE SECOND WORLD WAR, unlike the First and unlike other wars for several centuries in the history of Europe, was not terminated by any general treaty, since agreement between the victors —the Soviet Union and the Western Allies—soon proved to be impossible on fundamental matters.

Soviet Expansion

As early as 1940, after the Nazi-Soviet Pact, but anticipating war with Germany, the Russians carried their frontiers farther to the west. After a short war with Finland, they pushed the Finnish border, which had run very close to Leningrad, back about a hundred miles from that city; later they also took the port of Pechenga on the Murman coast. In 1940 they annexed Estonia, Latvia, and Lithuania, independent since 1918, and converted them into member republics of the Soviet Union. Dividing Poland with Hitler, they added its eastern portion to the White Russian and Ukrainian Soviet Republics. This region, conquered by Poland in 1920, was in fact largely White Russian or Ukrainian in population. They also at this time seized Bessarabia and Bucovina. These regions, occupied by the Germans from 1941 to 1945, all emerged again after the war as integral parts of the Soviet Union.

The Division of Germany

Soviet and Western armies met along the Elbe River in 1945. With Germany in total collapse, the Soviet Union annexed the northern part of East Prussia (where Königsberg was renamed Kaliningrad), and allowed Poland to annex southern East Prussia and other German territories to the Oder River and its tributary the Neisse. Germans in these areas fled or were expelled. Not since the twelfth century (see page 46) had Poland reached so far west. Germany west of the Oder-Neisse was divided into zones of military occupation, roughly determined by the position of the victorious armies at the close of hostilities. The Soviet zone extended west of the Elbe and contained the old German cities of Leipzig and Dresden. Berlin, administered jointly by the victors, became an enclave a hundred miles deep within territory under Soviet control. The western zones of Germany—American, British, and French—were recognized by those powers, in 1949, as the German Federal Republic. The Soviet zone turned into the German Democratic Republic. Thus Germany was divided, the western part associated with western Europe and the United States; the eastern part, with the Soviet Union and what were called the people's democracies of eastern Europe.

The Division of Europe

These people's democracies were the new regimes in Poland, Czechoslovakia, Hungary, Rumania (Romania), Albania, and Bulgaria, in addition to eastern Germany. These states, except for Albania,

had been occupied by Russian forces in pursuit of the Germans in the closing months of the war. At the Yalta Conference, early in 1945, the Americans and British believed that they reached an agreement with the Soviet Union to allow future governments of these Russian-occupied states to be established and conducted by free elections. Provisional governments were set up, in which the native communist and pro-Soviet parties at first allowed participation of others; but since anticommunists were often barred as ex-fascists and former pro-Germans, since the only military force on the spot was the Russian, and since communists in the new governments held the ministries of the Interior and of Justice (and hence controlled the police and the courts), the communists in these countries were able to introduce regimes modeled on, and supported by, that of the Soviet Union. Yugoslavia became independently communist while resisting Russia. Greece remained noncommunist only after a violent civil war; first the British, then the Americans, intervened against communism in Greece. Austria avoided communism because, like Berlin, it was jointly administered by the Soviet and Western powers in the postwar years.

The war left only the Soviet Union and the United States as first-class military and industrial powers. Production and transportation on the Continent had been brought to a standstill by the combined effects of Nazi occupation, land fighting, and Allied bombing. The United States soon came to favor the rebuilding of the German economy, notably in the decisive Ruhr industrial area, as a means of reviving Europe. With the Marshall Plan of 1947, the United States granted economic aid for this purpose. The Russians feared the revival of Germany and of Europe under American or any anticommunist auspices. In 1948, by a communist coup, Czechoslovakia was aligned with the people's democracies. In 1949 most of the west European states, as shown on the map, formed with the United States and Canada the North Atlantic Treaty Organization to prepare common military defenses. It became known in that year that Russia, like the United States, possessed atomic weapons. The success of communism in China, and war in Korea in 1950, heightened the tension between the two alliances. An iron curtain was said to separate the communist and Western worlds; not in centuries, if indeed ever, had there been so little trade, movement of persons, or cultural and intellectual intercourse between western and eastern Europe. In the 1950's western Europe took cautious steps toward greater economic and even political unity, in the hope both of resisting the Soviet Union and of reducing western Europe's dependence on the United States. In eastern Europe the people's democracies became increasingly interlocked with the Soviet Union, but the abortive Hungarian revolution of 1956 revealed the element of force necessary to maintain this state of affairs. There were flickers of hope, often disappointed, for a renewal of contacts between east and west. In a deep sense, as shown by preceding pages in this book, the historic border of European civilization lay east of the people's democracies, not to the west of them. This fact presented difficulties for Russia, and caused instability in the whole international situation.

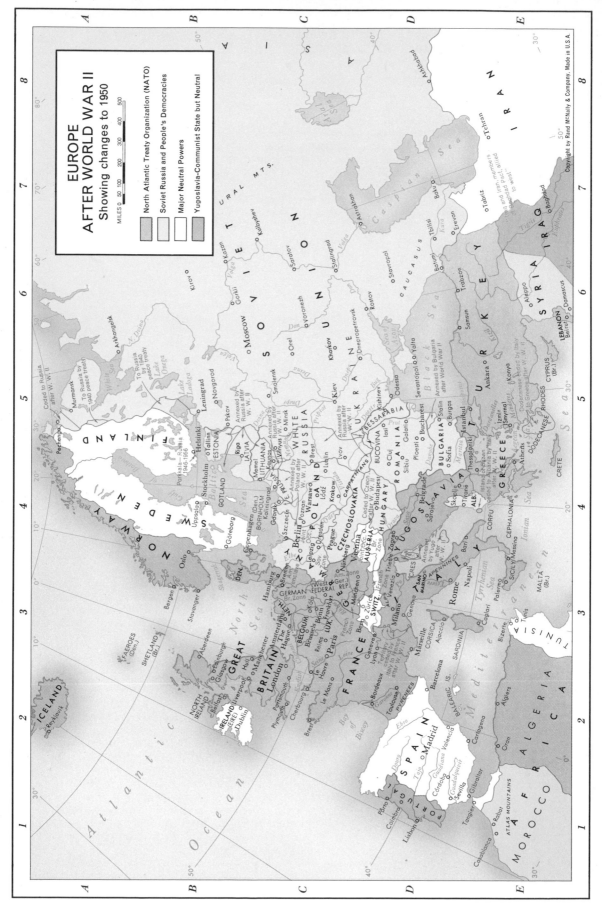

EUROPE
AFTER WORLD WAR II
Showing changes to 1950

MILES 0 50 100   200   300   400   500

North Atlantic Treaty Organization (NATO)

Soviet Russia and People's Democracies

Major Neutral Powers

Yugoslavia–Communist State but Neutral

Copyright by Rand McNally & Company, Made in U.S.A.

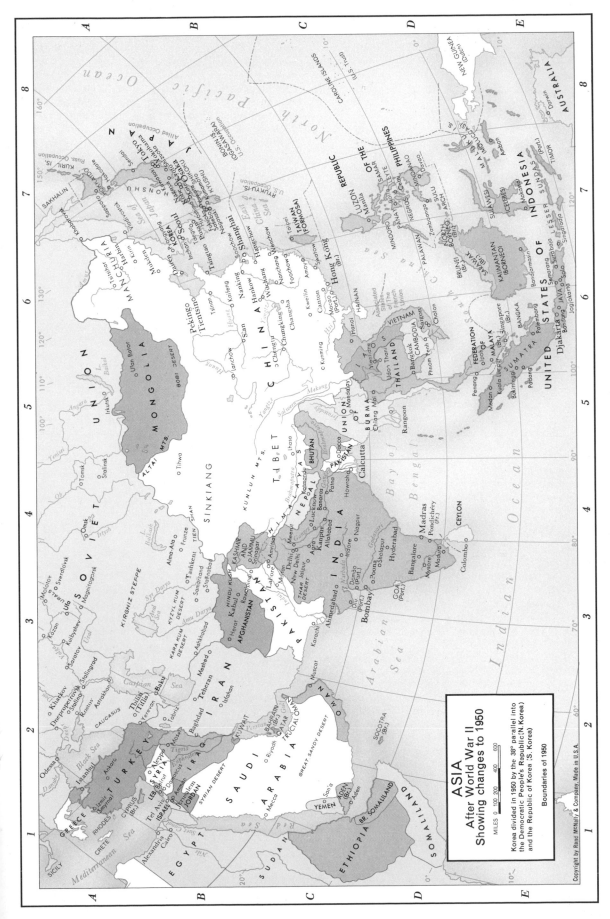

ASIA
After World War II
Showing changes to 1950

MILES 0 100 200   400   600

Korea divided in 1950 by the 38° parallel into
the Democratic People's Republic (N. Korea)
and the Republic of Korea (S. Korea)

Boundaries of 1950

Copyright by Rand McNally & Company. Made in U.S.A.

THE WORLD IN THE
MID-TWENTIETH CENTURY

▶ MAPS ON PAGES 187 AND 190-91

THE WORLD in the mid-twentieth century, after the Second World War, had changed beyond anything that the boldest or most informed observer in 1900 could possibly have foreseen. Europe was no longer the center from which political power and economic influence went out. The old pattern of international relations, the "great-power" system of Europe, no longer existed. Two continental powers, the United States and the Soviet Union, predominated instead. They were divided by ideological differences, each fearing the spread of the other's influence in the world; and they were armed with atomic and thermonuclear weapons, which put an entirely new face on all calculations of the use of military force. The colonial empires of 1900 (see pages 170–71) were disintegrating; Western civilization itself was successfully challenged; the white races were obliged to remember their minority status in the world as a whole.

South and East Asia after the Second World War
▶ MAP ON PAGE 187

On a map the greatest changes could be seen in Asia, where empire after empire in a brief half-century disappeared. The Ch'ing or Manchu dynasty collapsed in China, and the Ottoman Empire gave way to the Turkish republic. Soviet Asia became more populous and industrialized. The Asian empires of the British, French, Dutch, and Japanese were dissolved, and the Philippine Islands became independent of the United States.

India received independence in 1947, dividing into two parts: India itself, predominantly Hindu, though constituted as a secular state; and Moslem Pakistan, itself divided into two parts, the main part being along the Indus River, with East Pakistan at the other side of the subcontinent in the Ganges delta. Kashmir was claimed by both India and Pakistan. India and Pakistan both remained in the British Commonwealth of Nations. Burma, administered in 1900 as part of British India, became independent outside the Commonwealth. Ceylon, always separate from India under the British, became an independent dominion in the Commonwealth as did Malaya in 1957. British rule in Asia was confined to Hong Kong, northern Borneo, Singapore, and a few small places like Aden.

The Dutch, who had been in the East Indian islands for over three hundred years, were obliged in 1949 to recognize the Republic of Indonesia. The Dutch retained only western New Guinea, which Indonesia claimed.

The French, as noted below, lost Indo-China.

The Portuguese still managed to retain their four-hundred-year-old holdings in Timor in the East Indies and at Goa and Macao on the coasts of India and China.

Japan, in consequence of the Second World War, lost everything but its home islands. The Kurile Islands and southern Sakhalin went to

Russia. The United States occupied Okinawa and the Ryukyu and Bonin islands. The Caroline and other Pacific islands which Japan had seized from Germany during the First World War were administered by the United States as a United Nations trust. Japan also lost its interests in Manchuria, and conceded the independence of Korea. Formosa, or Taiwan, held by Japan since 1895, was returned to China.

Mongolia, formerly part of the Chinese empire, became the Mongolian People's Republic, associated closely with the Soviet Union.

China became a republic in 1912 upon the fall of the Ch'ing dynasty. There followed a long period of internal stress and of difficulty with Japan in both world wars. During the Japanese invasion before and during the Second World War the Chinese Communists gained power, while the Chinese Nationalists, or Kuomintang, lost it. In 1949-50 the Chinese Communists triumphed, and the Nationalists retired to Formosa. Both governments claimed legitimate rule over both Formosa and mainland China.

The success of communism in China revolutionized the ideological balance of power in Asia, and accentuated the difficulties of smaller countries along the Chinese border. In Korea, where communism had entrenched itself in the north during Russian occupation after the war, it proved impossible to form a unified republic, so that a North Korean and a South Korean republic were established. The communist North Koreans invaded South Korea in 1950. The United Nations, pronouncing the case to be one of aggression, called on member states to defend South Korea. The United States supplied most of the military force for this operation. Communist China aided the North Koreans. A truce in 1953 re-established the boundary between the two Koreas at approximately the 38th parallel.

In the former French Indo-China, after the war, the French recognized as independent units within a French Union the three states of Laos, Cambodia, and Vietnam, the last comprising Annam, Tongking, and Cochin China (see page 135). A war followed between the French and communists of Vietnam. In 1954 a truce divided Vietnam, of which the northern part became communist.

West Asia after the Second World War
▶ MAP ON PAGE 187

In west Asia the main developments were the continuing modernization of the Turkish republic, established in 1923; the final independence of the Arab states, with the abolition of the British and French mandates granted after the First World War; the establishment of the republic of Israel against Arab resistance; and the enormous increase in oil production, after 1945, in Saudi Arabia and Kuwait, by which these regions became vital to the daily life of Europe at a time when Europe was losing its ability to secure lines of communication.

Africa
▶ MAP ON PAGES 190-91

In Africa, too, there was restlessness under the old colonial system, both in the north along the

Mediterranean coast and in Negro Africa below the deserts. Egypt gained complete independence, and took steps to control the Suez Canal. Libya became independent after the defeat of Italy in the Second World War. The native rulers of Tunisia and Morocco shook off the protectorates imposed before 1914 by the French. In Algeria there were no native authorities, and the country had in many ways been assimilated legally to France. There were about 1,250,000 permanent European residents in a population of 9,500,000, and considerable French enterprises and investments, all greatly endangered by the fierce Algerian revolt that began in 1955.

The Union of South Africa was like Algeria in that a large permanent European population lived among even more numerous nonwhites. In the 1950's there were 2,800,000 of Dutch and British origin in a total population of 13,000,000, of whom all the remainder were Negroes, except 400,000 East Indians. The Dutch, or Afrikaners, having been there since 1652, longer than many of the Negro tribes, had developed a strong nationalism, and a racial exclusivism which in the twentieth century was increasingly difficult to maintain without violence. The Union had been a self-governing British dominion since 1910, in the sense that the whites governed the country, independently of London, with a minimum of political, civil, and economic rights for non-Europeans.

In 1953 the two Rhodesias and Nyasaland formed a loose federation, with a measure of political representation for native Africans. In the Congo the Belgians exercised a kind of enlightened despotism in which Africans were encouraged to make use of economic, educational, and occupational advantages. Of the pre-1914 German colonies, Tanganyika was administered as a United Nations trust by Britain, the Cameroons by France; but the Union of South Africa refused to recognize such a trusteeship for Southwest Africa. The former Italian Somaliland became a UN trusteeship administered by Italy.

The Sudan, peopled largely by Moslem and Arabized Negroes, became a republic in 1956, independent both of Egypt and of Great Britain.

In 1957 the former Gold Coast colony became the independent dominion of Ghana within the British Commonwealth. Dominion status was thus conferred for the first time on an all-Negro community. It was anticipated that Nigeria and other British African countries might eventually follow.

The Americas

▶ MAP ON PAGES 190-91

A map of the Americas at mid-twentieth century reveals only two territorial changes: Newfoundland joined Canada in 1949, and Ecuador in 1942 ceded its easternmost territories to Peru. Preparations were under way for a self-governing federation of the British West Indian islands, which when completed might form a mixed white and Negro dominion. The importance of the worldwide color question was strongly felt in the United States, where American Negroes, after the Second World War, made great progress toward enjoying the usual rights of American citizenship. For the United States, one of the basic difficulties in its

foreign policy was to sympathize with the aspirations of non-European peoples throughout the world, without antagonizing the European colonial powers whose good will was essential in the conflict with Soviet communism.

Some General Facts

It may be that never in world history has population grown so rapidly as in the twentieth century. It is estimated that the number of living human beings rose from 1,810,000,000 in 1920 to 2,691,000,000 in 1955. This represents an increase of about half in little more than a generation, a rate which, if continued, would have very serious consequences. Population in these years increased by a quarter in Europe without Russia, by about a half in Asia, three-fifths in Africa, and three-quarters in the two Americas. For individual countries see the Appendix.

Certain figures presented in the Statistical Yearbook of the United Nations offer a compact summary of the relationship between parts of the earth in the twentieth century, and even a résumé of the outcome of world history to that time. These figures are the estimates for consumption of energy in various countries—of energy derived from coal, lignite, petroleum, natural gas, and water power—converted to an equivalent in metric tons of coal. Energy from draft animals and the burning of wood is excluded, as is atomic energy. The energy here measured is what is used in modern industry and transportation, and for heat, light, motor cars, and domestic conveniences. The total such figure for a country is a rough measure of its potential strength. The per-capita figure is a rough index of its degree of modernization and its standard of living.

The United States in 1955, on this scale, consumed energy equivalent to that yielded by 1,363,834,000 tons of coal; the average for each American was 8.25 tons. For the United Kingdom the figures were 249,343,000 and 4.87. For France they were 105,847,000 and 2.44. For the Soviet Union they were 441,689,000 and 2.02. For China, a large but poor country, they were 96,440,000 and 0.16.

For big parts of the world they were:

	TOTAL TONS: MILLIONS	TONS PER CAPITA
North America	1,515	6.37
South America	69	.56
Western Europe	790	2.52
Eastern Europe, USSR, and Mainland China	770	.85
Asia without USSR and Mainland China	183	.22
Africa	57	.26
Australia-Oceania	42	2.86

The ascendancy thus shown for North America gives ground for both confidence and trepidation. It would appear that the weakness of western Europe is more political than economic, and that communist countries are by no means the strongest or the most comfortable. The inequality for the world as a whole is very marked. Attempts to rectify this inequality will doubtless furnish some of the chief themes for history in the future.

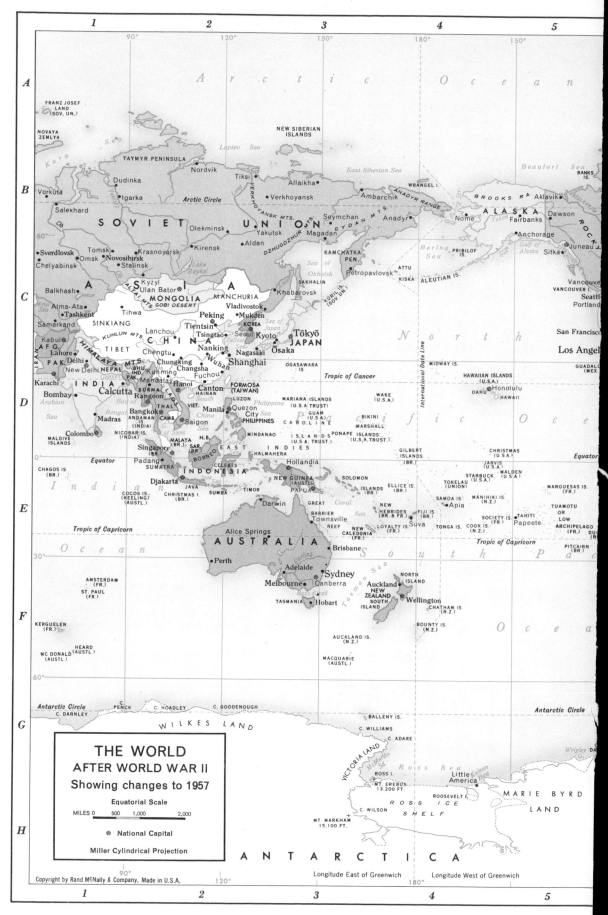

THE WORLD
AFTER WORLD WAR II
Showing changes to 1957

Equatorial Scale

MILES 0   500   1,000   2,000

⊗ National Capital

Miller Cylindrical Projection

Copyright by Rand McNally & Company, Made in U.S.A.

Longitude East of Greenwich   Longitude West of Greenwich

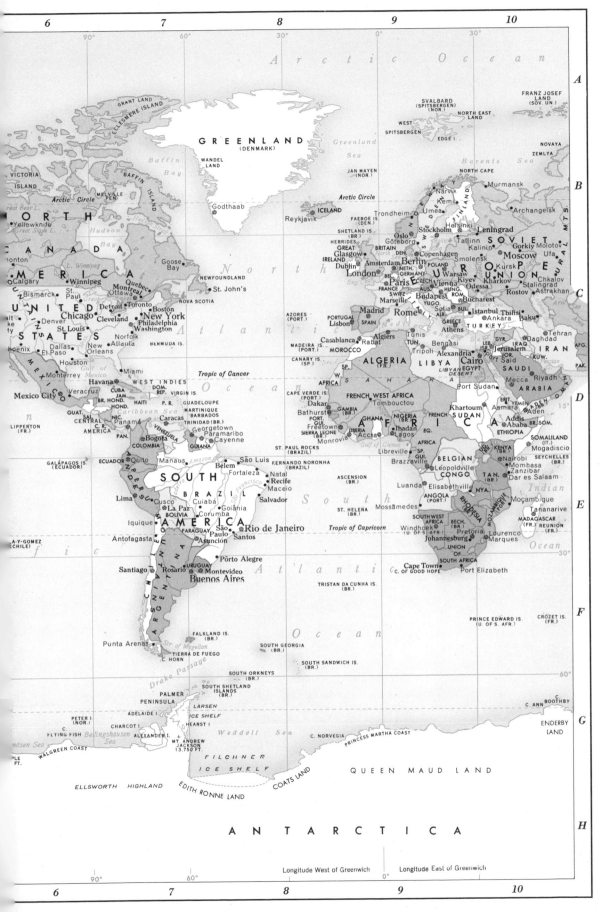

A

Arctic Ocean

SVALBARD
(SPITSBERGEN)
(NOR.)

FRANZ JOSEF
LAND
(SOV. UN.)

NORTH EAST
LAND

GRANT LAND

ELLESMERE ISLAND

WEST
SPITSBERGEN

EDGE I.

NOVAYA
ZEMLYA

Greenland
Sea

GREENLAND
(DENMARK)

WANDEL
LAND

Baffin
Bay

Barents   Sea

B

VICTORIA
ISLAND

JAN MAYEN
(NOR.)

NORTH CAPE

Murmansk

Archangelsk

Great Bear L.

Arctic   Circle

MELVILLE
PEN.

Godthaab

Arctic Circle

ICELAND

Reykjavik

Narvik
Kemi
Umeå

Helsinki

Tromso

FAEROE IS.
(DEN.)

Trondheim

Stockholm

Leningrad

Gorkiy
Molotov

SOVIET

Ural Mts.

Chkalov

NORTH
CANADA

Yellowknife

Great Slave L.

Oslo
Göteborg

SHETLAND IS.

HEBRIDES

GREAT
BRITAIN

IRELAND
Dublin
Glasgow

Copenhagen

Amsterdam
Berlin

Kalinin
Moscow

Smolensk

Ufa

Hudson
Bay

Goose
Bay

NEWFOUNDLAND

Winnipeg

L. Winnipeg

Quebec
Montreal
Ottawa

St. John's

London
Paris

EUROPE

Warsaw

UNION

Kiev

Kursk

Odessa
Kharkov

Rostov

Stalingrad

Astrakhan

AMERICA

Calgary

Bismarck

St.
Paul

Detroit
Toronto

Boston

NOVA SCOTIA

Vienna
Budapest

Bucharest

Istanbul
Tbilisi

Baku

UNITED

Denver

Chicago
Cleveland

New York

Philadelphia
Washington

Madrid
Rome

Sofia

Athens
TURKEY

Ankara

Tehran

STATES

St. Louis

Norfolk

AZORES
(PORT.)

PORTUGAL
Lisbon

SPAIN

GREECE

Baghdad

IRAN

AFG.

Dallas
El Paso

New
Orleans

Atlanta

BERMUDA IS.

Casablanca
Rabat

Algiers
Tunis

Bengasi

Alexandria
Cairo
Port
Said

Jerusalem

IRAQ

PAK.

Phoenix

Houston

Gulf of
Mexico

Miami

MOROCCO

MADEIRA IS.
(PORT.)

ALGERIA
(FR.)

LIBYA

EGYPT

SAUDI

KUW.

MEXICO

Monterrey

Havana

WEST INDIES

CANARY IS.
(SP.)

Tropic of Cancer

LIBYAN
DESERT

Mecca
Riyadh

ARABIA

Mexico City

Veracruz

CUBA
JAM.

BR.
HOND.
HAITI
DOM.
REP.
P. R.
VIRGIN IS.

SAHARA

Port Sudan

Aden

GUAT.
SAL.
NIC.
C.R.

CENTRAL
AMERICA
Panamá

Caribbean Sea

GUADELOUPE
MARTINIQUE
BARBADOS
TRINIDAD (BR.)

CAPE VERDE
(PORT.)

AFRICA

FRENCH WEST AFRICA
Tombouctou

GAMBIA
(BR.)

Khartoum

SUDAN

ERIT.

Asmara

YEMEN

SOMALILAND
(IT.)

Addis
Ababa

Mogadiscio

LIPPERTON
(FR.)

PAN.

VENEZUELA
Caracas

Georgetown
Paramaribo

Dakar
Bathurst
PORT.
GUI.

Freetown

SIERRA LEONE

GHANA

NIGERIA
Ibadan
Lagos

FRENCH
EQ.

ETHIOPIA

KENYA

SEYCHELLES
(BR.)

Bogotá

COLOMBIA

Cayenne

GUIANA

Monrovia

LIBERIA
Accra

AFRICA

Libreville

Gulf of Guinea

GUI.

Brazzaville

BELGIAN
CONGO

Nairobi

Mombasa
Zanzibar

Dar es Salaam

GALAPAGOS IS.
(ECUADOR)

ECUADOR
Quito

Manaus

Amazon

São Luis

FERNANDO DE NORONHA
(BRAZIL)

ST. PAUL ROCKS
(BRAZIL)

Léopoldville

T.A.N.
(BR.)

Belem
Fortaleza

Natal

Luanda
Elisabethville

NYA.

SOUTH

BRAZIL

Recife
Maceió

ASCENSION
(BR.)

ANGOLA
(PORT.)

Moçambique

Tananarive

Lima

Cusco
La Paz

Cuiabá
Goiânia

San Francisco

Salvador

ST. HELENA
(BR.)

Mossâmedes

MADAGASCAR
(FR.)

REUNION
(FR.)

Corumba

South

E

Indian

BOLIVIA

AMERICA

Iquique

Antofagasta

PARAGUAY
Asunción

São
Paulo

Rio de Janeiro

Santos

Tropic of Capricorn

SOUTH WEST
AFRICA
Windhoek
(U. OF S. AFR.)

RHODESIA

BECH.
(BR.)

Johannesburg

Pretoria

Lourenço
Marques

Ocean

A-Y-GOMEZ
(CHILE)

Pôrto Alegre

Atlantic

UNION
OF
SOUTH AFRICA

Santiago
Rosario

URUGUAY
Montevideo

Buenos Aires

TRISTAN DA CUNHA IS.
(BR.)

Cape Town
C. OF GOOD HOPE

Port Elizabeth

Ocean

F

Ocean

FALKLAND IS.
(BR.)

PRINCE EDWARD IS.
(U. OF S. AFR.)

CROZET IS.
(FR.)

Punta Arenas

Str. of Magellan

TIERRA DEL FUEGO
C. HORN

SOUTH GEORGIA
(BR.)

SOUTH SANDWICH IS.
(BR.)

Drake Passage

SOUTH ORKNEYS
(BR.)

SOUTH SHETLAND
ISLANDS
(BR.)

C. ANN

BOOTHBY

PALMER
PENINSULA

ADELAIDE I.
CHARCOT I.
HEARST I.

LARSEN
ICE SHELF

ENDERBY
LAND

G

PETER I.
(NOR.)
FLYING FISH *Bellingshausen*

ALEXANDER I.

MT. ANDREW
JACKSON
13,750 FT.

Weddell   Sea

C. NORVEGIA

PRINCESS MARTHA COAST

Amundsen Sea

WALGREEN COAST

FILCHNER
ICE SHELF

QUEEN MAUD LAND

ELLSWORTH HIGHLAND

EDITH RONNE LAND

COATS LAND

ANTARCTICA

H

BIBLIOGRAPHY

Readers in search of more detailed information on particular subjects may wish to consult one of the following historical atlases, which are more specialized than the present volume. A few in foreign languages are included, since place names are usually recognizable in any language written in the Latin alphabet.

For classical and Near Eastern antiquity: Heinrich Kiepert, *Atlas antiquus: twelve maps of the ancient world*, an old German work published in English translation (Chicago: Rand McNally, 1892); and other editions. Valuable maps are in the separate volumes of the *Cambridge Ancient History*, 12 vols. (Cambridge, Eng.: The University Press, 1923–39). *Westminster Historical Atlas to the Bible* (Philadelphia: The Westminster Press, new ed., 1956). Emil G. Kraeling, *Rand McNally Bible Atlas* (Chicago, 1956). Two new German atlases, with many regional, local, and city maps: *Grosser Historischer Weltatlas: Teil I, Vorgeschichte und Altertum* (Munich: Bayerischer Schulbuch-Verlag, 1954); and *Westermanns Atlas zur Weltgeschichte: Teil I, Vorzeit und Altertum* (Brunswick: Georg Westermann Verlag, 1956).

For medieval and early modern European history, there is still much of value in William R. Shepherd, *Historical Atlas* (8th ed.; New York: Barnes and Noble, 1956). See also the maps in the *Cambridge Medieval History*, 8 vols. (New York: Macmillan, 1911–36), and Part II of the German *Westermanns Atlas* mentioned above. For the history of the Christian Church in all periods there is Karl Heussi and Hermann Mulert, *Atlas zur Kirchengeschichte* (3rd ed.; Tübingen: Mohr, 1937).

For modern European history there is the very useful *Cambridge Modern History Atlas*, which is volume XIV of the *Cambridge Modern History*, 13 vols. and atlas (New York: Macmillan, 1903–12). C. Grant Robertson and J. G. Bartholomew, *Historical atlas of modern Europe from 1789 to 1922* (2nd ed.; London: Oxford University Press, 1924). Part III of the *Westermanns Atlas* may also be mentioned.

For Islam: Harry W. Hazard, *Atlas of Islamic history* (Princeton: Princeton University Press, 1951).

For Asia: Albert Herrmann, *Historical and commercial atlas of China* (Cambridge: Harvard University Press, 1935). C. Collin Davies, *An historical atlas of the Indian peninsula* (London: Oxford University Press, 1954). R. R. Sellman, *An outline atlas of Eastern history* (London: Edward Arnold, 1954).

For the United States: Charles O. Paullin, *Atlas of the historical geography of the United States* (Washington and New York: Carnegie Institution and American Geographical Society, 1932). Clifford L. and Elizabeth H. Lord, *Historical atlas of the United States* (New York: Henry Holt, 1953).

For Canada: Lawrence J. Burpee, *An historical atlas of Canada* (Toronto: Nelson, 1927).

For Latin America: Alva Curtis Wilgus, *Latin America in maps, historic, geographic, economic* (New York: Barnes and Noble, 1943).

For facsimiles of old maps, illustrating the history of cartography and the growing knowledge of the earth: Roberto Almagia, *Planisferi, carte nautiche e affini dal secolo xiv al xvii esistente nella Biblioteca Apostolica Vaticana*, 2 vols. (Vatican City, 1944–48). Konrad Kretschmer, *Die Entdeckung Amerikas in ihrer bedeutung für die geschichte des Weltbildes. Mit einem atlas von 40 tafeln in farbendruck* (Berlin: Kühl, 1892). Nils A. E. Nordenskiöld, *Facsimile atlas to the early history of cartography* (Stockholm: Norstedt, 1889). Edme François Jomard, *Monuments de la géographie: ou Recueil d'anciennes cartes européennes et orientales* (Paris: Duprat, 1862).

POPULATION OF SELECTED COUNTRIES
(*In Millions*)

	England & Wales	Scotland	Ireland	Netherlands	Belgium	France	Germany	Switzerland	Austria
13th–early 14th century	3.8	.5	.8			22.0	12.0	.6	
15th century	2.5				3.0	16.0	12.0		
About 1700	5.5	1.2		1.1	1.6	19.0	15.0	1.2	
About 1750	6.3			1.5	2.1	24.0	17.0		6.0
1800	8.9	1.6	5.2	2.0	3.0	27.0	25.0		14.0
1820	12.0	2.1	6.8			30.0			
1840	15.9	2.6	8.2	2.9		33.4	32.8	2.2	16.6
1860	20.0	3.1	5.8	3.3	4.5	35.8	38.1	2.5	18.0
1880	26.0	3.7	5.1	4.0	5.5	37.7	45.2	2.8	22.1
1900	32.5	4.5	4.5	5.1	6.7	39.0	56.4	3.3	26.1
1920	37.9	4.9	4.1	6.9	7.5	39.2	59.2	3.9	6.5
1940	42.0	5.0	4.2	8.9	8.3	39.8	70.1	4.2	6.7
1954	44.3	5.1	4.3	10.7	8.8	42.8	49.7	4.9	7.0

	Hungary	Portugal	Spain	Italy	Greece	Bulgaria	Romania	Russia	Poland
13th–early 14th century			6.5	10.0					
15th century			10.0	10.0					
About 1700		1.7	6.0	11.0				12.0	
About 1750		2.5	8.0	16.0					
1800		3.0	10.5	18.1				30.0	
1820		3.0		19.7					3.7
1840		3.4		22.0					
1860	13.7	4.2	15.7	25.0	1.3		4.4	63.7	4.8
1880	15.6	4.5	16.6	28.5	1.7	2.0		89.0	8.0
1900	19.3	5.4	18.6	32.5	2.4	3.7	6.0	103.6	9.4
1920	8.0	6.0	21.3	38.0	5.5	4.8	16.3	108.2	27.2
1940	9.3	7.7	25.8	43.5	7.3	6.3	15.3		
1954	9.7	8.7	28.7	48.7	7.9	7.5	16.5	216.0	26.5

	Czechoslovakia	Yugoslavia	Finland	Sweden	Norway	Denmark	Canada	U.S.A.	Brazil	Argentina
13th–early 14th century					.4	.8				
15th century										
About 1700				1.6	.6	.6		.3		
About 1750				1.8	.7	.7		1.0		
1800			.8	2.3	.9	.9		5.3	3.2	.3
1820			1.2	2.6	1.0		.6	9.6	3.8	.8
1840			1.4	3.1	1.3	1.3		17.0		.8
1860			1.7	3.9	1.7	1.6	3.1	31.4	7.8	1.2
1880			2.0	4.6		2.0	4.3	50.2		
1900			2.6	5.1	2.2	2.5	5.4	76.0	14.3	5.5
1920	13.6	12.0	3.4	5.9	2.7	3.3	8.8	105.7	31.2	8.7
1940	14.7	15.8	3.7	6.4	3.0	3.8	11.7	132.1	41.1	14.2
1954	12.9	17.4	4.2	7.2	3.4	4.4	15.4	162.4	57.1	18.9

	Mexico	Egypt	Algeria	India	Australia	New Zealand	Japan	China	Union of South Africa
1800	6.5	2.5		200.0					
1820		2.5							
1840	7.0				.2				
1860					1.2				
1880	9.6	6.8	3.3	253.9	2.3	.5	37.4		
1900	13.6	9.7	4.7	294.4	3.8	.8	46.7		5.2
1920	14.3	12.8	5.8	318.9	5.4	1.2	56.0		6.9
1940	19.8	16.9	7.5	385.3	7.0	1.6	71.4	458.3	10.3
1954	28.9	22.5	9.4	375.0	9.0	2.0	88.5	480.0	13.4

Population statistics are subject to a wide margin of error, especially for earlier dates. The use of these tables lies in comparison of gross magnitudes: to suggest, for example, that France may have been six times as populous as England in the Middle Ages, that Spain declined under the Hapsburgs, that France was more populous than Germany in the time of Napoleon, or that growth in the past century has been exceedingly rapid in all countries. A bar drawn across a column is a reminder that the difference between preceding and following dates is to be explained in part by a change of boundaries.

POPULATION OF SELECTED CITIES

Note: All populations are in thousands. Figures before 1850 are from the best discoverable estimates but are subject to a wide margin of error. A few ancient cities were very large; Rome is thought to have had about one million population in the 1st and 2nd centuries A.D. For European cities before 1800 the present table mainly follows R. Mols, *Introduction à la démographie historique des villes d'Europe du 14e au 18e siècle*, 3 vols., Gembloux (Belgium), 1954–56. Two 1950 populations appear for each city; the first for the city proper, and the second for the entire metropolitan area, including suburbs. Populations marked with a dagger (†) include certain suburbs annexed at a later date.

	London (*Greater London)	York	Bristol	Norwich	Liverpool	Manchester	Birmingham	Edinburgh	Glasgow	Dublin	Belfast
14th century	50	12	12	10	under 3	under 3	under 3	15			
15th century											
16th century	150										
17th century	500		30	under 15	under 15	under 15	under 15			40	
18th century	750							80	36	150	
1800	*959	16	61	36	82	77	71	85	77	200	30
1850	*2681	36	154	69	397	303	242	162	329	255	87
1880	*4767	50	207	88	553	341	401	236	511	250	208
1900	*6581	72	329	112	685	544	522	316	736	291	349
1950 (city)	*8325	105	442	120	800	700	1110	466	1088	522	443
1950(metro.)	10200	125	525	150	1445	1965	2400	515	1600	630	550

	Paris (*Seine Dept.)	Lyon	Marseille	Rouen	Bordeaux	Lille	Toulouse	Strasbourg	Bruges	Antwerp	Brussels (*Greater Brussels)
14th century	80			35					35	5	25
15th century							30		40	35	35
16th century									40	100	50
17th century	200	over 50	over 50	50	over 40	50		30		50	
18th century	500	100	90	70	60	60	60	40	30	50	80
1800	600	90	111	87	91	60	50	50	35	62	*90
1850	*1422	177	195	100	131	76	93	76	40	88	*251
1880	*2799	377	360	106	221	178	140	104	45	172	*424
1900	*3670	459	491	116	257	211	150	151	53	277	*604
1950 (city)	*4950	470	655	115	258	195	265	205	52	261	*929
1950 (metro.)	6350	740	715	265	445	755	285	275	91	630	1115

	Amsterdam	Lisbon	Seville	Barcelona	Madrid	Rome	Naples	Palermo	Milan	Venice	Florence
14th century		over 20	35	35	under 5	under 30	over 50	over 50	over 50	over 50	over 50
15th century	under 20					50	over 100	50	over 100	over 100	60
16th century	35	100	120	40	60	100	230	100	180	160	65
17th century	over 100	73	80	60	80	130	300	90	200	150	75
18th century	150	120	80	95	120	150	320	120	115	140	75
1800	201	180	90	115	160	153	350	140	134	140	84
1850	224	240	113	175	281	175	449	180	200	127	114
1880	317	250	134	346	400	300	494	245	322	135	169
1900	511	356	148	533	540	463	564	310	491	152	206
1950 (city)	845	783	374	1277	1528	1625	1010	480	1270	315	375
1950 (metro.)	1125	1100	405	1550	1575	1625	1230	480	1575	315	400

	Geneva	Zurich	Cologne	Frankfurt am Main	Hamburg	Berlin	Munich	Leipzig	Essen	Vienna	Prague
14th century											
15th century	over 10		35	over 10	over 10	under 10				20	over 25
16th century			35		over 40	12				over 40	over 40
17th century	17	12			60	20	20	over 20		100	over 40
18th century	20		40	40	100	100	40	30		220	75
1800	22	12	50	48	130	172	49	30	5	247	75
1850	†38	†42	97	59	132	†500	110	60	9	444	†206
1880	†70	†87	†160	†165	†410	†1321	†250	†250	†95	†1104	†250
1900	†97	†168	373	289	706	†2712	500	456	†216	1675	†382
1950 (city)	146	390	600	535	1621	3345	840	617	610	1615	940
1950 (metro.)	170	420	1125	850	1800	3900	950	800	3175	1900	980

	Copenhagen (*Greater Copenhagen)	Stockholm	Christiania = Oslo	Helsinki	Warsaw	Cracow	Budapest	Belgrade	Athens	Sofia	Bucharest
18th century		60			70	16					
1800	101	76	9	4	100	24	†54	25	12		40
1850	130	93	35	21	150	50	†178		31		100
1880	*266	169	119	43	383	†78	371	35	63	21	225
1900	*469	301	228	91	700	91	732	70	125	68	282
1950 (city)	*975	745	434	367	810	350	1650	425	565	460	1025
1950 (metro.)	1215	985	515	410	925	385	1670	460	1370	550	1225

	Constantinople = Istanbul	St. Petersburg = Leningrad	Moscow	Kiev	Odessa	Tashkent	Peking	Canton	Shanghai	Tokyo	Osaka
18th century		100			(Founded 1794)						
1800	600	220	250	20	6	35	700	600	300	800	350
1850		485	365	61	72				250		
1880	600	877	612	150	200	85			300	†1050	325
1900	1100	1150	1000	275	450	156	800	900	600	1600	900
1950 (city)	1000	2500	4700	900	550	725	2000	1500	5500	5425	1975
1950 (metro.)	1025	3250	6500	925	550	750	2000	1500	5500	8200	4425

	Hong Kong	Manila	Saigon-Cholon	Singapore	Batavia = Djakarta	Calcutta	Bombay	Delhi	Karachi	Cairo	Algiers
18th century	(Founded 1841)			(Founded 1819)			50		(Founded c. 1725)		
1800		15					200			200	60
1850	40	†140		25	70	300	500		35	250	50
1880	102	150	70	139	97	612	773	173	74	375	†84
1900	200	200	175	193	116	848	776	209	116	570	†134
1950 (city)	900	1000	1400	725	1300	2525	2810	910	900	2425	330
1950 (metro.)	1850	1600	1400	975	1600	3700	3050	1400	1050	2675	535

	Cape Town	Johannesburg	Sydney (*Greater Sydney)	Melbourne (*Greater Melbourne)	Santiago de Chile	Buenos Aires	Rio de Janeiro	São Paulo	Potosí	Lima	Mexico City
16th century	(Founded 1652)				(Founded 1541)	(Founded 1580)	(Founded 1565)	(Founded 1554)	120	25	10
17th century			(Founded 1788)		5	1	10		150	25	30
18th century				(Founded 1835)	6	20			25	55	110
1800	20		8		40	40	43			50	130
1850	20	(Founded 1886)	60	25	80	76	266	22	16	90	160
1880	35		*225	*283	190	236	375	35	12	110	230
1900	77	105	*482	*496	297	821	745	240	21	130	345
1950 (city)	440	625	*1775	*1400	660	3290	2450	2275	46	825	2275
1950 (metro.)	575	1175	1800	1425	1400	5300	3050	2600	46	950	3100

	Boston	Philadelphia	New York	Baltimore	Washington	Chicago	Detroit	San Francisco	Los Angeles	Montreal	Toronto
17th century	(Founded 1630)	(Founded 1682)	(Founded 1614)				(Founded 1701)			(Founded 1642)	
1700	7	4	5	(Founded 1729)							
1770	16	28	21	5	(Founded 1791)	(Settled 1816)		(Founded 1769)	(Founded 1781)		(Founded 1793)
1800	25	†81	64	27	3					15	
1850	137	†409	†696	169	40	30	21	30	2	58	28
1880	363	847	1912	332	†178	503	116	234	11	†175	†96
1900	561	1294	†3437	509	279	1699	286	343	102	†326	†219
1950 (city)	790	2075	7900	952	813	3630	1860	790	2175	1015	675
1950 (metro.)	2490	3350	13300	1350	1550	5325	3275	2325	4275	1400	1150

INFANT MORTALITY

Deaths per Thousand Infants under One Year Old

	U.S.A.	England & Wales	Sweden	Germany	France	Hungary	Japan	Australia
1840			154		155			
1850			153		162			
1860		154	146		173			
1870		154	139		178			
1880		149	130		172			
1890		142	111		166			
1900		153	102		164	234	170	112
1910		128	84	186	132	208	156	87
1920	76	76	60	123	95	188	161	60
1930	68	68	59	94	89	172	137	52
1940	47	57	39	64	91	130	90	38
1950	29	30	21	55	47	?	60	24

Source: Annuaire Statistique de la France, 1954, Partie Internationale, p. 23

LIFE EXPECTANCY AT BIRTH (Females)

(Number of Years)

	U.S.A.	England & Wales	Sweden	Germany	France	Austria	Japan	Australia
18th century			36		27			
1825			44		41			
1845		42	47		41			
1875		45	49	39		34		
1885		47	51	40	44			51
1895		48	54	44				55
1905	51	52	57	48	49	41	45	59
1920	57	60	60		56		43	63
1930	61	63	64	60	59	58	46	65
1950	71	72	72	69	69	67	60	71

Source: Annuaire Statistique de la France, 1954, Partie Internationale, p. 18

CONQUERED AND UNCONQUERED DISEASES

Deaths per Million of Population from Typhoid Fever and Cancer

	United States	England & Wales	Denmark	Belgium	France	Italy	Japan	Australia
TYPHOID FEVER								
1860				928				
1870			672	755				
1880		325	478	775				
1890		179	192	397		790		
1900	313	175	111	258		497	138	358
1910	225	70	38	110	114	272	130	160
1920	76	13	13	48	59	227	223	45
1930	45	9	9	31	48	192	145	24
1940	11	3	2	12	26	89	104	4
1950	1	*	1	8	8	29	9	1

* Less than .5 per million

	United States	England & Wales	Denmark	Belgium	France	Italy	Japan	Australia
CANCER								
1860				270				
1870		386		335				
1880		471	947					
1890		632	1083			425		
1900		800	1140			509	446	564
1910		940	1363	620	755	636	613	717
1920		1251	1417	789	813	669	707	907
1930	990	1411	1429	908	930	632	706	953
1940	1200	1723	1479	1187	1371	866	737	1167
1950	1359	1907	1557	1461	1697	1072	743	1290

Source: Annuaire Statistique de la France, 1954, Partie Internationale, pp. 25-35.

BIRTHS, DEATHS, AND POPULATION
England and Wales

	Births	Deaths	Natural Increase	Population	
		(per 1000 of population)		Number	Per cent increase in 20 years
1740	37	33	4		
1760	37	31	6	6,500,000	
1780	37	31	6	7,200,000	11%
1800	37	27	10	8,900,000	23
1820	37	21	16	12,000,000	34
1840	37	23	14	15,900,000	33
1860	34	22	12	20,000,000	26
1880	35	21	14	26,000,000	30
1900	30	18	12	32,500,000	25
1910	27	15	12	36,100,000	..
1920	22	14	8	37,900,000	17
1930	18	12	6	39,900,000	10
1940	15	12	3	42,000,000	9
1950	16	12	4	44,300,000	11

Source: World Population and Resources: A Report by Political and Economic Planning (London, 1955), pp. 19–20.

IMMIGRATION INTO NEW COUNTRIES
Thousands of Known Immigrants

Year	United States	Brazil	Argentina	Australia	New Zealand	Canada
1830	23	2				
1850	370	2				
1870	387	5	40	16	4	25
1890	455	107	30	25	17	75
1910	1042	89	209	38	5	287
1930	242	67	64	−11	5	105
1950	207	87	129	175	18	77

Figures for the United States, Brazil, and Canada are for total immigration; those for Argentina Australia, and New Zealand are net, after deductions of emigrants and returned immigrants.

EMIGRATION FROM EUROPE
Number of Known Emigrants per 100,000 of Population

Year	England & Wales	Scotland	Ireland	Denmark	Norway	Sweden	Russia	Austria
1853	342	770	3107		417	75		
1860	133	293	1045		119	1		
1870	469	686	1371	197	855	374		
1880	435	595	1800	287	1053	796		90
1890	487	516	1218	474	550	630	100	144
1900	318	461	1026	147	490	321	67	241
1910	708	1685	1174	325	798	448	87	487
1925	242	775	738	134	255	159	..	70
1937	65	84	60	8	22	17	..	23
1950	273*	..	..	593	71	184	..	10

Year	Hungary	Switzerland	Germany	Netherlands	France	Spain	Portugal	Italy
1853			390					
1860			...		28			
1870		131	155		13			72
1880	58	...	260		12		271	118
1890	228	258	197	78	54	347	580	380
1900	286	116	40	37	14	315	394	515
1910	564	139	39	55	12	937	683	1165
1925	36	89	99	41	5	253	364	255
1937	17	57	21	..	..	...	...	70
1950	..	173	130**	..	15	211	260	319

* United Kingdom.
**Western Germany, 1953.
Sources: Annuaire Statistique de la France, 1938; United Nations Demographic Yearbook, 1954.

GROWTH OF GOVERNMENT
Expenditures of Central Governments with Estimates of Government
Expenditures as Percentage of National Income

Annually About	United Kingdom *Millions of Pounds*		France *Millions of Francs*		Sweden *Millions of Kronor*		United States *Millions of Dollars*	
1697	2	7%						
1747	11	10%						
1790			500				4	1%
Napoleonic Wars { 1800	58	40%	835				9	1%
1815	112	50%	931	35%			34	4%
1865	65	7%	2,147	15%	34	5%	1,298	?
1900	182	10%	3,747	14%	152	8%	521	3%
World War I 1918	2,696	68%	54,537	50%	1,720	21%	12,697	22%
World War II 1944	6,086	75%	346,000	?	4,072	22%	95,315	52%
1953	4,847	33%	3,850,000	37%	9,145	25%	74,607	25%

Source: Woytinsky and Woytinsky, *World Commerce and Governments* (New York: The Twentieth Century Fund, 1955), pp. 688–700.

CRUDE PETROLEUM PRODUCTION
(Thousands of Metric Tons)

	U.S.A.	Venezuela	Mexico	U.S.S.R.	Iran	Kuwait	Saudi Arabia	World Total
1860	66							67
1870	701			28				774
1880	3,504			410				4,013
1890	6,110			3,980				10,314
1900	8,482			10,339				20,156
1910	27,941		520	9,625				44,093
1920	69,122	68	24,410	3,830	1,685			99,000
1930	123,117	20,109	5,662	18,451	6,036			177,200
1940	182,867	27,497	6,271	31,000*	9,765		700	262,000**
1950	270,353	78,235	10,363	37,800*	32,259	17,291	26,904	486,600**

* Estimated.
**Not including U.S.S.R.

Source: Annuaire Statistique de la France, 1954, Partie Internationale, pp. 113–14.

COAL PRODUCTION
(Thousands of Metric Tons)

	U.S.A.	U.K.	U.S.S.R.	Germany	France	Japan	India	World Total
1860	13,358	81,322		12,348				
1870	29,978	112,197		26,398	13,180			
1880	64,850	149,021	3,240	46,974	19,362			
1890	143,100	184,529	6,015	70,238	26,083	2,640	2,203	474,000
1900	244,600	228,784	16,156	109,290	33,405	7,489	6,217	700,000
1910	455,000	268,677	24,930	152,828	38,350	15,681	12,241	1,059,000
1920	597,178	233,205	7,642	131,356	34,672	29,245	18,243	1,165,000**
1930	487,078	247,775	48,817	142,699	68,293*	31,376	24,185	1,150,000**
1940	462,045	227,898	166,000	173,043	40,984	57,318	29,860	1,183,000**
1950	505,313	219,796	260,000	111,137	67,620	38,459	33,269	1,209,000**

* includes Saar.
**not including U.S.S.R.

Source: Annuaire Statistique de la France, 1954.

SHIPPING THROUGH THE SUEZ AND PANAMA CANALS

| | SUEZ | | PANAMA | |
	Number of Vessels	Tonnage, in Millions	Number of Vessels	Tonnage, in Millions
1871	765	.6		
1880	2,026	3.1		
1890	3,389	6.9		
1900	3,441	9.7		
1910	4,533	16.3	1,058	3.5 (1915)
1920	4,009	16.8	2,393	7.9
1930	5,761	31.4	6,027	27.7
1940	2,589	13.5	5,370	24.1
1950	11,751	81.8	5,448	28.0

Source: Woytinsky and Woytinsky, *World Commerce and Governments* (New York: The Twentieth Century Fund, 1955), pp. 471, 472.

RAILWAY MILEAGE
(Thousands of Miles)

	United States	Canada	Brazil	Argentina	Great Britain	Germany	Spain	Russia	India
1850	9.0	.1	.0	.0	6.6	3.7	.0	.4	.0
1860	30.6	2.1	.1	.0	10.4	7.2	1.2	1.0	.9
1870	52.9	2.5	.4	.4	15.5	12.2	3.4	7.0	4.8
1880	93.3	6.9	2.0	1.4	18.0	21.0	4.7	15.0	9.3
1890	163.4	14.0	5.9	6.1	20.0	26.7	6.2	20.2	16.8
1900	193.3	17.9	9.2	10.2	21.9	31.9	8.3	31.7	23.7
1910	240.3	24.8	13.3	16.5	23.4	38.0	9.3	41.2	32.1
1920	252.8	39.0	17.8	22.5	20.3	35.9	9.5	36.6	37.0
1930	249.1	42.6	19.7	23.7	21.4	36.4	10.1	52.0	41.5
1940	233.7	42.6	21.3	26.6	19.9	36.7	. . . .	62.5	41.0
1952	223.4	41.3	23.1	27.0	19.4	18.9*	11.1	76.6	39.5**

* Western Germany only.
**Includes Pakistan, 5.5.

Source: Woytinsky and Woytinsky, *World Commerce and Governments* (New York: The Twentieth Century Fund, 1955), p. 342.

SPEED OF TRANSPORTATION
(Miles per Hour)

	Horse Coach	Canal Tug	River Boat	Ocean Ship	Railroad	Automobile	Airplane
1840	5	2	5	10	31		
1860	5	2	6	15	40		
1880	5	3	8	20	50		
1900	5	4	10	25	60	30	
1910	5	4	10	30	60	45	50
1920	5	4	11	30	65	55	110
1930	5	4	11	30	70	60	185
1940	5	4	11	35	100	75	300

Source: Woytinsky and Woytinsky, *World Commerce and Governments* (New York: The Twentieth Century Fund, 1955), p. 308.

The following universal index lists all place names appearing on the maps in the *Atlas of World History*. In addition, it contains the names of peoples and tribes, empires and civilizations, and those explorers, adventurers, and military leaders whose routes are traced on the maps. Cultural data and the names of famous men in the arts and sciences, such as appear on the Civilization maps and elsewhere are not given. The written text is not indexed.

Of the names which appear on more than one map, those of cities, sites, and physical features (including most islands and island groups)—whose locations and boundaries remain relatively constant—are indexed to one map only, usually that covering the

first period in which the place flourished or the first map on which the item appears in some prominence or detail. The reader who wishes to follow a particular locality through successive periods of history may then consult the Table of Contents. Countries and regions, however, are indexed to the several maps which portray their areal and political development at successive periods.

In general, each index entry includes a map reference key and the page number of the map. Where two maps fall on one page, the letter "a" or "b" following the page number refers to the top or bottom map, respectively. Alternate names and spellings are added in parentheses.

PRINTED IN U.S.A.